THE
10th MAN

THE
10th MAN

THE FAN IN BASEBALL HISTORY

Donald Dewey

CARROLL & GRAF PUBLISHERS
NEW YORK

THE 10TH MAN
The Fan in Baseball History

Carroll & Graf Publishers
An Imprint of Avalon Publishing Group Inc.
245 West 17th Street
11th Floor
New York, NY 10011

First Carroll & Graf edition 2004

Library of Congress Cataloging-in-Publication Data is available.

ISBN: 0-7867-1361-5

Designed by Paul Paddock
Printed in the United States of America
Distributed by Publishers Group West

For Nick Acocella
Friend and Partner

CONTENTS

INTRODUCTION   IX

GENESIS TALES   1
The First Fans—No Fun and Games—Attendance Must Be
Paid—Pros and Cons—War Games—The Enclosure Movement—
The Betting Game

THE PROFESSIONAL GAME   41
Smartening Up—Guilt by Association—Krank Cases—
Territorial Rites—Blue Collars—Stars and Idols

PATRONAGE AND PATRONIZATION   73
Cultural Stability—Krank Cases: The Deadball Era—Sex in
the Grandstand—At the Ballpark—For the Good of the Fans—
God and Country

CLOSE ENCOUNTERS   115
The Star System—The Sultan and the Child—Eyes and Ears—
All the Stars—Gashouse Days—Night Shifts—Krank Cases:
Between the Wars

MINORITY IMAGES   157
Home Fronts—The Disappeared—The New New York Game—
The Stuntman—Goodbye to All That—Broadcast News

MARKET LURES   197

Bum Steers—Liquid Capitals—The New Breeds—
Box Office Hits—Going to Market

FANS AND PHANATICS   227

Winning Ways—On the Page—Reserve Causes—Battling the
Blues—Free Agency—Krank Cases: The Late Century

THE NEW COMPULSIVENESS   265

Getting Involved—Seeing Rose—Hexes and Complexes—
Gambling Fantasies—By the Numbers—Noise! Noise! Noise!—
Weather or Not—Krank Cases: Today's Game

CONTRACTION PAINS   317

Calling All Cals—Neighborhood Plays—Contractions—
Bonding Necessities—Foreign Affairs

EPILOGUE   353

ENDNOTES   361

ACKNOWLEDGMENTS   377

ABOUT THE AUTHOR   379

INDEX   381

Introduction

Baseball was the first successful mass entertainment medium in the United States. It merits that distinction for having appealed to audiences that dwarfed the numbers attracted to other entertainment forms in the middle of the nineteenth century (theater, circus, and so forth), for having maintained its popularity over successive generations on a nationwide level, and for having wet-nursed from its urban delivery rooms the fan culture that was subsequently exploited to far greater influence by the technologies of motion pictures, radio, and television, to name only three. Baseball's relationship to the technologies of industrial and post-industrial society has not merely been the traditionally ascribed one of furnishing external material for blanket electronic transmission and distribution; in its formative years, in its parallel development with the telegraph, the daily newspaper, and the railroad, as well as in the league structures that preceded vaudeville's chain booking practices, its parks and stadiums served as *the* prototypical vehicle for the country's mass entertainment consumerism. The open air was its cathode ray tube, the grandstand its chassis.

Baseball's pioneering role as a mass entertainment producer sprang most conspicuously from promoting, in its spectators, the purely imaginative and emotional participation (and the practical limitations to that participation) so fundamental to the workings of the media as we know them; in other words, the cry of "Play Ball!" might have sent players scurrying out to their positions on the field, but its message as a medium was directed primarily at those who *didn't* play. This is the most important context for grasping, among other things, the sport's superior social impact over such popular rivals as horse racing; its fabled identification with the pastoral and the seasonal; its proclaimed uniqueness from other organized sports for being "timeless" in nature; its affiliation with declared and undeclared sponsors; its peculiar history of gambling scandals; the self-righteousness and chauvinism of its official spokesmen; inane debates over its status as a business; its celebrity cult; and, ironically, the claim, especially besieged in recent decades by professional football, that it is the "national pastime." In fact, in more ways than Albert Spalding and Yogi Berra ever intended, baseball has never had serious competition for that honorific title.

It ought to go without saying that any ring of mass entertainment would be little more than sawdust without an acknowledgment of the customers encircling it. But baseball researchers have been markedly negligent about according recognition to the extent of the fan's organic involvement in the game. Some of this might seem understandable. The *game*, as such, remains most vivid as a chronicle of dramatic moments on the diamond and of the personalities contributing to those moments. The baseball *business* commands attention as a century-and-a-half calendar of franchise and league maneuverings with metropolitan, regional, and state ramifications and for the personalities achieving or failing at these manipulations. In the best of cases, even the *sport* has won deserved due as more than its constituent game and business elements, as a social dynamic binding together statistics, stadiums, and grandstand memories. But, that said, the fan has remained a minor figure in most of baseball's accountings. When not an abstract number or a nebulous demographic attesting to markets and trends, he typically has been seen only as a component of civic fervor or civil disorder, as a stereotype of generational sentimentality or class disgruntlement. Like the mass entertainment industry it specializes in, baseball history has found it convenient to idealize or caricature *the fan* (the father soft-tossing in the backyard with his son) as some entity removed from *fans* (the T-shirted fools spilling beer on one another while they reach over the railing to grab for a ball still in play), and vice versa. The result has been the caging of folklore and sociology in separate parts of the zoo, making it easier to claim insufficient time for visiting both on the same trip.

Viewed within a broader mass entertainment framework, even some of the most familiar politics of baseball history appear to develop an extra wrinkle or two. For example, attitudes toward the origin of the very word *fan* have always been more about ideological assumptions than established etymological evidence. The wisdom that *fan* is the shortened form of *fanatic* has prevailed since the close of the nineteenth century, when advocates of baseball as an immaculately conceived American sport abhorred the notion that it might trace back to *the fancy*, an English term for followers of boxing that, according to such researchers as William Henry Nugent, gradually spread to other sports. But more than just another possible instance of the zealotry of turn-of-the-century baseball powers to divorce the sport, even in its most casual language, from all things foreign, especially British, the fan as an abbreviation of *fanatic* also suggests a consumer ravenous for what the market can provide, the more and the quicker the better. Long before the New York Mets could peddle more than 70 different kinds of caps with the team logo, this was not an image to be discouraged.

As in the case of other mass entertainments, baseball could lend itself to an exhaustive from-the-beginning-to-now history solely around the concern for image. Some might say its preoccupations in this area have been even more accentuated than elsewhere, that its aspirations immemorial to be thought of as standing between Mom and apple pie as American Virtue have made it all but paranoid on the subject. For sure, the sport has only reluctantly left to disinterested eyes the characterization of its own fans, preferring to having them described in the nineteenth century as "quiet and respectable strangers," in the twentieth century as hardworking middle-class breadwinners, and in the twenty-first century as luxury box season-ticket holders. In the official version, the rowdies, gamblers, and drunks glimpsed in the lower deck have been as endemic to baseball as Fatty Arbuckle was to Hollywood: unfortunate aberrations and uglinesses rooted to eras long since overcome.

As much as the motion picture industry, baseball celebrates fiction as reality; as much as the recording industry, it depends for profit on the repetitive play of its fiction; as much as the station break announcement of "Details at eleven!" or a splurge of movie trailers, the constitutional theme of its fiction is expectation. Its rules, rituals, and skills make for a commodity demanding total suspension of belief in any world other than its own. The first function of the fan is to commit to this self-contained illusion as completely as he would to a Russell Crowe movie; in other words, he has to embrace the presupposition that the game, from organization through tactics to result, matters. As Leonard Koppett has put it, "the caring . . . *is* the entertainment."

This caring touches upon more than the immediate gratifications and despondencies occasioned by a specific game, season, or team. It dwells within a cultural premise ranging far wider than some economic or athletic concoction, occupying its fictional space so thoroughly—even arrogantly—that there is little room left for those who do not share the same impulse. For the true believer, there is something vaguely *off* about people who don't like baseball, as there is about people who don't like children or who hate animals. For poet Walt Whitman, it was imperative to care because baseball "belongs as much to our institutions, fits into them as significantly, as our constitution's laws; is just as important in the sum total of our historic life." A fugitive member of the Weather Underground made it clear where he came from when, while being hunted by the FBI in the 1960s for alleged political terrorism, he lamented to a friend that what he missed most was being able to see Willie Mays play regularly. Even other fictions that might appear to be superficially compatible are mainly irksome in their attempts to distract. The notorious failure of most fictional baseball movies to impress, for example, stems in substantial part from cross-wired fantasies, from the over-charging task of laying one set of imaginative conceits over another; cloned fiction isn't normally perceived as delivering much in terms of stimulating character or plot development.

The fan is called upon for more than caring, however. As routinely as radio and television, baseball also breaks through the fourth wall of its fictional programming for news bulletins stating that it expects more than metaphor back for its organizational enterprise. Like the mass media that succeeded it, the sport has always wanted it both ways, institutionalizing the fictional as actuality and its prominent players as emblems of the fantasy while letting no one forget the commercial springs of the romance, on the contrary emphasizing them as an integral part of the experience. Disreputable idleness, a solitary pursuit, became acceptable leisure, a socially controlled activity, in the middle of the nineteenth century only with a proliferation of ticket windows, box offices, and cash registers, and the fan has fulfilled his second vital function ever since by standing in line.

As anonymous as he might be at a stadium gate, the baseball fan passing through a turnstile brings an experience to his spectating role that the movie patron normally cannot bring to a Cinemascope screen. Unless he is an actor, or has been ambushed while riding with a posse, the average movie-house patron does not have the equivalent of the baseball fan's background of having played at some junior level the professional spectacle he has paid to watch. Even before he has taken his box or bleacher seat, personal currencies—yearning, embarrassment, nostalgia—are part of the equation. On the one hand, this sharpens the empathetic focus between the grandstand and the field; on the other hand, abetted not a little by the game's deliberate pace, it fosters an acutely opinionated watchfulness. It is not merely the spectacle as a whole that is judged, but every scene, line, and bit player within it. Approbation and antagonism, enthusiasm and disappointment shadow every moment. The sport's technical intricacies and strategic complexities notwithstanding, the departing spectator is rarely given to just an uncertain "Well, I guess it was all right" or an awed "That was magnificent!" For good or bad, an assumption of expertise calls for more layered analyses.

For all the odes written to baseball's seasonality, the spectator's combined distance and knowledge has nourished a speculative habit that is in season twelve months a year. If the first batter has yet to hit a home run in the Hot Stove League, conjecture about his ability to do so and about the next team he might do it for has kept daily newspapers in baseball mode every offseason since the founding of the National League in 1876. When New York's huge-circulation *Daily News* can devote ten different stories to baseball in one December edition, only one of which contains an announcement of completed fact, public absorption is clearly presumed to extend beyond wins and losses, beyond what takes place on the diamond in any immediately tangible way. In fact, as the ubiquity of everything from homegrown baseball dice games to elaborate computer programs has amply demonstrated, the fan has had little trouble inflating his speculative role to create personal fictions within the most visible one. Whether or not baseball is as "timeless" as has been claimed, such fantasies-on-the-fantasy have gone a long way toward making it placeless; whether or not they offer any more real control over what can unfold on a playing field, they provide a semblance of it in the living room.

Call-in talk shows have come to represent a similar consolation. When these radio programs first became popular about 25 years ago, there were undoubtedly callers who harbored genuine hopes their gripes or proposals would reach some authoritative ear, prompting concrete action in one arena or another. Indeed, there were isolated cases where that was so, at least when it came to an easily corrected public-relations boner involving some particularly obtuse team employee. With time, however, the talk shows have settled mechanically into a theatrically purgative role, broadcasting the complaints and epiphanies of callers less energetically than their commercials before saying goodbye-until-the-same-time-tomorrow. The fan, the supposed reason for the programs, comes across as predictably exasperated and powerless, one whose hopes in life have been reduced to having his 60 seconds on the air a more permanent record of his depression than might be provided by a psychiatrist's notebook or bartender's memory. Of course, even the most dejected or alienated fan theoretically retains one significant political weapon—the wallet power to stop supporting baseball through tickets, cable TV, and taxes. To date, however, and in spite of the volubility of pocket protest groups, the smarmy hectoring of media commentators, and the defensive sanctimonies of the baseball establishment, he has been demonstrably reluctant to wield it. No matter how many perpetual boycott warnings he has issued over threatened or enacted player strikes and owner lockouts in the last 30 years, he has done little to carry through on them, remaining captive to his emotional and speculative commitments. At most, as in the wake of the most disruptive of all labor troubles in 1994–95, attendance declined for only a brief period, and even then as much because of eleventh-hour pre-season settlements and exacerbated impatience with specific mediocre teams as because of some popular coast-to-coast resistance. More telling, over the last decade or so, since boycott threats have been especially vocal, all but a handful of clubs have established season attendance records, with any overall league numbers down from immediately before the 1994–95 strife due chiefly to such profit-by-suicide franchises as Milwaukee and Kansas City.

There has also been another curiosity about the usual fan stance on labor agitations. More often than not, it has reflected a plague-on-both-your-houses view—that the players are greedy and the owners deserve whatever grief they get. One political implication of the fan's stated indifference to union demands is that it leaves him closer to the status quo—a view exploited propagandistically by management more than once over the years. But the plague-on-both-your-houses stance also insinuates that the fan himself is outside the entire process—that *he* hasn't been the one to gobble up season tickets at higher and higher prices every year, that *he* hasn't been the one to parade his Cardinals jersey on the streets, that *he* hasn't been the one willing to stand on long lines for the opportunity to hand over $20 for the autograph of a one-time .276-hitting shortstop. In short, the fan himself has sometimes found it just as convenient as researchers to estrange himself from baseball's historical process.

At other times, fans have not been at all shy about dramatizing their own role in the sport. If one collected all their testimonials together, for example, there were about a million people (not the officially counted 34,320) on hand at the Polo Grounds on October 3, 1951, to witness personally Bobby Thomson's playoff-winning home run against the Dodgers. Another story approaching the dimensions of urban legend depicts the fan as having lost potentially tens of thousands of dollars because his mother threw away his baseball cards. This particular tale has played to some of baseball's most traditional institutional themes—that all true American boys collected cards; that there were aberrant moments growing up (going off to college, meeting girls) when baseball was not the chief priority it should have been; that women didn't appreciate the game as much as men (fathers have never been accused of doing the dumping); and that mild ruefulness (not matricide) is the price for such neglect. The first rule of fan identification with baseball is that, no matter how badly things have gone, there will always be another game tomorrow. For all his captivity, however, the fan entered the new millennium amid noise of being an endangered species, of being a kindred spirit to those *merely* 10 million viewers who have a favorite show cancelled because television network executives conclude such an audience doesn't translate into high enough ratings. The sport's economic strategists have been recorded as going so far as to regard the whole concept of a *fan* as injurious to their long-range interests, contrasting him unfavorably to the preferred *customer*. Although there have been minor variations in the explanations of the difference, the general idea has been that the customer might not always enter through the turnstile with the fan's emotional and imaginative baggage; but once he has pocketed his ticket stub, he is far more likely to take an escalator to the most expensive seating section, whip out a credit card for spending on corporate clients at the souvenir stand, and buy a commemorative tile in the team's Hall of Fame Room or a parking space in its VIP lot. As commonly suggested, the customer need not be a passionate follower of the club he is patronizing, need not know anything more about baseball than the nineteenth-century burghers in Cincinnati who sensed only that Harry Wright's Red Stockings were good for local business. The main thing is that the customer spends more than the fan, so therefore deserves greater attention.

There is a neat David-versus-Goliath ring to this. There is a lot of obfuscation to it, as well, since if *customer* has an etymological root, it is *custom*. What the propagandizing of the fan-customer distinction has left is the implication that only in the last couple of decades have the sport's business policies been tilted toward the especially well-heeled—that, for example, a Charlie Ebbets at the beginning of the twentieth century didn't make a science out of minimizing the number of cheap seats at Ebbets Field or that a Larry MacPhail after World War II didn't give unprecedented emphasis to season-ticket sales and open a club restaurant for the express purpose of attracting more business executives and their clients to Yankee Stadium. If stock boys or waitresses have had prestige seats at any World Series or playoff game in the last hundred years, it means they not only robbed the till where they worked, but found under all the bills the tickets that had been set aside for some business or political crony of the team owner weeks in advance. For a good 40 years, since the vogue for freestanding stadiums in peripheral areas encouraged greater use of automobiles, there has been little danger of a first pitch being held up because a city bus or train strike marooned riders on the way to the ballpark.

What baseball *has* been doing with greater frequency, on the other hand, is working to ensure that the rank-and-file fan in the stands, still the backbone of any franchise in sheer numbers, becomes as much of a financially predictable asset as the season-ticket holder who interrupts sipping his Pinot Grigio in his luxury box to look earnest about listening to "The Star-Spangled Banner." Although the tickets may nominally cost the same, there is a significant difference in profit for the club among those sold to a walkup on the day of the game, those purchased and reserved by telephone days and weeks ahead of time, and those mailed out as part of a season-ticket plan before the start of the season. Sammy Sosa and Pedro Martinez may have been the single biggest gate attractions around the turn of the millennium; but, because they drew mainly walkup fans who wanted to be sure the Cubs outfielder was in the lineup and the Red Sox righthander was pitching that particular day, they didn't add all that much bank interest from presold tickets for the host clubs. It has been in an effort to close that valve that teams have come up with multiple ticket plans, the most striking of which has been the Mets' scheme as of 2003 to peg prices to the identity of the opposition team. In short, it isn't that baseball has developed the hallucination that it can do without a traditional fan base of favor of the Fortune 500 and selected friends; it is that it has stepped up its reminders to fans that, since the days when 50-cent versus 25-cent admissions were a *casus belli* between leagues, they have always been regarded as customers, that there have always been turnstiles to fields of dreams.

GENESIS
TALES

The First Fans

Baseball's evolutionists have long since won the day from Albert Spalding and its creationists. Anyone who still believes Spalding's early-twentieth-century diktat that Abner Doubleday got up from bed one morning in 1839 and discovered a bat and ball in his sock drawer is most likely to be found keeping an eye on his chimney the night before Christmas. When last heard from, the evolutionists had traced generic children's games involving bases and balls back to 1744, had uncovered a suggestive quatrain entitled "Baseball" dating to 1774, and had dug out the journal of a Revolutionary soldier who attested to playing ball at Valley Forge in 1778. In 1825, 14 years before Doubleday was supposedly yelling "Eureka!" in his Ballston Spa bedroom or behind a tailor's shop in Cooperstown, another upstate New York community in Hamden was taking on challengers for what it called "Bass-Ball" at a dollar a game. The evolutionists have also brought forth evidence of baseball's direct siring by the British game of rounders from a sports book for boys published in London in 1829 and reprinted that year in the United States, as well as demonstrating that the first known use of the term *base ball* in its modern application was in a couple of other sports manuals issued in New England in the mid-1830s. According to researchers, none of this information or the games feeding from it could have been unknown in New York City in the early 1840s, when two squads, the New York Nine and the Knickerbockers, gained status as the first organized adult baseball teams. One person in particular who had to have known something about this recorded trail, it has been generally agreed, was Alexander Cartwright, a young bank clerk widely credited with inspiring some of the sport's most essential ground rules and regulations while serving as the vice-president, secretary, and head cheerleader of the Knickerbockers.

A clerk for the Union Bank, Cartwright was one of a group of professionals and white-collar employees who took advantage of their mid-afternoon quitting times in the early 1840s to gather on the East Side of Manhattan for a little exercise. These doctors, lawyers, and company men of various kinds and office levels started off by playing classic rounders, but then gradually changed some rules to accommodate their restricted playing space, first at Madison Square and then, trying to keep a step ahead of Manhattan's northward commercial expansion, a little further uptown in the Murray Hill section. When Murray Hill also began falling to land developers, the Knickerbockers shifted their games out of New York altogether, leasing the Elysian Fields in Hoboken, New Jersey, a brief ferry ride across the Hudson. A narcotic blend of woodlands, pastures, and waterfront, the Elysian Fields was a five-acre recreation park built in 1831 on the estate of gambler and bon vivant John Cox Stevens. In the years that followed, the tract became home to the New York Yacht Club, the New York Athletic Club, and the St. George's Cricket Club. In providing a playing area and dressing rooms for Cartwright's club, Cox received an annual rental of $75.

By the time they got around to drafting a formal constitution for their Knickerbocker Base Ball Club on September 23, 1845, members had been settled for some time on three major departures from rounders—a diamond rather than a square shape to the playing field; no retiring of runners by plugging them with the ball as they ran between bases; and, in a change with vast implications for those both playing and watching the game, the introduction of foul lines.

Contrary to the assertions of Cartwright's Hall of Fame plaque, the constitution's 14 regulations (the other 11 were more or less paraphrases of the rules for rounders) said nothing at all about 90 feet between bases, about contests lasting 9 innings, or about each team taking the field with 9 men. Moreover, although he undoubtedly had a hand in their formulation, Cartwright himself did not even sign off on the regulations that accompanied the formal chartering of the club, leaving that to fellow members William Wheaton and William Tucker.

To judge from surviving Knickerbocker scorebooks, the first contest played under the reformed rules took place less than two weeks after their codification, on October 6, 1845, at the Elysian Fields. Presumably because that match fielded only seven men a side, however, it—and several others in between—have been given the historical brushoff in favor of The Game, also played in Hoboken, on June 19, 1846, in which the New York Base Ball Club (apparently the core of the New York Nine) clobbered the Knickerbockers by the margin of 23–1.

As hallowed as it has become in baseball lore, the milestone significance of the June 1846 contest remains moot a century and a half later. Although the game did feature nine men on a side, the Knickerbockers played before and after that with different-sized teams, attributing no magical importance to the number. The score would also indicate the clubs were playing under the rounders rules of continuing only until some agreed-upon winning tally was reached. Then there is the issue of Cartwright's own role in the game. He definitely didn't play. Claims that he umpired, even fining player James Whyte Davis six cents for swearing, might or might not be true; the club scorebook leaves that line blank, as it frequently did.

Whether in October 1845 or June 1846, however, the Cox estate played host to the first true baseball fans. History has not recorded their names or numbers. What we can surmise about them is that they were New Yorkers or Jerseyans; that, unlike the billions that would follow them, they had no park or sandlot playing experience of their own; that the majority had received personal invitations from the players or other spectators; that because these included the wives and girlfriends of the players, a high proportion of them were women; and that a minority—cricket enthusiasts, water sportsmen of one kind or another—dropped by out of curiosity over the variation on rounders the Knickerbockers had devised. Give or take a few corsets, top hats, and horses, the scene would not have been unlike that at a community softball game today.

With the addition of special sun-screening pavilions for the women, the tableau would remain largely the same for the next decade or more. Applause was as much for encouragement as for congratulation, groans connoted sympathy more than disillusion. If gentility was in abundant supply, there was little reason for it not to be. The games were free, they were more novelty than impassioning cause, and they were an excuse for friends to get together in the fresh air. Rare was the contest that wasn't a prelude to dinner or drinks at McCarty's Hotel or the Odd Fellows Hall in Hoboken, or to some gathering back across the river in Manhattan. If the spectator was still only an onlooker at the evening function, it had more to do with his personality than with celebrity hierarchies.

Crossing over to Hoboken on the 13-cent Barclay Street Ferry, those first spectators didn't know it, but they were about to provide 160 years of livelihoods for historians, sociologists, psychologists, economists, entrepreneurs, city planners, bookmakers, architects, stadium managers, players, trainers, equipment suppliers, publicists, ushers, ticket sellers, souvenir vendors, beer distributors, scoreboard manufacturers, reporters, writers, marketers, advertisers, broadcasters, media executives, and the Phillie Phanatic. For doing nothing but sitting down and looking, they would be made symptom, emblem, and vanguard of vast internal changes in the United States. Long before they flirted with the baleful identity of couch

potatoes, they would be courted as eral benchmarks and proposi-
tioned as cushion revolutionaries. They would become synonymous
with the consequences of urbanization, the social structures of mass
leisure, and, to close a devolutionary cycle from the phenomenal to
the pestilent, a syndrome labeled "spectatoritis." They would look
forward to next year, wait 'til next year, and, in cities like Boston and
Chicago, wait through generations of years. The Hudson wasn't
always as narrow as it looked.

As complementary as their relationship has been, baseball players
and baseball fans have not had identical histories. Three early differences are particularly noteworthy. It has become a truism, for example, that the sport flourished in the middle of the nineteenth century in tune with a mood shift by the dominant Protestant culture
toward non-working activities; i.e., the realization by clerical scolds
that athletics might not have been *that* bad for the soul when the
most available alternatives for men with free time on their hands
were saloons, casinos, and bordellos. But this liberalized thinking
had no automatic application to people merely watching others
indulge in sports; the elaborate rationalizations for "muscular
Christianity" imported from British churches were all but irrelevant
when the only muscles being exercised were gluteal. Secondly,
through the excuse of fees for groundskeepers or other third parties,
the fan was paying money to see baseball long before the player was
receiving it, at least openly. And thirdly, the stigmas attached to
playing as a *profession* were conveniently divorced from the convention that people with "serious jobs" had a right to be entertained
when they weren't working. In one way or another, all three of these
differences would exert a permanent influence on interactions
between the diamond and the grandstand.

No Fun and Games

A censorious mood hovered over organized recreational activities in the United States in the early 1800s. In the words of historian Donald Mrozek, "To Americans at the beginning of the nineteenth century, there was no obvious merit in sport—certainly no clear social value to it and no sense that it contributed to the improvement of the individual's character or the society's moral or even physical health." One good reason for this was that most of the popular sports of the period—horse racing, boxing, animal fights of one kind or another—were magnets for gamblers and their usual train of rowdy bettors, desperate losers, and seedy collectors. But even such budding team games as cricket did not find hearty acceptance from the churches. At the core of the cultural somberness were the persisting Puritan and severest of Calvinist strains in American Protestantism that, even diluted by given sects, generally viewed man as wholly sinful by nature and capable of good only by unremitting discipline. Hard work wasn't only a social and economic necessity, it was a religious obligation for the continuous honing of self-discipline: playing was for children, and not too much of that, either. As Britain's Thomas Macaulay once quipped about this gloomy outlook: "The Puritan hated bear-baiting, not because it gave pain to the bear, but because it gave pleasure to the spectators."

At the same time, however, there were other components of the Puritan perspective that helped to reanimate the Republic after the near-disaster of the War of 1812 and that, later, were deployed as a decidedly unreligious alibi for the abuses of territorial expansion and industrialization. Usually ticked off as *self-reliance, energy,* and *industry,* what these qualities ultimately offered was a loophole in the austere Protestant behavioral code; to wit, God didn't demand merely that unworthy man get up every morning to work hard at some job; God demanded that, *whatever* he did, unworthy man work at it industriously. Ideologically, a wagon train could have been driven through the distinction.

The frowning didn't end overnight. Through an initial phase in the 1820s and 1830s, a new concern with the importance of physical conditioning—relayed from an England that had already seen some of the deleterious health and hygienic effects of industrialization—went little beyond individual running and calisthenics. For appeasing the old-guard sentries against idleness and narcissism, the justification was that the exercise not only constituted an act of respect toward a vessel of creation, but was both a practical preparation and a symbol for the nation-building tasks confronting all Americans. It was only with the steady clustering around growing cities and the rise of single-industry communities in the forties and fifties that team games became prized simultaneously as extracurricular representations of the work ethic and needed relief from actual daily toil. Guardians of the old censoriousness tried to act satisfied with the compromise that, whether viewed as an informal extension of labor or as physical and mental therapy for keeping the worker fit, the playing had an ulterior purpose, was not indulged in as an end in itself.

This still left open the moral dubiousness of merely watching a game. How did the churches reconcile the growing number of spectators drawn to baseball with the allowances they had made for muscular Christianity? For baseball historian Harold Seymour, "sitting in ball parks passively watching others perform was perhaps not the best form of recreation . . . but at least it was much better than some far less wholesome activities that might have been pursued." In fact, the churches were markedly resourceful in elaborating reasons for condoning the spectating habit.

One important justification was drafted from the game itself—that a spectator could learn a great deal from emulating the combination of discipline, energy, and self-reliance displayed by players and, ideally, would apply that insight to his own daily life. That he could observe such model behavior in the fresh air and within a setting of decorous comradeship might not have been right up there with godliness, but it confirmed the virtues of attentiveness (and its big brother obedience). Such graspings became easier as the years went on and the game assumed increasingly patriotic airs; eventually, social reformers adopted the same language for praising baseball's impact on city dwellers. Despite its various scandals in the second half of the nineteenth century, it wasn't long, either, before ministers were reaching for baseball metaphorically to drum home Biblical messages for those who sat both in pews and bleacher seats. Typical was a Methodist preacher cited by the weekly *Sporting Life* as telling his parishioners: "A recent writer in a popular magazine has characterized the scientific game of baseball . . . as the 'most perfect thing in America,' the idea being that for directness of aim and concentration of effort, it is the highest instance of efficiency attained in the life of the nation. This picture of efficiency must be transferred from the ball ground to the church of the living Christ that thus it may fulfill its glorious mission in achieving the redemption of all mankind."

Protestantism's apologetic contortions around the first fans were, by its lights, a social necessity. A game wasn't even needed for early spectators to be intrigued by diamond events. While searching for a serious opponent in the late forties and early fifties, the Knickerbockers would go over to Hoboken two or three times a week to keep in shape and, according to team member Daniel

Adams, "sometimes we had as many as a hundred spectators watching the practice." When the Knickerbockers finally found organized adversaries in such teams as the Gothams and the Eagles, Adams told the *Sporting News* years later, "there were thousands of people present." There seems little reason to doubt that this "hundred" and those "thousands" came primarily from the same social strata as the players—white-collar workers largely from Manhattan who had finished their work by mid-afternoon and didn't have to save up for the ferry fare.

But once the Knickerbockers were able to demonstrate their New York Game against the Gothams and Eagles in the fifties, they also began losing their monopoly on play and on the crowds in the New York area. The sport's first true hotbed was Brooklyn, where the number of organized teams was estimated as jumping from 12 to 71 over the last half of the decade. It was in this light that one New York daily joked in 1857 that the so-called "City of Churches" was about to change its sobriquet to the "City of Base Ball Clubs." The first Brooklyn squad of note was the Eckfords, shipwrights and mechanics who worked for the richest shipbuilder in the country, Henry Eckford. Although sometimes depicted as proletarians, the Eckford players were decidedly middle-class. Many were nonmanual workers, with a significant portion of them earning twice as much pay as the Knickerbocker clerks who were perceived in some quarters as upper-class. As popular ideas about Dodger fans would illustrate decades later, the misconception about the Eckfords and their following was rooted in biases about Brooklynites in general.

The Eckfords were merely one of the numerous teams formed along occupational lines or as after-work extracurricular activity in the 1850s. Among the more notable were the Mutuals (the firemen of Mutual Hook and Ladder Company No. 1), the Metropolitans (teachers), the Manhattans (policemen), the Pocahontases (dairy workers), the Phantoms (bartenders), the Excelsiors (merchants and countermen), and the Atlantics (butchers). The most popular playing locations included the Capitoline Grounds, Carroll Park, and Wheat Hill in Brooklyn; Red House and Hamilton Square in Manhattan; and Englewood in New Jersey. Clubs with vocational identities or company connections inevitably attracted similar categories of workers and colleagues as rooters, this in turn producing a little more us-against-them boisterousness from outside the foul lines. Among the keenest of early rivalries was that between Brooklyn's Excelsiors and the Knickerbockers. For one game played on the grounds of the Excelsior Club at the foot of Court Street, more than six thousand people were reported as perching on housetops and even clinging to the masts and spars of the vessels docked in the harbor. The *Brooklyn Daily Eagle* took the opportunity to remind its readers that baseball was not only "an excellent school for the physical training of our youth, but also . . . a rational and manly pastime, which our wives, sisters, and sweethearts can witness, and enliven us with their presence, without the fear of a word or deed that would call the blush to the cheek of the most fastidious."

As early as 1855, *Porter's Spirit of the Times* pronounced baseball a "national game," even though most of the adult playing at the time was confined to the East Coast. There were decidedly more misgivings about spectators, especially the kind who didn't want the action on the field to speak for itself. As *Spirit of the Times* scolded after hearing a little too much shouting at one game: "Respectable and quiet strangers could witness either play or practice as long as they understood that their presence on the ground was a privilege, not a right." Harold Seymour cites another reporter who, after seeing the behavior of onlookers at the first games to charge an admission price, the 1858 Fashion Course series on Long Island, "complained acidly that the crowd seemed to think that the games were got up for their special entertainment and that they were conferring a favor on the players by their presence." As bizarre as this criticism of a paying public might seem, it demonstrated the degree to which some reporters were slow to view baseball as an entertainment comparable to the theater or a minstrel show; for them, the only consideration was their "manly, scientific" sport, with the onlookers very dispensable extras. The debate over organized sport's place in the fictional entertainment universe was under way. It also wouldn't be the last time in baseball history that the public grasped what it was seeing before the game's publicists did.

The proliferation of the clubs in Brooklyn and New York turned out to be a poisoned time capsule for cricket, which had preceded baseball as a team entertainment in the late 1830s. Much of the writing about American cricket has tended to be historistic: Such a snobby English game couldn't possibly have succeeded against baseball's profound American ethos, so it didn't. This was certainly the point of view of late nineteenth-century notables who had economic or philosophical allegiances to baseball. Albert Spalding, who had both, spoke for many when he declared: "Cricket is a splendid game, for Britons. It is a genteel game, a conventional game—and our cousins across the Atlantic are nothing if not conventional. They play cricket because it accords with the traditions of their country so to do; because it is easy and does not overtax their energy or their thought."

It was a little more complicated than that. For starters, cricket wasn't all that snobby. Its primary athletic and fan appeal in cities like New York and Boston was to the same white-collar and professional groups that had gravitated toward the Knickerbockers, while its foundation in places like Philadelphia, Lawrence, and Lowell was the textile mill. Blue-collar workers from Portsmouth, New Hampshire to Cincinnati knew a bowler wasn't always a hat. Open betting was a steady feature of games, hard drinking a regular postgame occurrence. Nor was it just British diplomats who continued to make it baseball's chief rival as a spectator sport in the fifties. Thousands flocked routinely to the Elysian Fields to see the Dragonslayers from Staten Island take on visiting elevens from Montreal and Toronto. In 1859, extra ferries had to be put on to handle an estimated 24,000 people crossing the Hudson to see an exhibition between American all-stars and a British club. On the eve of the Civil War, there were at least ten cricket associations playing regularly in Manhattan or Brooklyn. Before the end of the century, clubs would be playing out schedules as far away as San Francisco.

The usual explanation given for baseball's ascendancy over cricket, alluded to by Spalding, has been the former's faster pace. "Baseball . . . was an exhilarating game that took under two hours to complete and thus did not prevent fans from a full day's work," as Steven A. Riess has put it. "By comparison, the British game of cricket . . . was so leisurely that it sometimes took days to complete." Americans haven't been the only ones captive to that argument. When R. A. Fitzgerald, captain of the English cricket team, visited the United States in 1872, he resorted to similar language. "Cricket," Fitzgerald asserted, "has to contend against the business habits of Americans. They will not give the time necessary for the game. . . . Time is money there, and there is no denying that much of that valuable commodity is egregiously cut into ribbons at cricket."

Such explanations have always seemed a little pre-cooked. While there is no doubt, for instance, that cricket would have cut heavily into the working day of both players and fans, that didn't prevent it from finding enthusiastic acceptance in the industrial cities of England, where labor hours were equally fierce. Nor did exhausting work schedules deter passionate players of either cricket or baseball from rising as early as four o'clock in the morning to get in some practice before reporting to the factory or firehouse. It has also been curious that some of those discerning a fatal flaw in cricket's open-endedness have been quick to romanticize baseball's "timelessness."

Baseball surpassed cricket's popularity in a period of intense nativism in the United States. But even assuming social predispositions against a sport that never masked its British origins, they were aggravated by practical problems emanating from cricket itself. The boom in baseball clubs might not have caused an immediate crisis for cricket attendance, but it posed a longer-term problem of playing space—for practice as well as for games. In 1856, papers were already reporting that every green plot within ten miles of New York was being used as a playing field. Cricket's response, as the populations of Brooklyn and Manhattan continued to swell, was to remain content with its principal patches in Hoboken and on Staten Island. Nor did the sport make any serious attempt in the New York area to recruit among the trades, leaving that territory exclusively for baseball; baseball's resultant ubiquity in fields and parks turned out to be its own best advertising, as much cause as effect.

It was upon these premises, rather than upon some predetermined cultural or spiritual logic, that the comparative rhythms of the two sports assumed the importance they did. And the most critical of these rhythms for flourishing in the U.S. were not those measured on the field of play, but those emanating from the stands. American cricketers, as much as American ballplayers, could think of their sport as an engaging pastime moving according to its own ebbs and flows; but cricket spectators had to make the additional commitment of returning two or three days in a row to have their entertainment concluded satisfactorily. That was not the easiest of commitments in an industrial society where the clock ruled leisure as much as work. If there was anything less "American" about cricket than about baseball, in short, it wasn't in the games, but in the pressures around the availability of audiences. What was made to seem a fated cultural choice by Spalding and other nativist critics was primarily a social and economic one. Baseball over cricket was, in fact, the first significant ratings win achieved by the baseball medium.

Attendance Must Be Paid

On July 20, 1858, baseball recorded its first paying fans. The place was the Fashion Race Course in Corona (or West Flushing), now part of the Queens borough of New York City but then part of Long Island. The occasion was the first of a three-game series between all-star squads from Brooklyn and New York. For 50 cents a head, the 1,500 customers (as they now were) were seated in the track's stone grandstand. Those who had arrived in buggies and carriages had also left dimes and quarters with the game's first parking-lot attendants outside. All the money collected went to the groundskeepers who had been pressed into service on short notice to convert the course into a playing field. More than four thousand people attended the series, which the New Yorkers won two games to one.

The success of the Fashion Course games opened more than one gate. Most obviously, it spurred the owners of race tracks and other substantial tracts of land around the East to convert their facilities for baseball, usually charging a dime (but sometimes a quarter) for admission. The heavy use of buses and the recently instituted Long Island Rail Road for getting to the games also opened some eyes to the fact that ferry boats to Hoboken and Staten Island didn't have to be the only public conveyances feeding off spectator sports. In the years to come, traction executives seeking collateral profits from games played at city outskirts would make up a disproportionately large share of baseball team investors. In addition, the crowds willing to travel lengthy distances and to pay for the pleasure of sitting in a grandstand made an impression on William Cammeyer, a Brooklyn skating-rink proprietor who a few years later would open baseball's first enclosed ballpark.

And then there was the gambling. Betting was said to have been so frantic during the series that, according to one astonished chronicler, "even women were seen exchanging wagers" openly in the grandstand. This appeared to refer to the common practice of single-batter (will he reach base or make an out?) and single-inning (how many runs will Brooklyn score during this at bat?) bets. Beyond this individual activity, there was the growing "pool" gambling that had been going on since well before the Fashion Course series, which certainly had hundreds of adepts in the Corona stands. By purchasing a ticket for as little as a dime from a tobacco shop, pool hall, or other retail enterprise, a bettor could win money by correctly selecting the club that won the most games, scored the most runs, or attained some other numerical high. When the games had special importance, daily newspapers provided invaluable assistance to pool sellers by publishing up-to-the-hour odds. The dailies didn't get their lines out of the air: Professional gamblers had wasted little time buzzing around this sport that was still organizationally amateur. By 1860, the bookmakers were infestive enough to attract attention to themselves by trying to get the Excelsiors to throw championship games to the Atlantics.

It went without saying that, together with other identification factors, the gambling made for less disinterested spectators. This in turn made for a lot of short tempers when diamond events didn't please the onlookers. One of the worst eruptions took place on August 23, 1860, during the rubber match of the three-game series between the Excelsiors and Atlantics played under the auspices of the National Association of Base Ball Players (NABBP). As clubs of the period went, the champion Excelsiors projected an image of sprightly decency, not least because of an earlier identity as the Jolly Young Bachelors. By contrast, the Atlantics were pretty much viewed as Brooklyn toughs—in part because many of its members were open-air butchers, in part because of their ties to gamblers and corrupt local politicians. Thus, there were all the elements for a morality play when almost 20,000 people jammed the Atlantics' turf at the Putnam Club in the Fort Greene section of Brooklyn for the contest that would decide the local championship. Also on hand were about a hundred cops, alerted not only by the anticipated size of the crowd but also by some ugly incidents over the first two games, in which supporters of the Atlantics had made it clear to the Excelsiors that they expected to win their bets. The tension was thick enough, according to the *Daily Eagle,* that although the attendance was larger than that for either of the first two games, fewer ladies were on hand.

Despite constant heckling from Atlantics fans, the Excelsiors sailed into the fifth inning with an 8–4 lead without too much trouble. But then the Atlantics rallied for two runs and appeared on the verge of scoring further when one of their baserunners overran third base and was tagged out. Rather than leave the field, the runner staged enough of a scene with the umpire to arouse the stands, sending nightstick-twirling policemen into one potential trouble spot after another. Peace was finally restored, but only briefly. In the sixth inning, the Atlantics first baseman made two misplays that seemed to assure the Excelsiors of a rebuilt lead. But it never came to pass. The pro-Atlantics bettors became so unruly that the Excelsiors had to leave the field, leading the umpire to declare the contest a draw. The gamblers didn't collect, but at least they went home no poorer. The Excelsiors refused to play the Atlantics again within the NABBP.

Some of the press reaction to baseball's first major public-relations crisis was predictable. "If the admirers of this manly pastime desire its future welfare," the *Daily Eagle* warned, "they should at once proceed to adopt stringent rules among the various clubs *against betting on the result of the matches played [original italics],* for it was unquestionably a regard for their pockets alone that led the majority of those peculiarly interested in the affair, to act in the blackguard manner they did." The *New York Clipper,* however, sounded an additional note by steering some of the blame for the outburst away from baseball's traditional middle-class fan base toward what it termed "the foreign element of our immense metropolitan population"—an apparent reference to Irish immigrants. Beyond its knee-jerk xenophobia, the gratuitous charge reflected a growing uneasiness among the worthies of the press about baseball's class appeal. For all the taffy talk (then and ever after) about how presidents and paupers, lawyers and laborers, bankers and delivery boys belonged to the same class when they watched action on a ball field, the prospect of testing so much classlessness regularly did not thrill the stalwart citizenry. As Warren Goldstein has observed, "the cult of respectability among artisans, clerks, and petty proprietors gave them just as much dread of 'the poor' and 'the roughs' as was expressed by those much further up the class ladder."

The brouhaha at the Excelsiors-Atlantics game was not an isolated incident. Less than two weeks later, a similar scene unfolded in Bergen, New Jersey, during a game between the Brooklyn Resolutes and Jersey City Mechanics. Once again, gamblers spent most of the contest cursing out the team they had bet against (the Resolutes), this time going home with a win *and* money. In the same year, a visit by the New York Mutuals to Irvington, New Jersey, attracted between 6,000 and 7,000 fans—and enough pickpockets to service most of them. It didn't take long for disturbances among the spectators to spill out onto the field into a full-blown riot. Before police arrived on the scene, players took to swinging bats in self-defense. The era of genteel baseball was drawing to a close.

Pros and Cons

By 1860, baseball wasn't quite the New York–centric affair it had been only three years earlier with the formation of the NABBP; clubs as far away as Chicago and St. Louis had become organization members in the interim. Nevertheless, few would have denied that the level of play in New York and Brooklyn was higher than elsewhere, making even the provincial claims of teams in the area to being "national" champions a commercial asset. A few weeks before encountering the Atlantics and their disagreeable fans, the Excelsiors decided to exploit this with the sport's first two barnstorming tours—an initial swing through upstate New York followed by visits to the Middle Atlantic states of Pennsylvania, Maryland, and Delaware. The two tours proved to be as vital to the shaping of the sport as the Fashion Race Course series. Together, they underlined the influential role of the railroad and the telegraph in baseball's growth, as well as consolidating its popularity beyond the biggest cities of the East Coast and communities with NABBP representation. It was almost incidental that their fifteen straight road victories without a defeat also confirmed the Excelsiors as the best team in the country.

Two decades earlier, the trips would not have been possible—at least not without the willingness of the players to go barnstorming for more than a thousand miles by horseback or coach. In 1830, for example, there had been merely 32 miles of track in the entire country. But by 1860, with 30,000 miles of track laid down, the venture was not such a gallop into the dark. Nor was it conducted in privacy. Thanks to local telegraph operators, the particulars of every game were relayed around the country within minutes of its conclusion. Albert Spalding, then a ten-year-old in Illinois, would credit those reports with seeding a passion in him and other boys in the Midwest for baseball. More than what they brought practically through their technology, the railroad and the telegraph put the sport on the fast track to *imagination*. Not only didn't the fan have to be in the vicinity of the playing field to know what was going on, he didn't have to know anything about the place where the team was, other than its being a venue for victory or defeat. Box scores became maps.

From Albany to Baltimore, the Excelsiors paraded more than their championship reputation; they were also able to put on murderous display Jim Creighton. The game's first bona fide star as both a pitcher and a batter, Creighton was to spark as many misty stories as Abner Doubleday. Was he really the first paid professional, or just one of several players the Excelsiors were paying under the table? Did he truly go through the entire 1860 season without making an out, or was it merely four outs in 1862? Did he actually start the game's first triple play after making an acrobatic catch in the outfield against Baltimore on July 22, 1860, or was that just the triple play the most people had seen up to that point? In the end, these became details swallowed up by a charisma that made him the single biggest attraction in the pre–Civil War period.

What was less debatable was that his pitching mastery was based on a combination of speed, wile, and larceny. In the era when pitchers were obligated to underhand 45-foot deliveries to the plate, Creighton perfected an illegal wrist snap that amounted to throwing the ball. For much of the 1858 and 1859 seasons, this made his fastball all but unhittable. When batters began catching up to him, he reasserted his dominance by varying the wrist snaps to come up with off-speed pitches. All of this produced frustrated protests from opponents, secret copying from other pitchers, and bigger lines outside ticket booths.

The spectating pastime within the pastime at Excelsior games was to try to pick up the wrist snaps, prompting learned and not-so-learned discussions among the onlookers. Those with weaker eyesight had to be content watching his power feats with the bat, since, along with his dazzling pitching, Creighton was one of the earliest arguments for slugging as the biggest box-office lure. In the words of one newspaper at the time, the long ball "cannot fail to elicit applause." The bottom line was that, whether or not he was literally the very first to be paid for his services, Creighton was certainly the most profitable player investment of his time.

The triumphant tours by the Excelsiors represented some serious thread-pulling at the sweater of amateurism then covering baseball. First, there were the trips themselves, which added up to extended time away from the jobs most members of the club were still holding down. Even the players not being paid under the table had to work out arrangements with employers or customers without making it sound as though their jobs had become the extracurricular activity. Then there was the unabashed promotion of Creighton, which suggested to anyone paying attention that his box-office value must have been worth *some* compensation. However rarely they were enforced, NABBP regulations forbade players not only from receiving remuneration of any kind, but also from being involved "directly or indirectly" in any form of betting on games. And beyond the NABBP, there were all the public perceptions—from the crypto-religious apologetics to the moralistic pep talks to the carefree recreativeness—that would have been blurred by the mere mention of money. What the Excelsiors tours were basically gambling on was that the time had come for fans to concede that a Jim Creighton playing on the most polished of clubs was worth the price of their admission, that the superiority rather than familiarity of playing skills was the attraction, and that this level of athletic ability both required and deserved full-time professional concentration.

A response from the public was still in the offing when, on April 12, 1861, Union troops fired back at the Confederate forces around the Fort Sumter garrison in the harbor of Charleston, South Carolina. The Northern batteries were under the command of Abner Doubleday.

War Games

The Civil War years (1861–65) have often been portrayed as baseball's incubation. More accurately, they were a weaning period from which the sport was able to assert for itself the national presence East Coast cities had been claiming for it for the better part of a decade. Because of the countless thousands of small-town recruits exposed to the New York Game for the first time by soldiers, prisoners, and stockade guards from one side or the other, the North-South conflict also nurtured the fable of baseball's rural roots. Both exaggerations, the military and the rural, blended into postwar national reunification themes that the increasingly brutal realities of Eastern cities, especially within the true baseball cradle of New York, repudiated. In the years to come, they also fed off one another for the layered image of a pastorally innocent but profoundly honorable pastime worthy of an ideal American institution. No less a figure than the log-cabin president, Abraham Lincoln, would be evoked as the First Fan.

Beyond all the rhapsodies, what was clear by the end of the sixties was that the war had gone a long way toward democratizing the sport's players and followers, if not its operators. The mass in the baseball medium no longer had to be measured by single-game attendances in Brooklyn or Jersey City, but could be projected as a potential market for any population center between the Atlantic and the Pacific.

Given his lifelong proclivity for associating baseball with military virtues, it was hardly surprising that Spalding emphasized the Civil War's impact on the sport's development. In a typically florid passage in his autobiography, he declared:

> *[Baseball] received its baptism in the bloody days of our Nation's direst danger. It had its early evolution when soldiers, North and South, were striving to forget their foes by cultivating, through this grand game, fraternal friendship with comrades in arms. It had its best development at the time when Southern soldiers, disheartened by distressing defeat, were seeking the solace of something safe and sane; at a time when Northern soldiers, flushed with victory, were yet willing to turn from fighting with bombs and bullets to playing with ball and bat. It was a panacea for the pangs and humiliation to the vanquished on one side, and a sedative against the natural exuberance of the victory on the other. It healed the wounds of war, and was balm to stinging memories of sword thrust and saber stroke.*

As recently as October 1985, Yale president A. Bartlett Giamatti delivered a speech to the Massachusetts Historical Society containing similar themes. According to the future baseball commissioner, the sport "grew in the surge of fraternalism, to fraternal societies, sodalities, associations, and aggregations, that followed the fratricide. Baseball showed who had won the war and where the country was building. . . ."

Over in reality, meanwhile, things were a little less neat. Few were the recruits, even from the deepest South, who had never seen some version of the game played somewhere. The Mexican War (1846–48) had already introduced it to many in Texas and the Southwest. By his own journal accounting, Alexander Cartwright himself had spread the gospel to "mountain men and Indians" during an 1849 trek from New York to California. Even remote Los Angeles claimed to have been playing since before the North-South hostilities. Below the

Mason-Dixon Line, Augusta and New Orleans were just two of the cities that had been sending teams out on the field for a few years. Seymour cites a report of one 1859 contest in New Orleans during which "polite stewards" served refreshments within "commodious tents for the ladies spread under the umbrageous branches of the fine old live oaks."

What the War Between the States did bring was extended exposure to the New York Game—not only at military installations and in concentration camps, but in the towns and cities through which the Union Army marched. In the words of folklorist Tristram Potter Coffin, the war helped the sport spread "like dysentery." Widely circulated anecdotes paint Yankee soldiers as marching off against the Confederacy with bats and balls in their bags; Abraham Mills, a future National League president, liked to say he used his baseball equipment as much as his sidearms. For their part, Confederate soldiers hardly had to wait to be captured and clapped in Union stockades, as has often been insinuated, to get the knack of the game. Seymour cites the testimony of one "Captain James Hall of the 24th Alabama" who recalled playing in Dalton, Georgia, on the eve of General William Sherman's Atlanta Campaign in the summer of 1864. One Massachusetts infantryman was recorded as having "come to view Confederate soldiers in a more favorable light after he witnessed their skill as baseball players."

Not even the war put an end to the baseball entertainment offered by the NABBP teams, though it did curtail schedules and drastically reduce the number of member squads. The 62 clubs playing under the NABBP banner in 1860 dropped to less than half that for the war years, with many teams suiting up for only a handful of games over the summer. The trailblazing Knickerbockers didn't play at all for two years. But the games that did go on continued to draw, and to draw big. On October 21, 1861, three months after the First Battle of Bull Run, a Brooklyn all-star squad attracted more than 10,000 fans to a game against Hoboken at the Elysian Fields. On July 10, 1862, the Brooklyn Excelsiors became the first team from the New York area to go to Boston, where they defeated a Bowdoin squad by the handy score of 41–15. On Independence Day in 1863, thousands turned out for an intramural game staged by the Baltimore Pastimes. The contest was noteworthy insofar as the battle of Gettysburg was raging less than 60 miles away and the city was torn between sympathizers for the North and the South.

The drafting of Lincoln as the First Fan didn't begin in earnest until the early twentieth century, after his assassinated figure had begun to dwarf the pragmatic Republican politician, as much despised as admired while he was alive. The campaign was of a piece with Spalding's maneuvers to mythologize the sport through the person of Abner Doubleday. The success of the campaign was such that, as late as the 1940s, radio fabulist Bill Stern was deliriously portraying Lincoln as being on his deathbed and begging (who else?) Doubleday: "Don't let baseball die!"

In fact, though, baseball had come to Lincoln before he had come to the sport, at least within the popular media. In the wake of the November 1860 presidential elections, Currier and Ives issued a print depicting the future sixteenth president and his vote rivals— Southern Democrat John Breckinridge, Northern Democrat Stephen A. Douglas, and Unionist John Bell—as ball players. Entitled "The National Game: Three 'Outs' and One 'Run': Abraham Winning the Ball," the print had Lincoln holding a ball and a long rail labeled "equal rights and free territory," with his foot on a "home base." All four men, in dialog clouds discussing the election results, speak in the baseball slang of the day, with Lincoln warning the others that if they want to challenge him again in 1864, they must have "a good bat and strike a fair ball to make a clean score and a home run." The Currier and Ives lithograph makes it clear that baseball was already enough of a cultural currency in the country not to need a Lincoln for popularizing it in any introductory sense, that his impressment later on would be to strictly ideological ends.

A running motif in the depiction of Lincoln as the First Fan is that he acquired his interest in the sport through playing it himself— making him the baseball equivalent of Renaissance Man. The most popular of all Lincoln baseball tales concerned his alleged reaction in Springfield when told a delegation was on its way to inform him officially that he had won the Republican nomination for the 1860 presidential race. As passed on by Spalding, the nominee's reply to the messenger supposedly was: "Tell the gentlemen that I am glad to know of their coming; but they'll have to wait a few minutes till I make another base hit." As the complete fan, Lincoln was also the subject of a noted "fathers playing catch with sons" story. On July 12, 1914, five decades after the reputed fact, Winfield Scott Larner told the *Washington Evening Star* he had been present in 1862, when Lincoln and his nine-year-old son Tad had showed up for a game on an old circus lot in the capital at Sixth and K streets. In Larner's account, Lincoln led his son by the hand "modestly and unobtrusively," making his way "up to where he could see the game and sat down in the sawdust left over from the late circus." For the rest of the game, the president was said to have held the boy between his knees, pointing out this and that, every so often cheering and waving his hat like "the most enthusiastic fan of the day." The Larner story would eventually inspire cartoons and other representations of the president as an attentive spectator.

The Enclosure Movement

B efore it was so ideologically, baseball was enclosed physically. In 1862, war or no war, William Cammeyer saw enough profit in the offing to convert his lucrative ice-skating rink in the Williamsburg section of Brooklyn into the first ballpark. Beyond the novelty of the facility itself (inspired by the grandstand at the Fashion Race Course in Corona), the Union Grounds at Lee Avenue and Rutledge Street assumed significance for the financial leverage it gave the entrepreneur over both fans and teams and for the formalization of the game-going ritual.

Benches placed beneath a long wooden shed and at various vantage points around the field enabled the Union Grounds to seat roughly 1,500. Standees, still the overwhelming majority for big games, had to watch from their usual places behind the foul lines. Aside from the grandstand shed, there were structures used as clubhouses and for storage, as well as a saloon. Fences estimated as six or seven feet high encircled the field, which, when drained and dried, was an enormous pasture extending more than 500 feet away from home plate in all directions.

When the park opened on May 15, 1862, Cammeyer was on hand to collect a dime from every spectator who walked through the main entrance to see the Eckfords take on the Putnams. He could do little about an embankment outside the outfield fence that made it possible for freeloaders to follow the proceedings, if at an appreciable distance. On the other hand, the saloon on the grounds and the vendors circulating among the seated patrons amounted to another commercial wall, this one blocking out street peddlers who had come to count on baseball crowds for important income: In effect, the concessionaire business, another big source of profit, had also been formalized. In acknowledgement of the war raging in other parts of the country, Cammeyer had a band kick off the day by playing "The Star-Spangled Banner," the first time music was known to have been part of pre-game ceremonies.

In its first year of operation, the park was used mainly by the Eckfords or for all-star contests involving Brooklyn and other area players. When military conscription began to deplete the Eckford forces, Cammeyer invited the rising Atlantics to use the facility. That proved to be a smart move, insofar as the Atlantics were soon on their way to becoming one of the dominant teams of the decade, going through 1864 and 1865 without suffering a defeat; however, it proved taxing when they began demanding a slice of the gate receipts. Cammeyer resisted at first, contending that he had earned the right to pocket the full admission by furnishing a field and a clubhouse. But faced with an ultimatum from a club that had never hesitated to use its political connections to get what it wanted, he was forced to relent and cut the Atlantics in for a portion of the ticket sales. In the view of such pioneer baseball publicists as Henry Chadwick, Cammeyer's concession amounted to the real beginning of professionalism in baseball. Once teams perceived gate receipts as a measuring stick, they could hardly wait for the war to end in order to play more games, schedule more tours, and recruit more skilled players for enhancing their box-office appeal. As for the fan, the necessity of paying also, at least in theory, gave him a weapon.

The opening of the Union Grounds was the first brick in what was dubbed the "enclosure movement," a sardonic reference to the eighteenth-century privatization measures in Britain for closing off public grazing and farming lands. Before the end of the year, Reuben S. Decker and Hamilton Weed converted a second ice rink, also in Brooklyn, in the Brownsville section around Nostrand and Putnam Avenues, into a ballpark at the Capitoline Grounds. Before long, parks were popping up in other parts of the country. What also popped up was the debate over how discriminatory toward fans the enclosure movement sought to be, proved to be, or failed to be.

On one level, the paid seating pioneered by Cammeyer privileged more than the affluent carriage trade as sedentary spectators. This was not to the total comfort of the carriage trade, which in the years ahead would find more and more reasons to try to revive cricket as a vibrant national pastime at baseball's expense. The gentry that wanted to watch a game had no choice but to buy a bench place, and if that made for closer quarters with neighbors than was desired, that was too bad; their only other options were to sit on one of the special terraces usually provided for women (and at higher cost), or to stay home. The Cammeyers of the day didn't worry too much about the choice made, since however much the press liked to dress up the economic and social standing of the grandstand patrons, the upper middle class was no more vital to the success of the enclosure movement than it had been to the success of the Knickerbockers in Manhattan and Hoboken. At the other end of the scale, the fixed seating made it increasingly difficult for those without money to get any closer to the action than the kind of embankment that skirted the Union Grounds. The haves had seats and shade, the have-nots needed more income or binoculars. The closest most of them came to home-plate sightlines were in the panegyrics about how baseball games supposedly brought together all classes in some Edenic democratic assembly. It was the nature of the sport, as one paper asserted, to attract "judges, lawyers, bankers, doctors, clergymen, merchants, clerks, mechanics, students, railroad men, laborers, farmers, officials, editors, printers' devils, bootblacks, and so on. . . ." One of the funniest of these lion-with-the-lamb descriptions ran in *Wilkes' Spirit of the*

Times, which told its readers that the 5,000 people attending a game in Paterson, New Jersey, between the hometown Olympics and the Unions of Morrisania (the Bronx) included "a large number of young ladies and a few old ones; men of all grades, ages, and standing—the young and strong, the aged and feeble, crippled, blind, and maimed; garrulous, patient, enthusiastic, combatible and non-combatible [sic], in truth a motley group comprising everything."

Meanwhile, it was hardly a secret that the principal target of the new parks were the same white-collar workers, tradesmen, and professionals who had been drawn to the Knickerbockers as players a couple of decades earlier. Just the starting times of games—in the late afternoon when these groups were free—made that evident. Indeed, for the rest of the century, through the organization of the first professional leagues, game starting times would be based on the quitting times of the workers most likely to attend. In New York, this meant "prime time" was 4:00, after Wall Street had closed for the day. In Washington, it was a half-hour later for accommodating government clerks who got off at 4:00, while in Chicago it was an hour earlier since the Board of Trade closed at 1:30 and the Stock Exchange at 2:00. The 4:30 first pitch in Washington was about as late as park owners waited since the assumption was that most of the spectators were family men who had only a couple of hours to spare between leaving their offices and sitting down to dinner with their wives and children.

At first, it was the starting hour of the game more than its cost that conspired against attendance by the blue-collar working class; most factory hands and other laborers toiled 10 ½ hours a day every day except Sunday. Enclosed late afternoon matches were not so much a deliberated escalation of a class policy as they were just the latest step in the development baseball had been following since its inception. Claims by some historians that the dime admission at parks like the Union Grounds and Capitoline Grounds was a calculated discouragement to the working class overstate the social planning of the Cammeyers and Deckers, understate their profit motive, and overlook their business comfort zone. Ten cents was ten cents—wherever it came from, because the "wherever" had already been fairly predetermined. It was only later, from the the mid-1860s on, that ballpark operators felt the need to justify their price increases to a quarter (and yet later to 50 cents) with the argument that this would serve as a deterrent to "unruly elements." Even then, few were buying that. As the *New York Chronicle* observed, all the talk about attracting better-behaved crowds through a higher admission was so much camouflage; the public was being forced to pay more, the paper said, "simply because the proprietors of the grounds have had to share the gate receipts with the ball players."

Where the classism of the early entrepreneurs was manifest right from the start, on the other hand, was in their preconceptions about character, especially in their deep-rooted biases about the source of any rowdyism in the stands. And rowdyism there was—plenty of it—set off by everything from disagreements over what took place on the field to fisticuffs over somebody's view being blocked. The situation became so acute that Henry Chadwick anticipated the current practice of television directors not to show field streakers by scolding newspapers for reporting grandstand fights in any detail, pointing out that this only encouraged what he termed the "brutal tastes . . . [of] the blackguards." Notwithstanding the fact that the overwhelming majority of those mixed up in the fracases were the middle-class patrons cultivated by the park owners and despite the fact that professional bookmakers and gamblers (other regular sources of friction) could gain entry to the grandstand by forking over the thinnest of coins, the disturbances still frequently ended up being blamed on the social stratum least represented at the park. Class codewords like "roughs" and "unprofessional element" littered accounts of disorderly scenes. What seldom crept into such stories, on the other hand, was the drinking that was encouraged by on-site saloons and vendors. Least of all was there any explicit questioning of the philosophy, espoused sincerely or not, that higher personal profits for a business producer equalled a policing instrument for the greater social good. This was as much a glib premise of capitalism in baseball as it was in other American sectors.

As the century wore on, the dance around the social background of baseball fans would become more acrobatic, especially with the increasing interest shown in the game by newly arrived immigrants. By contrast, the problems posed by gambling fans and their favorite bookmakers were already in full flower before Lee surrendered at Appomattox.

The Betting Game

Fussy disclaimers by its officials notwithstanding, baseball has been joined at the hip to gambling throughout its history. The next big-league game not to draw some fan's betting interest will be the first one since the formation of the National League in 1876. The first recorded one-on-one wager goes back even further than that, to September 10, 1858, when two unidentified fans put up $100 on whether or not Brooklyn Eckfords infielder John Holder would clout a home run in a game against the New York Mutuals. Holder was told about the bet and was offered $25 of the winnings if he delivered. He did.

The same two teams, the Eckfords and the Mutuals, were implicated in the first player gambling scandal seven years later. In order to assure a victory by Brooklyn over his team and to win a bet, Mutuals catcher William Wansley went hitless in five at-bats and committed six passed balls during a game on September 28, 1865. His defensive play became so embarrassing that, before the raucous reaction of New York fans, he had to be switched to right field midway during the game. It later came out that the receiver risked the public furor for $40—what remained from an original $100 bribe after he had given $30 each to complicitous teammates Tom Devyr and Ed Duffy to guarantee Brooklyn's 23–11 win. Although all three players were ordered suspended for dumping the game, the NABBP's bureaucratic procedures, helped along by arm-twisting from Mutuals backer Boss Tweed, got them all eventually reinstated.

Tweed's Mutuals figured at the center of a great number of gambling and fix stories in the NABBP era, but they were anything but alone. As illustrated by their fractious series against the Excelsiors in 1860, the Brooklyn Atlantics were another favorite nesting place for gamblers. In 1866, an October championship series between the Atlantics and Philadelphia's Athletics occasioned even more tumult than the games against the Excelsiors, with estimates of up to 30,000 spectators and "an immense amount of betting" accompanying every pitch. These games got so out of hand that one of them had to be called off after the crowd surged onto the field. "The disorder and rowdyism manifested at the match today are deeply regretted by the members of the baseball fraternity," a statement said following the chaos. "It was chiefly caused . . . by the heavy betting of certain parties."

A year later, the *Newark Daily Advertiser* described a game between the same two teams during which "a few men, with their hands full of greenbacks, were walking around the skirts of the crowd calling for takers of bets at a hundred dollars to twenty that the Athletics will beat two to one." The Jersey paper reckoned that "over $100,000 changed hands." In 1868, Philadelphia's *Sunday Mercury* termed "lamentable" a "betting mania that pervades all classes." At a Manhattan contest between the Mutuals and Troy Haymakers, it said, passing along information from an upstate New York daily, "women brought their money and bet on their favorite Haymakers to the last cent in their possession. We hear of Lansingburg sewing girls who sent down their five, ten, and twenty dollars each by their male friends to bet on the Haymakers."

For the most part, mid-century accounts of gambling displays betray a tone of dismay—itself something of a surprise since, for all its attributes as mass entertainment, baseball was still also a sport and sports in America had meant heavy gambling since the horse races of colonial Maryland and South Carolina. The offended wonder was a stew of several vegetables. First, there was the sheer outlandishness of some crowd actions to protect bets. When there was clear danger of some longshot cleaning out bookmakers, for example, a common solution was to stage a riot that would cause the game to be called off. A western variation on this tactic, Seymour has noted, was California gamblers waiting for a fly ball to be hit, then pulling out their guns and firing into the air just as the outfielder was lining himself up for the catch. Then there was the segment of the press that shared the outlook of a minority of players, especially those from the original Knickerbockers, that baseball should have been primarily a recreational exercise with no overbearing concern about winners and losers. Linked to that was the corollary attitude, evident well into the twentieth century, that even fan enthusiasms for one team over another should have been discreet. As Yale football coach Walter Camp stated: "It is not courtesy upon a ballfield to cheer an error of the opponents. If it is on your grounds, it is the worst kind of boorishness. Moreover, if there are remarkable plays made by your rivals you yourselves should cheer." Allen Guttman has cited another early twentieth-century writer, Ira Hollis, who complained about how "discourteous" and "unfair" it was for a home crowd to root against a visiting club. According to Hollis, "not everyone wants to see a good game. There are those, perhaps a perennial majority, who prefer winning at all costs and humiliating the opponent whenever possible." Although both Camp and Hollis were talking most directly about college football, their sentiments echoed those around the "manly good sportsmanship" that had prevailed at the Elysian Fields in the 1840s.

Closer to home, the press astonishment was also a product of its own propaganda—the perspective that baseball was second to no social activity as a symbol for reunifying the nation after the Civil War. If betting was anything, it was partisan; if it abetted passions, they were all of a sectarian kind. Chadwick's repeatedly stated confidence that baseball would weld the North and South back together through friendly competition looked like spitting into the wind next to an 1867 *Harper's Weekly* conclusion that "so common has betting become that the most respectable clubs in the country indulge in it to a highly culpable degree and so common . . . the tricks by which games have been 'sold' for the benefit of gamblers that the most respectable participants have been suspected of baseness."

But the biggest adaptation problem of all for the sportswriting fraternity was accepting baseball as the mass spectator entertainment it had rapidly become. Even after the Civil War, in an indication of persisting uneasiness with the social and religious rationalizations for condoning mere watching, the game's most ardent advocates remained preoccupied with the physical, psychological, and moral benefits *playing* was supposed to confer. If sportswriters were no longer as peremptorily dismissive of spectators as some had been during the Fashion Race Course series, they didn't waste too much print on them, either, except when their behavior approximated that of a rabble; they barely existed as crowds, let alone as individuals. By conscious design or not, this reluctance to take in baseball's full breadth as a social institution involving full-time watchers made it easier to ignore the very consistent gambling history of spectator sports in the country.

The spectators themselves had little reason, incentive, or background for ignoring it. Once in the role of onlookers, within a leisurely ambience of predominantly male camaraderie, beers and whiskies close at hand, they were as vulnerable to the vicarious excitements of betting on baseball as they would have been to wagering on a horse, a boxer, or a cock. It was precisely in awareness of the usual consequences of such a male ambience that baseball guardians began calling for greater attendance by women as early as the midfifties. Nor was it coincidence that the Knickerbockers, the most devoutly amateur NABBP club, established the prototype for the Ladies Day tradition in 1867 by asking players to make a point of inviting their wives, daughters, and girlfriends to the games played the last Thursday of every month. This only made the scandal greater when, as in such cases as the Fashion Race Course series and the Haymakers-Mutuals game, women were observed doing some of the most serious wagering.

In the end, however, it wasn't women who provided the antidote to the gambling problems of the 1860s. The solution turned out to be the most venerable one of all where mass entertainment tastes were concerned—the audience deciding it didn't want to be entertained any more by this particular show. So the show had to be changed.

THE
PROFESSIONAL
GAME

Smartening Up

To read raw numbers, baseball couldn't have flourished more than it did in the immediate postwar years. After its drastic membership losses during the Civil War, the National Association of Base Ball Players rose back up to 91 clubs in 1865, more than doubled that number to 200 for 1866, and kept going to some 300 the following year; indicative of its sweep west, the NABBP could claim nine members from Des Moines, Iowa, alone by 1867. Employers in Chicago became so convinced the game produced better workers that they gave them time off for practice and became active supporters of some 50 teams in the city. By 1868, popular clubs like the Brooklyn Atlantics, New York Mutuals, and Washington Nationals were known to be divvying up a good $100,000 each from ticket sales (and, in the case of Washington, plate passings through the crowd during games).

The press sent out one sanguine bulletin after another on the receptivity of fans to the paid admission policies instituted by Cammeyer at the Union Grounds. In 1866, the *Brooklyn Daily Eagle* declared that the sport had "attained a higher position in the present season than it ever before held." A report on a Mutuals-Athletics match in 1867 noted that not even the generally adopted decision after the war to raise ticket prices from a dime to a quarter had discouraged fans. "One would imagine that in these times of high rents and low wages that the patronage of the base ball arena would be somewhat limited at such a high tariff as a quarter of a dollar," it said, "but the fact is a quarter is nothing for such an hour or two's exciting sport as a well contested ball match yields." In 1869, the *New York Times* estimated that some 200,000 spectators could be counted on for attending the biggest games every year. By the following year, *Wilkes' Spirit of the Times* could say there "never was greater activity" when it came to the game's popular pull.

Fan enthusiasm was so marked that not even the seasons limited play. On February 4, 1861, more than 10,000 people flocked to Litchfield's Pond in south Brooklyn to watch the first of many ice baseball games, this one featuring the Atlantics against the Charter Oaks. In covering the 36–27 victory by the Atlantics, the *Daily Eagle* described the scene in part:

> *The abutting embankments presented a triple row of spectators, and as the day wore on, the tide of population continued steadily to increase. Hooped and ribboned loveliness was out in full blow, and while many ladies courageously braved the perils of the treacherous ice, very few adventured the skates. Quite a number of carriages pulled up in the street skirting the pond—a position which afforded the inmates a good view of the ballplayers who full of enthusiasm and excitement, dreamed not and cared not for broken bones and bruised flesh. . . .*

When Brooklyn fans weren't blaspheming against baseball's seasonal character, they were showing up for games more knowledgeably in warmer temperatures. Already in 1860, Henry Chadwick had come out with the sport's first annual guidebook, *Beadle's Dime Base Ball Player*. In part, it was a rehash of his newspaper articles, the NABBP rules, and the inevitable declaration on the physical and moral benefits of baseball. More important, it contained the statistics gathered from the previous year's play—the first significant publication foray into baseball numbers. Most important of all, the guide found an avid market for its odds and ends, selling a reputed 50,000 copies the first year and, once the war was over, building from there. On October 11, 1866, fans had access to their first scorecards, printed up in Brooklyn for what was billed as "The Great Game for the Championship of the United States"—the turbulent series between the Atlantics and Athletics that drew up to 30,000 fans. Although consisting of little more than the names in the day's expected lineups, the scorecards marked an important step in the game's programming—both in the literal sense of listing what performers would be appearing in the afternoon show and in the figurative one of the public commitment by clubs to the spectator. There could be no more illusions about dispensable extras.

Even some of the game's problems in the 1860s seemed more a product of success than failure. The tremendous growth in the number of its teams made some sportswriters worry that the NABBP was going to be pulled apart at the center, leaving regional clubs to form rival mini-groups that would defeat the association's goal of a single nationwide organization. Daily papers and sports weeklies became so inundated with material during peak summer months that they presented only the briefest of summaries of most matches. Toward the end of the 1860s, dailies were demanding fees for printing club announcements. The *Philadelphia Press* went further than that by refusing to cover any game unless the clubs took out an ad in the paper. In baseball-mad Brooklyn, informal street games triggered so many complaints that the chief of police ordered the rigorous enforcement of an ordinance against using public thoroughfares for playing; he backed down only when an overzealous patrolman prompted press scoldings by also trying to apply the regulation to games organized in city lots. Not all employers shared the outlook of those in Chicago, either. Complaints started being heard from job applicants that they were being turned down for openings if they admitted to playing baseball or even attending games regularly. In New York, merchants and other employers held meetings for discussing the increasing absenteeism of employees off to play or watch a game. One meeting's resolution asserted it was "the duty of employers to do what could be done to impose . . . a proper restraint."

But excess wasn't the sport's only ailment. When they weren't just passing along numbers as signs of the NABBP's thriving, reporters had begun to notice something else—that only the first-class clubs like the Washington Nationals and Brooklyn Atlantics were drawing big crowds. This in turn prompted concern about the divisions that effectively existed within the association—with the Nationals, the Brooklyn teams, and a small handful of others exhausting the top register. It was in this context that the NABBP erupted in joyous denial when a young pitcher named Spalding led the severely underdog Forest Citys of Rockford, Illinois over the touring Nationals in a July 1867 game at Dexter Park in Chicago. It was the only defeat for the Nationals during a streak that saw them outscore the opposition by a margin of 735–175. Only after a week of local celebrations was Rockford informed it had won merely a game, that since Washington had had no standing as national champions, it had been in no position to lose that title, either.

Especially where growing fan disinterest was concerned, the sport's chief affliction was *hippodroming*—fixing a game or series of games for maximum payoffs with the connivance of players and officials on one or both teams. The first whispers of such rigging dated back to the 1858 Fashion Race Course series, with allegations that the Brooklyn and New York all-star squads had split their first two games to guarantee a big gate for the decisive third game. Even if true, that would have netted the players involved only minimal cuts from the revenues ostensibly ticketed for the groundskeepers at the Long Island track. But with the new revenue-sharing system in vogue a decade later, there was substantial money to be pocketed from any hanky-panky. For Chadwick, in fact, "the primary evil of the gate-money system is the temptation it offers for dishonest practices in the way of getting up bogus matches, or of playing games on the 'hippodrome' principle." By the latter part of the decade, the atmosphere had become sufficiently murky for even the victory by the Rockford Forest Citys over the Nationals to be interpreted as part of a plot. When Washington subsequently went on to thrash the far superior Chicago Excelsiors, Second City newspapers accused the Nationals of having lost to Rockford deliberately, to build up the box office for their next game. Chicago dailies retracted the charges only after receiving indignant visits from representatives of the touring team.

Fans weren't so quick to retract their suspicions. The *Clipper* noted after the 1869 season that matchups that had previously attracted crowds of 10,000 and 15,000 had drawn only 5,000 that year. *Wilkes' Spirit of the Times* discerned the same trend the following year. With particular reference to the mere 1,000 spectators who had showed up for an Atlantics game against the visiting Chicago White Stockings, the paper blamed the Brooklyn club for the diminished attendance—for "getting into such bad repute, from the constantly flying rumors of 'sells' and 'thrown' games, that few people care to expend their time and money in going to witness what may turn out to be merely a 'hippodroming' exhibition." The games didn't even have to be fixed in order to be at the mercy of gamblers. Probably the single most notorious game of the period was an 1869 contest between the Troy Haymakers and the Cincinnati Red Stockings that spoiled the latter's perfect record for the year. It ended in a 17–17 tie after Haymakers backer John Morrissey, a Tammany Hall cohort of Boss Tweed's, got his players to trump up a dispute with an umpire and go marching off the field in high dudgeon over one of his calls. The tie enabled Morrissey to hold on to $17,000 he had developed second thoughts about risking on a bet.

The hippodroming plague touched spectators on more than one level. Most obviously, bettors found themselves "planting their tin," in a phrase of the day, on a predetermined outcome. This did little for the adventuresomeness of the gambling instinct, while even those who happened to be in on the special of the day or who guessed right couldn't have many fantasies about borrowing a sense of control over destiny for a couple of hours. One way or the other, fixes did not dangle any long-range enticements before the eyes of the casual bettor. Then there was the far greater number of people affected by the playing of the rigged game itself. Here there was much more at stake than a wagered dollar or two—an onlooker's identification with a team, an aesthetic appreciation of the game, perhaps even a captivity to the relentless propaganda about what baseball was supposed to mean to the national soul. One didn't need John Calvin waiting at home to realize that watching a fixed game had involved more idleness than even the most mentally nimble of muscular Christian pastors could have excused. At bottom, hippodroming put a lie to spectatorship itself.

More sophisticated rationalizations were required for keeping people in the grandstands. Albert Spalding, for one, never doubted that the solution lay with professionalization. As he would write in his autobiographical *America's National Game* some years later: "I was not able to understand how it could be right to pay an actor, or a singer, or an instrumentalist for entertaining the public, and wrong to pay a ballplayer for doing exactly the same thing in his way." It was an analogy some would find hard to accept well into the twentieth century.

Guilt by Association

A t its 1868 convention in Washington, the NABBP formally acknowledged its losing battle against professionalism, declaring it a "dead letter" and announcing that the organization would henceforth be divided into "two distinct classes of players"—the professional and the amateur.

The move ended years of hypocrisy during which players had been receiving direct cash payments, been given no-show jobs by club operators, or been paid off in some other way, such as sharing in a game's gate receipts. What the association preferred not to address was that its structural bisectioning turned the second-tier amateur clubs into attractions for only true baseball diehards and regional boosters, in effect creating the first major-minor divergence of franchises and fans of any significance.

Any doubts the NABBP might have had about its decision seemed to dissolve during the triumphant run of the openly salaried Cincinnati Red Stockings in 1869. The biggest advertisement for baseball up to that point in its history, the squad managed by Harry Wright attracted huge crowds from coast to coast, generated tons of newsprint both on the sports pages and in non-sports publications, and was received at the White House by President Ulysses S. Grant. For all the earlier successful runs by teams like the Excelsiors and Nationals, the Red Stockings gave off an unprecedented aura of champions—making them both magnetic at ticket windows and the favorite hate object of opposition rooters. They were also the first team clearly to benefit an entire city by association. While previous winning clubs (in Brooklyn, for example) had accomplished much of their damage against intracity or area rivals, making it something of a civic wash, Cincinnati rode the success of the Red Stockings to multi-layered commercial profit in both small and big businesses. Before the club had ever embarked on its triumphant tours of the East and West, a local businessman was quoted as saying: "Glory, they've advertised the city—advertised us, sir, and helped out business, sir!"

But the very success of the Red Stockings widened even further the gap between the professionals and the amateurs, and not only because of the frequently lopsided scores Cincinnati ran up against poorly skilled clubs. While in Philadelphia, for instance, the team drew some 15,000, following that up with houses of more than 23,000 for six dates in the New York area. But other appearances weren't so profitable. In Mansfield, Ohio, the Red Stockings earned $50, in Cleveland only $81. In Syracuse, the team arrived at the field to discover a pigeon shoot under way and general ignorance about any game. In Rochester, there were fans waiting, but also teeming rain, forcing the Cincinnati players to do their own groundskeeping in order to go on with the scheduled contest. Experiences of the kind convicted Wright that the professional-amateur divide existed in more than just an NABBP decree, and he was soon talking about eliminating the teams stipulated as amateur from his schedule. At the same time, other cities like Chicago were becoming openly envious of the popular receptions accorded the Red Stockings. When the club wasn't creating mob scenes in ballparks, it was doing so on main streets and boulevards during finely produced rides back and forth to the diamond. According to the *Chicago Tribune*, it was a disgrace that the metropolis didn't have a "representative club; an organization as great as her enterprise and wealth, one that will not allow the second-rate clubs of every village in the Northwest to carry away the homers in baseball."

The upshot, in 1871, was the gutting of the NABBP for the National Association of *Professional* Base Ball Players—a nine-team league that promised fans only the highest professional standards for a 50-cent admission cost. The engine behind the new circuit was Wright, who moved with most of his best players from Cincinnati to Boston, taking along the red socks that would become as synonymous with Massachusetts baseball as with that in Ohio.

In its five years of chaotic existence, the NAPBBP gained attention for several things where fans were concerned. In having at least one local politician in the board room of all its teams, it showed that the "pride by association" lessons imparted by Cincinnati had not fallen on deaf ears. Whatever the specific party badge involved, the political presence tightened relations between the diamond and city hall in the name of community and, for at least the first year or so, this helped build attendance. The association's Chicago franchise was also the first to promote season tickets, guaranteeing that $15 would insure that a seat wouldn't be resold even if its holder couldn't make a game. Given its proclaimed standards, the league additionally made it clear that it didn't regard winning as some incidental goal to exercising in the afternoon air. Winning meant crowds, and crowds were the only way for teams to pay off their salary commitments, let alone produce a profit. If the sport had not quite reached the "winning at any cost" attitude that informed the final years of the century, the NAPBBP did a good job of reducing the list of compensations for losing.

For all that, however, the league worked overtime to estrange its fans. However professional they might have been in terms of paying salaries, the majority of member teams were all but inept before the stronger clubs, especially Wright's Red Stockings, making for rare suspense in games involving Boston and usually finding it only in encounters between mediocrities. Games were sometimes held up for an hour or more before increasingly irritated spectators while clubs argued over a mutually acceptable umpire. Fights among drunken fans were regular sideshows, and more than one umpire was assaulted for making an unpopular call. Scheduling was left up to individual clubs, meaning the acutely downcast among them didn't bother announcing much of anything to anybody near the end of a season. Formulas for deciding a champion borrowed too much from the obscure works of mathematical wizards.

Even if the Red Stockings made some of these considerations moot, there were the persisting problems of players jumping from team to team whenever an extra dollar was waved at them, and of hippodroming—neither of which did much for fan identification. Whatever the prominently displayed signs in ballparks said to the contrary, gambling was everywhere: Brooklyn and Philadelphia permitted pool selling even in the grandstand. Bookmakers clustered together so predictably at the Capitoline Grounds that their favorite section in the Brooklyn ballpark became known as the "Gold Board." Boss Tweed's New York Mutuals were such a scandal that their every win and loss was analyzed as part of a scheme. Spalding, whose pitching was a major reason for the success of the Red Stockings, admitted in his autobiography that "the spirit of gambling and graft held possession of the sport everywhere." The *New York Times* didn't have to wait for that twentieth-century reflection, deciding in 1872 that the kind of player on exhibit with the NAPBBP was "a worthless, dissipated gladiator; not much above the professional pugilist in morality and respectability." Against such a backdrop, the NAPBBP might not have needed any external pushes, but it received one anyway with the onset of a national economic depression. "By the end of the 1875 season," as William J. Ryczek has said, "the drawing power of teams such as the Mutuals, Philadelphias, and White Stockings was virtually nil. Fans were reluctant to gamble a 50 cent admission price when they couldn't be assured of seeing an honest game."

Touching on the "pride by association" theme, Benjamin Rader has pointed out that "although fielding a baseball team could on occasion attract more attention to a city than building hospitals, opera houses, or libraries, it could also boomerang. . . . A losing team could evoke negative publicity, feelings of inferiority, and even depression among the city's residents." In the specific case of the bankruptcy of the NAPBBP and the clubs affected by it, with the arguable exception of Boston, the depression blanketed *all* of baseball's prominent communities and beyond them to the sport's standing as a mass entertainment industry. In the words of Alfred H. Spink: "In 1875, competition among the professional clubs ran so high that bribery, contract breaking, dishonest playing, poolroom manipulation, and desertion of players became so public that the highly respectable element of patrons began to drop out of the attendance until the crowds which attended the games were composed almost exclusively of men who went to the grounds to bet money on the results. . . . The game fell into a state of demoralization which threatened its existence. . . ."

Since mere commercialization and professionalization didn't work, yet another remedy was needed for keeping "the highly respectable element" in its seats. Very much in keeping with the times, that solution was monopolization.

Krank Cases

Before being swallowed up by its own disorder, the NAPBBP inspired the first writer to make a conspicuous effort to characterize baseball fans. The scribe was Thomas W. Lawson, who fell as prey to his passions as to gambling, and was as overbearing as any grandstand shouter could be.

Writing was only one of several pursuits the mercurial Lawson took up after moving to Boston from Nova Scotia as a child. By the age of 17, he had made his first fortune through canny investments, only to lose it again within days through some uncanny ones. He rebounded and then some, mainly as a broker who could work for or against Standard Oil depending on the profit potential, and by 1900 was estimated as being worth up to $50 million. Lawson didn't let the money sit. When he wasn't buying the right to have flowers named after his wife or personally financing the publication of a Republican party history in a special silk-paper limited edition for his friends, he was trying to buy his way into the America's Cup races. When the New York Yacht Club made the mistake of barring his participation on a technicality in 1901, Lawson turned his writing skills to magazine articles denouncing the "money kings" ruling Eastern business and social circles. The fact that he was sporting a pretty big coronet of his own didn't deter him from relaying the kind of executive corridor chatter that, where the insurance industry in particular was concerned, triggered a major criminal investigation in 1905. When such exposés made him *persona non grata* in top financial circles and (coincidentally or not) his investments began collapsing, he devoted more of his time to writing, including a couple of novels. He had gone through most of his money by the time he died in 1925 at the age of 68.

Lawson became fascinated with baseball after moving to Boston as a boy and seeing Wright's Red Stockings. His equal attention to fans emerged some time later, in 1888, with another tiny-circulation endeavor (designed in the shape of a baseball and bound in horsehide) entitled *The Krank: His Language and What It Means*. A satirical look at a fan as he arrives for a game, the booklet begins:

> *The Krank is a heterogenous compound of flesh, bone, and baseball, mostly baseball. He came into existence in the early seventies. He came to stay.*

> *The Krank is purely American. He is found in no other country.*

> *The Krank is of the masculine gender. The female of the tribe is known as the Kranklet. The Krank has reached a high state of cultivation. The Kranklet is at present only partially developed.*

The fan is depicted as "knowing it all" and "telling it all"—to the ticket seller, to the ticket taker, to the pool seller with whom he places a bet, to the players who limber up too close to where he is standing, to other fans. The responses of the krank's targets are not recorded; they are assumed to be accustomed to his loudmouth behavior.

Lawson's allusion to the birth of the true fan during the NAPBBP era of the "early seventies" wasn't entirely based on restrictive boyhood memories. Certainly, prior to the NAPBBP, there was scant mention in the press of spectators other than as an amorphous collection of enthusiasts, bettors, rowdies, or some combination of the three. Even after the circuit had dissolved to make room for the National League in 1876, fans were heard from—positively or negatively—in general Letters columns of the newspapers more than on the sports pages. It would take several more years—as well as a few more leagues and a lot more teams—for the know-it-alls to be known as well as they wanted to be.

Territorial Rites

Between 1846 and 1876, baseball spectators journeyed from the amateurs they could see for free, to the amateurs and professionals they could see for a dime, to the professionals and amateurs they could see for a quarter, to the professionals they could see from a seat for a half-dollar. The next stage was the professionals they were told they couldn't see at all for any price. At least that was one of the effective aims of the National League of Professional Baseball Clubs, which superseded the NAPBBP following behind-the-scenes maneuvers during the offseason of 1875–76. Specifically, the NL brought with it three new elements—control of the game by the teams rather than the players, designs of a territorial monopoly that banned members from playing games with non-member clubs, and a shift of the sport's organizational center from the East Coast to Chicago. All three goals were eventually attained to one degree or another, but not without a few more junctures at which going to the circus or taking up cycling seemed a more fruitful way of passing leisure hours.

The engines behind the NL's ascension were Chicago White Stockings owner William Hulbert and the ever-commercial Harry Wright, who had both come to the conclusion that allowing players to run the game was akin to (as more than one critic of the NAPBBP put it) leaving the patients in charge of the asylum. There was never any attempt by Hulbert or his fellow owners to hide their monopolistic intentions. Their charter blueprint called for each club to have exclusive control over its city and the surrounding area within a radius of five miles. Members were forbidden to play exhibitions against non-league teams since that would have given the latter too much notoreity. In theory, the league was open to any club that could pay a $100 admission fee and came from a city with a population of at least 75,000, but since there was a ceiling on eight teams, candidates couldn't even bother to apply until an existing member fell out. All of this, of course, represented a very idiosyncratic concept of the "democracy" Spalding and legions of officials were to find common to baseball and the United States of America. Or, as NL President John Tener would declare during World War I: "Baseball is the very watchword of democracy. There is no other sport or business or anything under heaven which exerts the leveling influence that baseball does. Neither the public school nor the church can approach it." Something else not approaching it for a while were fans.

Hulbert had something to glow about in 1876 when, led by Spalding's 47 victories, the White Stockings captured what has been recognized as the first major league pennant. He had something to glower about when only the White Stockings showed a profit for the year. While Chicago was jubilant enough about its team to project new steamcar routes for carrying more passengers to the 23rd Street Grounds for the 1877 season, other member cities were simply steaming. Before the season was over, two clubs, the Mutuals and Athletics, begged off from road trips for being too costly, leading to their expulsion and leaving the league without the critical New York and Philadelphia markets. Hartford became so desperate for ticket sales that it prohibited sportswriters from telegraphing the score until the game was over, hoping this would draw more afternoon barflies and pool shooters to the Hartford Ball Club Grounds; it didn't. The Connecticut team was finally forced to switch operations to

Cammeyer's Union Grounds in Brooklyn, where it also remained through the following season. The ban on exhibitions against non-NL squads was shelved as soon as it became obvious franchises would sink altogether without such income. For all his earlier insistence on this stipulation, Hulbert was among the first to realize that any visiting team to New York that could play only the Mutuals during its stay was not going to leave town with much of a profit.

The fact that the league survived through an even worse season in 1877 owed more to fan expectations than to what was delivered at the ballpark. For one thing, telegraphed play-by-play reports to every paper in the country kept the NL's modest six-team organization the most visible game in town even though the towns themselves were few in number; more than any baseball enterprise before it, the NL owed a great deal to its media *image* as an ongoing, serious, organized undertaking. In this, the league was helped by the name value of its players (Spalding, Harry Wright and his brother George, Cap Anson, etc.) and by its uncompromising stand on both the franchises in New York and Philadelphia that hadn't lived up to their commitments (immediate dismissal) and the involvement of four Louisville players in a major game-throwing scandal (lifetime bans). In the eyes of the fan, a business that would rather sacrifice lucrative markets than abide whimsical or irresponsible decisions by individual members presented a picture of righteousness more powerful than the separate details of crisis. This was an especially appealing posture to a white-collar, middle-class clientele that was feeling buffeted at the time by wave upon wave of labor strikes and corruption investigations around the country; the player as mere worker, as he had become in the NL, could be seen without having to be heard. Whatever else it might have been short on, the NL knew its audience.

It also knew the right politicians. The league's grab for territorial exclusivity, for equating a community with a single team, might have irked baseball purists and those of an anti-trust bent, but it was welcome fodder for civic leaders for whom the benefits of pride by association were at their most concentrated in one representative club. Hardly the starry-eyed Babbitts and minor parasites they have sometimes been depicted as, these political and business forces proved indispensable for disguising as mere boosterism the monopolistic nature of the territoriality principle—sometimes by funneling private finances in the direction of an elected club, other times by favoring a team through real estate and tax manipulations, still other times by using legal machinery to discourage the unwanted. Like it or not, the late nineteenth-century fan had to be as aware of the strengths and weaknesses of his neighborhood alderman as of his favorite third baseman.

Of course, not even these elements would have been sufficient for survival if the league had not known when to be measured about its most austere demands (such as in playing non-NL clubs), or if there had been a serious organizational alternative. It did, and there wasn't. At its very nadir, the league could have still boasted that its clubs-first structure had created entirely new premises for the sport—turning it into a production company bigger than any of its single performers, identifying its generic activity with the particulars of a given impresario as much as P. T. Barnum's "Greatest Show on Earth" had come to mean the circus. The National League of Professional Baseball Clubs had achieved the ledge of a cultural reference point—future rivals would have to combat it not only as an organization that had gotten there first, but as *baseball* itself.

When the fan needed further incentive for identifying the NL with the best baseball had to offer, Spalding and the Wright brothers, in particular, were on hand to furnish it. For his part, Spalding moved from the pitching mound to financial control of the White Stockings and, more important, to the launching of a national (and later international) sporting goods business. If the league had a Cinderella story in its darkest days, it was in 1879, when George Wright left his brother's pennant-winning Boston team to take over a humpty-dumpty Providence franchise and, against all expectations, wrested the flag away from Harry. Wright was the first to admit that part of his incentive in making the move was to open the Wright and Ditson sporting goods company in Rhode Island.

What both Spalding and George Wright would profit from was their intuition that the baseball industry had grown well beyond the field or the teams paid to take that field. By the 1880s, the game had become just the centerpiece of a business meant to draw in the fan outside the ballpark as much as inside it, grandstand seats or not. That there was a market for such ambitions, despite general economic pressures and the failures of individual franchises, could not have found clearer confirmation than in 1881, when Spalding, deciding they were superfluous, stopped issuing instruction guides on baseball rules. The main question in the next phase of the sport's development was not whether people knew how the game worked, but what people would be encouraged to watch others working at it.

Blue Collars

The growing corporate climate around the NL at the beginning of the eighties encouraged more than one market analysis of the fan. The main conclusion of the surveys was hardly surprising—that profitability lay with the white middle-class that had free hours to attend games and the discretionary income not only for tickets, but for the publications and sporting goods that demonstrated its absorption in the sport. What these relatively unsophisticated studies were slow to catch up on was that the gradual introduction of half-day Saturdays in retail outlets and even some plants, along with soaring literacy rates, might not have made blue-collar workers any richer, but it certainly gave them a little more free time and more points of contact with the game. By maintaining its exclusionary devotion to the middle-class profile, the NL left the field open for others to cultivate working-class spectators. At the same time, it abetted the arrival of entrepreneurs who were not at all shy about treating fans as strollers down a carnival fairway. Most of these pitchmen were concentrated within the American Association, the NL's rival and then partner between the early eighties and early nineties.

Practically from its inception in 1876, purists accused the league of Spalding, Hulbert, and the Wrights of being more about the "amusement business" than baseball. But the NL stacked up as the most immaculate of athletic endeavors compared to the carousels, animal acts, and Wild West shows organized by the American Association as lures to watching baseball (or to have baseball as a lure for *them*). The Spaldings and the Wrights had enough money-making satellite interests to pretend that games could speak for themselves; AA owners such as Chris Von der Ahe and Erastus Winman didn't have the stolid instincts for that confidence, relying more on Magic Carpet rides and Buffalo Bill. If the game they produced never completely slipped down into the cranny of pitching balls at milk bottles, it wasn't because it was venerated as a Christianity-building enterprise or respected as a mythic expression of militant patriotism, but because profits from such a step weren't regarded as promising enough.

Thanks to the unmistakable aversions of the National League, the AA didn't have to finance any surveys for locating potential audiences for its more flamboyant approach. For starters, there were the immigrant populations of New York, Cincinnati, and St. Louis that were heavy on the Irish and heavier on the Germans or vice versa. The prospect that these resettlers might constitute the next fan base for baseball not only agitated the NL mandarins with their Presbyterian, Episcopalian, and Methodist preconceptions about the best users of grandstand seats, but also stirred to louder action outside antagonists who had watched the baseball-as-the-"national-game" joke go on too long. One who had done so was landscape architect Frederick Law Olmsted, who had made allowances for cricket grounds in his masterpiece of Central Park, but who had also seen fit, as a Public Parks functionary, to bar from his Manhattan greenery as equal evils baseball, Irish church suppers, and German singing-society picnics. Olmsted was typical of the upper-class urbanite in the East for whom the alleged crudities of baseball inevitably appealed to what was sometimes referred to as the country's growing "Celtocracy." Zoss and Bowman have suggested many of the attacks of the period on the "rowdies" at ball games were coded Anglophiliac attacks on Irish immigrants. While there is undoubtedly some truth to this, ethnic biases never completely took over the field from class prejudices, or even from the conflicting religious outlooks that found the largely Catholic Irish perplexed by the Protestant mania about not playing ball on the Sabbath. In short, Irish laborers were convenient targets on any number of levels.

It was in the same anti-immigrant vein that the *New York Times,* which had never stopped championing cricket as a more desirable sport, was able to find new excuses for attacking baseball in the early eighties. In an August 30, 1881, editorial, the daily claimed the sport was "gradually dying out in this country," that it had been surpassed by cricket, and that it had from its beginning been a sport "unworthy of men" and in its developed state "unworthy of gentlemen." To bolster its contentions, the paper dipped into the Irish bog, asserting that the game had been taken over by immigrants who didn't worry too much about the physical injuries their adopted sport caused. It came up with such statistics as that "37,518" people had been involved in some kind of baseball accident in the previous decade and that "eight percent" of these casualties had died.

All of this was mere grist for the mill for the American Association. In setting up a rival six-team league in 1882, it offered three things that the National League did not—Sunday baseball, beer and whiskey at its ballparks, and a 25-cent admission price (as opposed to the NL's 50 cents). It also offered the opportunity for players to win higher contracts either through direct offers or by playing one circuit against another and jumping back and forth. Primarily because of the player ploys, the NL held its nose and signed a peaceful coexistence agreement with the AA for the 1883 season. As it turned out, however, trouble from AA grandstands didn't live up to stereotypical expectations. The major exception was at the double-decked entertainment complex at Baltimore's Union Park, where the Von der Horst brewing company kept the suds flowing frantically at an adjoining restaurant and dance hall as well as at the ballpark and where somebody thought it prudent to separate the grandstand from the field with barbed wire. But the AA franchise wasn't confirming some fated social predeliction even on that score, since the NL Red Stockings had taken the same precaution in Boston. Militant Sabbatarians took aim at the AA's Columbus franchise for playing on Sundays by exhuming an ancient ordinance prohibiting any kind of work on the day, but the club beat back the threat with demands that City Hall be consistent by also suspending public transportation on Sundays. When all the propaganda smoke cleared, in fact, it turned out that the sober, white-collar NL, not the AA, was the setting for most of the friction and ugliness in the decade.

Umpires were a particular focus of trouble. In 1882 alone, spectators mobbed arbiters on ten different occasions. (One of the most common refrains of the day was: "Mother, may I slug the umpire/May I slug him right away?/So he cannot be here, Mother/When the clubs begin to play?") But these disturbances were equally divided between NL and AA ballparks. If there had been an election for the single worst park of the eighties for seeing a game, the winner would have been League Park in Kansas City—part of the dry, middle-class NL. The Cowboys were members only for the 1886 season, but that was long enough for every umpire in the league to threaten resignation if he had to return to work a game before Kansas City's vituperative fans. The NL was also the scene of the single worst fixing scandal of the decade, involving umpire Dick Higham. Higham was expelled following the 1882 season after telegrams to gamblers provided strong evidence that he had been making calls against the Detroit Wolverines to protect bets on their opponents.

The AA didn't supply all that many blue-collared drunken fans, but it did furnish more than a normal share of rogues, hustlers, and clowns as owners. The character-in-chief was Chris Von der Ahe of the St. Louis franchise—the prototype of the owner who attracted as much print as his players. Von der Ahe ultimately won greatest attention for his Coney Island of the West—carousels, carnival rides, band contests, and boxing matches slotted before and after games as part of the total Sportsman's Park experience. But the saloonkeeper by trade provided much more material for the reading public than that first in the American Association, then in the National League. Unlike his buttoned down colleagues, whom the press was usually careful about attacking by name, he had all the credentials of excess for being a daily target on some sports page somewhere almost every day of the year. Among other things, he was extravagant, greedy, shameless, shrewd, stupid, a German immigrant, and didn't pronounce his English consonants all that precisely. His serendipities and fiascos sometimes seemed like the same thing, with the laughable, the sad, and the cruel constantly being remixed for the occasion. Cartoonists were drawn to him regularly for his checked slacks, spats, and diamond kingpins; for his ever-present greyhounds Snoozer and Schnauzer; for his references to himself in his comic-book German accent as Der Poss President; and for an aggressive Jimmy Durante nose turned scarlet from his incessant samplings of his own tavern's hops. Von der Ahe didn't do anything unless it could be done loudly, at least where his person was concerned. His indulgences included a sequence of very expensive and very public mistresses and a life-size statue of himself that ended up on his grave.

Von der Ahe had nobody to blame but himself for much of the ridicule he attracted during his career. But not all the criticism was the product of humanitarian outrage at his frequently crude treatment of his players, either. Most obviously, his habits accommodated the Katzenjammer Kids caricature of German immigrants—an easy laugh for any reporter not employed by *Anzeiger des Westens*. Equally symptomatic, he was what passed for a "personality" in a game conspicuously bereft of many. Well into the eighties, the game remained pretty much all there was. The fan who wanted more than that had to wait for Michael "King" Kelly.

Stars and Idols

The solemn rationalizations resorted to for justifying baseball's very existence still lingered fifty years later. The game's most prominent figures were so worried about their sober image that, when they weren't talking about going into saloons only for a lemonade (wink, wink), they gave the impression of living in church basements between games. That was fine for sanctimoniousness, but not so great even for the then-modest demands of sports page color. Certainly, there was no player of the early eighties with the charisma Jim Creighton had emanated briefly 20 years earlier, let alone of the stature of boxer John L. Sullivan, the period's greatest sports luminary. The one who came closest was Chicago's Anson, but he was more star than idol, earning his every round of applause through what he did as a player-manager on the field rather than through what dreamers thought he had done or would do off it.

Press-promulgated nicknames were one early attempt to personalize players for fans. Here again, though, Anson's long tenure with the White Stockings pushed him somewhat prematurely into such secure, homespun tags as "Pop" and "Unk." Bob "Death to Flying Things" Ferguson aside, most of these pre-twentieth-century efforts were either about as colorless as the player's given name (Big Jim, Black Jack, Smiling Billy) or so forced by some writer showing off his classical education (The Gladiator for Pete Browning, The

Apollo of the Box for Tony Mullane) that they did little for imaginative identification.

And then along came King Kelly, the first fan idol in the major leagues—the prototype of the player who triggered as many crowd scenes on streets as in ballparks and who never underestimated his own magnetism on the people drawn to him. Before his career was over, he and his grandstand following would define most of the player-fan customs still observed today.

Charisma may never be merely the sum of individual addends, but they are a starting point. Kelly's first fortune, after spending two years with Cincinnati, was to come into his own as a player with the White Stockings, the most prominent team in the country. In contrast to the reserved, strait-laced figures of manager Anson and owner Spalding, he was a constant reminder to Chicago fans that there were laughs in winning—a point he illustrated over and over again on the field with baserunning that spanned the inventive (he introduced the hook slide) to the fraudulent (he saw little reason to touch third base on his way home if an umpire wasn't watching); with game-long give-and-take with fans in the stands or with such antics as protecting himself from wet outfield grass by carrying a board out to his position to stand on; and with such pre-Baltimore Orioles tricks as tossing his catcher's mask in a runner's path to gain an extra second or two for a tag. Kelly's mercurial image was also abetted by being baseball's first star utility player; he was liable to be manning any position on the field when the game got under way. Although often identified as a catcher, he actually appeared more frequently in the outfield (758–583), also playing all the infield positions and even pitching 12 times during his 16-year (1878–93) career. It was as he moved from one position to another that he won two batting championships, in 1884 and 1886.

That would have been enough to add up to stardom, but Kelly had more going for him. Physically, he had a fullback's build, sported a full mustache and wavy black hair, and was rarely pictured on or off the field without a prankster's gleam in his eye. His pre-baseball career in a silk mill resurfaced in the ascots and high hats he affected as soon as he was out of uniform, and his high-button shoes and walking stick were the equal to any dandy's on the boulevard. If his lessons from the silk mill weren't enough to get him noticed, his habits in the gin mill were. The main break he took from buying drinks for himself was buying them for others, and this quickly made him a popular downtown figure not only in Chicago, but in the other National League cities as well. He considered it a wasted night when he ended up sleeping in his own bed, and routinely had sections of women cheering him on in Chicago and elsewhere.

After winning the batting title in 1886, Kelly demanded a $10,000 contract from Spalding. Spalding's retort was to sell him to Boston for that amount—not absolutely the first player sale in the major leagues, but the biggest, both in terms of the money involved and the player being peddled. Kelly added to his legend by refusing to approve the deal until he had an agreement with the Red Stockings that paid him the league maximum of $2,000 plus another $3,000 under the table for the team's "use of his photograph." Stunned White Stockings fans made the sale the talk of Chicago during the offseason. A popular tune in the city at the time went:

> *Arab Kelly's gone and left us*
> *Of his presence he's bereft us.*
> *Kelly of the diamond bold*
> *He's deserted us for Boston.*
> *Although Albert laid the cost on,*
> *Ten thousand clear in Puritanic*
>   *gold.*
> *We surely have the pity*
> *Of every sister city.*
> *In our loss of Kel,*
> *The tricky and the bold.*

The sale prompted considerable talk of boycotting White Stockings games in 1887, but, except for the first few home dates, that didn't come to pass to any significant degree. What did happen was that, without Kelly, Chicago dropped from first to third and that, with him, Boston doubled its attendance despite laboring along at a .500 pace for a fifth-place finish. In fact, the player who became known as "The $10,000 Beauty" after the Spalding sale was even more popular in Boston than he had been in Chicago. It was there, in his first season at the South End Grounds, that, according to autograph expert Charles Hamilton, he likely started the craze of players giving out signatures to kids waiting outside after a game. It was also there that fans began the chant of "Slide, Kelly, Slide" whenever he was on first base with second base unoccupied. Two years later, John Kelly (no relation) wrote a popular period song by that name for vaudeville star Maggie Cline, who made it part of her Irish musical repertoire along with such ditties as "Throw Him Down, McCloskey," "How McNulty Carved the Duck," and "Down Went McGinty to the Bottom of the Sea." Even though the lyrics of "Slide, Kelly, Slide" had nothing to do with the King, the song would follow him for the rest of his life, and not to his displeasure; Cline even performed it at his memorial service.

As suggested by the Cline song, no small part of Kelly's popularity in Boston was due to the city's heavy Irish population. He also worked at it. For attention, ambition, or both, he showed up umpires on the field, took up an acting career on the stage, and put his name to the first ghosted tell-no-evil autobiography. He had no compunction about quoting himself as having once chided Red Stockings teammates for maintaining too low a profile, asking them: "Why don't some of you dubs break a window and get yourselves talked about?" Another favorite story revolved around the Brotherhood war of 1890 during which rebellious players established their own Players League in competition to both the NL and AA. A tale substantially confirmed by Spalding said that the Chicago owner offered Kelly $10,000 to defect from the dissidents, that Kelly took a long walk to mull over the offer, came back to say he was rejecting it, then went on as a player–manager to lead the Boston entry in the Players League to a pennant. As a reward, fans chipped in to buy him a (mortgaged) house and a coach with two white horses; he added his own touch shortly afterward by buying a monkey that became a constant companion.

Not even Kelly's decline under the twin weights of drinking and faded skills reduced his extravagance or the eagerness of crowds for seeing him indulge it. As he wandered from Boston to Cincinnati to New York in his final major-league years, his returns to a previous base inevitably triggered ballpark welcome-home ceremonies or lavish banquets. His offseason stage work included not only such period melodramas as *A Rag Baby*, but SRO recitings of "Kelly at the Bat," his customized version of "Casey at the Bat." It was on route to a Boston vaudeville engagement in November 1894 that he was bedded for pneumonia; he died a few days later at the age of 37. Some 5,000 mourners were said to have paid their respects to his remains at Boston's Elks Hall.

Kelly's death made the front page of the *New York Times*—a sign of both his fame beyond the borders of baseball and the paper's resignation to the sport's ascendancy in American society. His involvement with the theater also encouraged theatrical producers to sign other baseball personalities as specialty acts in the hopes of adding to their traditional audiences. One of the biggest catches was none other than Anson, who had been driven to distraction by Kelly's antics and drinking during their time together in Chicago. Anson appeared in Charles Hoyt's 1895 play *The Runaway Colt*, a work replete with allusions to baseball's ongoing gambling scandals. Specialty performances of the kind continued well into the World War I era, with such notables as Ty Cobb, Hughie Jennings, Christy Mathewson, and any number of Mathewson's New York Giants teammates treading the boards. It wasn't much of a jump from there for Hal Chase, John McGraw, and others to figure in silent movies.

The readiness to pay to see players not playing baseball cemented the celebrity status of the big leaguers while speaking to the heightened impressionability of their fans. Theater producers were not alone in shouldering their way into the players' extended marketability. From the late 1880s, for example, tobacco companies such as Old Judge, the Mayo Tobacco Works, Buchner, and Kimball's issued baseball cards with their wares; the typical tobacco shop also displayed large-sized black-and-white cabinet cards of star players for assuring customers they had come to the right place. Board and table games with baseball motifs, which had actually been around since the 1860s, also found more devotees with the association of the most noted players of the late nineteenth century. Product endorsements became an income staple for many stars.

As gifted as he was, Kelly was not baseball's greatest player of the nineteenth century by any technical or athletic standard. There were better hitters, much better fielders, and even some runners who could outdo him on the basepaths. What singled him out was his ability to wrap his gifts within so many of the era's permissible excesses. His larcenous flair on the field might not have met the test of Henry Chadwick's gentlemanly values, his drinking might have contributed mightily to his early demise, and his flirtations with the Gaiety Girls on and off the stage might not have been Shakespearian in their profundity, but they were all part of a male Ragtime model of life short of indictable felony. Even some of the predictable cant in his as-told-to book came with the acceptable winks of the day. In that most expansive of American ages, King Kelly was the stuff of dreams because he did not insist that trait had to be synonymous with a divinely blessed mission.

PATRONAGE
AND
PATRONIZATION

Cultural Stability

By the earliest hours of the twentieth century, 29 American cities could claim to have hosted 89 teams officially recognized as being of major-league caliber. What they could not claim was that most of the clubs had lasted long, that their sponsoring leagues had always been as major in fact as in name, or that many of the departed franchises had left behind indelible moments for the grandstand spectator.

Fans in Altoona, Richmond, and St. Paul had awakened one morning to find big-league baseball in their hometown, only to have it gone again before lunch hour. Fans in Cleveland and Washington had lost scheduled home games to the road when local club owners had abruptly decided there were bigger gate prospects there. Fans in Baltimore and Cleveland had watched entire rosters shipped overnight to bigger markets as part of crossownership stock-syndication schemes. Even fans not deprived of teams through quick-buck ploys had to have wondered about the conditions under which they were being entertained. In New York, for instance, city entries in both the National League and American Association had been owned by the same John B. Day, making for a lot of instant trades and contract reassignments when one franchise appeared to be in more need than the other. On May 12, 1890, there had been the even more bizarre circumstance of Giants outfielder Mike Tiernan bringing the fans of two stadiums to their feet for the same home run. Tiernan's shot had cleared the wall of the NL Polo Grounds and landed in adjoining Brotherhood Park, where a Players League game had been under way. The Players League spectators had been as appreciative of the blow as the Giants fans because they had been peering over the fence at the progress of the neighboring game, which till then had been a scoreless 13-inning duel between period greats Amos Rusie and Kid Nichols. They might have also felt closer to the home run because the club they had paid to watch in Brotherhood Park was the New York Giants—the name of Tiernan's club, as well.

In short, being a baseball fan in the final decades of the nineteenth century could be a confusing—and not always rewarding—experience. Numbers told a deceiving story. Thanks in great part to the introduction of the American Association's 25-cent admission price, the eighties had been a boom decade—one of the most profitable (proportionately) in the history of the sport. Some of these numbers not only held through the dissolution of the AA in the nineties, when an expanded (to 12 clubs) National League ruled alone, but even appeared to rise for several teams. They did so, however, in as much of a dissolute atmosphere as baseball has ever known. "Quality of game" crimes implicated not only absconding owners, but gratuitously violent clubs and gambling-obsessed spectators. Fan harassment of visiting teams included rock throwing and threats on the lives of the players, and police assigned to ballparks didn't hesitate to pull guns in the name of maintaining order. If there were more (live) bodies around NL parks in the nineties than there had been around NL and AA fields in the eighties, they were more often than not cursing, brawling, guzzling, or wagering bodies, and in some parks that was just the ushers.

By most odds, the raucous scenes at ballparks in the nineties should have dealt an even deadlier blow to baseball than the frauds endemic to the National Association of Professional Base Ball

Players in the mid-seventies. As though the game's internal problems weren't sufficient, the decade produced an unprecedented horde of rivals for the entertainment dollar: vaudeville, football, light and comic opera, basketball, the theater, bicycle marathons, the circus, amusement parks, and the nickelodeon, to name ten. Between a national financial crisis at the beginning of the decade and a war with Spain at the end of it, the fan had no ceiling on his choices for seeking amusement. That he didn't defect, that he didn't disappear with the dozens of teams and several leagues that had claimed his loyalties in the eighties and nineties, owed to two principal factors— the settling of a baseball *culture* in the country and the establishment of Ban Johnson's American League.

However commercialized, professionalized, and industrialized it had become by the end of the nineteenth century, baseball maintained a personal link with its fans that only one other sport could claim to a substantial degree—the likelihood that the spectators had played it, if only at the most rudimentary athletic level. The only physical proficiency more natural than throwing around a ball for the American male growing up in the second half of the 1800s was running, and, long past an early-century infatuation with pedestrianism, track was not a professional sport. Until football and basketball assumed greater sway, baseball was unique as a train of experience starting from the backyard and stopping off at the schoolyard and the local green or lot before arriving at the ballpark. Where the rider got off as an athlete depended on talent and the time to hone that talent. When he did get off, the no-longer-player found ubiquitous reinforcement for maintaining a fan interest in the game. Not only had daily newspapers begun to capitalize on baseball as a significant circulation asset, but specialty weeklies put it at the center of entertainment coverage. The three most important periodicals of the kind were the *New York Clipper, Sporting Life,* and the *Sporting News,* the latter two launched within three years of each other in the mid-eighties, when it had become apparent that the National League and

American Association had created a hunger for baseball information in the public. At least in editorial address, none of the three papers agonized too much about how baseball might or might not have represented a moral advance on other mass amusements. The *Clipper* was, in fact, even more known as a theatrical weekly, its pages filled with Rialto news on openings and castings, ads for shows, and photos of amply proportioned actresses. For its part, Francis Richter's Philadelphia-based *Sporting Life* featured sections on billiards, hunting, and racing. From his St. Louis offices, *Sporting News* editor Alfred Spink, who had once thought of himself as a playwright and had written a show calling for a live horse race on stage, flanked baseball stories with his own weekly theater column and stories on cycling, racing, and hunting. As Warren Goldtsein has said, in the nineteenth century "the sporting . . . was the theatrical press." Indeed, the premier issue of the *Sporting News*, the so-called "baseball Bible," left open the possibility that its future content might depend on the public's reaction, an editorial asserting it would be up to readers to "guess out what [the paper's] aims and objects are." The guess was made easier after the debut press run of 3,000 on St. Patrick's Day in 1886 had blossomed to 60,000 readers within two years. Despite operating in a more claustrophobic regional market with the *Clipper* and the popular sex-and-sports formula of the New York-based *Police Gazette, Sporting Life* also managed to sell more than 40,000 copies a week.

Beyond the sheer availability of information provided by the weeklies for the fan, there was its specific content. On one level, this meant game summaries, individual franchise reports, profiles of players and executives, and independent league roundups. Equally important, as with any mass entertainment field, the baseball reporter had the built-in function of publicist: mention it and, no matter what is said, they might come. And baseball's nineteenth-century sportswriters went well beyond unintentional collaborations. On an individual level, crossovers were constant. Henry

Chadwick belonged to as many league rules committees as mastheads. *Cincinnati Commercial-Gazette* sports editor O. P. Caylor was not only one of the founders of the American Association, but took over the editorship of the New York *Sporting Times and Theatrical News* in 1890 when Spalding wanted to use the sheet for NL propaganda against the Brotherhood rebellion and Richter's championing of the Players League cause in *Sporting Life*. Richter himself arrived at those politics only after pushing an elaborate restructurization proposal that helped trigger the Brotherhood strike in the first place. Another Philadelphian, A. M. Gilliam of the *Record,* saw nothing untoward about asking teams in spring training to pass along regular items because "the games you play in the South mean nothing, but the score of even a five-inning practice game will be greedily scanned by the enthusiasts here and will boom your club for the coming season." A third Philadelphian, Al Wright, the first compiler of National League averages, also managed the Athletics in 1876 before they were expelled for not playing out their schedule. Before launching the *Sporting News,* Spink had bought Sportsman's Park with Chris Von der Ahe. One of his successors as *Sporting News* editor, Joe Flanner, supervised the writing of the 1903 peace agreement between the National and American leagues that served as the sport's foundation for the twentieth century; not a single word of the text approved by Flanner was amended.

None of this promised much in the way of in-depth journalistic examination of the major leagues. Players could be scolded, spectators could be chastised, and rival newspapers and their editors could be scorned, but front-office executives could be pretty sure that any mention of their names would be in the vein of positive instruction for the Republic. The resultant picture for the fan was of baseball the institution in capable hands precisely in those years when the frenetic coming and going of franchises and leagues was arguing the very opposite. By way of compensation, there were statistics and more statistics. The centerpiece of this absorption was the checkerboard standings grid devised by Al Wright for the *Philadelphia Sunday Mercury,* enabling readers to know at a glance where their teams stood vis-à-vis adversaries. If there had been any lingering nostalgia over playing the game without worrying about winning it, the Wright checkerboard put paid to it. And more than raw numbers, the statistics provided on everything from batting averages to the comparative ballpark distances of outfield walls played to the game's "orderliness," reassured its largely middle-class clientele that there was a rational, scientific dynamic beneath what might otherwise be construed as mere play.

If the press consolidated the sport's standing in the entertainment world, Spalding and other propagandists assured the fan that going to a game was the highest of patriotic acts. Even before Abraham Lincoln had been invoked as the First Fan and before war hero Abner Doubleday had been designated the sport's Adam, Spalding's publications were relentless in claims that the game owed nothing at all to such earlier sports as the British rounders or one old cat, that it had sprung up as a complete innovation on American soil. The key development in this campaign was an 1888 world tour undertaken by Spalding with his White Stockings for the avowed purpose of exporting baseball's "American spirit." Although it would subsequently be celebrated as a prime example of Spalding's promotional genius, the trip's cardinal achievement was ironic in the extreme—indeed demonstrating that baseball was truly an American sport, but chiefly in the sense that not too many other people were interested in it. But that detail was conveniently buried when the group returned to the United States and was hailed deliriously for what it had supposedly accomplished. Even the normally phlegmatic Mark Twain congratulated Spalding for bearing "the very symbol, the outward and visible expression of the drive and push and rush and struggle of the raging, tearing, booming nineteenth century . . . to places of profound repose and soft indolence." Rhetoric of the kind not only told the fan he was being an American by supporting baseball, but that this support made him *better* than the other peoples of the earth who couldn't get excited about an opposite-field double. There was no timelier theme in the expansion urges that gripped the country in the nineties.

If the press and the Spaldings made baseball the law of the land, Ban Johnson sold himself as the guarantor of the sport's order. Another former newspaperman, Johnson had been tuning up for several years at the turn of the century with a minor league circuit for taking on the NL; in 1901, he made his move. The new American League announced franchises in Milwaukee, Detroit, in three markets only recently abandoned by the NL (Baltimore, Cleveland, and Washington), and, even more defiantly, in three cities (Boston, Philadelphia, and Chicago) still occupied by the existing league. From the start, Johnson painted the AL as a corrective to all the rowdyism and instability of the nineties, banning gamblers from his grandstands and players from his fields if they engaged in any violent confrontations with umpires or opponents. His stated and restated objective was to restore respectability to major-league baseball.

Such pronouncements were hardly revolutionary. Throughout the nineteenth century and early twentieth century, there was not a single branch of the mass entertainment field, sport or non-sport, that didn't introduce itself as a "clean" alternative to what it was seeking to replace or rival. The NL itself had posed as morally as well as organizationally superior to the NAPBBP in going into business in 1876. Similarly, vaudeville's earliest organizers in the eighties and nineties were adamant they were bringing "wholesome" entertainment to communities marred by the sleazy stag ambience of variety halls; the Tony Pastors, B. F. Keiths, and E. F. Albees routinely described their stage productions as "refined" and "legitimate." Protestant ministers might have been complaining that cities like New York had one church for every 4,500 parishioners and one saloon for every 150 patrons, but their ethic was far from dead. Rarely was entrepreneurial initiative not pitched as moral progress.

Practiced as it was in Johnson's rhetoric, the NL had no qualms about trying to drive him back to journalism. But after two years of hostilities, featuring contract jumping at a level not seen since the worst days of the NABBP and NAPBBP, more wholesale gutting of clubs, and processions in and out of courtrooms, the sides forged a partnership that the American Association, for one, had never dreamed of contracting with the NL. Moreover, in establishing a ruling three-man National Commission, the leagues handed Johnson powers only slightly shy of dictatorial since the swing vote between the league presidents belonged to Reds owner Garry Herrmann, who had learned the virtues of compliance as a tool of Cincinnati political boss George Cox. A notorious gourmand, Herrmann disagreed with Johnson about as often as he missed a meal.

The so-called National Agreement opened the way for the AL in 1903 to move its Baltimore franchise to New York, where it was renamed the Highlanders and then the Yankees. That would mark the last franchise move for some 50 years; over that time, big league baseball became the exclusive domain of seven states and the District of Columbia, with 11 of the leagues' combined 16 teams concentrated in five cities (Boston, New York, Philadelphia, Chicago, and St. Louis). For the fan who happened to live in one of these selected areas, it was a stability without comparison in any other mass entertainment medium. For the fan outside these regions, it meant the addition of 16 significant American cultural spots to be visited one day.

Krank Cases:
The Deadball Era

The chief exception to the anonymity of early baseball fans was in the occasional article citing the presence of noted figures at games, usually in the key of implying that their interest in baseball confirmed its legitimacy. This was nowhere more marked than in the pieces reporting the fan habits of government officials and prominent politicians—the double suggestion between the lines being that they gave importance to baseball, and baseball made them men of the people. The *Washington Gazette*, for example, thought it was worth mentioning even during the offseason that many of President Benjamin Harrison's cabinet members would be attending games in 1892, declaring in part:

> *Among the Cabinet officers, Secretary [Charles] Foster of the treasury can be found at every game, seated high up in the scorer's box, quietly munching roasted peanuts and keeping tally with as much care as he does in counting the cash of Uncle Sam. [Agriculture] Secretary [Jeremiah] Rusk is another member of the Cabinet who can always be seen at games. Indeed, it is said of him that he was the most faithful attendant at the games in the last four years. [Navy] Secretary [Benjamin] Tracy is also a devotee of base ball, while the latest addition to the cabinet, [War Secretary] Stephen B. Elkins is as fond of the game as he is of a fine terrapin dinner.*

Also attractive to editors was the show-business clientele at the Polo Grounds—a regular feature of Giants games until the franchise pulled up stakes for California after the 1957 season. Regulars at the end of the nineteenth century and early in the twentieth included De Wolfe Hopper of "Casey at the Bat" fame; stage star Helen Dauvrey, before and after her divorce from future Hall of Famer John Montgomery Ward; George M. Cohan, then starting his career; and Maggie Cline, the "Bowery Brunnhilde" and "Daughter of Hercules" who was as popular in New York as she was in Boston with "Slide, Kelly, Slide" and her other Irish ditties.

Among the first characters to acquire their fame from the grandstand itself were Frank H. Wood in New York and General Arthur Dixwell in Boston. A Giants fan who rarely missed a home game in the 1880s and 1890s, Wood had the curious habit of leaping to his feet after every play, good, bad, or indifferent, and yelling out "Well! Well! Well!" This study in enthusiastic quizzicalness eventually earned him an appearance in Zane Grey's *The Redheaded Outfield and Other Baseball Stories.* Just as Wood became known as Well! Well! Well! Wood, Dixwell's gingerly cries of "Hi! Hi!" at the South End Grounds prompted his rebaptism as Hi! Hi! Dixwell among Boston fans and writers. The wealthy general didn't leave his fervor at that, however: He not only rewarded Boston players with expensive cigars for special feats on the field, but also established an annual trophy for the best minor-league club in the New England area. Another early fan was Andrew Rudolph, known as "Detroit Andy" for his compulsive absorption with the early twentieth-century Tigers. Rudolph was one Thomas Lawson krank know-it-all who apparently did know something: After George Mullin followed some pitching pointers shouted down from the fan's bleacher seat, he turned in three consecutive 20-win seasons. Mullin was so grateful he helped Rudolph get the scorecard concession for Bennett Park—a mixed blessing, insofar as the business ultimately ruined "Detroit Andy."

The fan who caused the biggest commotion in the early part of the century, Claude Luecker, also had a Detroit connection. On May 15, 1912, his relentless taunts of Ty Cobb at New York's Hilltop Park led the outfielder to climb into the stands and start pounding away at him. At a stirring from nearby fans to go to Luecker's aid, Sam Crawford and other Tiger players grabbed bats to make sure the fight stayed private. When stadium police finally intervened, Cobb was sent off the field, where he told reporters Luecker had called him "a half-nigger." Informed that the fan had lost four fingers in a printing-press accident, the Georgia Peach shrugged that he didn't care "if he had no feet." When Cobb was suspended for the episode, teammates sent a telegram to Ban Johnson warning they would boycott a May 18 game against the Athletics if the outfielder wasn't reinstated. Johnson ignored the threat, and the players did what they said they would. Rather than cough up a $1,000 fine for not fulfilling the club's schedule, Detroit owner Frank Navin ordered manager Hughie Jennings to round up some Philadelphia amateurs for the game. The Athletics trounced the makeshift team, 24–2, after which Cobb implored his teammates to go back to work.

Boston was home to the first prominent fan club—the Royal Rooters of Michael T. McGreevy, whose imperious judgments of when an argument had run its course earned him the nickname of "Nough Said." "Nuf Ced," as it was usually written, operated out of a Roxbury saloon called the Third Base that was close to both the South End Grounds and the Huntington Avenue Baseball Grounds occupied by the Red Sox after the launching of the American League. The bar, as Stephen Fox has described it, was "an overstuffed shrine to the game":

> *A life-sized statue of a ballplayer in a Boston uniform, in full mustache, holding a bat, stood guard above the door. Inside, scattered among the inevitable spittoons, brass rail, and dark paneling, a random riot of noteworthy balls, bats, trophies, and baseball photographs covered the walls and ceiling. The lights, in globes that resembled overgrown baseballs,*

hung down from bats donated by famous ballplayers such as King Kelly,
Cy Young, and Nap Lajoie. The clock behind the bar kept baseball time
with a bat-and-ball pendulum. . . .

McGreevy's first big foray with the Royal Rooters came late in the 1897 season, when he followed the home team to Baltimore for a pennant-deciding series with 125 fellow groupies; the party included a brass band and John "Honey Fitz" Fitzgerald, a future Boston mayor and the grandfather of John F. Kennedy. When the Beaneaters, as they were known at the time, won two of the three games for what proved to be the difference in the race, the Orioles were the first to credit the Royal Rooters and their games-long antics for influencing the outcome. In the words of Baltimore catcher Wilbert Robinson: "It's a certainty that Boston could not have beaten Baltimore without them. Little bags of beans pelted every head in sight, and the Boston contingent went mad with joy." Although the Orioles came back to beat the Beaneaters in the post-season Temple Cup series, the games in Baltimore proved to be the start of something big and noisy for the Royal Rooters for the next couple of decades.

The Rooters specialized in pennant-decisive and World Series games. With McGreevy and Fitzgerald at their head, they made a show of marching military style into ballparks in solemn blue suits and ties; only those who got too close to them might have detected they had done their drilling at the Third Base or its road equivalent. Their grandstand whistling, hooting, and cheering were all preliminaries to the rendering of their club anthem— "Tessie," a turn-of-the-century song from the popular musical *The Silver Slipper*. With more preparation than they were wont to admit, the Rooters altered the lyrics to suit the Boston foe of the moment. Against the Pirates and their star Honus Wagner in the 1903 World Series, for instance, the grandstand chorus went: "Honus, why do you hit so badly?/Take a back seat and sit down/Honus, at bat you look so sadly/Hey, why don't you get out of town?" Like Wilbert Robinson, Tommy Leach of the Pirates insisted the booster club was a factor in the Red Sox victory over Pittsburgh. "I think those Boston fans actually won that Series," Leach said years later. "They started signing that damn 'Tessie' song. . . . Sort of got on your nerves after a while."

Between 1903 and 1916, "Tessie" provided the accompaniment for six pennants and five World Series championships by either the Red Sox or Braves. It was also chorussed out for other signal baseball moments, such as when Jack Chesbro of the Highlanders fired a wild pitch in the ninth inning of the 1904 season finale to give Boston another flag. As a group, the Rooters took themselves as seriously as the Robinsons and Leaches did. When they discovered their usual places had been occupied by visiting New Yorkers in the 1912 World Series against the Giants, for instance, they marched around the field later to be known as Fenway Park, trumpets and trombones wailing and holding up the start of play; it took two charges by police, a near-riot, and the threat of a forfeit to the Giants to restore order. After the game, the Rooters trooped ceremoniously to the Boston dugout with their megaphones so they could boo club secretary Rob McRoy for the seating mixup and demand his firing.

At the same time, however, they rarely got embroiled in nasty scenes with rival fan clubs, even after making it their first order of business upon arriving in a city to parade down its central thoroughfare with Boston banners; on the contrary, their jousting in Pittsburgh in 1903 and in Brooklyn during the 1916 World Series with the locals won them a great deal of sympathetic press. Because of World War I and a hastily arranged postseason championship in 1918, the Rooters didn't get a chance to perform "Tessie" in the games against the Cubs. When the Red Sox won anyway, the charm appeared to be off the tune. But that was also the last time a Boston club captured a championship, so that the Tessie Curse has ranked second only to the Curse of the Bambino as a New England explanation for the postseason failures of the Red Sox since the World War I era.

The Royal Rooters weren't the only fan club active in the early twentieth century; Cleveland had the Bards, the White Sox the Rooters, Pittsburgh the Stove League, and Brooklyn the Boosters. In themselves, the clubs didn't define a given team's following any more than an individual fan like Hi Hi Dixwell did. All sixteen teams of the period drew their fan base from the same preponderance of white-collar middle-class white males and from a smaller but steadily growing blue-collar presence, ethnic breakdowns determined by the population of the city in question. What the booster clubs did do was paint the particularities of a given baseball setting on an enlarged canvas in a way that, despite Ban Johnson's beliefs in greater or lesser respectability, the teams themselves couldn't always do. Though nobody in baseball had anything to gain by admitting it, most squads were average performers that could only be counted on to win about as much as they lost during a season. In terms of personality, their organizational distinction from one another stemmed from two or three stars or from an occasionally idiosyncratic way of managing (John McGraw's Giants) or of approaching the game (the "Hitless Wonders" of Chicago). If this was an inevitable component of athletic competition on a level playing field, the very essence of the drama known as a pennant race, it also posed something of a problem for owners trying to make a profit from their individual professional product, win, lose, or finish fourth; however exhilarating equitable competition could be, major league baseball did not have the same interests or goals as college baseball. Every source of recognition of the home team was therefore useful publicity; for that reason, the smarter owners not only tolerated the antics of the fan clubs, but encouraged them. The fan as paying publicist was a franchise asset long before somebody came up with the idea of Cap Day.

Sex in the Grandstand

For a good part of the nineteenth century, sportswriters advocated increased attendance by women at games as the ideal deterrent to grandstand rowdyism. A typical comment by the *Ball Players' Chronicle* in 1867 was that a female presence "purifies the moral atmosphere of a base ball gathering, repressing . . . all outbursts of intemperate language which the excitement of a contest so frequently induces." "To realize the advantage of the attendance of the fair sex," another writer declared, "it is only necessary to contrast the behavior of a large crowd of spectators at a ball match during an exciting contest when no ladies are present with that of an assemblage in which are to be seen hundreds of bright-eyed fair one. . . . At the former, profanity, ill feeling, partisan prejudice and other characteristics of 'stag' gatherings are conspicuous features, while at the other the pride of gentlemen which curbs men's evil passions in the presence of ladies frowns upon all such exhibitions of partisan ill will, and order and decorum mark the presence of the civilizing influence of the fair sex." If there was any variation in this perspective for a good 30 years, it was in the occasional wink implying that the single woman might find attending a game profitable for herself, as well. According to *Porter's Spirit of the Times* for instance, it was a given that players would perform more energetically before women since "more than one of them attends the ground with the view of sharply measuring among the players the qualities of what might make a serviceable future husband."

By the early twentieth century, there was decidedly less press plumping for women as moral sentries and much less tea-party coyness about any sexual shopping. One reason was that, while rarely more than a fraction of a gate, women had indeed been going to games all along; even the 1908 anthem, "Take Me Out to the Ball Game," was about a woman telling her date to forget about taking her to a show instead of to the ballpark. The trouble was, their attendance had done absolutely nothing to curb the male habits that bothered the fretting writers. Another problem was that their very presence had occasioned grandstand incidents—mashers, fights over lower-priced Ladies Day seats, and so forth.

Then there was the demographic disillusion that many of the women who did attend were not the wives and daughters primarily intended by the sportswriters, but single women in pairs or in larger groups who weren't quite so sheepish about sizing up the talent on the field. Two of these factors came together in 1897, when Washington set out to exploit the good looks of pitcher Win Mercer by announcing free admission for women at Boundary Field for one of the righthander's starts. After Mercer was thrown out of the game in the fifth inning by umpire Bill Carpenter for arguing, women protestors began tearing up seats and smashing ballpark office windows. Carpenter had to be smuggled off the premises in disguise. After the incident, the Senators announced the cancellation of all Ladies Day promotions.

A particular source of irritation to the sportswriting fraternity from the 1880s on was that women were going to ballparks not only as spectators, but as players on all-girl teams. This found the writers in regular battle with themselves not to sound like frothing misogynists—and usually losing. One pet target was the touring "Female Base Ball Club," which was organized in the early 1880s after promoter Harry H. Freeman took note of the crowds that had attended earlier all-girl games in Decatur, Illinois, and New Orleans. For Francis Richter in *Sporting Life*, there was no question the bottom had been reached. "The female has no place in base ball, except to the degradation of the game," he thundered. "For two seasons now various sections of the country have been nauseated with the spectacle of these tramps, who have been repeatedly stranded and the objects of public charity. . . . [In Georgia] their conduct was of such character that respectable ladies got off the cars and waited for the next train."

Ridicule often substituted for censure. In 1883, the *New York Times* seized upon the female teams for the double objective of mocking them and providing still another reason why baseball couldn't be taken seriously. In one game report, it said "no casualties either among the girls or spectators occurred, for the reason no girl was able to throw the ball swiftly enough to inflict a severe blow. . . . They could not have caught it if they tried, for the simple reason they were standing on their feet and were without aprons." A month later, the paper reported at length on what it headlined as "A Base-Ball Burlesque." The *Times* said in part:

> *A crowd of about 1,500 people assembled at the Manhattan Athletic Club's grounds . . . yesterday afternoon, and laughed themselves hungry and thirsty watching a game of base-ball between two teams composed of girls. One side was composed of brunettes, whose costumes were of an irritating red; the other was of blondes who wore sympathetic blue. . . . These young ladies . . . were selected with tender solicitude from 900 applicants, variety actresses and ballet girls being positively barred. . . . They were of assorted sizes and shapes. Some were short and stout, some were tall and thin; others were short and thin, and still others tall and stout. They played base-ball in a very sad and sorrowful sort of way as if the vagaries of the ball had been too great for their struggling intellects. . . .*

Criticism of women as spectators came for everything from their understanding of the game, to their readiness to be part of crowds, to the size of their hats. Especially on Ladies Days, which attracted female fans beyond the hard-core regulars, women were scored for cheering "oddly" and "inappropriately," the implication being that they were ignorant of what they were watching. Indignation wasn't confined to the major leagues, either. In the late eighties, a reporter for the *San Francisco Examiner* voiced dismay that women would allow themselves to be part of the mob transportation scenes to and from parks. "Men hung on to the poles supporting the roofs of the dummies and were as thick as monkeys in a South American forest," he wrote of a ride to a local game. "Women stood up on the car platforms tightly sandwiched between men whom they had never seen before, but it was no time to be squeamish or even particular."

Another favorite early turn-of-the-century peeve was the size of the hats worn by women to games. Although fashionable outside a ballpark, the women were told constantly, the millinery was good inside only for obstructing views and causing grandstand disputes. One writer obsessed by the subject was E. H. Simmons of the weekly *Sporting Life,* who devoted two lengthy articles to it within the space of three issues. "The women's hats at the ball games are getting to be a serious menace, and if the trouble grows worse the managers will find they will have to do something about it," he said in his opening shot. "The number of women who attend ball games is steadily increasing and the style of headgear that some of them wear is simply appalling. One would think that the commonest kind of consideration for others would prevent women from wearing hats of a size that makes it impossible for anybody sitting behind them to get even a glimpse of the ball field. But, unfortunately, the average woman does not seem to be affected by any such consideration, and so the unfortunate victims of her vanity and selfishness have no redress. But the time is coming when the worm will turn, and when the man who pays his money to see a ball game and sees instead nothing but the back of a woman's hat will make his protest felt and heard."

In his followup attack, Simmons was able to report some slight progress to his *Sporting Life* readers:

> *A gratifying feature of Saturday's game was the large number of women who removed their hats during the game, thus allowing those behind them to witness the game as well as themselves. There was, unfortunately, still a large number of women who kept their hats on, to the great discomfiture of those in their vicinity. And such hats as some of the women wear! One woman walked across the grounds with a headgear construction of such immense size and hideous appearance that the crowd in the grandstand rose en masse to look at it and voice its disapproval. The writer often wonders what proportion of women who go to these games understand and enjoy what they are witnessing. Many, of course, do. It is probably those who do not, and who go merely to be seen rather than to see, who make themselves so conspicuous and who display such complete disregard for the rights of others.*

Simmons's rancor emanated from a baseball press climate in which public devotion to upholding family values was often juggled with personal night-crawling habits. To a great degree, the double standard was dramatized through two New York players who represented the opposite extremes of box-office sex appeal in the early part of the century. Giants pitcher Christy Mathewson's handsomeness was routinely described as being part of the makeup of the ideal son—the one who, among other things, had attended Bucknell, sung in the university choir, and promised his dying mother (a militant in the Woman's Christian Temperance Union) that he would never pitch on Sundays. On the other hand, Highlander first baseman Hal Chase's good looks were those of the suave rogue—the one who, among other things, swaggered around as The Prince, couldn't spend money fast enough, and had a predilection for spending it on all-night poker games and chorus girls. When Mathewson took the mound at the Polo Grounds during his Hall of Fame career, he sold "family" tickets; when Chase took up his position at first base at Hilltop Park during a career that would be sabotaged and eventually sunk by a series of fixing scandals, he sold chorine tickets. Some of the same writers who were routinely included in Chase's all-nighters were the first to suggest in print he was attracting the "wrong element" to Hilltop Park; that is, the women weren't mothers and wives. And sometimes they wore big hats.

If anybody topped this moralistic Babel, it was Spalding. On the one hand, while still operating the White Stockings in the early eighties, he had given the first significant baseball job to a woman. Suspicious that some of the performance statistics submitted to his annual guide had been doctored under pressure from players, he announced that Chicago's official scorer would remain anonymous, from the league as well as from the team. Only a number of years later did it emerge that the scorer was Elisa Green Williams and that she had not even told her family precisely what she did for a living.

While coming down against women as players, Spalding also subscribed to the need for a strong female presence at games—not for the widely espoused purpose of keeping male spectators calm, but for having them contribute "smiles of derision for the Umpire" in cases of bad calls and "perfectly decorous demonstrations when it became necessary to rattle the opposing pitcher." He didn't spell out the nature of the "decorous demonstrations."

In a *New York Times* interview after he had withdrawn from day-to-day league affairs, Spalding also suggested another benefit in having the right women attend games. According to baseball's premier myth-maker, the sport's beneficial effects on the nation would remain permanent because just as racing had resulted in better horse breeding, baseball players should lead to "improvement in man breeding."

At the Ballpark

For all the hand-wringing about crude behavior and gambling, the biggest threat to baseball at the onset of the twentieth century came from shoddy wooden ballparks that put fans at risk for a lot more than a few dollars. Between 1889 and 1911, franchises in Brooklyn, Boston, Chicago, Cincinnati (three times), St. Louis (twice), New York (twice), Louisville, Cleveland, Philadelphia (twice), and Washington all suffered extensive home grandstand fires or collapses. Many of the facilities weren't all that inviting even when they weren't crumbling. In Brooklyn, stenches from the nearby factories made attending a game at the first version of Washington Park an endurance contest—an experience re-created with a later move to Eastern Park and its proximity to the acrid smells of Jamaica Bay. Then there were the playing fields, often not much better than the seating arrangements. Swampy outfields were the norm. In Pittsburgh, the Allegheny River could be counted on to flood Exposition Park at least six times a season, making normal play impossible; absurdity was reached on July 4, 1902, when the Pirates ownership, determined to hold on to a holiday crowd despite a standing lake in the outfield, ruled that all balls hit out there would be automatic singles. Detroit's Bennett Park posed another kind of problem: an infield that was barely covered cobblestone, making for a surfeit of errors and sliding injuries.

One of the worst disasters occurred at Philadelphia's Baker Bowl in August 1903, when taunting by children set off a chain of events that ended with twelve deaths and injuries to 200 others. As the Philadelphia *Inquirer* put the scene together from eye-witness accounts:

> *Ten thousand persons were in the park. . . . Shrieks of help and murder from the street below were heard. Some little girls had been teasing two drunken men, the latter had turned on them, and one of the children had fallen. The crowd on the top left field bleachers . . . rushed to the three-foot-wide wooden balcony that overhangs the top of the wall, twenty-five feet from the ground, to see what happened. Suddenly, jammed with an immense, vibrating weight, a hundred feet or more of the balcony tore itself loose from the wall, and the crowd was hurled headlong to the pavement. Those who felt themselves falling grasped those behind and they in turn held on to others. Behind were thousands still pushing to see what was happening. In the twinkling of an eye the street was piled four deep with bleeding, injured, shrieking humanity struggling amid the piling debris.*

The collapse of the Baker Bowl balcony and the other disasters brought baseball owners more than bad publicity and apprehensive fans; they also brought higher insurance rates and lawsuits. Most of the plaintiffs had a case since, going back to the days of William Cammeyer in Brooklyn, ballparks had been erected in mere weeks with the help of politically protected winking at this building code provision and that fire ordinance. Equally hurried repairs with the same flimsy materials didn't help. Indeed, for long years, ballparks were the forest nobody could see for all the trees of amenities and distractions that had been put in place for the entertainment of the fan. And the distractions never stopped multiplying.

Although Chris Von der Ahe's "Coney Island of the West" received the most attention, Sportsman's Park was far from being the only facility that expected ticket buying to be merely the start of ballpark spending. The St. George Grounds on Staten Island, which hosted two New York teams briefly, featured a restaurant, ice cream parlor, tennis courts, fireworks, geysers, and a picnic ground. Baltimore's park not only had a dance hall and restaurant, but various promotion deals with an adjacent amusement park. The Polo Grounds had a prominent bar behind the first base seating section. The Olympic Grounds in Washington had had a first-class restaurant as early as the National Association of Professional Base Ball Players in 1871. More than a century before the opening of Bank One Ballpark in Phoenix, the Phillies boasted a swimming pool in Baker Bowl that helped make the complex so popular that the franchise shattered all previous baseball attendance records with almost a half million people in its inaugural year of 1895.

In many cities, the Ballpark Experience began even before getting to the game. Because most parks were located on the cheapest real estate on urban outskirts, owners found it good business to sell tickets through more centrally located retail operations, especially bars and pool halls; some drug stores also played agent, mainly for women customers, as part of advertising campaigns to dispel the image of long ticket-window lines at the ballpark. While managing the Phillies in the eighties and nineties, Harry Wright remained true to his commercial instincts by persuading Philadelphia's owners to open the gates earlier so fans could take in the pre-game batting practice he had instituted; the proposal proved to be a boon for concession stands.

As today, the early-century grandstand fanned out from home plate down the first and third base lines toward the outfield and its increasingly cheaper seating. Since players didn't wear numbers, let alone names, on their uniforms, fans identified them as they came to bat from a scoreboard number announcing their place in the lineup and matching that number to a scorecard name. Those who stood behind outfield ropes commonly as far as 500 feet away from home plate (the forerunner to bleacher seats) were generally regarded as either zealots who didn't need any scoreboard to know the players or as passersby who would have survived without knowing them.

Most parks had special facilities for women, including bathrooms with attendants. In Cincinnati, enclosed steps from the field to the grandstand allowed women to get to a ladies section without having to parade past the boys with the beers. The Reds also had enough misgivings about a twelve-beers-for-a-dollar policy that they literally confined their bibulous customers within chicken-wire pens dubbed "rooters' rows" along the first and third base lines. Men were usually barred from the ladies' sections unless accompanied by a woman, and, even if admitted, couldn't smoke or drink. But not even escorts always succeeded in protecting women from harassment. "Guying women as they pass in front of stands at ball games is a fine display of chivalry, a truly hoodlum species of chivalry," the *New York Sun* scolded of an early-century Polo Grounds practice.

Ballpark concessions became synonymous with Harry M. Stevens, a Briton who had his epiphany while traveling through Ohio in the late eighties peddling a biography of Civil War general and U.S. Senator John Logan. Taking a break from his door-to-door odyssey to attend an Ohio State League game in Columbus, Stevens realized that it wasn't just because he was a stranger that he was unable to distinguish the players, that locals were also stymied by hastily printed-up lists of names that had little relevance to the day's batting order. His initial proposal to take over the printing and selling of scorecards came up against an impossible $500 licensing demand by the ownership of the Columbus Discoverers. But then he hit upon the idea of selling advertising in the programs to local businesses and, a couple of days later, was able to hand the team a check for $700 in exchange for the scorecard franchise. That was the end of General Logan and the beginning of a multimillion-dollar business.

From Columbus, Stevens quickly branched out to major and minor league parks in Pittsburgh, Wheeling, Toledo, and Milwaukee. When Von der Ahe asked him to print up scorecards for the 1887 postseason championship series between St. Louis and Detroit, he had the invitation to major league circles he needed. Within a few years, a Stevens program was a regular feature at ballparks all over the country, as well as at race tracks, indoor arenas like New York's Madison Square Garden for bicycle races and kennel shows, and vaudeville houses. At the same time, the growing company expanded its food and beverage lines to include beer, soda, peanuts, popcorn, ice cream, sandwiches, and pies. The most controversial fare was the soda, regarded by the macho fans of the day as an effeminate alternative to the beer that was usually served in the stands in big-handled glasses. But it was also the pop that, according to some historians, inspired Stevens to devise drinking straws—a way for fans to go at their sarsaparilla without having to drop their eyes from the game.

The most noted commodity associated with Stevens is the hot dog, which has as many creation myths as baseball itself. H. L. Mencken, for one, claimed he had been eating them in Baltimore as early as the 1880s and that they had been popular before then. Other have traced them to World Expos in Chicago and St. Louis. But according to the tale with the widest currency, while overseeing his Polo Grounds operation one day in 1901, Stevens was so disturbed by the decline of soda and ice cream sales during a cold snap that he had an assistant run down the street to a butcher's shop in the then-German neighborhood to buy several boxes of the red frankfurters known as dachshund sausages. After a quick heating of the franks, they were slapped into pointed Vienna rolls and hawked by vendors with the cry "Get your red hots! Get 'em while they're hot!" As much of a favorite as the sausages became with Giants fans, it was not until several years later that they were called hot dogs. The first use of the term at all was in the *New York Sun* in 1906 with a reference to the "hot dog sandwiches" then being sold—not at a ballpark, but at the Coney Island amusement park. That precedent has made highly improbable the often-recounted story that sports cartoonist Tad Dorgan popularized the expression *hot dog* in 1915 only because he didn't know how to spell *dachshund*. While the term did become commonplace after a Dorgan cartoon, it would seem to have already occupied at least a modest niche in the language for the better part of a decade. The hot dog's identification with ballparks has sometimes been made to sound genetic. If anybody has ever been recorded as saying hot dogs tasted just as good elsewhere as from a grandstand seat, the testimonial has been lost. The strength of the association has been such that romantics of the game have claimed an exclusiveness for the phenomenon that, in fact, it doesn't have; to cite just one obvious parallel, moviegoers have some ideas of their own about where popcorn has to be chomped to be enjoyed fully. But on its own terms, the hot dog unquestionably acquired ritualistic status for the fan at the ballpark, as such adding to the spectating entertainment, enriching the baseball industry, and amplifying the sport's institutionality.

The ballpark security issue, meanwhile, finally prompted the building of the first complete steel-and-concrete facilities in 1909—Shibe Park for the AL Philadelphia Athletics, which opened in April, and Forbes Field, for the NL Pittsburgh Pirates, which opened two months later. It was hardly coincidental that both trailblazers were from Pennsylvania, the state with the biggest investment in the steel industry, but the ramifications of the new installations went beyond that. For one thing, Pittsburgh owner Barney Dreyfuss seized the occasion of the new park to earmark an unprecedented percentage of his 25,000 seats for reserved booking, putting into practice his long-held contention that franchises could not prosper on the basis of the walkup trade. For another thing, the construction of the steel ballparks required an outlay of capital not required by the wooden structures, making owners far less whimsical about moving from here to there. There is little doubt the parks were a significant factor in the franchise and geographical stability of the two leagues for the first half of the twentieth century, with even the most elaborate structural innovations (second decks, outfield stands, and the like) subjected to existing contours. (Conversely, the depreciation of ballparks—through natural attrition or calculated neglect—would figure prominently in late-century maneuvers to transfer franchises.)

Within five years of the openings of Shibe Park and Forbes Field, ten more steel-and-concrete structures would be built. But ballparks weren't the only thing getting bigger and more deeply entrenched in the early 1900s.

For the Good of the Fans

The biggest problem baseball had with pool sellers and bookmakers was that they were pocketing money that fans could have spent on the sport directly. The fan who bet $10 on the Cardinals over the Braves at the neighborhood poolroom risked having $10 less to spend on other games or at the concession stands during the ones he did attend. It was in this spirit, as much as any other, that baseball officials announced a new crackdown on gambling at the beginning of the twentieth century. Of course, they weren't about to say as much. Nor were they about to admit to any concern that more gamblers around ballparks meant more chances of corrupted players. The foremost aim of the campaign, league executives swore, was to help the fan help himself.

"The war against gambling on baseball now being waged by the National Commission and all leagues under organized ball is not intended to protect the players and umpires from falling into temptation, and any insinuations to this effect are insults to both players and umpires and to the national game itself," NL president Thomas Lynch told the *New York Sun* in June 1912. "The crusade against this gambling evil is to protect the patrons who attend the game and to stamp out the poolrooms where pools are sold on the results of games." Similarly, the *Boston Globe* insisted the crackdown had nothing to do with suspect players or even with big-time gamblers, but was aimed solely at rescuing the everyday fan from his own worst tendencies. "The big gambler, the man who follows this for a living, does not knock a club when it falls from under his wager," the paper found. "He isn't built that way. If he loses, he takes his medicine. . . . But the little tinhorn, the two-bit fellow, makes life miserable for the unfortunate athlete who does something that costs him money. . . . Gambling has killed horse racing, it killed foot racing, and a few other perfectly good sports. Therefore, if they wish to gamble, let it be done quietly and in secret, not in the open grandstands." The *Globe* also decided that "base ball has been singularly free from scandal and suspicion of dishonesty, and the magnates are wise trying to keep it that way."

What made these pronouncements noteworthy, aside from the *Globe*'s slippery grasp of baseball history, was that they came amid indications that gamblers had never been stronger in clubhouses; in fact, Lynch's unctuousness was in response to an editorial warning from the *Sun* that both players and umpires were becoming increasingly bold about conniving with gamblers in fixes. Certainly, the period saw numerous incidents that raised questions about the honesty of the game and some of its most stalwart figures; a suspiciously high number of accusations centered around John McGraw and his NL champion Giants. The charges continued up to the doorstep and through the door of the super-scandal of the 1919 World Series. But rather than admit any institutional problem, executives and compliant sportswriters hid behind the kind of cant that greeted Philadelphia fans returning to the Baker Bowl after repair work had been completed on the collapsed balcony in 1903. A sign at the entrance declared:

> *The same business management which catered only to the respectable and refined classes in the past will continue to do so in the future. Our park rules prescribe temperature, order, and discipline. They proscribe gambling, betting, profanity, obscenity, and disorderly conduct, as well as*

*Sunday ball playing at home or abroad. Our players, proud of their past
reputation, prefer to sacrifice both championship and place rather than
win either by trickery, rudeness, or other conduct unworthy of their good
name or the approval of the ladies and gentlemen whose refining presence
honors their contest for supremacy on the ball field.*

The presumption that it was the fans whose proclivities required
the emergency action represented more than diversionary tactics by
baseball owners. Although some of them (Pittsburgh's Dreyfuss was
one) were genuinely convinced that gambling was detrimental from
both a moral and a business standpoint, and had little hesitation
about calling in the police to conduct regular sweeps of their grandstands, most were not so sure. Betting was simply too widespread to
know with absolute confidence to what extent its elimination
would affect mass enthusiasm for the sport. One estimate passed
along by Seymour was that in 1911 some 40,000 New Haven factory
workers held pool tickets amounting to $10,000 and that a Philadel-
phia pool that same year sold some 20,000 tickets on the World
Series. The owners' doubts were deepened by state law disparities,
specifically by anxieties that a rival team would gain an economic
edge because of the greater tolerance of betting habits in its market.
And then there was the need for many of the owners to go up
against political powers that might have been protecting the gambling rings: Ward heelers were not ideal municipal foes for a public
entertainment industry.

In this context, the announced crackdown in the early 1900s, as
with those twenty and thirty years earlier, was as much a stress test
of fans as it was some unalterable commitment to the values proclaimed by the Baker Bowl sign. The result was that, within mere
months of the "crusade," after almost daily dispatches reporting
police raids in minor-league as well as major-league parks, with the ink
still drying on a *Sporting Life* headline about "Every Resource to Be
Employed in a Herculean Effort to Put an end to an Evil," even more

money was being wagered in the pools. By 1919, the raid stories had been replaced by regular reports of families going into hock because dad (or sometimes mom) had cashed in Liberty Bonds to back a Walter Johnson start against the Tigers. A year later, the *Chicago Tribune* could say that 400,000 pool tickets were being sold every week in that city alone. The upshot was that the teens years before, during, and after World War I eclipsed the first decade of the century for gambling activity. It was also the teens that heard charges that two World Series *before* the Black Sox fiasco had been fixed and that even an entire pennant race had been rigged. The fans had spoken; they had said "no" to no gambling.

Sincere or not, the public posture by baseball officials that it was their duty to save fans from themselves confirmed a more paternalistic phase in the relationship between the two sides. Previously, even the most flexible of pontifications had carried an exclusionary ring: Fans who were interested only in having their team win, in gambling, or in making crude spectacles of themselves had no place within a respectable sport, period. In the national reformist breezes of the early 1900s, however, that attitude was far too absolutist, not to say counterproductive at the ticket window. If the owners weren't altogether secure about the importance of gambling to fans, they had at least developed another self-confidence—that *whatever* fans wanted, they were the ones to provide it. Their monopoly wasn't just over geographical markets, but over personal tastes, inclinations, and habits translated as mass demand.

The numbers seemed very reassuring on this score. Not counting the Boston Braves, which were being run as a major league farm club for McGraw and the Giants, every franchise in both leagues in the period could count on a minimal 200,000 fans a year, with most teams doing better that that for an average of six million people walking through turnstiles every season. Profits mounted so much between the signing of the National Agreement in 1903 and 1911 that the annual publications with particularly close ties to baseball, such as *The Spalding Guide,* started becoming evasive about precise attendance figures, the better for leaving the tax collector in the dark. There was only one small glitch: When fans got the opportunity to reaffirm their special allegiance to the NL and AL, they didn't take it. On the contrary, they clearly indicated a willingness to watch just about any winning team, whatever its league banner or professional credentials.

The opportunity was provided by the Federal League, an eight-team circuit that sought to compete in 1914 and 1915 with the NL and AL with clubs formed around such veterans as Hal Chase, Joe Tinker, and Mordecai "Three-Finger" Brown. To varying degrees of enthusiasm the first year, the Feds set up for business in Chicago, Indianapolis, St. Louis, Kansas City, Pittsburgh, Baltimore, Brooklyn, and Buffalo. The biggest Feds attraction turned out to be the Whales of Chicago, which had both its best and worst day on the final afternoon of the 1915 season. While it lost a pennant-deciding game, the club did so before 34,000 fans at the same time that the White Sox and Cubs, also both home for the day, were drawing 5,000 between them. Although other FL franchises were nowhere near as popular (some of them were forced to sell tickets for a dime to try to fill seats), the most embarrassed club of all was the 1914 AL Indians. Hearing rumors that the Feds had designs on the Cleveland market, owner Charles Somers sought to head them off by switching the home games of his minor-league Toledo team to League Park during Indian road trips. The result was heavier turnouts for the minor-leaguers than for the last-place Indians. In addition, a single amateur game held at the Brookside Park amphitheater in October between the city champion White Autos and the Luxus team from Omaha drew 80,000 spectators, while Cleveland managed to attract merely 186,000 for its entire home schedule.

The Federal League lasted only through the 1915 season. But that was time enough to create three important legacies and a clarion reminder to the sport. The first legacy came about when the Baltimore franchise refused to accept a $50,000 payoff for liqui-dating itself and began a years-long court fight against Organized Baseball; the litigation went on until May 22, 1922, when the U.S. Supreme Court ruled that Organized Baseball was not vulnerable to anti-trust provisions because its activities did not constitute inter-state commerce. The second and third developments stemmed from the permission given Whales owner Charles Weeghman to buy the Cubs. One of Weeghman's first moves for ingratiating himself with NL fans was to allow them to keep any foul balls or home runs hit into the stands; at least in Chicago, there would be no more scenes of stadium personnel wrestling with fans to retrieve balls—a not-uncommon occurrence around both leagues. Weeghman also moved his new franchise out of West Side Park and into Weeghman Field, the North Side facility he had been using while with the Feds. Later renamed Wrigley Field, the ballpark became the model for "field of dreams" reveries about the once-upon-a-time innocence of major-league baseball (not to mention a memorial to the last serious attempt to break Organized Baseball's monopoly).

The reminder came from fans: that in their readiness to watch new teams, minor-league teams, or amateur teams, they still thought the only thing really good for them was winning entertainment.

God and Country

The fan was seldom allowed to forget how far from—or close to—God he was because of his passion for baseball. If not as relentlessly as before, Protestant ministers still took to the pulpit in the early twentieth century to denounce the sport's links to gambling, drinking, and women of the night, while the Woman's Christian Temperance Union charged into every pathetic tale about such alcoholic players as Bugs Raymond and Rube Waddell as a vindication of its mission. One clergyman told the Presbyterian Ministers' Association in 1900 that so many Pittsburgh players had been injured during the year because the Lord had taken over as the team's manager to punish them for having dared to play on a Sunday. Like vaudeville operators, baseball owners worried enough about the attacks to make it a policy to hand out free passes to religious leaders, the hope being that their presence would be an advertisement for respectability. But since most of those who availed themselves of the passes in cities like New York, Boston, and Chicago were Irish Catholic priests who had never regarded baseball as one of the seven deadly sins in the first place, the free passes didn't do much to reach the gesture's prime targets.

The leagues didn't leave it at that. If any minister anywhere in the country had something positive to say about the sport, it received full attention; the same was true of any newspaper editorial discerning the eschatological meaning of an extra-inning game. Thus, in May 1910, when NL secretary-treasurer John Heydler found something along these redeeming lines in the smalltown *Franklin (Pennsylvania) Evening News,* Francis Richter didn't hesitate to devote the entire front page of *Sporting Life* to reprinting the article. Its theme was "That which is religion is essential to baseball. Justice, truth, obedience to law, cheerfulness in serving, faith, hope, good will toward those opposing us, action, soul-expression, are all characteristics and fundamental in religion and baseball." *Sporting Life* itself was not beyond posing for its readers as a vivid example of how purity was next to godliness; or, as Richter declared on one occasion, "*Sporting Life* is not only one of the cleanest papers issued, but . . . it is absolutely the cleanest paper on earth."

No amount of reprinted treacle or editorial self-aggrandizement, however, could solve the thorny issue of Sunday baseball. Although the five clubs representing the NL and AL in Chicago, St. Louis, and Cincinnati received permission to play Sunday ball in 1902, various lay and clerical movements came together to make sure local blue laws were upheld in the other cities of the leagues in the name of the Christian sabbath. Not for the first time, much of what passed for religious debate defined a class conflict between a WASP gentry and a working class that had only Sunday for playing or watching sports.

The contradictions and paradoxes stemming from this faceoff were worthy of *Alice in Wonderland.* Within the same city park, adults could ride horses, hit a golf ball, or return a tennis serve, but children were liable to arrest for tossing a baseball. The same Sabbatarians who linked the game to beer and liquor sales marched past open saloons to close down ballparks. Some of the cities with the highest number of working-class Catholics, such as New York and Boston, were among those with the toughest blue laws because most such legislation also covered the variety halls and theaters that priests tended to look at more disapprovingly. Although most owners logically enough supported the elimination of the blue laws so they could make money on

Sundays, not all did. Pittsburgh's Dreyfuss, for instance, took the line that weekend games would ultimately work against the weekday attendance clubs had come to depend on for the overwhelming majority of their income. (This was probably his way of saying that, just as he sought to play down the gate's reliance on walkup customers, he didn't want working-class spectators accounting for too much of his business.)

Most owners took furtive ways around the statutes. The Yankees solidified their following in New Jersey by playing Sunday games there during the 1918 season. Another charade was the staging of special "free" concerts or other benefits during which a baseball game would be played and collection baskets circulated through the grandstands. When Brooklyn's Charlie Ebbets came up with too many buttons and slugs when he used that ruse, he switched to the scorecard tactic—admitting fans for free but obligating them to buy scorecards that just happened to be color-coded according to the seating section desired. That gambit came to an end when the police marched onto the field to arrest the Brooklyn battery and the leadoff batter for Philadelphia in an April 1904 game. When both the players and the two teams were fined, the NL warned Ebbets not to repeat the ploy with any other visiting club. More than a decade later, however, McGraw and Mathewson were hauled out of the Polo Grounds after the Giants attempted the same trick—in their case, an advertised benefit for the 69th Regiment, about to go overseas for the World War I hostilities.

The plying of politicians had only lukewarm results for many years. The most shameless graft episode was in Ohio in 1910 and 1911, where Cleveland and some of the state's minor-league teams were permitted to host Sunday ball only after season passes were handed out to lawmakers like matchbooks. What finally turned the tide was the war and the impetus provided by the District of Columbia's decision to drop the Sunday ban so homefront workers in and out of the Federal government could enjoy their one day off however they wanted. A year later, New York State Senator James Walker pushed through a local options bill in Albany that brought Sunday games to the Giants, Yankees, and Dodgers. Walker was later elected mayor of New York City behind the slogan "He Gave Us Sunday Baseball."

The last holdouts were Boston, Philadelphia, and Pittsburgh. Boston did not get a green light until 1929, mainly because of a years-long melodrama in which owners of the Braves and city council members swapped charges about who had tried to corrupt whom in getting ordinances waived. Pennsylvania cities unspooled another saga; before it was over, Athletics owner Connie Mack threatened to move his club across the Delaware River to Camden in more liberal New Jersey. As with World War I and Washington, the strife finally ended because of an outside factor—in this instance, the Great Depression. In 1933, Philadelphia was sinking in unemployment and financial problems that had left it more than $30 million in debt. The realization that the city could collect more than $1.25 million in taxes by permitting Sunday sports and other amusements pushed the state government in Harrisburg into approving a local options bill. In November 1933, after a seven-year struggle, Sunday ball was approved for most Pennsylvania communities.

As prickly an issue as Sunday games was, it wasn't the only one that forced clubs to tread carefully with their communities early in the century. The entry of the U.S. into World War I in 1917 triggered enough ugliness in ballparks and hypocrisy in baseball's executive chambers to embarrass the bones of Abner Doubleday. On the one hand, there was the determination of National Commission members Ban Johnson and Garry Herrmann to have baseball declared a critical war industry, thereby winning exemptions from the draft for players; on the other, there was the growing anger by fans into the 1918 season about the fact that the players had remained relatively untouched by conscription while they, friends, and family members were being routinely shipped to Europe to take on the Kaiser. Coming in for special abuse as "slackers" were players who took civilian war-industry jobs in factories and shipyards in the hope of putting off a military callup. Many of them ended up doing more ball playing than painting or screw tightening, and newspapers didn't let either them or their fans forget it. Typical was a *Chicago Tribune* attack on Shoeless Joe Jackson, which said in part:

> *We need shipbuilders to win the war, but when a man on the eve of being drafted into the Army suddenly finds that he can best serve the nation by painting ships, good Americans will not be very enthusiastic over seeing him in baseball after the war is over. The special gifts that disqualify him for the Army will likewise disqualify him for special popularity in the great American game.*

White Sox owner Charles Comiskey, among others, would later use such editorials in negotiating contracts with his players. What many commentaries of the kind neglected to point out was that the Comiskeys were working feverishly behind the scenes to prevent their players from having to work even in shipyards, at least during the baseball season.

The biggest stage for both fan acrimony and ownership two-steps was Cincinnati, where the heavy German immigrant population sparked a conflagration of ethnic hatred. The least of it was the changing of family names from Schultz to Stratford and Holtzinger to Holt or of street names from Bismarck to Montreal and Berlin to Woodrow; library books in German were consigned to sub-basements, city ordinances put an effective end to performances of Beethoven's Ninth Symphony with the condition that all public gatherings be conducted in English, and all teachers of German descent were fired from public schools on what was known as "Pink Slip Day." The tarring and feathering of perceived enemies and collaborators had stopped being news by the summer of 1918, and there were at least two attempted lynchings.

Through all the xenophobia, Reds owner and National Commission member Herrmann tried to be all things to all people: a German-American who was more American than German; an enthusiastic backer of Johnson's notion to have all teams organize benefits for the armed forces and precede games with grotesque military drills on the field, bats substituting for rifles; and a spokesman for keeping players out of the draft and keeping baseball going. As Herrmann put it in one piece for *Sporting Life*:

> *Organized baseball, it must be remembered, is not only a sport, it is a gigantic industry involving the investment of millions of dollars and giving employment directly and indirectly to many thousands of men. As a mere industry, it is entitled to the same consideration as other industries of like dimensions, for the revenue derived solely from business is a vital concern of any nation in time of war. . . . There is nothing frivolous, nothing discordant, nothing out of harmony with the serious public situation in a game like base ball. It tends to develop athletic activity and encourage love for athletic prowess, which are the foundations of a strong military organization. In short, baseball is essentially a war game, and its activities, far from being curtailed, should rather be stimulated by the present war.*

This was more than an attempt to stand on its head the baseball-military analogy so dear to the Spaldings and Chadwicks. It asked for belief that the fiction of the baseball game and the profits of the baseball business added up to a literal patriotic struggle—with fans presumably duty-bound to attend games. It didn't work, with either the government or the fans. In July, Secretary of War Newton Baker ordered all diamond activity, including any World Series, to be concluded by September 12. Johnson's snit of a response was to threaten to close down the American League indefinitely, but owners ignored him and continued playing. The baseball press was just as livid as the AL president over the early shutdown order. "Baker Rule a Blow to Nation's Morale," the *Sporting News* headlined one issue. Next to that front-page story was another claiming that the chief beneficiaries of the ruling would be "gloating" shipyards that could now count on having professional players for company teams.

Fans weren't too pleased, either—with anybody. Not only did attendance drop radically around both leagues during the season, but the Cubs–Red Sox World Series games averaged almost 10,000 fewer spectators than normal, and this despite Chicago's use of the much larger Comiskey Park for its home contests. The notion that the Cubs would need a bigger facility than Weeghman Field was itself a commentary on the sport's awareness of the fan mood.

As it turned out, the end of the war in November precluded further fissures, and the *Sporting News* and baseball officialdom were soon back to boasting about how many players had been in uniform in support of the war effort. But some things were not normalized so easily. The Germans of Cincinnati held on to their Americanized names. The "slackers" were still booed the following season. And more than ever, fans demonstrated that their sources of scandal were not necessarily those of the owners.

CLOSE
ENCOUNTERS

The Star System

n 1914, playwright Edward Davies Schoonmaker called on the theatrical world to emulate baseball as the most effective way of establishing an American national theater along the lines of those in many European countries. According to Schoonmaker, baseball's organizational fluidity and democratic appeal were what had allowed it to "meet the needs of our national life." Almost a century later, there is still no national theater in the United States—meaning either that no one in the theater has given much thought to the dramatist's proposal or that the organizational model he pointed to has proven to be more defective than he anticipated. On the other hand, it wasn't too long after Schoonmaker's call that Organized Baseball began to zero in on fans with a staple of the commercial theater— the star performer as bigger than the play around him.

Stars were nothing new. Among the many to have fit the bill in baseball's earliest years were Harry Wright, Cap Anson, Nap Lajoie, Cy Young, Honus Wagner, Christy Mathewson, Walter Johnson, and Ty Cobb. Fans had celebrated more than one of them with special days at the ballpark during which the player was festooned with gifts; in 1911, his followers went so far as to present Philadelphia Phillies outfielder Sherry Magee with an automobile as compensation for not having won one as the National League's Most Valuable Player the year before. The presence of Cobb in Detroit and Mathewson in

New York meant longer lines through the turnstiles, as well as significant sales for ghosted biographies.

But for all the fan adulation they received, star players remained ticks on the team clock. In the words of Steven Riess: "Ballplayers might gain individual glory by their accomplishments, but they learned that in the end it was the team effort, the sum of all individual parts, that counted." To suggest otherwise wouldn't have been mere *gaucherie* as it would be today, but a subversion of the one-within-the-all "science" that prompted so much admiration for the game in everything from newspapers and literature to academic journals and child-raising brochures. Consequently, player profiles in the period usually verged on the nondescript, with even flamboyant matinee idols like King Kelly and Hal Chase coming across as bland spokesmen for the sport. They might have thrived on the personal attention they received, but, whether through their quotes or through the handling of the quotes by sportswriters, the team concept imposed vanilla reserve.

And that was just fine with the owners who, let alone the theater, only had to look at the fledgling movie industry to see how much stars could cost employers. Some owners were even wary of having hometown players as regulars for fear they would have too much "favorite son" clout from the grandstands when they made their contract demands. The bottom line was that hardly a week went by that one of baseball's semi-official organs didn't attribute a player's slump to some self-delusion that he had become "bigger than the team"—the ultimate criticism.

But paradoxically, it was also acceptance of the baseball culture as it was then known that encouraged the growing attachment of fans to individual players. In the Chadwick-Spalding perception of the game, the players stood only slightly below war heroes. The geographical stability of franchises as of the early twentieth century made players familiar local faces. The need to fill up daily sports sections since the *New York Journal* had paved the way in the nineties meant that even the most colorless profiles betrayed something personal about the subject, if only by accident. A customary seat in a ballpark could acquaint a fan with the idiosyncrasies of the players positioned closest to him. Ethnic points of identification brought not only the Irishman with a special passion for Hugh Duffy or the German with one for Honus Wagner, but the Italian eager to see an Ed Abbaticchio, the Jew a Johnny Kling, and the Native American a Lou Sockalexis. Even when fan groups weren't throwing dinners or organizing special days for one-time countrymen or ethnic similars, they were reading about them with immigrant pride in foreign community newspapers or simply talking about them at a neighborhood tavern or cafe. Recognition wasn't synonymous with stardom, but it was a necessary first step.

At the same time, the team-over-the-player concept suffered erosion from another direction. For decades, the 1877 Louisville Four scandal had traumatized officials not because a Grays player had been discovered fixing games (hardly a revolutionary occurrence), but because *four* of them—the guts of an entire club—had been implicated. However well-founded they might have been, subsequent suspicions about individual players, managers, or umpires had never chomped at the sport's basic unit the way the four nineteenth-century Grays supposedly had. The obsession about the Louisville Four became such that well into the second decade of the twentieth century, sportswriters as well as owners could be commonly quoted as claiming that that had been the *only* baseball scandal of note.

But then the Louisville fix returned twice over with the charges that eight members of the White Sox had colluded with gamblers to throw the 1919 World Series to the Reds. The case, which took two years to play out inside and outside courtrooms and from beneath avalanches of press conjectures, contradictory accusations, and self-serving recreations of events, left few unscathed. Although the eight players were acquitted by a jury, they were banned for life by Commissioner Kenesaw Landis anyway. What it all added up to were two new baseball legends—that the owners had been so horrified by the rigging that they had brought in Landis to clean house, and that the corruption had crushed fans around the nation, as epitomized by the plaintive cry of "Say it ain't so, Joe!" allegedly uttered by a youngster to Shoeless Joe Jackson, one of the compromised Chicago players. Both legends had a fruit drink's dosage of real juice for fact.

On November 12, 1920, all big-league owners except Phil Ball of the St. Louis Browns agreed to give full powers to Landis as commissioner in place of the three-man National Commission. One journalist of the period characterized the powers as those of "a Czar, a Kaiser, and a Chinese Mandarin rolled into one." Since it came two months after the first public confirmation of the "Black Sox" briberies, it didn't take long for the Landis appointment to be interpreted as baseball's stride toward moral rearmament, with the judge coming in to do what neither the National Commission nor individual owners had been capable of doing up to that point.

But actually, amid rumors of rampant fixes, especially involving the Cubs and Giants, owners had been quietly blackballing potential embarrassments on their rosters for more than a year *before* giving Landis his authoritarian powers. His role in this area, at least initially, was supposed to have been to provide an image of rectitude for what was taking place behind the scenes; it was only after the owners realized the ramifications of the powers they had surrendered, and after the judge employed them in such an utterly public way against the Black Sox players, that everyone seemed to remember that this had been the intention from the start. Credible front aside, what Landis had mostly been needed for was for repairing the game's deteriorating administrative structure, in which one league president (Johnson) was behaving more and more like everyone's crazy Uncle Bob, the other (John Heydler of the NL) spent most of his time refining his enemies list, and the chairman (Garry Herrmann) had been impressing everyone for years with how he didn't want the job and, with Johnson given to a weaker guiding hand, had the indecisiveness to show why he shouldn't have it.

Whatever the expectations upon his appointment, Landis brought a public sobriety to his post that the windy Johnson and constantly munching Herrmann had not always managed. He also brought a tendency to respond primarily to his own quirks, one of which was making sure the star players didn't get in the way of the bulldozer justice he meted out to lesser diamond figures named in connection with shady play. The nearest he came to making an exception was outlawing the slugging Jackson with the other seven White Sox players, and that came under another of his priorities: not to think too much about matters that had taken place before he had succeeded the National Commission.

Without question, some baseball—especially White Sox—fans grew up fast in the wake of the disclosures over the 1919 World Series; novelists James T. Farrell and Nelson Algren were only two of the Chicago writers who recorded their shock at the first news that a boyhood hero had been losing to the Reds deliberately. With the core of their team outlawed and the rest of it dropping down to seventh place in 1921, Chicago fans in general found something better to do than to go to Comiskey Park that season. In various ways, the press singled out Jackson for the worst attacks, making it a small miracle that he wasn't actually assaulted personally. One pet motif was recalling the outfielder's World War I days as a shipyard "slacker," another was the well-known fact that he was illiterate; for the particularly inventive news commentator, these two points could add up to questions about how much of an American Jackson could have been while playing that most American of games. The slugger's longest-lasting problems, though, would stem from fictions depicting him as a destroyer of youthful dreams. The most noted of these was Hugh Fullerton's romance, typical of the sensationalist New York *Evening World,* about the boy who wanted Jackson to say it wasn't so as the player was emerging from his grand jury testimony. Not many remembered Jackson's denial (supported by witnesses) that he had ever encountered such a boy or such a request. More indelible was Fullerton's account:

> Jackson gulped back a sob, the shame of utter shame flushed his brown face. He choked an instant, "Yes, Kid, I'm afraid it is," and the world of faith crashed around the heads of the kids.

Walter Camp threw in another well-circulated tale about a Chicago teenager who was found in his backyard "breaking his bat into kindling wood and crying silently" after hearing of the fix. Taking the Fullerton story as fact, the *Chicago Herald & Examiner* went so far as to indict Jackson for the inevitable criminal path to be taken by the youngster he had disillusioned. "It is possible to believe that Jackson's example may outweigh the teachings of his parents, of his Sunday school teacher, all the other good influences in his life, just at this stage of that life," the daily declared. "Why should the kid go straight? If the grand jury has him to deal with some day, would it be unfair to Jackson to carry the blame back to the dirty money that sold out Comiskey and the Sox fans?"

The press zealotry to nail the "sinners" (as they were called, as often as crooks) and to do so in the name of fans didn't blanch at suppressing inconvenient details. The *Chicago Tribune*, for example, conducted a poll asking whether the indicted players should be imprisoned as well as banned from baseball, and went on to print pro-prison letters by a 2-to-1 margin; what the paper neglected to point out was that respondents had voted against any harsher steps by a 60–40 ratio. The simple truth was, fans were not nearly as exercised about the bribery disclosures as some of the game's moral sentries wanted them to be. The Landis decision to bar the Chicago Eight followed scenes of general jubilation in the courtroom and outside the courthouse over the acquittal announcement, not to mention incidents of jury members asking the defendants for autographs while the trial was still going on. Attendance throughout the Roaring Twenties soared, not only in the AL because of the

Babe Ruth–led Yankees, but in the NL as well. 1921 also turned out to be the worst of it for fallen attendance at Comiskey Park, at least until the end of the decade, when even the most ardent loyalists cottoned to the fact that the White Sox were on a 15-year roll as a second-division doormat for the rest of the AL. If not happily, some news outlets acknowledged the obvious. Thus Tom Rice told his *Sporting News* readers:

> *It is astonishing to note the contradictory attitude of so many baseball men and baseball fans regarding the persons who were tried in Chicago. On the one hand, there has been a vehement demand from all fandom that professional baseball should purge itself of every suspicion of evil. On the other side, thousands of fans have gone to see and rooted for players on a semi-proteam around Chicago who were accused of throwing a World Series and numerous small towns sent these players offers of engagement to play in exhibition games. How is one to account for the moral attitude of the fans who encourage future crookedness by giving their support to those charged with crookedness in the past?*

The only way Rice himself could account for it was the suspicion that "for 20 odd years . . . we have been unconsciously boosting a potentially crooked gambling game whose players, owners, and fans are unmoral, and who regard detected cheating in sport as annoying but not reprehensible."

But baseball's institutional voices didn't let the Rices get them down. In the same *Sporting News* a month later, there was the familiar editorial thought that, Black Sox or not, baseball not only remained a clean sport, but an organizational model other American social sectors would be smart to emulate. The weekly asserted in part:

> *This new moral sense in baseball, when one considers the general let down in morals, is something striking. It encourages us to believe that the game is reaching the plane it should be on, approaching the standard*

when it can be said of the game as operated and played that it sets an
example for politics, business, and society generally.

At the very least, editorials of the kind indicated the persistent gap between the baseball establishment and fans in how seriously baseball was to be taken—a difference demonstrated most tumultuously over the World War I conscription issue. On the one hand, Organized Baseball and its press satellites continued to pitch the sport as a paragon of morality and patriotism; crookedness such as that in Chicago in 1919 didn't happen, it just got overcome, once again proving the honesty of the sport and the strong moral fiber of its officials. Nobody would have nodded more sympathetically than Spalding over a pledge by the owners in 1921 that the president of the United States himself would be consulted about a successor if Landis happened to die in office because "nothing is good enough for baseball that is not good enough for America." In the meantime, fans gave every sign of thinking of baseball primarily as an entertainment that, with such help as the daily odds splashed across front pages by the press during the 1919 World Series, could even net a few betting dollars from the crooked affair they were told to loathe. The establishment point of view relied mightily on a combination of denial, arrogance, and paternalism; the point of departure for the fan was how much amusement—from the game, from an afternoon out with friends and family, from memories of former games, from small bets—could be gleaned for the price of a ticket. The man on the street still didn't have as much invested in baseball mythology as the man in the front office did.

In many ways, it was a gap that had been growing wider with every passing year, with few bright signs for baseball's long-range development as the nation's most prominent spectator sport. But then, to the relief of the owners and the exhilaration of the fans, along came the star of stars.

The Sultan and the Child

Babe Ruth's impact on baseball was half cyclone, half magnifying glass—what he didn't destroy, he enlarged several times over. The dynamics of the game on the field, the game's preoccupation with statistics, the crowds in the grandstands, the literal creation of grandstands, player salary structures, the press's depiction of players off the field, baseball's prominence around the world as well as nationally, even the English language—the Baltimore problem child deposited in an industrial school by his parents at the age of seven and grown to the build of a barrel on stilts affected them all. People who knew nothing about baseball knew who Babe Ruth was; tourists thought of him as a sight to be visited; Japanese soldiers in World War II who couldn't think of any better obscenities to scream at American soldiers fell back on "Fuck Babe Ruth!" even though he had been retired for a decade. It was almost the least of his legacies that, with the Murderers Row Yankees of the 1920s, he set the fuse for the explosion of the most successful professional franchise in the history of any sport in any country.

On the field, the price for Ruth's exaltation as baseball's first great power hitter was the abandonment of an initial career as the most dominating lefthanded pitcher in the American League. In his first three full seasons with the Red Sox, he won 65 games, leading the league in ERA in 1916 and for one stretch tossing 29 straight scoreless innings in World Series competition. Once he moved to the outfield as a regular for Boston in 1919, however, his mound feats were largely behind him, thanks to an unprecedented 29 home runs and top rankings in various hitting categories. A few months after the end of the season, Boston itself was behind him when Red Sox owner Harry Frazee, needing cash after some bad Broadway play investments, sold him to the Yankees for $100,000 (double the highest previous amount ever paid for a player) and a $300,000 loan with Fenway Park as collateral. The deal eventually gained the aura of a curse on the New England franchise because of Boston's failure to win a World Series from that time on. Less magically, it plunged the Red Sox into a decade in which it would be the only big league team not to make a profit.

Ruth's 54 home runs for the Yankees in 1920—more than the total of every other *team* in the major leagues except for the Phillies—were mere prelude. Over his 15 seasons in a New York uniform, the lefthanded hitter topped the AL in home runs a record twelve times, swatted 40 or more (including the magical 60 in 1927) eleven times, led the league in runs batted in six times, in runs scored eight times, in slugging average thirteen times, and threw in a batting championship. None of this took place in private. In 1920, the Yankees obliterated previous attendance marks by drawing 1,289,422— the first of five straight seasons of at least one million and the highest turnstile count until after World War II. Any doubts about the source of the attraction were dissipated in 1925, when a combination of mysterious ailments and a disciplinary suspension reduced Ruth to 98 games and the turnout to less than 700,000. Response around the AL was equally fervid; during the decade, Chicago, Detroit, Philadelphia, and St. Louis all doubledecked their facilities or added extra seating in part because of the bigger crowds expected during the visits by Ruth's Yankees. The slugger's greatest influence, though, was in New York, where his gate appeal became so overwhelming at the Polo Grounds that in 1922 the landlord Giants terminated a leasing agreement with the Yankees in a sulk because they were being outdrawn in their own park. This forced the ousted tenants to go across the Harlem River to the Bronx and, within sight of the Polo Grounds grandstand, put up Yankee Stadium—a facility dubbed "The House That Ruth Built" not merely because he made it popular, but because he had necessitated its erection in the first place.

Ruth also contributed decisively to a portrait of the typical baseball fan. Although no single player came close to his statistics, his slugging in the twenties keyed an offensive onslaught on pitchers in both leagues. The assault, aided by the introduction of a livelier ball and by the banning of such important pitching weapons as the spitball, proved as galvanizing for what it appeared to mean as for how it actually affected the game. While not even Ruth's Murderers Row could claim that its seven pennants and four World Series championships were solely the result of aiming for the fences and eschewing the offensive and defensive niceties of the game, both the press and team promotions played up that feature as a gate lure in tune with the times. It would become all but impossible afterward to argue against offense, and especially the home run, as baseball's most important fan attraction.

For sure, amassing big statistics and compiling big scores wasn't in counter-argument to the philosophy of the decade of conspicuous consumption; it fit so neatly that it spawned a sub-literature among historians, psychologists, and sociologists in which Ruth, as the unquestioned bellwether of the offensive movement, was dissected as an American manifestation of (take your pick) unbridled animal instincts, corrupting hedonism, or Nietzsche's superhero. From some pen or other, he would be cited as a proof of what Charles Darwin had discovered, the perfect illustration of what Sigmund Freud had furrowed his brow about, and a benign exemplar of what Adolf Hitler was shrieking. He was the Babe, the Bambino, and the Sultan of Swat, but most of all he was found to be America—an America that no longer felt obligated to the conventional Protestant virtues associated with Chadwick–Spalding baseball, that even went out of its way to flout them and what they were supposed to represent.

In the Prohibition era, when newspapers couldn't print enough crime, sports, and sex for avid readers, Ruth carried his burden blithely. When the press wasn't reporting on his gargantuan eating habits that mocked gluttony, it was being careful not to say anything about his sexual appetite satisfied only by an endless buffet. His dalliances with women were so constant and varied that any prolonged absence from the lineup, such as in 1925, was rumored to be due to venereal disease. To help offset those rumblings, the Yankees built up his genuine affection for children, most famously in the case of eleven-year-old Johnny Sylvester. A New Jersey boy gravely ill from osteomyelitis, Sylvester inspired numerous sentimental tales in books, movies, and magazines about how a baseball hero bought a second lease on life for a doomed, hospitalized child with a timely home run. (In real life, Sylvester survived not because of the home run, but because he had already been home and on his way to recovery when visited by the outfielder.)

Ruth's natural informality was another publicity asset, especially around American and foreign dignitaries whom he was wont to address as "Prez" or "kid." But what might have seemed genuine and unaffected to the public was rarely allowed to stand on its own, and not only because of academics intent on studying the progress of Ruth's genes from the Pleistocene epoch to the speakeasies of Al Capone's Chicago; for sportswriters, the secret to his magnetism for children was that *he* was a child, too—somebody who could astonish and who gave pleasure, but also somebody whose naughtiness had to be kept in check. This paternalistic tone, by baseball officials as much as the press, continued throughout Ruth's career and beyond, when he vainly sought managing assignments. He might have been the Bambino on the field, the only retired player ever to have special tickets sold for his batting practices, but off the field he was simply the *bambino*—according to baseball's boardrooms, something still a little too foreign to be entrusted with heavier responsibilities. However fortuitous his arrival for erasing some of the bad taste from the Black

Sox affair, he was still a production of employers who knew what was good for him and for fans. Babe Ruth might have been a folk hero; but as a folk hero who belonged to a corporate entity, the New York Yankees of the American League, he was also a logo.

Eyes and Ears

The millions who thronged to games in the twenties weren't the only ones who saw players in action or were able to follow every drive hit into an outfield gap. Thanks to technical advances in photography and the dawning of radio coverage, baseball's home audience could be literally that—no longer having to hover around telegraph offices, newspaper buildings, or bars to read the up-to-the-minute scores being posted.

Photographers had been hanging around baseball diamonds since the days of the Knickerbockers at the Elysian Fields. The earliest known daguerreotypes show a posed Alexander Cartwright and his teammates (presumed to be from the late forties) and a combined group of Knickerbockers and Brooklyn Excelsiors (thought to trace to the mid-fifties). With the introduction of Kodak's Brownie box camera in 1900, however, photography became a national obsession and more of a challenge to the professionals being paid to do more. By the 1920s, sports pages were routinely presenting closeups of tight-jawed shortstops dodging spikes or runners grimacing as they slid across home plate.

The daily graphics redefined fan appreciation of the game on several levels. Even those who had been in attendance had not been as close to the diamond action as the photographers, down on the field in foul territory; consequently, the photographs to be seen on sports pages, even more vividly than prose game accounts, could personalize dramatic moments on timed delay—either reinforcing the memory of grandstand emotions or rebutting what had seemed so exciting at the time. For those who had not been in attendance, the photos gave life to third-party accountings of the game played, as well as serving as a stimulus to go to those still to be played. For this reason, owners parried until after World War II criticism that photographers on the field posed both a safety risk and an interference threat. Like the telegraph and the newspaper before it and the radio and television after it, photography could not help publicizing baseball while acquitting its own function.

The greater familiarity of players because of photographs coincided with calculated efforts by teams to abet grandstand recognition of local heroes and to make an outing to the ballpark a friendlier, more informed experience. One thing clubs did was to emulate the Cubs by putting an end to their greedy chases after foul balls—long a source of bruised feelings, but an absolute disaster in 1934 when a Lou Gehrig foul ended with Yankee Stadium personnel fracturing the skull of teenage fan David Levy as he tried to extract the ball from the screen behind home plate. When a court awarded Levy $7,500 in damages, clubs in both leagues decided spectators could keep whatever they caught. Special promotions, such as offering any seat in the grandstands for a dollar, were de rigueur. Bargain doubleheaders, especially on Sunday, became standard, to the point that Monday effectively replaced the sabbath as no-baseball day. Twin bills proved particularly tonic for bad clubs (and didn't hurt concession-stand sales, either). To encourage attendance by children, the Senators offered the regular sideshow of former pitchers Al Schacht and Nick Altrock doing clownish routines before games and between ends of a doubleheader.

Increasingly elaborate scorecards underlined the new major advantage of uniform numbers. Thirteen years after Cleveland had experimented with sleeve numbers, the Yankees introduced full back numerals in 1929. The system adopted by the team began with the usual batting order of the eight regular position players, then filled out the rest of the roster from there; for this reason, third batter Ruth was given No. 3 and cleanup hitter Gehrig No. 4. Although hailed by the press as a welcome move for increasing fan enjoyment of the game, it took years for the numbers to win total acceptance. One reason was an attitude around both leagues by the early thirties that whatever the Yankees did smacked of arrogance and was worth rejecting just because they had done it. As a profound foe of the Babe Ruth slugging approach and of anything else connected to his former Polo Grounds co-tenant, John McGraw surprised nobody by dismissing the uniform numbers out of hand, insisting that "real fans" would know players without any such help.

A more serious objection to the numbers came from players worried they might be taken as bull's-eyes for impatient fans. The concern had some legitimacy since, despite all management's public relations gestures, there was a great deal of grandstand restiveness in the period. President Hoover, for one, became less enthusiastic about going to Griffith Stadium during Prohibition after enduring choruses of "We want beer! We want beer!" whenever he showed up. Heated exchanges between fans and players became almost a daily occurrence. The situation, which only got worse with nerves frayed by the Depression, degenerated so badly that the leagues forbade players from conversing with fans in 1932. But that diktat proved so unenforceable that it was dropped by the end of May.

What photography and uniform numbers did for the eye of the fan, radio did several times over for his imagination. The first broadcast of a game took place from Forbes Field on August 5, 1921, when Harold Arlin did the play-by-play of a Pirates–Phillies game for pioneer Pittsburgh radio station KDKA. A couple of months later, a wire was laid between Pittsburgh and New York, enabling Grantland Rice to relay the World Series between the Giants and Yankees. With one exception, broadcasts were limited for the next few years to Graham

McNamee's reporting of Series games. A concert baritone, McNamee became the first in a long series of play-by-play men who had the voice and the backing of his station and/or sponsor, but something less than complete command of baseball's intricacies. This delighted sportswriters, whose fears of being put out of business by radio drove them to constant mockery of the medium.

Listeners weren't of the same opinion, however; following McNamee's coverage of the 1925 World Series between the Pirates and Senators, he received 50,000 letters from around the country.

As in the case of foul balls hit into the stands, Cubs fans were the first to gain a regular-season benefit from the World Series broadcasts. In April 1924, Chicago owner William Wrigley hired *Chicago Daily News* reporter Hal Totten to broadcast Wrigley Field games. Alone among owners at the time, Wrigley viewed free radio broadcasts as more useful than harmful to ticket sales. He also had the business room for playing out his hunch because, at worst, he would have been able to sell his chewing gum for a couple of hours. The Cub owner didn't take the plunge gingerly: At various junctures over the last half of the twenties, he gave permission for as many as five Chicago stations to relay the broadcasts simultaneously.

The instant popularity of the aired games didn't go down easily with other teams. The Cardinals and Browns insisted they were to blame for keeping Midwesterners home instead of journeying to games in St. Louis and, worse, would create a demand for radio coverage in their area as well. In 1925, Ban Johnson banned radio microphones from all American League parks—a step immediately endorsed by the Johnson-friendly *Sporting News*. "Baseball is more an inspiration to the brain through the eye than it is by the ear," the weekly claimed. "The greatest value of baseball, next to playing it, is to look upon it. There is nothing about it which appears to appeal to wave lengths. A nation that begins to take its sports by ear will shortly adopt the white flag as its national emblem and the dove as its national bird."

Cubs fans rebutted such twaddle with their feet, by walking

through the turnstiles at Wrigley Field. Between 1925 and 1931, with the games on the air, they numbered 7,845,793 for a team that ran, very roughly, in the middle of the pack, winning one pennant. This was an increase of 117 percent over the previous seven-year period, when none of the games had been broadcast and the club had played at only a very slightly lesser pace, again with one pennant. The Chicago showing persuaded some of the weaker teams, such as the Braves, to strike small broadcast deals, but clubs confident of their drawing power because of their talent continued to resist. The onset of the Depression steeled the antis even more against anything remotely threatening ticket sales. Particularly opposed were the two markets that would one day gain the most from broadcasting—New York and St. Louis.

It fell to Larry MacPhail, Cincinnati's chief operating officer, to wage the decisive battles, beginning in 1934. MacPhail's first resource was Reds owner Powel Crosley, who, aside from automobile interests, both manufactured radios and had an extensive broadcasting operation through local station WSAI. His second asset was Mississippi-born announcer Red Barber, who had never seen a major league game before being hired to broadcast Cincinnati's Opening Day game in April 1934. More than delivering play-by-play, Barber used his down-home twang and dry humor to underline the game's dramatic values and personalize players beyond their statistics. Many of his stock phrases—"sitting in the catbird seat" (having an edge or lead); "runnin' like a bunny with his tail on fire" (speeding around the bases); "havin' a rhubarb" (being in a brawl); "tearin' up the pea patch" (scoring heavily or excelling)—became part of the baseball lexicon. Along with the rustic manner went an adamant credibility: Unlike other sportscasters, for example, Barber refused to pretend that the studio recreations he did of Reds road games were anything but readings off the news wires; to this end, he insisted that the clacking teletype machines from which he was pulling his copy be heard by his audience. What the listener received, instead of the fiction of being at a ballpark, was the arguably more exotic sensation of being in a radio newsroom.

As in Chicago, the result of the Cincinnati broadcasts was more fan interest in a club for which a pennant was only a flag on a grandstand roof. Listeners projected themselves into Barber's detailed descriptions of field action, establishing more nuanced identifications with players. Inflection was all, and nobody learned it faster than Reds fans. Rises and falls in the voice, sometimes merely an extra second of silence, conveyed far more tersely than a sportswriter's paragraph whether a ball should have been caught or a pitcher should have been lifted. Player character, at least as judged by Barber, could be divined by something as elementary as his use of first and last names; for example, if "Babe" and "Ernie" could strike out, but "Bottomley" pop out, it was a pretty safe assumption that the announcer found Messrs. Herman and Lombardi a little more sociable than first baseman Jim Bottomley. On radio, the baseball information shared with fans could also be implicit. It conveyed the game between the lines far more vividly than newspapers because its immediacy left less time for the traditional political filters adopted by sportswriters. For good *and* bad, instant impressions replaced studied opinions.

While rooters in cities like Chicago and Cincinnati could always measure their radio impressions by going to a local ballpark, the medium also created another kind of fan—the kind in non–major league cities who never got to see the players he heard about continuously from April to September. For these fans more than for those with relatively easy access to a big league park, players assumed grand dimensions. A pitcher's fastball was faster, a slugger's home run longer, a third baseman's error more inexcusable. The expectations fostered by one mass medium mingled with the anticipatory emotions around another to create timeless fantasy—the one *out there,* infinitely renewable. What the telegraph had done for Spalding and his friends in Illinois, radio did for millions all around the country.

All the Stars

The promotion of individual stars as a fan lure didn't stop at the ballpark. One beneficiary of this new stress was Christy Walsh, a Los Angeles reporter who turned sports-licensing pioneer. In the early twenties, Walsh set up a syndicate specializing in books, magazine articles, and newspaper columns ghosted by writers for the diamond's big names. Well into the thirties, he employed dozens of writers to manufacture the "personal insights" of such stars as Bill Terry and Harry Heilmanns in regard to World Series games, while the players themselves were most likely off in the mountains hunting. One of those collecting paychecks from the syndicate was Ford Frick, the future baseball commissioner who would remember his ghosting days with Babe Ruth in 1961 when he insisted on planting an asterisk next to the name of Roger Maris in the record book. Some of the book-length hagiographies churned out by the Walsh stable became best-sellers; many more ended up on the lists of books recommended for children.

The culminating acknowledgement of the new status of diamond stars came in 1933, through Chicago *Tribune* sports editor Arch Ward. While holding down one of the most prestigious sports jobs in the newspaper world, Ward wasn't much of an editor and less of a writer: When he was expected to devote a column to some special event, he always brought along a staffer who typed out the words to which Ward attached his own name. What Ward was good at, and what made him valuable to press baron Robert McCormick, was promoting, making him the ideal recourse when City Hall told the *Tribune* it wanted to add some kind of spectacular sports event to Chicago's centennial exposition, "A Century of Progress." Ward's proposal was for an all-star contest between the leagues—what would soon enough become known as the "fan's game."

As on the question of radio coverage, it wasn't an easy sell. Although the Baseball Writers Association of America had been selecting annual all-star teams since 1925, owners had not accorded much public attention to the dream lineups for fear it would only encourage higher salary demands. Working to Ward's advantage, on the other hand, was that both Landis and American League president Will Harridge had their offices in Chicago, at the epicenter of the attempts to make the upcoming exhibition a symbol of how the city was prevailing over the Depression. It also helped that the *Tribune* began leaking particulars of the plan, creating a clamor for the game among fans in Chicago and other cities. The last obstacles were overcome when the newspaper agreed to cover all expenses and Landis ruled that all proceeds would go to the Professional Base Ball Players of America charity.

Fans elected the teams to the first all-star contest, through ballots published in 55 newspapers across the country and tabulated at the *Tribune* offices. With McGraw and Connie Mack managing the squads on July 6, 1933, the AL scored a 4–2 victory before more than 49,000. The decisive blow in the game, appropriately enough, was a two-run home run by Ruth. For the *Sporting News*, the game and a subsequent agreement between the leagues to make it an annual event was evidence that owners had the best interests of fans in mind. "The decision indicates a tendency to give the public what it wants," the paper said, "and when that course of action is followed to its logical conclusion there will be no reason for anybody writing a series of articles on 'What's the matter with baseball?'"

But some people continued to write them, anyway.

Gashouse Days

I t took the Depression a couple of years to slow baseball down. Against all expectations, 1930 was a banner season, registering combined attendance totals for the two leagues at more than 10 million—a plateau that wouldn't be reached again for fifteen years. Even when grim reality set in the following season, shaved ticket prices and the larger number of unemployed in the afternoons kept ballparks relatively filled, certainly in comparison to the theater and higher-priced entertainments. From that point on, however, lassitude gradually gained the upper hand in the grandstand, with an occasional break here and there for crowd anger. As Giant third baseman Freddie Lindstrom recalled:

> People avoided eye contact. . . . It was like everybody had his own thoughts and was in deep concentration upon them; or maybe it was that people were so self-conscious of their problems they were ashamed to look at one another . . . at the ballpark the cheering sounded forced, like it was expected of them rather than spontaneous, as it had always been. Maybe it's my imagination, but it always sounded like it was a split second later than it should have been, as if their minds were out of synchronization with what they were seeing.

Other players talked about playing in "eery silences," especially in the bigger stadiums with more empty seats. Lloyd Waner thought the subdued fan reaction was a reminder of what he called "the real world." "Remember, we went from the hotel to the ballpark, back to the hotel, and then on to the train for the next go-round," the Hall of Fame outfielder told Donald Honig. "All our reservations were made for us, all of our meals were paid for. Did that for six months. Then the season would be over and my brother Paul and me would go back to Oklahoma, and then we would realize how bad things were. The farms were abandoned, their owners off to Lord knew where. Stores that had been doing business in the spring were boarded up. People were glum and poor. That was the real world."

But the players weren't completely insulated. Because most of them were sending their salaries home and getting along during the season by counting pennies, they came to regard even a three-cent newspaper as a frivolous expense. This enabled fans to ingratiate themselves by handing over their own (read) papers, which were then passed from player to player. In exchange for the donation, the fan would receive an autograph or get a few minutes of conversation. He would also get to confirm first-hand the traditional image of the ballplayer as a cheapskate.

Fans themselves were no less thrifty when it came to extras like the *Sporting News*. The weekly's circulation dropped so precipitously in the mid-thirties that it began running contests for bats, balls, and game tickets, while devoting pages to jigsaw puzzles, crosswords, and other come-ons. Those who kept up their subscriptions could rarely turn to the paper's "Voice of the Fan" section without encountering a letter complaining about the price of attending a game. One W. H. Milton, for example, warned the White Sox that they were cutting off their nose to spite their face by maintaining pre-Depression prices during the days of misery. Referring to a recent experience at Comiskey Park where only an estimated 1,200 people had been on hand for a doubleheader against Philadelphia, Milton wrote:

I figured up what I had spent to get into the park, not counting transporta-
tion. The ticket was $1.10. I spent ten cents for a cushion and bought two
score cards at ten cents each. That made a total of $1.40. . . . Had the
White Sox received 50 cents, and filled half those vacant seats, it would
have been much better than charging $1.10 and then playing to such a
small crowd.

Not every fan confined grievances to letter-writing. One of the more boorish scenes of the decade took place in Cleveland in 1935, when fans turned against crowd favorite Earl Averill for publicly defending unpopular manager Walter Johnson against rebellious teammates; instead of the cheers he was used to, Averill was booed every time he stuck his head out of the dugout. As for Johnson, he was near the receiving end of so many pop bottles that the Indians began serving soda in paper cups and assigned him a police escort in and out of League Park until he was finally fired.

Short tempers in the grandstand were particularly in evidence where the Cardinals were concerned. The emblematic club of the Depression years, St. Louis gained its nickname of the Gas House Gang from a Willard Mullin cartoon of players holding clubs (not bats) in a train yard filled with gas tanks, gleefully making their way across the tracks to wreak havoc on the better part of town. The cartoon itself was inspired by St. Louis shortstop Leo Durocher, who had described his team as "gas house players" unwanted by tonier base-ball people. The class suggestions of the gas house image sounded a sympathetic note among more than Cardinals fans, while also stoking up adversaries, especially the Giants and their followers, with equal pretensions to being a team for the times.

Much of the passion for and against the Cardinals stemmed from an astute massaging of public opinion. The least of it was that the Cardinals were the first club to hire a full-time publicist and the first to promote doubleheaders in a big way as offering fans a "free" game. Owner Sam Breadon had established his credentials in demagoguery shortly after taking over the franchise in 1920, when he announced he wanted out of ramshackle League Park before its rotting grandstands added to the stadium disasters of the period. He was persuasive enough that the city asked the Browns to allow the Cardinals to share Sportsman's Park. When Browns owner Phil Ball rejected the idea, Breadon rented an abandoned quarry in South St. Louis and took out newspaper ads urging fans to bring pails of dirt to the location so he could build a park with genuinely popular support. The prospect of thousands of people descending on the quarry with pails, shovels, and spoons lit a fire under City Hall, which did the same to Ball until the Cardinals were accepted as tenants at Sportsman's Park.

But not even Breadon was up to the manipulations of team general manager Branch Rickey, who ascribed his every deed to some greater social good. One of Rickey's pet projects, borrowed from insurance company executive W. E. Bilheimer, was the Knothole Gang—getting community leaders to buy bleacher seats for use by youngsters who couldn't afford to get into the ballpark otherwise. While the ostensible purpose of the program was to fight juvenile delinquency, it also created generations of Cardinals fans. In the arena of believe-what-you-want-to-believe, there was Rickey's enlistment of Allie May Schmidt for the public relations boast that St. Louis always acted on solid proposals from their fans. According to the executive, it was the church worker Schmidt who, while supervising preparations for a luncheon to which Rickey had been invited, noticed two cardinals perched on a snowy limb outside a window and instantly made cardboard cutouts of the tableau for each table. Rickey said he was so taken with the design that he ordered the familiar birds added to the team uniform.

When it came to the Gas House Gang, Rickey's tales took a full leap into lies. From the start of spring training in 1934, he fed sportswriters endless hokum about the manic, bruising doings of the club's most conspicuous players, inventing out of whole cloth such nicknames as The Wild Hoss of the Osage (Pepper Martin) and Ducky (Joe Medwick). Abstemious as Rickey was personally, he titillated the public by depicting his personnel as inveterate drunks who were better at their jobs than their sober counterparts around the league. It didn't take long for some of the players to believe in their own publicity, making Rickey's fables redundant. Road trips resembled a traveling carnival, thanks to the presence of a band called the Mississippi Mudcats, which could never hear enough of "The Wreck of the Old '97," and of fellow passengers who wanted to be able to say that they had shared a flask with baseball's most raucous team.

Unfortunately for Rickey, his players and NL fans weren't the only ones who bought the image of the Cardinals as good-time swaggerers. In the 1934 World Series, Detroit fans appeared to have gained a breather from the Depression's particularly crushing impact in their area when the Tigers went up three games to two and had 19-game winner Schoolboy Rowe on the mound for the clincher. But Rowe lost the sixth game, and the Cardinals came up with a seven-run inning early in the finale, dooming Detroit hopes. The one drop too many came when, during a sixth-inning rally for more St. Louis runs, Medwick slid into third, Detroit's Marv Owen stepped on his leg, and, from his prone position, Medwick kicked Owen back in the chest. A punchup didn't get too far, but when Medwick returned to his left-field position, he was clobbered with fruit and other objects from exasperated Tigers fans; some of them had to be stopped from climbing down to the field to get at the outfielder. The ugliness ended only when Landis, in attendance, asked St. Louis manager Frankie Frisch to remove Medwick from the game before the World Series ended in an unseemly forfeit, unseemly riot, or both.

What all the sound and fury over the Gas House Gang disguised was that the 1934 world championship was that particular club's only one. Far more durable was the impact of the farm system on fans in St. Louis and around the country.

Rickey's pioneering approach to developing young talent arose from years of frustration with minor-league owners who, once they heard that St. Louis was interested in a player, would contact the richer Giants or Cubs and offer them the prospect for more money than the Cardinals could afford to pay. Rickey's countertactic, which he claimed was also for "saving the minor leagues," was to persuade Breadon to purchase an 18-percent interest in Houston's Texas League team, giving St. Louis an insider's edge on at least that team's talent. That trickle took less than a decade to become a flood: By the thirties, the St. Louis chain of complete or partial ownerships and contractual agreements totaled 32 franchises scattered from New York to California, from Minnesota to New Mexico, at AA, A, B, C, and D levels; the team even owned two entire leagues (the Nebraska State League and the Arkansas-Missouri League).

Most obviously, the farm system permitted the Cardinals to remain pennant contenders for decades—whether through promotion of prospects, trading them for proven talent, or sometimes just selling them to put off financial constraints. It also served as a breeding ground for fans outside the organization's home market. A farm team in Paducah or Kinston developed St. Louis rooters in Kentucky and North Carolina—an association more often than not reinforced by the uniform colors of the minor leaguers and the wares available at souvenir stands. For fans, the picture was much more mixed. For those in St. Louis, the chain concept opened a more continuous avenue for identification with the parent club, keeping up expectations about the prospects presumably on their way to Sportsman's Park. This in turn encouraged the fan's psychological possessiveness toward both player and team; in other words, the catcher who had made his way to St. Louis through stopoffs at Midland, Decatur, and Rochester was "ours" in a way that one obtained through a big-league trade could never be. By contrast, supporters of one of the farm teams had to accept that players would be moving on and up once they had shown themselves to be too skilled for those currently applauding their feats. While nothing new in itself, since bush leaguers had always sought advancement to a higher level of play, the farm system's clearly ranked promotion levels never allowed minor-league towns and the fans in them to forget exactly how minor (temporarily instrumental) they were. The lettered classifications of play served to grade more than the players.

Night Shifts

For all practical purposes, the last of the Protestant rationalizations for enjoying baseball as a spectator sport evaporated on May 24, 1935, when Larry MacPhail staged the first big-league night game, in Cincinnati. In the process, he flooded out justifications about how the game afforded fans the opportunity to enjoy the sun and fresh air. As much as radio had, night games entrusted baseball spectatorship to utility companies.

Night ball as such was not all that revolutionary. Experimental games under the lights had dated back to the previous century. Right before his death and the dissolution of the Federal League in 1915, Robert Ward, owner of the Brooklyn Tip-Tops, had built five 80-foot stanchions at Washington Park with the intention of attracting after-twilight customers. Only Phil Ball's resistance to accommodating anything proposed by the Cardinals had thwarted a Sam Breadon initiative for introducing lights at Sportsman's Park a few years earlier. Already in the thirties, several minor-league clubs had been able to point to night games as their financial salvation. But for most big-league owners, the minors were one thing and their franchises another. Among their various concerns was the danger of tinkering with their model fan—the middle-class breadwinner who squeezed in visits to the ballpark between work and the family dining-room table. After-supper game fans might not have all been creatures of the night, but the sport's business still centered around the kind of people who made sure they got enough sleep so they could be up early for work in the morning.

MacPhail's biggest card in persuading other owners to go along with night ball was his own bad club; for years, the NL had been making only nickels and dimes with its forays into Cincinnati anyway. When the historic evening arrived, MacPhail wasn't content just to advertise the game and nod to some groundskeeper to switch on the lights; the show organized for the chilly, foggy evening started with military bands and fireworks displays, the latter culminating in configurations of an American flag and a gigantic C with REDS in the middle. Then there was an elaborate presentation of the special guests, who included George Wright, the last surviving member of the 1869 Red Stockings, and George Cahill, a technician who had tried to win Cincinnati over to night ball twenty-five years earlier. Finally, the signal for turning on the lights was given—not to a groundskeeper on the premises, but telegraphically to Washington, D.C., where President Franklin Delano Roosevelt activated the $50,000 system with a remote control button from the White House. The Reds put the finishing touches on the evening by defeating Philadelphia, 2–1, before a crowd of 20,422. Most of those on hand echoed the sentiment of National League president Ford Frick: "It was swell."

However much he has been depicted as an executive with exceptional foresight into baseball's development, MacPhail was also enough of a showman to prize night ball as an amusement novelty for the here-and-now. In this connection, he had a suspect role in the case of the only fan ever to take up a playing career in the middle of a game. The bizarre incident occurred during one of the other night games scheduled in Cincinnati in 1935, a July 31 contest against St. Louis. Because of overflow crowds drawn by the Gas House Gang, management had to accommodate many spectators behind ropes on the playing field. With St. Louis leading 2–1 in the eighth inning, singer Kitty Burke ducked under the rope, got a bat from Reds outfielder

Babe Herman, and went up to the plate against Paul Dean. On a lark, the Cardinals pitcher lobbed the ball across the plate, and Burke slapped a grounder to Frisch. The manager-second baseman threw to first, then raged at umpires for a while that the out should have counted. (He lost the argument, then the game.) While scolds predictably denounced the episode, MacPhail couldn't have been happier for the extra publicity. Indeed, the ease with which Burke got the bat from Herman suggested to some that the stunt had been planned all along. One way or another, the singer ended up with a Cincinnati uniform that she wore in a burlesque act billing her as "the only woman to bat in the major leagues."

The generally enthusiastic reviews it received from Frick and other spectators in 1935 didn't mean night ball had gained universal acceptance, even among fans. Players wasted little time griping that their strikeout or error at a critical moment was due to bad lighting. The Yankees and Cubs, regularly among attendance leaders, were the most adamantly opposed to tampering with tradition. Fans wrote to the daily papers warning about some of the night owls brought out by the light stanchions—in effect, the old "bad element" allegation, but this time emanating from the grandstand itself. For the first time, there were also laments that baseball was estranging future fan generations by scheduling games beyond the bedtime of children. All of this provided enough grounds for the other teams to continue to sit on the fence. While the Reds ended up drawing about 10 times more fans for their seven night games in 1935 than they would have in the afternoon, no other club hurried to emulate them. It wasn't until MacPhail himself moved over to the Dodgers that, in 1938, a second club adopted night ball. Only from that point on did other teams get into line—the Phillies, Athletics, Indians, and White Sox in 1939; the Giants, Browns, Cardinals, and Pirates in 1940. More than 40 years later, the Cubs would fight a last losing battle for the novelty to *not* have lights.

Krank Cases:
Between the Wars

Kitty Burke wasn't the only fan drawing publicity in the period. For some time, a standby of sports pages around the country had been the zealot who had earned the title of Mister Cub or Mrs. Tiger for a fervid pursuit of a team. The typical article sketched in the fan's background recounted some astonishing number of games attended, and ran down the subject's favorite players and greatest ballpark moments. Texas businessman Hyman Pearlstone became the "champion Athletics fan" for planning 32 consecutive vacations around Philadelphia's spring training schedule and for accompanying the club on at least one road trip each year in that time. At least Pearlstone had the honor when it wasn't going to James Penniman, touted by the monthly *Baseball* as the "country's greatest baseball fan," not only where the Athletics were concerned, but also the Phillies. A retired surgeon named Lucas R. Williams could tell a reporter in 1931 that he had been present for just about every Cubs home game since the days of Al Spalding and had also gotten into the habit of taking road trips with them. In 1935, on the 50th anniversary of having seen his first game, the Yankee Doodle man, George M. Cohan, was singled out by sportswriter Tom Meany as the "greatest Giants fan of all time." The *Sporting News* got to the point of adding a periodic feature on what it called "The Champion Fan"—for the most part minor-league boosters, enabling the paper to build up its readership in smaller cities. Explaining the purpose of the profiles, the weekly said it wanted to "bring fans out of the grandstand and stand them up at the plate so everybody can see them."

Like a house organ whose company was the entire country, the St. Louis weekly also added fans to its obituary and birth announcement columns, territory previously restricted to baseball personalities. Once again, it included minor league boosters in such items as:

> *Daniel Cahill, 64 years old, known for many years as the Cubs' No. 1 fan, died from a heart attack in Chicago the night of May 9.*

> *Bill Sparrow, whose real name was Frank William Wroblewski, died in Milwaukee February 14 at the age of 54. Bill was known as the No. 1 fan in the Brewer City.*

> *George Beech, owner of George's Cafe at Cardiff, California, near San Diego, was killed in an automobile wreck at San Diego, December 8. Beech was an ardent fan, always watching the Padres' games, and each time a player hit a home run he gave him $5.*

Harry Potts, the paper told its readers, was the biggest Cub fan in Calumet City, Illinois, and who could doubt it after Harry named his first son Rogers Hornsby Potts and his second one Hack Wilson Potts? Then there was eight-month-old Kenneth Tuckness from Amarillo, proclaimed as the "game's youngest fan" because his grandfather attended every single game played in the town by the West Texas–New Mexico League club and insisted that the infant be with him in his miniature uniform.

Fan clubs mushroomed in the thirties, around both teams and individual stars. Many of the clubs were started by teenage girls along the lines of those common to the motion picture industry, and for the most part the players limited their involvement to some annual pre-game meeting with their boosters and to autographing photographs. Among the players drawing substantial personal followings, as much for their looks or the quirky tastes of a club organizer as for on-field skills, were Lou Gehrig, Joe Medwick, Babe Dahlgren, and Johnny Vander Meer. Fan clubs set up on behalf of teams usually cost would-be members a dime for receiving some kind of periodical and membership card. There were enough of these clubs by 1940 for organizers of the Phillies, Giants, and Yankees groups to wear second hats as directors of an American Association of Baseball Fan Clubs. Explaining the objective of one such club, a Philadelphia reader told the *Sporting News:*

> *[The Phillies Fan Club] was formed by a bunch of dyed-in-the-wool fans who felt sheepish about seeing the team finish in the cellar every year, and in the red, also. We thought that what they needed the most, outside of playing talent, was some diehard fans to give them encouragement.*

By the 1930s, most clubs had their "Detroit Andys"—the grandstand extrovert who had the wit or sheer relentlessness to impress surrounding spectators, players, and the pressbox as an artisan in fandom. Setting the standard for abusiveness were the Kessler brothers, who seated themselves on opposite sides of the infield at Shibe Park and honked at each other throughout the game about the inadequacies of both home and visiting players. The Kesslers reserved their worst attacks for Philadelphia native Jimmy Dykes, who became so distracted by the taunting that Athletic owner Connie Mack offered the brothers a bribe of season tickets. When even that failed to shut them up, Mack took them to court for harassing Dykes. That didn't get him anywhere, either, and the Athletics finally traded the third baseman to the White Sox. Taking the opposite tack was Lolly Hopkins, who liked to stay so "positive" during her regular trips from

Providence to Boston that she used her megaphone to praise opposition players as much as those with the Red Sox and Braves. Both Boston teams eventually gave Megaphone Lolly a season pass.

Another Boston regular was Lucy Swift, who at the age of 80 was still keeping assiduous score of as many Braves and Red Sox games as she could. A poignant notice upon her death in 1943 noted:

> Today in New Bedford, Miss Lucy Swift, 81, will be buried, and baseball has lost in her one of its most faithful and colorful fans. As a little girl in a whaling family of repute in New Bedford, she started going to ball games because her mother would not allow her two brothers to go unless they took along Lucy. . . . For several decades she had lived in Back Bay's Trinity Court, right near the depot from which the Sox and the Braves would often start their road trips through the West. Every time they left, she watched them from her apartment window, waved them goodbye and wished them luck, even though they did not know she was giving them a fare-thee-well.

In Detroit, Patsy O'Toole didn't need a Lolly Hopkins megaphone from his customary seat behind the Tigers dugout. The classic foghorn-voiced fan, O'Toole spent 25 years bellowing "Boy, oh, boy, boy, oh, boy! Keep cool with O'Toole!" punctuating this irritating refrain with hollers of "You're a bum!" to every visiting player and "You're a great guy!" to every Tiger. Invited to Washington for the 1933 World Series, O'Toole's mantra, adapted for the AL Senators, so annoyed Franklin Delano Roosevelt, sitting nearby, that the President had him removed to another section of Griffith Stadium.

Mary Ott and Henry Hoffman did the honors in St. Louis. Ott was known as the Horse Lady for a vocal whinnying that was nuanced enough for those around her to figure out whether she was emitting praise, criticism, or something in between. She once claimed it took her about three innings to drive a visiting pitcher to the showers—which was three innings more than it took her to start downing prodigious amounts of beer. Hoffman, who liked to be addressed as the Count, wasn't happy unless he was organizing pre-game ceremonies paying tribute to a Cardinals player. But he abruptly lost enthusiasm for his avocation when he happened to overhear a newly honored player complaining about having received only a gold watch. Hoffman died of a heart attack at Sportsman's Park when he became too excited over an extra-inning victory by St. Louis.

Cincinnati's cheerleader was retired bricklayer Harry Thobe, who showed up at Crosley Field wearing a white suit with red trouser stripes, one shoe matching the suit and the other the stripes. Before games, Thobe dashed around the bases and slid into home. Even after management put an end to that routine, he continued, well into his seventies, to dance jigs from the first to the ninth inning as a means of spurring on the Reds. Nightclub owner Jack White reigned from the left-field stands of the Polo Grounds. If the Giants won, he posted the score above his bandstand in the evening; if they lost, diners and dancers stared at a sign declaring NO GAME TODAY

The team with the most colorful grandstand presences, however, was Brooklyn. Restaurateur Jack Pierce was obsessed with third baseman Cookie Lavagetto, a regular at his Brooklyn Heights eatery. When he wasn't handing out cards calling for Lavagetto to be elected president, Pierce was arriving at Ebbets Field with two cartons of balloons, a helium tank, a giant banner, and two bottles of scotch. Ensconced in a box seat behind third base, he would belt down his scotch, scream out *"Cookie!"* then puncture one of his inflated balloons for emphasis. When Lavagetto was drafted during World War II, Pierce turned his attentions to the recently acquired Joe Medwick, but without the same enthusiasm. The Ebbets Field grandstand also provided music with a band calling itself the Dodger Sym-Phony. The Sym-Phony's most requested tune for years was "Three Blind Mice," which it played when the umpires walked onto the field and whenever an arbiter figured in the middle of a controversial call against the Dodgers. After the assignment of four umpires per game made that ditty inaccurate, "The Worms Crawl In, The Worms Crawl Out" went to the top of the Sym-Phony's charts. It was played when an opposition batter made an out and returned to his bench; the moment he sat down, the Sym-Phony let go with clanging cymbals and a booming bass drum. Some players teased the musicians by refusing to sit or making feints at doing so for long minutes, but always ended up being kaboomed down anyway.

The most famous of all fans throughout baseball was Hilda Chester. A one-time peanut sacker for the Harry M. Stevens company, the plump, raspy-voiced Chester was forced into retirement by the first of two heart attacks. Forbidden by doctors to excite herself by yelling for the Dodgers, she took to showing up in the Ebbets Field bleachers with a frying pan and iron ladle, banging away from the first pitch to the last out. With the support of every other fan in the bleachers and NL outfielders, the Dodgers presented her with a cowbell as a replacement for the frying pan, and that quickly became her signature. Chester was so enamored of Leo Durocher that she perjured herself during a trial over the Brooklyn manager's assault on a fan, claiming to the judge that the victim "called me a cocksucker and Leo came to my defense."

Although Durocher gave her a season's pass for the grandstand, Chester rarely used it, preferring to remain in the outfield seats. On one occasion, she yelled for outfielder Pete Reiser to pick up a note she had thrown on the field and to take it to Durocher. On his way to the dugout, Reiser paused to say hello to Brooklyn boss Larry MacPhail, sitting along the first-base line, then handed the note to Durocher. As soon as the manager read it, he ordered Hugh Casey to get up in the bullpen. Although Brooklyn starter Whitlow Wyatt had been sailing along to that point, Durocher brought in Casey, who was promptly knocked around. After the game, a furious Durocher warned Reiser never to hand him another note from MacPhail during a game. The note had said, "GET CASEY UP, WYATT'S LOSING IT." That made Chester the only bleacher fan ever to change pitchers.

Not all fan-team interactions in the thirties and forties were at the benign level of horse laughs and cowbells. The trial at which Chester perjured herself, in 1946, had been convoked to hear charges that Durocher and an Ebbets Field security guard had beaten up World War II veteran John Christian for heckling the manager. Although a not-guilty verdict was returned, it was in good part because of Chester's testimony and in even greater part because of $6,750 paid to Christian by the Dodgers. In 1940, Frank Germano got so disgusted with umpire George Magerkurth's calls against the Dodgers that he leaped out of the stands and slugged the arbiter; sentenced to six months in jail for the assault, Germano shrugged that at least he would be "out in time for Opening Day." That same year, Detroit and Cleveland fans traded disturbances over the press branding of the Indians as "Cry Babies" for revolting against manager Ossie Vitt. In Detroit, the visiting Indians were pelted with baby bottles—an attack returned later in the year when Cleveland fans unleashed fruit and bottle barrages against the Tigers. Some fans took losses so hard they had murder in more than in their minds. On July 12, 1938, for example, Dodger fan Robert Joyce became so morose over a loss to the Giants that even fellow Brooklyn rooters began ribbing him in a Park Slope bar. Joyce excused himself, went home, then returned with a gun, killing one of his taunters and seriously wounding another.

The availability of the Baseball Annies who attached themselves to teams could also lead to trouble. On July 6, 1932, Cubs shortstop Billy Jurges received a visit at his Chicago hotel room from dancer Violet Valli, who claimed to be in love with him. The rest of Jurges's subsequent story to police was that he spurned Valli's advances, she pulled a gun and threatened suicide, he tried to wrest the gun from her, and she wounded him in the ribs and hands. Seventeen years later, an eerily similar tale was played out in another Chicago hotel. This time, an insurance company clerk named Ruth Ann Steinhagen sent a note to Phillies first baseman Eddie Waitkus, saying it was "extremely important" he visit her room. When Waitkus went to the room on the evening of June 14, 1949, Steinhagen was waiting with a knife, intent on killing both of them because, she said, "I knew I would never get to know him in a normal way." But when the player walked briskly past her at the door, according to the 19-year-old, she went to her backup plan by pulling a .22-caliber Remington rifle out of the closet and shot him in the chest. It was only Steinhagen's call to the desk that prevented Waitkus from bleeding to death. She ended up in a mental hospital for three years. The Jurges and Waitkus shootings served as the basis for the misadventures of Roy Hobbs in the Bernard Malamud novel *The Natural*.

Even without gunplay propelling their interest, psychologists and sociologists have produced warehouses of analyses of the manias peculiar to baseball fans. One study, for example, distinguished what it termed the "eight most common" reasons why people go to ballparks:

1. Group affiliation (an opportunity to spend time with others).
2. Family (an opportunity to spend time with family members).
3. Aesthetic (fan enjoys the artistic beauty and grace of sports movements).
4. Self-esteem (an opportunity for the fan to feel better about himself or herself).
5. Economic (the potential economic gains afforded by gambling).
6. Eustress (the excitement felt while watching a game).
7. Escape (a diversion from the rest of the fan's life).
8. Entertainment (the game perceived as enjoyable pastime).

But while inarguable on a general level, such motivations could also apply to watching weekly state lottery balls roll out of their bird cage and down the chute to somebody's great fortune. The spectator is presumed from such lists to have only incidental interest in what exactly he is watching. And that, as Al Spalding would have been the first to point out, has never been the (American) case.

MINORITY
IMAGES

Home Fronts

Major league baseball's continuation during World War II owed to a decision by President Franklin Delano Roosevelt, with a big assist from Washington Senators owner Clark Griffith. On January 15, 1942, following more than one lobbying talk with Griffith, Roosevelt formally informed Commissioner Kenesaw Landis that he was in favor of keeping the game going in the interests of relaxing war-industry workers after they quit for the day. What the decision did not do was exempt players from the military draft or accommodate World War I–like attempts by baseball officials to have their industry declared essential to the nation's welfare. Still, there was similar grandstand resentment that players were being rejected as physically unfit for military service at suspiciously high rates. By the final year of the war in 1945, 281 of the 400 players on the field had been declared 4-F.

The preponderance of 4-F players has fed a misconception that Organized Baseball was something of a freak show throughout the war, exclusively featuring the lame, the halt, the too-fat, the too-tall, the too-young, and the too-old. But in 1942 and 1943, most clubs still had their key players. At the same time, it was also in these years that fans stayed away in the biggest numbers. On the other hand, when fans might have had more cause to resent having to pay customary prices for the patchwork lineups put on the field as of

1944, teams in both leagues began drawing again, to the point that 1945's combined attendance for both leagues of 10,841,123 was at that time the greatest in baseball history. This was not as anomalous as it might have appeared. In the opening years of the war, people were not only preoccupied with how the hostilities might affect family members already drafted or about to be drafted, but also about their own vulnerability in going to some sparkling-lighted stadium very visible from the skies; it was still a period of precautionary blackouts and brownouts, and not even the opportunity to see a Mel Ott home run convinced everyone the risk was worth running. Conversely, as the war news got better after D-Day in June 1944, there were fewer worries about seeking the relaxation Roosevelt had deemed important. The last two war years also featured suspenseful pennant races, including the unlikely St. Louis Browns beating out the Tigers in 1944 and the Tigers coming back to nose out the equally unlikely Senators in 1945; there was also a tight race in the NL in 1945.

Before getting to that point, though, owners were seldom without a thought for some gimmick that would keep the public interested, no matter whose feelings were bruised in the process. One of the longest-standing quests by the Yankees, Giants, and Dodgers, for instance, was finding a Jewish player who might stir attention in New York City's substantial Jewish community. The search had been going on since the twenties, when John McGraw had sought to eclipse the publicity around Babe Ruth with Moses Solomon. But the Rabbi of Swat, as Giants beat writers were encouraged to call him, not only couldn't live up to McGraw's boast of being a better hitter than Ruth, but disappeared back into the minors for good after a mere eight plate appearances. Faring little better was Andy Cohen, who replaced Rogers Hornsby at second base in the Polo Grounds in 1928. The infielder made things worse for himself by stroking a couple of game-winning hits in April, prompting Hornsby haters in the pressbox to print daily comparisons of Cohen's play with that of the future Hall of Famer in Boston. The pressure on Cohen built to the point that even the normally disagreeable Hornsby intervened to ask the Polo Grounds writers to let up on him.

The search for a Jewish star was still on during World War II, mainly because both the Yankees and Giants had blown chances to sign Detroit's Hank Greenberg. The mistake by the Yankees had been in inviting Greenberg to Yankee Stadium as a prelude to signing him; the James Monroe High School standout took one look at Lou Gehrig and decided the home team wouldn't need a first baseman for some time. The Giants had spat in their own plate by refusing a request by Greenberg to shag flies at the Polo Grounds before a game; according to the team's front office, he had not been a major-league prospect. In 1942, the Yankees contributed to the absurdity further by ballyhooing first baseman Ed Levy as the Jewish favorite son New York had been waiting for. When Levy explained his surname was that of a stepfather, that he had actually been born as the Roman Catholic Edward Clarence Whitner, he was told by club president Ed Barrow to keep quiet. Levy-Whitner batted .215 in less than 200 at-bats over two war-time years. As it turned out, none of the New York teams ever did find the box-office magnet they were looking for. The closest to the objective, Sandy Koufax of the Dodgers, did not blossom into a star until after the team had moved to Los Angeles following the 1957 season.

While the New York teams were trying to hedge their bets against World War II attendance dropoffs by playing the ethnic card, Chicago's Phil Wrigley played the sex card with women's baseball. Wrigley's original notion had been that fans might continue filing into big-league stadiums for women softballers when home teams were on the road. When that idea was quashed by other owners, he settled for the alternative of funding four teams for the All-American Girls Softball League in more modestly populated mid-western cities—Kenosha, Racine, Rockford, and South Bend. He also modified standard softball rules by moving back the pitcher's mound and allowing runners to take leads, as well as bringing in such former big-leaguers as Max Carey, Jimmie Foxx, and Dave Bancroft as managers. By midseason in 1943, the clubs had proven so popular that the Cubs owner changed the name of the circuit to the All-American Girls Professional *Baseball* League. The official gate count for the initial campaign's 108-game schedule was 176,000; or, as more than one baseball historian has noted, the AAGPBL drew a higher percentage of its home communities to local parks than any major-league team ever had up to that point.

The AAGPBL continued expanding and thriving even after the end of the war and the return of stars from the armed forces to the big leagues. Its biggest year was 1948, when a 10-team league drew more than a million customers; a nine-game tour in Puerto Rico alone drew 100,000. From the beginning, the AAGPBL was at pains to deny it was recruiting "tramps" (hookers) or "tomboys" (lesbians). Clubs nicknamed the Peaches, the Daisies, and the Lassies, the public was told, were constantly chaperoned and had experts like Helena Rubenstein around to instruct them in the finer arts of being "ladies." To the same end, the uniforms designed for the women (by Wrigley's wife) consisted of thigh-revealing skirts but with satin shorts that covered everything else. "Femininity is the keynote of our league," as league president Ken Sells declared. "No pants-wearing, tough-talking female softballer will play on any of our . . . teams."

The "respectability" emphasis made for male fans who knew better than to look forward to anything but baseball when they entered a park. It also encouraged attendance by wives and girlfriends (if not by children, since they might not have read Sells's statements and might have gotten the wrong idea about a woman's place). It was shortly after women began attending AAGPBL games that reporters began noticing, at major league games, how adept many of them had become at whistling down at the field by putting fingers in their mouths. Off such impressions, as much as from the league's very existence, books published at the close of the twentieth century, not to mention the successful film *A League of Their Own* (1992), depicted the

AAGPBL as a pioneering force for women's rights. But it was also true that the circuit had a great deal more official sponsorship (and less daily harassment) than numerous earlier female teams dating back to the nineteenth century; that its profits went to male owners; and that, once the minor leagues were back to full throttle at the end of the forties and start of the fifties, the AAGPBL players were deemed expendable.

Other players didn't have to wait that long to be considered unnecessary.

The Disappeared

n 1891, the weekly *Sporting Life* observed that "probably in no other business in America is the color line drawn as in baseball. An African who attempts to put on a uniform and go in among a lot of white players is taking his life in his hands." What was obvious to *Sporting Life,* however, was regarded as a dirty secret in other precincts, and, for the better part of eighty years, a lot of people labored mightily to put the best possible face on the sport's segregation policies. One of the first rationalizations came from the 1868 edition of *Beadle's Dime Base Ball Player,* when it defended the National Association of Base Ball Players' ban on black teams the previous year as aimed solely at "keeping out . . . the discussion of any subject having a political bearing." When Toledo catcher Fleet Walker was dropped by the American Association franchise in 1884, it was because he was suffering from (a previously undisclosed) injury. When the minor International League barred blacks a few years later, it was only because it was helpless before pressures from white stars who didn't want to be photographed, let alone play, with African Americans. When Kenesaw Landis turned down pleas from Negro National League founder Rube Foster to include a black team in Organized Baseball, it was because the black clubs weren't "organized" enough.

Not all the justifications were so blatantly spineless. There was also the "realism" school that extolled the skills of Negro-league players as some kind of consolation prize for the supposedly unchangeable destiny of their separation from the big leagues. Fans, sportswriters, and officials—both black and white—often took this attitude to the point of suggesting that American baseball history was divided into two parallel chronicles of the equally gifted and merely racially diverse. Glossed over by this romantic view were critical differences between the NL-AL and Negro leagues in such areas as access to financing and to stadiums and team travel conditions, not to mention general social barriers. For the upbeat, it was more important that white stars from Babe Ruth to Bob Feller sang the praises of the Josh Gibsons and Buck Leonards; that sportswriters like Damon Runyon wove legendary tales around black players out-pitching, outhitting, and outrunning the best the established white leagues had to offer; and that white fans descended on Comiskey Park, Griffith Stadium, and other ballparks for Negro league games in open admission they were likely to see better playing than if they waited for their home team to return from the road. For their part, black fans routinely denied they were being demeaned in any way by not being able to see the Judy Johnsons or Cool Papa Bells in major-league uniforms. One such fan, Lee Franklin, recalled sitting in an Atlanta stadium with white rooters who had come to see a local minor-league team take on a Negro squad. "They (the whites) were there to cheer for these kids who might someday become major lea-guers," Franklin said. "But we figured we were watching major league players already."

This prevailing "accommodation without acquiescence" stance on the part of the black community, together with Organized Baseball's pretensions to symbolizing American values, produced some impressive acrobatics in civics logic in the baseball press in the first part of the twentieth century. One of the most bizarre editorials ever to appear in the *Sporting News* sought to balance a concession that African Americans were blacklisted and a doubt that this was fair—

to arrive at the conclusion that there was no discrimination in the game! The editorial asserted in part:

> *In Organized Baseball there has been no distinction raised except tacit understanding that a player of Ethiopian descent is ineligible—the wisdom of which we will not discuss except to say that by such a rule some of the greatest players the game has ever known have been denied their opportunity. No player of any other "race" has been barred. We have had Indians, Chinese, and Japanese playing ball and if a Malay should appear who could field and hit he probably would be welcomed. All shades from lightest blonds to darkest brunette have been admitted, with the one exception of the woolly-haired race.*

Black fans had little time for such jabberwocky. From the first all-salaried black clubs (late 1860s) and the first African-American circuit (1887) to the start of the Negro National League (1920), the reconstitution of a stronger Negro National League (1933), and the formation of the Negro American League (1937), they had shown no hesitation in embracing local squads as a community event. And there was plenty of baseball to see. A typical Negro-league club played some 200 games between February and late fall. Opponents included not only league adversaries, but white minor and semipro squads, as well as assemblages of major leaguers for special all-star exhibitions. Tripleheaders were common; players recalled taking the field for even four games on holidays. Because only the games with league opponents (about one-third of the total) counted in the standings and some teams were known to cancel them at the last minute if a barnstorming date promised to be more profitable, the clubs were frequently dismissed with the "disorganized" label affixed to them by white officials like Landis. But an equally strong case could have been made that, by being able to cope with a relentless schedule that took in rural fields and big-city stadiums from one end of the country to the other from one week to the next, most of the clubs gave new meaning to the travails of organization. As Buck Leonard once rebutted the Landis objection: "We weren't disorganized. We just weren't recognized."

If recognition wasn't a problem in the black communities, it was in good measure thanks to the *Kansas City Call, Chicago Defender, Pittsburgh Courier,* and other African-American newspapers that circulated well beyond their immediate markets to provide all the news on black ball that white newspapers rarely passed along. Because the players were on some diamond for almost the entire year, the best of them couldn't help but become ghetto celebrities through the regular reporting and occasional photographing of their field feats. Even the insufficiencies of the black press could work to the advantage of teams: Since the papers didn't have the budgets to assign beat writers to barnstorming tours, they were dependent on managers or local enthusiasts as stringers—the first of whom were unlikely to denigrate their own players, the second of whom were given to exaggerating the significance of the contests played in their home towns. For a league game between good clubs, any gate below 10,000 was considered a disappointment and 15,000 was often reached. In terms of spectators, though, the highlight of every season was the East-West all-star game in such settings as Yankee Stadium or Comiskey Park; it attracted between 40,000 and 50,000 customers.

The impact of black teams was hardly confined to the number of people who passed through turnstiles. As Donn Rogosin has noted:

> The Negro leagues were among the largest black businesses in the United States before the breakdown of segregation; in their prime they were a multi-million-dollar operation. The cafes, beer joints, and rooming houses of the Negro neighborhoods all ben- efited as black baseball monies sometimes trickled, sometimes rippled through the black community. The management of two leagues with 12 to 15 teams, each league playing across the entire nation and employing hundreds of people, may rank among the highest achievements of black enterprise

during segregation—a sorry comment on segregation, but a tribute to the world that Negro baseball made.

The arrival of a Negro league club was usually the signal not only for festivities, but socially prestigious festivities. Charlie Biot, an outfielder for the New York Black Yankees, recalled: "Everybody got dressed to the nines to go to the ballgames, not like today when people dress like they're going to rake leaves." Dress codes were, in fact, all but published, and the black press didn't ignore offenders. When a shirtless spectator was caught by a camera attending a Chicago American Giant game, the local *Defender* was indignant. "No matter how hot it might be, and it wasn't that warm," the weekly declared, "men naked to the waist have no place in audiences at our baseball games. Notice the woman sitting next to the man in question."

The bigger the venue, the more elaborate the welcome. Quoting the *Chicago Defender,* Rogosin reports that the 1937 Opening Day meeting between the American Giants and Monarchs in Kansas City started off with a parade that featured "500 decorated cars, the Lincoln High School Cadets, two 50-piece bands, a group from the Veterans of Foreign Wars, and the Kansas City Monarchs Booster Club." None of that distracted from the main business at hand, however. Speaking of his own youthful experiences in Atlanta, Lee Franklin remembered that one of the first differences he noticed between the black and white fans who went to see the Black Crackers was that the former were usually all in their seats for batting practice, while the latter tended to drift in only minutes before the first pitch. "The other thing that was different than all the white games," Franklin said, "was the arguing. Man, there was always a lot of arguing going on! I don't mean people getting mad or fighting or anything, but a lot of friendly arguments about the players, the game, the umpires, the rules. . . . People got very excited even when the game didn't mean anything much as far as a championship. The colored fans treated every game like it was the World Series."

White fans were particularly numerous in northern cities and in areas where there were no major-or high minor-league clubs. "What I always thought was funny," Franklin said of his pre-WWII experiences in Atlanta, "was the way the white people at the ballpark had no problem with buying a beer, hot dog, or peanuts from one of the black vendors while they were sitting alongside the black fans. But outside the ballpark there wasn't a cafe in the city of Atlanta where a white person would sit down and eat with a colored person in the place. It was like the ballpark was something entirely different."

As with the white clubs, black teams had their problems drawing during the Depression, especially with a growing reluctance by towns to watch local semipro contingents being demolished by the overwhelmingly superior visitors. The most controversial solution to the gate problem was the resort to clowns and racial stereotyping for the promise of an evening of laughter as well as hardball at the local park. It was to become the ultimate vindication of anti-integration forces that the two teams specializing in such routines—the Clowns and the Zulu Cannibal Giants—had their extremely calculated show-business tactic turned against the Negro leagues as a whole as incontrovertible evidence that Landis had been right to think of black ball as not serious enough to compete in the same world as the Griffiths and the Wrigleys.

The Clowns and Cannibal Giants belonged to three traditions—minstrel stage farce, the Al Schacht–Nick Altrock kind of ballpark goofiness, and the fantasies of the nearest racist slug. Comedy stunts had been a part of black baseball since the 1880s, and juggling, hidden-ball tricks, and Harlem Globetrotter–type "shadow play" had always been viewed as a weapon for keeping beered-up fans of losing white teams in good humor. Before the Clowns in the early thirties, however, such antics had been pretty much between-innings distractions, very much subordinate to the game. Although still providing a superior show when it came to balls and strikes, the Clowns (originally from Miami, later to be identified with Indianapolis and Cincinnati) gave greater emphasis to their skits and set routines, often making the game an afterthought. Among the mainstays of the itinerant club were two nonplayers—a dwarf named Behop and a tuxedoed, high-hatted partner named King Tut—who worked the grandstand while the game was going on and then did numbers on the field between innings. Much of their routine was similar to that of the contemporary Phillie Phanatic; such as sitting on the laps of women and making silly runs around the bases. But they also kept up sharp minstrel-show banter that typically saw the pompous Tut being outwitted by his tiny nemesis. Other Clowns regulars included first baseman Goose Tatum, who would wear an oversized glove on his foot, and catcher Pepper Bassett, who would do his receiving on a rocker; Tatum became so renowned for his comic feints and dexterity that he was later signed by the Globetrotters. The standard highlight of the show was a routine in which Bebop, Tut, and Tatum teamed up as fishermen (on the pitching mound) who get outwitted by birds, fish, and flies. The low comedy included the comics reviving one another from bops on the skull by passing smelly shoes before their noses.

While black and white fans couldn't get enough of them, other Negro-league teams and black newspapers were not particularly amused by the Clowns. For veterans like Piper Davis, longtime player–manager of the Birmingham Black Barons, they were baseball's equivalent of Stepin Fetchit and all the negative connotations of his gape-eyed routines. "If you was black, you were a clown," Davis was quoted many years later. "Because in the movies, the only time you saw a black man he was a comedian or a butler. But didn't nobody clown in our league but the Indianapolis Clowns. We played baseball." Many voiced fears even in the thirties that the Clowns would end up becoming the symbol of the Negro leagues for those too lazy to question racial preconceptions. As Wendell

Smith of the Pittsburgh *Courier* put it on one occasion: "Negroes must realize the danger in insisting that ballplayers paint their faces and go through minstrel show revues before each game. Every Negro in public life stands for something more than the role he is portraying. Every Negro in the theatrical and sports world is somewhat of an ambassador for the Negro race—whether he likes it or not."

As disturbing as the Clowns were to such critics, the Zulu Cannibal Giants left them speechless. Not only did the Giants paint their faces, but they wore grass skirts, wielded African war clubs for bats, and often played barefoot—comforming to all the racial stereotypes popularized by Tarzan movies. Among the solid ballplayers under the greasepaint was Buck O'Neil, later the manager of the Kansas City Monarchs and still later the first black coach in the major leagues. Another team that attracted a following for more than baseball was the so-called Cuban House of David. In this instance, comedy was deemed superfluous for spectators who should have already been laughing at the mere sight of black and Latin players wearing the long beards of the white House of David sect. Among those who played for the Cuban Davids was the father of future American League pitcher Luis Tiant.

Fans weren't the only whites showing an interest in the caricatures of Negro league entertainment. Numerous were the whites who owned black teams or booked their tours; the stadium landlords who leased playing facilities to the barnstormers were almost exclusively Caucasian, as were the organizers of the exhibition swings with major-league all-stars. Paydays around the black franchises weren't the most appropriate moment for claiming that only the ball was white, providing still another reason for the white Establishment to resist any talk of integrating the NL and AL. But the talk continued anyway—in the black press, in the columns of a growing number of white sportswriters, and in black grandstands. The accommodation might have been having to play in dilapidated ballparks where the bugs were thicker than the grass, but the non-acquiescence was the belief that integration had to come sooner or later. In 1938, all these simmerings were heated up by the so-called Jake Powell Incident.

For what amounted to a five-word lie, Yankees outfielder Powell sparked protests from coast to coast, boycott threats against his club, and ugly eruptions at Griffith Stadium; through it all, baseball officials paraded sentiments usually associated with antebellum Southern plantations. The trouble started on July 29, 1938, when Powell cracked to White Sox radio interviewer Bob Elson that he spent his winters as a Dayton cop "cracking the heads of niggers." The fact that he wasn't a cop in Ohio or anywhere else got swallowed up in the ensuing furor. The Gladiator's Civic Club, a Chicago-based African-American service organization, immediately demanded an apology and Powell's ouster from baseball. Deluged by letters from Chicago blacks, the initially unperturbed Landis suspended the outfielder for ten days. While Powell was denying making the remark attributed to him, New York manager Joe McCarthy was insisting his player "meant no harm . . . just meant to get off a wisecrack." For his part, Landis was satisfied to say the quote had been uttered "carelessly, not purposely."

The McCarthy and Landis reactions succeeded in worsening matters. Black papers such as the *Chicago Defender* and the *Philadelphia Afro-American* saw in them the racism that had prevailed under the commissioner. One of the few white journalists who publicly agreed with them was Westbrook Pegler of the Hearst chain, who accused Landis of trying "to placate the colored clientele of a business which trades under the name of the national game, but which has always treated the Negroes as Adolf Hitler treats the Jews." Yankee president Ed Barrow couldn't see the comparison; on the contrary, he assured journalists, he had "consulted with two of my colored servants and they seem to feel that it was just an unfortunate mistake that cannot happen again." Only when black groups from as far away as California announced plans for boycotting the beer products of Yankee owner Jacob Ruppert did Barrow realize stronger action than his in-mansion consultations was needed.

The countermove by the Yankees was to send Powell and his wife on what was called "an apology tour" of black newspapers, businesses, and bars in Harlem. But while taking in such establishments as the *Amsterdam News,* the Rhythm Club, and Small's Grill, Powell continually mixed his "regrets" for what he termed a "slur" with denials of having made the crack in the first place. A signed statement passed to the *Chicago Defender* through its New York office concluded: "I have two members of your race taking care of my home while myself and wife are away and I think they are two of the finest people in the world. I do hundreds of favors for them daily."

The last scene was played out at Griffith Stadium on August 16, after Powell had completed his suspension. With the Yankees throttling the Senators in the first game of a doubleheader by a score of 16–1, exasperated locals turned their resentment on Powell, a native of nearby Silver Spring, Maryland, who had started his career with Washington. The hurling of pop bottles, fruit, and other missiles at him caused lengthy delays. Like other mainstream dailies that had had little to say about the suspension and the responses of Landis and Yankee officials, the *New York Times* decided that the bottle-throwers in the ballpark represented a worse menace than anything Powell had said.

Powell, who had been a mainstay of the New York lineup, was never the same after the episode. In 1940, a fractured skull during an exhibition game hastened his professional demise. His final appearances in a big-league uniform, for the 1945 Phillies, were not without a schematic touch. He was signed at the urging of Philadelphia manager Ben Chapman, whose anti-Semitic exchanges with Jewish fans at Yankee Stadium had so disturbed McCarthy in 1936 (while the Yankees were beating the bushes for a Jewish box-office draw) that the outfielder had been packed off to the Senators as soon as the manager had heard about them. In return for Chapman, New York had received none other than Powell.

In November 1948, Powell was arrested in Washington for passing a bum check. While in police custody, he pulled out a gun and killed himself. He was 40 years old.

The New New York Game

Branch Rickey signed Jackie Robinson to a contract on October 23, 1945, but it was much earlier that the foundations were laid for the sense of awakening community in Brooklyn that would make the signing as convulsive a development as it turned out to be. In 1938, Larry MacPhail arrived from Cincinnati to resuscitate a franchise that had been surviving for years on the sense of humor of Brooklyn fans. (It also helped if they were agile enough to dodge the chunks of corroded Ebbets Field strucutral metal and rust peels that fell regularly into grandstand seats.) MacPhail's first big move (after repainting the place) was to introduce lights to the ballpark; his first big piece of luck was to turn them on for the first time on June 15, the evening Cincinnati's Johnny Vander Meer wrote himself into the record book as the only pitcher to hurl back-to-back no-hitters. The 38,748 in attendance had a conversation piece an army of publicists could not have contrived, and the crowds built from there.

Aside from night ball, MacPhail also brought in the blue color that became synonymous with the Dodger franchise, Leo Durocher as manager, and Red Barber as the team's radio voice. At the time, the hiring of Barber was considered the most outrageous move since all three New York teams were in the middle of a pact not to broadcast games. MacPhail's unilateral jettisoning of the accord not only forced the Giants and Yankees to follow suit, but made the terse but dulcet Barber more of a force in the East than he had ever been in Cincinnati. As Robert Creamer once described his impact: "I was a Yankee fan in those days, but I never listened to Yankee games. I listened to Barber and the Dodgers. Everybody did." Especially when the team climbed to the peak of the NL standings. "In the summer of 1941 you did not need to own a radio to hear Red broadcast. You could thread your way through a crowd on the beach and get the game from a dozen different portables. In traffic you'd hear it from a hundred different cars."

While Brooklyn was getting better on the field, the equally fractious MacPhail and Durocher were involving the whole borough in their running feuds and theatrics, helped in the executive's case by bottles, flasks, and any bourbon chocolates he could import from Kentucky. Sportswriters close to the team estimated MacPhail fired Durocher 20 times during their evening tussles about players and games, only to rehire him again in the relative sobriety of the following morning. It was just as well he did, because it wasn't only Hilda Chester who saw Durocher as the symbol of Brooklyn's renaissance. On one occasion, fans took up a collection to pay a $25 fine levied against the manager-shortstop for slugging Giants first baseman Zeke Bonura. The intention was to change the money into pennies, then throw the coins on the field and have league officials crawl around to retrieve them. Only when NL president Ford Frick intervened with warnings to MacPhail and Durocher was the plan called off. To show his gratitude to fans for such gestures, MacPhail gave away a car before a game—then fired Durocher again after the game for starting a pitcher he didn't want starting.

As it turned out, Durocher lasted many more years in Brooklyn than his boss. In September 1942, just as the Dodgers were blowing a big lead to St. Louis for the pennant, MacPhail announced his resignation to accept an Army commission. To the dismay of beat reporters who had gotten used to all-nighters with the executive, his replacement was the teetotaler Rickey. While the shift in front-office style was as radical as it could be, and MacPhail's drinking companions from the press were there to cluck about it to readers every day, the ongoing war and the cuts beginning to be made into all teams by the military draft helped ease Rickey into his new post. And war or no war, the Ebbets Field turnstiles also remained relatively active. In 1943, the Dodgers outdrew every other team in baseball (661,739); through the four war years, only they and the Yankees never dipped below 600,000 for a season. Taking up much of the slack for drafted fans were the thousands of workers at the Brooklyn Navy Yard, the largest shipbuilding facility in the United States and only a twenty-minute trolley ride away from Ebbets Field.

Widespread predictions that Durocher's abrasiveness and Rickey's sanctimoniousness would produce a quick divorce overlooked what they had in common: experiences with the Gas House Gang, an aversion to alcohol, and a dedication to picking anybody's pocket in the name of winning. At least in retrospect, Rickey also always claimed he maintained his patience before Durocher's serial embroilments with umpires, players, gamblers, and sportswriters because he was the ideal manager for the first integrated clubhouse of the century. What he never said quite as explicitly was that Durocher would also help sell a black player to white Brooklyn fans, that his gritty personality would soften the impression that the move had been dictated from on high. He proved to be right, when Durocher killed a player rebellion against Robinson's joining the Dodgers before it got much beyond Ebbets Field favorite Dixie Walker.

Once Rickey had decided on Robinson as the player he wanted for breaking the color ban, he was able to introduce the infielder into Organized Baseball in 1946 not only in the minor leagues, but on foreign territory, since Brooklyn's AAA farm club was in Montreal. It didn't take long for Robinson and Royals fans to hit it off, with the then-first baseman leading the team to the International League flag while capturing the batting title. It was a different story on the road, with teams like Syracuse and Baltimore stirring their rooters into ugly scenes aimed not only at Robinson, but at "nigger-loving" teammates. The best and worst was saved for the end of the year, when Montreal took on Louisville of the American Association in the Little World Series. Louisville players began by staging a protest against Robinson's presence, then incited fans throughout the two games in Louisville to toss black dolls and other objects onto the field. When the series moved back to Canada, Montreal fans responded by booing every move by a Colonels player and cheering every one by Robinson. A three-game Royals sweep gave them the championship and ended with fans charging onto the field of Royals Stadium and hoisting Robinson and his teammates on the city's shoulders. One wag said it was the first time a mob ever went after a black man in love rather than hate.

On April 15, 1947, Robinson made his major league debut against the Braves at Ebbets Field before more than 26,000 fans. For the first few games, curiosity remained the prevailing grandstand mood; but as soon as the Dodgers hit the road, racial taunts began building from opposition benches and fans. The vilest demonstrations came from Ben Chapman's Phillies and Johnny Neun's Reds, but even these threatened to be a mere prelude to a threatened strike by Cardinals players. With the press in New York becoming more vocal in condemning the attacks on Robinson, NL president Ford Frick was finally galvanized into action, warning that any St. Louis player going on strike would be banished immediately from the league. Cardinals veterans like Enos Slaughter had to be content with taking long leads off first base, then sliding back hard into the bag in the hopes of nailing Robinson with their spikes.

Nobody was more abashed by Robinson's arrival than MacPhail, who had returned to baseball as a part-owner of the Yankees. All his innovations in other areas notwithstanding, he had been one of the most ardent foes of integration. Aside from some bedrock racism and his resentment that Rickey had been hogging the headlines,

MacPhail equated blacks in the sport with financial hemorrhaging, especially his own. To begin with, there weren't enough black executives for the corporate clientele he had been cultivating at Yankee Stadium with club restaurants, season tickets, and other perks for the affluent. Second, he had been among those making significant money in arranging and promoting offseason all-star games between major leaguers and Negro league stars. Third, he didn't mind sharing his opinion that black ballplayers equaled black fans equaled depreciated franchises. And fourth, there was his pursuit of radio (and later television) ad money and his apprehension that Madison Avenue would be less enthusiastic about a racially mixed audience.

As in the case of Babe Ruth 27 years earlier, Robinson's impact was so pervasive that the techniques, image, and popularity of the game became merely different sides to the same phenomenon. His speed was deployed not primarily for stealing bases, but for running the opposition into defensive mistakes. Surrounded as he was by a power-hitting lineup (Duke Snider, Roy Campanella, Gil Hodges, Carl Furillo), his thefts tended to be surgical cuts in late-inning situations rather than mechanical charges from base to base. Then there were the prancings and shoutings at the opposition pitcher, causing balks, wild pitches, and wild throws to the first baseman; the threatening moves toward the next base to pull fielders out of position; and the endless taunting, jockeying advances toward the next base on routine popups and singles in a dare to outfielders to throw behind him. These "tricky ball" maneuvers, a Negro league staple for years, flew in the face of traditional wisdom about riling the adversary—and also turned Ebbets Field crowds into the Dodgers' 26th Player whenever he got on base.

The Robinson style, and the brouhahas it precipitated, keyed the us-vs.-them climate that settled over Ebbets Field during the Boys of Summer years. The team was not only good and won noisily, it also lost pennants thunderously—most notably in 1950 on an extra-inning home run by Philadelphia's Dick Sisler on the last day of the season and in 1951 on Bobby Thomson's Shot Heard 'Round the

World in the playoffs against the Giants. In defeat as well as victory, the Dodgers *were* Brooklyn; or, in the characterization of cartoonist Willard Mullin, a bunch of Bums.

Especially after emphatic public demonstrations of solidarity from team captain and native Kentuckian Pee Wee Reese, Robinson became "our" black even to the small minority of fans who thought segregation should have been added to Moses's tablet. He earned special stars for the added ferocity he brought to games against the Giants, managed by his former protector Durocher, who had been shoved across the East River by Rickey during the 1948 season. Building on a half century of bitter rivalry going back to the days of John McGraw, the Dodger-Giant duels during the Robinson-Durocher era, featuring constant beanballs and regular brawls, were jihads in their fervor and crusades in their length. Even when the Giants weren't pennant contenders, the confrontations supplied the most boisterous sports entertainment in the city, sending thousands of New York fans to Ebbets Field and thousands of Brooklyn followers to the Polo Grounds whenever the teams met. It was also Durocher who summed up the Robinson aura so palpable to Brooklyn fans: "You want a guy that comes to play. But he didn't just come to play. He came to beat you. He came to stuff the goddam bat right up your ass."

But for all that intensity, what also remained noteworthy about the heat generated by Dodger-Giant games was that it rarely brought fans to the physical pitch the players reached. Unlike the rowdy ballpark scenes before the war in cities like Detroit and Cleveland, not to mention the periodic riots of the nineteenth century, there was an all-but-total grandstand sublimation in the violences perpetrated between the white lines, at worst challenging fans to produce can-you-top-this heckling. White or black, beered-up or not, fans in both New York parks had made their peace with the game and its characters—volatile or endearing, as the case might be—as drama or farce requiring no aggressive audience participation for entertainment.

The Stuntman

Branch Rickey might have had his Knothole Gangs and Allie May Schmidts, but nobody worked more tirelessly as the fan's best friend in the front office than Bill Veeck. For Veeck, baseball was nothing *but* entertainment, and he kept people laughing for some forty years with stunts, promotions, and even the odd winning team. The son of a long-time Cubs executive, he was the one to charm generations of visitors to Wrigley Field by planting ivy on the outfield walls, as well as the one to draw interest in a dumpy minor-league Milwaukee Brewers franchise through such giveaways as (instantly delivered) 200-pound blocks of ice. For game fun, there were such ploys as a winch that he used to raise the outfield walls in Milwaukee whenever the opposing team was up, then to lower them again when the weak-hitting Brewers came to bat. None of this Barnumism made Veeck a popular son in big-league boardrooms, where he plagued other owners for decades. More to his discomfiture, it also put him on a collision course several times with the very fans he claimed were his priority.

By his own accounting, Veeck made his first serious attempt to buy a big-league franchise in 1943, when he sought to take over the wretched Philadelphia Phillies. According to his autobiography, his plan had been to end decades of second-division play by Philadelphia by bringing in such Negro league stars as Satchel Paige, Roy

Campanella, and Monte Irvin and daring Landis or anybody else to stop him at the height of World War II. It was only because he made the mistake of confiding his intentions to Landis, he contended, that he was headed off by the commissioner and NL president Frick, with the Phillies being quickly sold to lumber magnate William Cox instead. The trouble with this widely circulated story, as a band of researchers pointed out in the late nineties, is that there has never been a shred of evidence to support it aside from Veeck's own word. On the contrary, all indications are that it was largely inspired by his irritation over the attention given Rickey for breaking the color barrier in Brooklyn. But whatever happened in Philadelphia, he definitely did make an offer to buy the Indians in June 1946, and even AL owners constitutionally wary of his flamboyance agreed it would be nice to have something better going in Cleveland than a moribund organization in which the widows of five directors sat on the governing board.

The promotions at Municipal Stadium started at once. Rarely did the Indians play back-to-back home games without something like Ethnic Night or midget racing. Clowns Max Patkin and Jackie Price were hired with the title of "coaches" so they could perform before games and during doubleheaders. Every radio station in the city was invited to broadcast games free. An orchestra filled in diamond lulls with the popular tunes of the period. Fans who weren't polled through radio stations or newspapers were accosted by Veeck personally to list the most urgent needs of the team. Only weeks after Jackie Robinson's debut with the Dodgers, he signed slugger Larry Doby as the first black player in the AL. The results were big numbers. With only half a season to work with, he managed to double Cleveland's attendance in 1946 from the previous year; in 1947, the total of 1.5 million was second in the league only to the Yankees.

Two Indians players had their doubts. One was Doby, who took some time to accept the idea that he had been signed for the club as a genuine talent rather than as another box-office gimmick. Even more ticklish was the situation of playing manager Lou Boudreau, the city's most popular player for years. In taking over the franchise, Veeck made it clear that he wanted to retain the shortstop only as a player, replacing him as manager with Casey Stengel. In what would become an increasingly important calculation for managerial appointments as the century wore on, the owner decided the stiff Boudreau wasn't sufficiently "media-friendly"—a charge never leveled against the garrulous Stengel. When Boudreau refused to step down as manager and pointed to a contract backing his position, Veeck bided his time until the end of the 1947 season, then began trade talks with the Browns for a multiplayer deal that would send Boudreau to St. Louis in exchange for slugger Vern Stephens. What happened next defined the limits of Veeck's populism.

Whether through Boudreau, the Browns, or some other party not ecstatic with Veeck's success, the proposed trade reached the Cleveland papers, prompting street-protest demonstrations and petitions that the owner be the one to go to St. Louis. When he realized what he had wrought, Veeck ran all over Cleveland, from bar to restaurant to bar, to admit as personally as he could that he had made a mistake, while also denying that a deal had been completed or that it had even been his idea to start with. Popular opinion continued to run against him until November, when he made a grand show of summoning Boudreau to a peace-making session and, rather than bouncing him as manager or trading him, gave him a new two-year contract in his double role.

Boudreau's response was to lead the Indians to a world championship in 1948, the first time they had appeared in the World Series since 1920. Along the way, the franchise recorded several crowds over 70,000, going on to eradicate all existing attendance records with a total of 2,620,627. One of Veeck's finishing touches to the pennant-winning team was the signing of Negro-league legend Satchel Paige, the oldest rookie (at least 42) in baseball history. But not even the fact that Cleveland was deadlocked at the top of the standings with

Boston and New York with mere hours left in the season stopped him from staging one of his most elaborate promotions on September 28. Joe Earley Night grew out of a letter written to the *Cleveland Press* on September 8 in which a Cleveland plant guard complained that all the special days and evenings held in ballparks were for honoring players, but never fans. Veeck's reply was to celebrate the letter writer, Joe Earley, as the model Cleveland fan prior to a game against the White Sox. Before a crowd of more than 60,000, Earley was given an automobile, a cow, a swaybacked horse, a calf, a goat, and eight pigs. Another $30,000 was spent on flying 20,000 Princess Aloha orchids up from Hawaii so they could be distributed to the women passing through the turnstiles. The team then completed the evening by thrashing Chicago, 11–0.

The Cleveland portion of the Veeck Show lasted only one more year. Although once again topping two million in attendance, the franchise was weighed down a good part of the season by the owner's personal financial problems. When it became obvious the Indians were going to be unable to repeat as pennant winners, Veeck staged the ritualistic burying of the 1948 championship flag in the Municipal Stadium outfield as one of his last promotions, then returned to negotiations for selling out.

Two years later, he was back as owner of the St. Louis Browns in another try at resuscitating a dead franchise. As in Cleveland, the stunts came first. His coming out as owner took place on July 4, 1951, when an enormous sign at Sportsman's Park greeted fans arriving for a doubleheader with the message: OPEN FOR BUSINESS. UNDER NEW MANAGEMENT. Then, while fans enjoyed free beers and sodas, the clowns Max Patkin and Jackie Price went through the same routines they had in Municipal Stadium. They were followed by Millie the Queen of the Air, who slid down a tightrope stretching from right field to third base, and a fireworks show. Another familiar ploy was the signing of Satchel Paige, complete with rocker for sitting in the bullpen. There were two differences from Cleveland, however: only

10,392 responded to the city-wide advertising of the big afternoon, and the 1951 Browns had none of the promise of the 1946 Indians.

Veeck didn't give up. Within the span of five days in August, he pulled off the two most famous stunts of his career. In the name of celebrating the 50th anniversaries of both the American League and his Falstaff Brewery radio sponsor, he wheeled an enormous birthday cake out on the field between games of an August 19 doubleheader against the Tigers. Out of the cake popped 3' 7" Eddie Gaedel wearing a Browns uniform with the number 1/8. Veeck then sent Gaedel up to pinch-hit for leadoff hitter Frank Saucier in the first inning of the second game. Assured by manager Zach Taylor that the dwarf had signed a valid contract, umpire Ed Hurley allowed Gaedel to stand in against Detroit's Bob Cain. With his laughter as much as Gaedel's size contributing to his wildness, Cain issued a four-pitch walk. None of the laughter from the Tigers, Browns, or grandstand was appreciated by league president Will Harridge, however, who solemnly decreed the following day that midgets were banned from the AL and that the Gaedel appearance was to be erased from the record book. Harridge was ignored on the latter count by the sport's most popular encyclopedias.

Five days later, Veeck held Grandstand Managers' Day, the closest spectators have ever gotten to running a big-league game. Originally, the promotion was to have been the selection of the Browns' starting lineup from mail-in ballots printed in the *St. Louis Globe-Democrat*; each voter received a free ticket to the game and the right to contribute to the strategy against the visiting Athletics. The daily's editors killed the balloting after only one edition and Philadelphia general manager Art Ehlers threatened to protest the gimmick to the league, but Veeck went ahead anyway. Each of the 4,000 special ticketholders, joined by Veeck and 89-year-old former Athletics manager Connie Mack, received a placard with a green YES on one side and a red No on the other. Browns' publicity director Bob Fishel held up cards with proposed moves—steal, warm up a pitcher, and the like—to which the grandstand managers flashed their opinions. A circuit court judge in attendance tabulated the results and relayed the consensus to the St. Louis dugout. All the while, manager Taylor sat in a rocking chair in street clothes and slippers, puffing away on a pipe. The fans called an excellent game: The Browns won, 5 to 3, to end a four-game losing streak.

In 1952, attendance climbed by some 80 percent—the highest for the franchise since 1924 with the exception of the 1946 general boom year. But it was still only a climb from the abysmal to the near-abysmal, leaving the Browns well behind the rest of baseball. When the Anheuser-Busch breweries and their deep pockets purchased the Cardinals, Veeck saw no future in St. Louis and entered into various negotiations to move the franchise to Milwaukee, Baltimore, or even Los Angeles. When word of his intentions got out, he became as unpopular as he had been in Cleveland during the Lou Boudreau debacle. Other AL owners spent a good year or more pushing him toward the edge, playing on his increasingly fragile relations with St. Louis fans. Veeck himself provided them with their biggest weapon when he demanded that home teams cut visiting clubs in for a share of TV revenues. When the Yankees, in particular, scoffed at the idea of paying the lowly Browns anything for being televised at Yankee Stadium, Veeck retaliated by refusing to sign a release permitting the airing of St. Louis road games. Herded together by the Yankees, the other owners immediately changed the league schedule to eliminate normally lucrative night games in St. Louis. Suddenly, such reliable draws as the Yankees and Indians were playing before a few thousand at Sportsman's Park on Friday afternoons rather than before packed houses later in the evening. Fans unaware of the behind-the-scenes manipulations producing such a schedule blamed Veeck for not being the smart promoter he claimed to be. They also blamed him when, after the 1953 season, he was forced to sell the club to Baltimore interests that immediately transferred it to Maryland.

Goodbye to All That

Browns fans were far from being the only ones abandoned in the fifties. In what became a rush to the door before the end of the decade, the first such defection actually took place a year earlier, from Boston.

Aside from the Cubs, the Boston Braves were the only original National League franchise still in business in the middle of the twentieth century. In all that time, however, the club had won pennants only in 1914 and 1948, and even then had failed to outdraw the Red Sox. In some seasons, Fenway Park turnstiles had clicked three times more often than those at Braves Field. One important factor in Boston's stronger identity as an AL city was the succession of penny-pinching owners who took over the Braves with the help of the Giants, who ran the New England franchise as a farm club for decades. A second was the stronger Irish aura emanating from Red Sox players and managers in that most Celtic of American cities. A third was the Grand Canyon known as Braves Field: Not only did the enormous distances of its outfield walls prevent the club from joining the power explosion in the 1920s and 1930s, but the smoke being constantly belched from the rail yards outside the park made fans as alert to the direction of the wind as to the progress of the game. It was against this background that the Braves ended baseball's half century of geographical stability and jumpstarted a wholesale movement of major league franchises in the 1950s.

Boston's owner at mid-century was construction industry millionaire Lou Perini, who was never reluctant to declare his aim of
winning Boston away from the Red Sox. Unfortunately, his team's
1948 pennant coincided with a sudden-death playoff game between
the Red Sox and Indians for deciding the AL flag, so there weren't too
many defectors from the action at Fenway Park. Perini's consolation
prize was that for the first time in the history of the coexisting franchises, Boston was alive with street-corner contentiousness about the
relative merits of the two clubs. The pennant victory also helped wipe
out the low point of his ownership: Opening Day in 1946, when 5,000
newly painted seats in Braves Field caused some 13,000 fans to file
claims of ruined clothing against the team. It took months for lawyers
to rebut some of the claims, but even then the slow-drying seats
appeared to have accommodated two fans each.

By the fifties, however, both the paint and the pennant had
receded some distance in Perini's rearview mirror, for he now faced
the more pressing business of buying out his partners in order to
have total freedom with the franchise. The general feeling was that
he wanted to move the team to Milwaukee, site of the organization's
chief farm club. But in continuing to procrastinate about his intentions, Perini infuriated Wisconsin, so much so that state legislators
began calling for his lease on Milwaukee's County Stadium to be
rescinded and local papers proposed a season-long boycott of games
played by the Braves' minor league team. Under such pressures,
other NL owners pushed Perini to Milwaukee less than a month
before the opening of the 1953 season, with the Braves already in
spring training.

The swift turn of events—adding up to the first transfer of a big
league franchise since Baltimore's move to New York at the beginning
of the century—shocked those left behind. "I threw myself across my
bed that day and wept so loudly that my mother shuffled in and bent
over me, her wide, aproned hips, like some black-padded umpire, and
ordered me to stop," as one Braves fan recalled. "At fifteen, I had

never disobeyed my mother, so I stopped crying and tried to focus on something in my room that wouldn't remind me of the end of my world." But while Braves Field was shuttered overnight and simply left to go to seed, County Stadium just as quickly became a symbol of Milwaukee civic pride. With the season opener only weeks away, tens of thousands besieged the park with ticket requests. When the Braves showed up from Florida, they were welcomed by more than 12,000 fans at the train station. An estimated 60,000 attended an official parade the following day, setting the pattern for a love affair between the field and the grandstand that would inspire the club for most of its time in the city. By May 20, in its 13th home game, the team had matched the attendance (281,278) it had drawn for its 77 games in Boston the previous year. The overall 1953 attendance of 1,826,397—more than the last three years in New England combined—would be topped in 1954, when Milwaukee became the first NL club to top two million customers. They weren't cowed fans, either. Hundreds, sometimes thousands, of boosters traveled with the team, taking delight at tooting their horns and ringing their cowbells in Chicago, Brooklyn, and New York. Since the Dodgers were the league's ruling club at the time, the descents on Ebbets Field were particularly boisterous, though without anything but vocal incident.

The ramifications of the move by the Braves went far beyond the team's attendance or new ability to pay for better players. A key aspect of Perini's decision to move was his trust in air travel and his recognition that planes had made it unnecessary to think of the big leagues merely in terms of trains snaking back and forth from the Northeast Corridor to Chicago and St. Louis. Although Larry MacPhail had arranged for the Yankees to take many road trips by air in the 1940s, most other owners thought flights were either too costly or too dangerous. Perini's decision to follow MacPhail's example not only stirred other teams to take to the air, but, once up there, to reflect seriously on the implications of air travel for the existent geographical boundaries of the major leagues. Dodgers owner

Walter O'Malley, for one, always said it was Perini's exodus from Boston that got him thinking about his options in Brooklyn.

More immediately, the move by the Braves spurred similar decisions by the poor relations in two other two-team cities. The following year, Veeck lost his St. Louis Browns to Baltimore. In 1955, it was the Mack family's sale of the Athletics to Arnold Johnson, a Chicago-based vending machine and real estate millionaire who had made clear from the beginning his intentions of transferring the club from Philadelphia to Kansas City. What Johnson had been cagier about— and which had disturbed other big-league owners enough to hold up approval of the sale for long months—were his connections to the Yankees. There was reason to worry. In their 13 years of existence, the Kansas City Athletics would prove to be even more of a major-league farm club for a New York team than the Braves had ever been for the Giants. Before that became farcically obvious, however, the team drew 32,147 for its opening game on April 12, 1955—at the time the single greatest attendance for any sports event ever staged in Kansas City.

Broadcast News

The franchise shifts by the Braves, Browns, and Athletics broadened baseball's geographical base at the same time as broadcasting interests were redefining in dramatic ways fan perceptions of major-league play. Although television's impact on the game at the turn of the fifties was still relatively primitive, that was not so for radio, where the image of the fan as someone who simply clicked a dial and roamed the bases with his favorite team for a couple of hours was fast receding into an age of innocence. In addition to their immediate market outlets, many clubs by mid-century had established elaborate networks for carrying games beyond their home cities. This had been done with the logical-enough intention of, say, creating Dodger fans in Binghamton or Cardinal fans in Memphis; that is, making the game synonymous with a specific franchise. But this umbilical relationship between individual teams and listeners around the country began fraying in 1949, when Gordon McLendon, operator of the Liberty Broadcasting System in the Dallas suburb of Oak Cliff, decided that major-league baseball offered enormously profitable programming for next to no cost. With 300 stations initially in the fold (the number would grow to more than 400), he launched his Game of the Day with each station paying him $10 for a daily production outlay (minus salaries) of no more than $27.50! The budget trick was that for three weeks out of every month, the games were recreations sent out from the Oak Cliff studios on the basis of Western Union play-by-play accounts. Only during the fourth week— when a host team would be happy to welcome visiting announcers for publicity in normally unreachable markets—was there live coverage of a series from an actual ballpark.

The Liberty broadcasts had no end of consequences. While receptive in theory to greater exposure, every one of the major league teams also invoked a 75-mile-radius blackout against them in the name of protecting both ticket sales and a club's local radio operation. This meant Liberty might have been heard by tens of millions of people in the Southeast, South, and West, but not by too many in the Northeast or Illinois. In effect, not all listeners were equal for the games being produced by the big leagues themselves—an early, albeit involuntary, version of multi-tiered electronic audiences. At the same time, the expansive networks set up by teams like the Cardinals and Dodgers suddenly had competition in their secondary markets, forcing them to improve production values to keep listeners. McLendon's success also spurred the bigger broadcasting webs, starting with Mutual, to investigate their own resources for daily and weekly games that would not be obligated to a specific franchise.

The Liberty broadcasts had a more subtle but equally profound influence on the fan. With the conspicuous exception of those emanating from New York, local broadcasts and team network feeds were in the "homer" vein—announcers who had no conscience crisis over expressly rooting for the clubs paying their salaries. If the Red Barbers, Mel Allens, and Russ Hodgeses from New York were not in that category, it was largely because they worked in a city with a huge non-native population. Their sponsors didn't care too much about journalism's "objectivity" ideals, but they did care about alienating those transplanted White Sox or Cub fans out there with purchasing power. With the various Game of the Day and Game of the Week formats, however, *all* broadcasts were assumed to be neutral since the announcers usually had no private contract with one of the clubs on the field (and even if they did, their goal for the day was disguising, not embroidering, that particular). This fostered much cooler perceptions of the players and teams at two levels: for the listener with no emotional stake in the outcome, in developing the sense that a game was a game, to be enjoyed or not on its own merits; for the listener with an emotional stake, in developing an awareness that not everyone was on his elation-despondency meter. There might not have been anything new in the realization that the baseball industry considered itself more important than any of its local market teams, but, through the network games, there was a new complicity for the fan in feeling part of that priority.

Television followed much of the path traced by radio. Although owner Bob Quinn had been urged (unsuccessfully) to consider televising Red Sox games as early as 1931, it fell to the radio pioneers Larry MacPhail and Red Barber to put together the first complete game telecast, between the Dodgers and Reds, from Ebbets Field on August 26, 1939. World War II interrupted more ambitious plans; but, as soon as the hostilities were over, the three teams closest to Madison Avenue wasted little time in attaching themselves to the new medium. The first significant local contract, in 1946, earned MacPhail's Yankees $75,000. But it was the Dodgers, in good part because of the curiosity generated by Jackie Robinson, that quickly became the medium's darling in New York and around baseball. By the early fifties, while the TV revenue average for teams was $200,000, Brooklyn was banking close to three times that amount and was the hottest ad attraction in all professional sports.

Nationally, television got its feet wet with the World Series duels between the Yankees and Dodgers in the late forties. But the real plunge came with the 1951 Giants-Dodgers playoffs, when 15 million viewers across the country were crouched over black-and-white sets in their living rooms or looking up from bar stools as Bobby Thomson rounded the bases to give New York a pennant. From that point on, the cameras were present for every World Series game and, later on, for a radio-like Game of the Week. Growth through the fifties was commensurate with that of the TV industry: While only 12 percent of U.S. households had sets for the 1949 World Series between the Yankees and Dodgers, 87 percent did for the 1960 series between the Yankees and Pirates.

The most conspicuous victims of the network coverage were the minor leagues. With fans in Butte and Tuscaloosa able to tune in a Saturday game between the Red Sox and Yankees from Fenway Park, interest in local C-level squads on the other side of town plummeted. In 1951, there were 59 professional leagues employing 8,000 players; by 1964, that number had plunged to nineteen leagues and 2,500 players under contract. Not all that surprising, this brought forth regular denunciations from Branch Rickey, the architect of the farm system, that television was making "major league fans out of minor league fans." More debatable was Rickey's assertion, repeated whenever a newsman was at hand, that the medium was also responsible for the sharp drop in major-league attendance between the late forties and the first part of the fifties. Although his opinion was shared by numerous owners, Rickey was not the most impartial spokesman for such a view: Not only had he been in charge of the Dodgers when Brooklyn had embraced the medium, but his subsequent move to Pittsburgh paired him with a catatonic franchise looking for alibis for an attendance slide of eight straight years that had started before television had ever entered the picture. Moreover, Rickey's blueprint for reanimating the Pirates consisted of signing hundreds of raw teenagers in the hope that at least a few of them would acquire major-league abilities while playing on the low-minor-league teams that were gradually being eliminated from existence.

But Rickey's biases weren't the only problem with the cause-and-effect TV-attendance criticism. Because of the pronounced feel-good atmosphere in the aftermath of the war, the bloated attendance figures of the late forties were in themselves a suspect point of comparison. Gate counts for the good teams of the period (Yankees,

Dodgers, and later the Milwaukee Braves) were anything but cata-strophic, anyway. When the Giants won pennants in 1951 and 1954, they drew more than a million; when they were also-rans in other years, they didn't. The same was true of the Phillies—the flag-winning year of 1950 on the one hand, the other seasons of the decade on the other. The Red Sox didn't even have to topple the Yankees to stay in seven figures, but when they couldn't play .500 in 1954, Fenway Park's seats got plenty of sun. If television could be accused of any-thing in such a context, it was that it sharpened grandstand tastes for winners. Sometimes this meant the small screen as a vehicle for deciding whether a trip to the ballpark for the next game or the next series would be worth the effort, sometimes it meant the medium as an alternative form of entertainment altogether (Milton Berle instead of the Cardinals).

Where television did weigh from the very beginning was in how it affected the fan's conceptualization of the game. In exchange for closeups of players, the early telecasts offered relatively static per-spectives from cameras placed behind home plate, isolating the pitcher and hitter as individual duelists. Even with the introduction of the centerfield camera in 1957, adding the masked catcher and his plate positioning as a pitch-by-pitch principal, the visual presenta-tion strengthened the impression of *mano-a-mano* showdowns at the cost of weakening the countless defensive nuances available to the ballpark spectator with a glance and to the radio listener through an announcer's description and his own imagination. It wasn't so much that the grandstand spectator and radio listener didn't also focus on the pitcher and batter, which of course they did, as that the cameras *imposed* the mound and batter's box on the eye, implying they were the only things worth watching. As with all live sports as opposed to, say, motion pictures, it was the viewers rather than the players being directed within the story line of the moment. Instincts developed through this kind of visual concentration could not help but be car-ried over to the ballpark, not least in the growing complaint over the years to come that "nothing was happening" on the field when the pitcher wasn't throwing or the batter wasn't swinging. Something else imposed on the viewer as television coverage intensified were so-called "game themes" that did not necessarily reflect what was happening before the cameras. One of the worst examples occurred during the 1986 World Series, when both Red Sox and Mets fans accused announcers Vin Scully and Joe Garagiola of being biased against their team. The actual culprits were pre-production meeting directives: to emphasize the sorry fortunes of New York after two losses (but while it was on its way to victories in the third and fourth games), then to stress the folding of Boston (while it was in the process of a fifth-game win). In light of the failure of Scully and Garagiola to depart from their script, preperception was all.

MARKET
LURES

Bum Steers

The 1950s lacked a little to be considered the Fan Appreciation Decade. In Boston, St. Louis, and Philadelphia, hundreds of thousands woke up one morning to discover that the team they had been rooting for since childhood had disappeared. The argument advanced for defending all three transfers was that there were many *more* fans waiting to support the clubs in their new venues. But sometimes not even overwhelming numbers in support were a guarantee of respect.

In 1957, for example, Cincinnati fans were so excited about their muscle-bound sluggers in sleeveless uniforms that they voted—and voted and voted—until the starting lineup of the National League All-Stars more or less consisted of Cardinals first baseman Stan Musial surrounded by Reds. With other clubs shrieking in his ear, Commissioner Ford Frick ruled that this was taking the concept of the "fan's game" too far, disqualifying some of the Cincinnati players. If that annoyed Ohio fans, those around the rest of the major leagues weren't much happier when Frick and the owners used the ballot stuffing as an excuse to confine All-Star voting for the next 12 years to players, managers, and coaches. The third indignity for Reds boosters was that no sooner had they given the franchise its first two million-plus seasons in 1956 and 1957 than owner Powel Crosley opened talks for moving the club, a descendant of the fabled Red

Stockings, to New York City. The plan was scrapped mainly because of renewed congressional investigations into baseball's exemption from antitrust laws and the fear of other owners that Crosley might be supplying embarrassing evidence that they all gave greater priority to lucrative markets than to fan loyalties.

By far, however, the period's least fan-friendly development stemmed from the opening Crosley had seen in New York—following the departure of the Dodgers and Giants for California.

Of all the franchise shifts in baseball history, none was more stunning than that of the Dodgers to Los Angeles following the 1957 season. Unlike every other transferred franchise in the twentieth century, Brooklyn had been drawing more than a million customers a year. Not only had it been making money at the gate, but its attractiveness to Madison Avenue and Broadcast Row had generated millions of additional dollars. Its roots in the community were deep to the point of folklore—whether it was Wilbert Robinson saying "Dodger fans always look for the dark cloud in the silver lining"; Bill Terry asking whether "the Dodgers are still in the league"; or a priest named Herbert Raymond dispensing with a Sunday sermon but asking his parishioners to say a prayer for slumping Brooklyn first baseman Gil Hodges. Even those not interested in baseball had been exposed for generations to Brooklyn jokes centered around the team, to nightlife columnists reporting the off-field doings of everybody from Rube Marquard to Leo Durocher, and to Lloyd Nolan and William Bendix portraying armies of motion picture characters who inevitably identified themselves by their favorite team. With the club's migration west, libraries had to clear shelves for a sub-literature analyzing the move as the principal cause of Brooklyn's economic and social plunge over subsequent decades. The shock was such that it came almost as an afterthought that, as a condition for the transfer, the Giants accompanied the Dodgers to California, abruptly ending 74 years of National League baseball in New York.

Brooklyn residents have never had any doubt about the villain of the story: Dodger owner Walter O'Malley, a corporate attorney with more than a touch of Tammany Hall who had bought out Branch Rickey in 1950 to assume day-to-day control of the organization. An apocryphal tale told of disillusioned fans years after the club's flight had two of them privately listing the three most evil men of the twentieth century, then comparing nominations to reveal that both had named Hitler, Stalin, and O'Malley. But the owner also had critical help from Robert Moses, in name the city's parks commissioner but in reality the overseer of any municipal project that required a jackhammer. A non-driver himself, Moses believed in highways and automobiles the way popes believed in Catholicism. When he wasn't building new expressways, he was decking them with low overpasses that made them unattractive to city buses. In his private moments, he cultivated a personal disdain for O'Malley usually reserved for riders on the A train. After being approached several times by O'Malley in 1953 and 1954 about condemning some downtown Brooklyn land as the prelude to building a stadium to replace the rundown, small-capacity Ebbets Field, for instance, Moses described him to an associate as "beefing, threatening, foxing, and conniving."

Throughout the O'Malley-Moses struggle over the need for a modern park with expanded parking facilities, the public took the role of the nitwit actors standing in a studio and staring off at a back-projection battle between a giant lizard and a giant armadillo in a prehistoric jungle. What was going on was unthinkable (a) because it was beyond reason and (b) because one didn't dare think it. In the interest of public relations, Moses established what he called the Brooklyn Sports Authority for the ostensible purpose of coming up with a stadium solution agreeable to all parties. As early as January 1956, however, he was telling an aide: "I think we can agree in advance on what the outcome will be as far as the Dodgers are concerned, but it is necessary to show that our opposition is based on something other than prejudice." O'Malley's countermoves revolved around ballparks. First, as a declaration of his seriousness to get a better facility, he transferred a handful of home games in 1956 to Roosevelt Stadium in Jersey City. What that got him were gripes from the players about the minor-league accommodations, protests from Brooklyn residents about being deprived of games in their neighborhood, and, given the tepid turnouts for the scattered week-day night games, confirmation that New Jersey was Yankees territory. Committed to his game of Chicken, however, he waited only until the end of the 1956 World Series before selling Ebbets Field to a real estate developer (with a lease for the team to continue playing there for three more years). Again in 1957, O'Malley shifted some games to Roosevelt Stadium, but by that time he had advanced beyond Chicken; in the interim, he had made the far more decisive move of swapping minor-league franchises with the Cubs, giving him title to Los Angeles's Wrigley Field and territorial prerogatives over that California city. If anybody still believed in his primary goal of remaining in Brooklyn, final disillusionment came when he turned around and traded Wrigley Field to the city of Los Angeles in exchange for the Chavez Ravine site where he intended building the stadium he had been denied by Moses.

The final practical obstacle to the defection of the Dodgers lay with the Giants. Unlike Brooklyn, the New York team had some real financial problems because of a sharp drop in attendance, its ranking as the city's third most popular big league team where advertising and broadcast revenues were concerned, and owner Horace Stoneham's profligate ways with a dollar. The fact that the Polo Grounds was located in Harlem did not help with the white suburban trade, either geographically or socially. Years after the episode, apologists for the franchise's relocation were still pointing to a tragic 1950 killing as a sign that the neighborhood around the Polo Grounds had become too dangerous (in other words, too black). The victim of the killing was a retired railway worker named Barney Doyle, shot in the forehead while watching a Dodger-Giant game on Independence Day. The shooter turned out to be a 14-year-old who had been firing a .45

automatic into the air from his rooftop some 1,200 yards away from the ballpark; police ascertained that, because of a parapet, the youth couldn't even see the Polo Grounds from his position on the roof, ruling out any thrill-killing motive. Nevertheless, the Doyle shooting was still a whisper in the background seven years later, the insinuation being that things could only get worse in Harlem. By early 1957, the question wasn't so much *if* the Giants would move, but *where* they would go. For some weeks, the likely destination was Minneapolis, but then in May the league gave the Dodgers formal approval to move to Los Angeles and the Giants to San Francisco if they could work out local deals. The one condition was that both clubs had to go, to justify continental road trips, or neither could. With O'Malley turning on the pressure, Stoneham received permission from his board of directors on August 19 to make the move.

O'Malley was astonished, when he arrived in southern California, to discover that not all Angelinos were glad to see him. Against all forecasts, a June 1958 referendum held to ratify the swap of Wrigley Field for Chavez Ravine and $4.7 million of city money for initiating stadium construction passed by the narrow margin of 345,435–321,142. Opposition to the deal was fueled by the realization that 1,800 Chicanos had to be thrown off the 315 acres for the building work to begin, and by disclosures that the area was rich in oil deposits. After years of being stranded at third base by other franchises that had appeared to be heading for California, however, city authorities closed their eyes to the dissent and welcomed the team. With the help of the gigantic Memorial Coliseum as its home over its first four seasons while the new stadium was being built, the franchise drew more than 2 million customers in seven of its first nine years. With a steady dose of Hollywood stars like Cary Grant, Doris Day, and Frank Sinatra in its box seats, it also moved quickly away from its Willard Mullin image as the Bums.

In San Francisco, the Giants also profited immediately, if relatively more modestly because of having to spend two years in ramshackle Seals Stadium (capacity: 23,000), then moving on to the frigid wind tunnel known as Candlestick Park. What both clubs found out, however, was that their East Coast stars were not automatic grandstand favorites in California. In Los Angeles, the Coliseum's barely visible right field stands disarmed lefty slugger Duke Snider more than a decade of NL pitchers had; in San Francisco, in both his history and his comments to the press, Willie Mays carried too much of New York with him, so the locals showed greater warmth first toward Orlando Cepeda, then toward Willie McCovey. Importing teams wasn't quite the same thing as importing heroes.

Liquid Capitals

Major-league teams have taken up residence in Washington much like congressional legislators: for terms of varying length, but always with a hovering expiration date. Only St. Louis has had as many as Washington's seven franchises since the establishment of the National League in 1876, and no city has had as many fold up or go elsewhere. And this has been without counting numerous others rumored on the verge of moving to the nation's capital and one that existed only in baseball trading cards.

It was the sixth Washington team, the American League Senators of Clark Griffith, that had the longest identity with the District of Columbia. It was a piebald identity—thick on U.S. presidents from William Howard Taft to Dwight D. Eisenhower cocking their arms to deliver the first ball for a new season, light on the number of voters sitting behind them. Between 1901 and 1960, the club drew one million fans only once (in the euphoric postwar year of 1946); it needed a quarter century and a pennant even to get to a half million (in 1924). The yearly apathy required little outside assistance: Unlike the even more miserable Browns, who shared St. Louis with the Cardinals, the Senators had market competition from a club in nearby Baltimore only at the very beginning and very end of their existence. That the franchise survived as long as it did was due to Griffith, his personal relations with U.S. government officials, and the AL's resolve not to lose that connection in conducting its affairs through two world wars, the Depression, and periodic congressional investigations into baseball's statutory standing. But the government character of the city also worked to stall the Griffith Stadium turnstiles. The elected officials, staff aides, and assorted bureaucrats who took up residence in the area brought their home rooting backgrounds with them—and, unlike in New York or Chicago, with an acute sense that they would eventually be returning from where they came. The result was that Griffith Stadium crowds usually had a high percentage of spectators cheering on the visiting team. This wouldn't have been all that negative if, say, an Indians fan living in the city had a pure enough baseball interest to see the Senators on their own between visits by Cleveland; but, outside indulging a whim to see how many runs the Yankees might score during a weekend bloodbath, Washington's drab squads didn't invite entertainment considerations of the kind. More than in any other big league city, the return customer in Washington was predictable—he would be back the next time his home team came to town.

With the death of Clark Griffith in 1955, the special relations with federal officials also died. What was left for his heir Calvin was a franchise that had become so synonymous with losing that it had figured in the musical fantasy *Damn Yankees* as the payoff in a Faustian bargain (the cost of a human soul is the Senators beating the Yankees for the pennant). In the same vein, headline writers enjoyed more than the brevity in referring to the club as the Nats. Victories were invariably the work of the "pesky" Nats, defeats always meant the Senators had been "swatted." The Browns might have been worse historically, but because of where they played, the Senators were losers in sculpted marble. Or, in the words of longtime team announcer Bob Wolff: "I never had to mention who was winning or losing, just give the score."

Unlike most of his contemporaries, Calvin Griffith didn't see a new stadium as the automatic answer to his attendance problems, and for good reasons. Given the unique administrative situation in Washington under which a federal commission had the final say on any municipal ventures, a new park in place of the privately owned Griffith Stadium would have required national government approval and been subject to its management. Moreover, any new facility under federal control would have usurped the chief revenue sources for the Griffith family—the money made from concession stands and from rentals to the football Redskins. The last straw for Griffith came when Congress agreed to look at a projected $6 million stadium, but only for the predominantly black northeast district of the city. For public consumption, he claimed he rejected the proposal because congressmen demanded it include a special free box-seat section for them, but the fact of the matter was that Griffith's perception of blacks was that they all spoke Spanish and should have been grateful for the chance to trade in their sugar plantation machetes for Griffith Stadium bats. The congressional proposal confirmed his fears that, as long as he remained in Washington, the franchise would become increasingly dependent on African-American customers. Throughout the mid- and late fifties, therefore, he flirted with cities from one end of the country to the other (Los Angeles, San Jose, San Francisco, Louisville, Minneapolis) while simultaneously assuring Washington residents he was going nowhere. One full-page ad appearing in the *Washington Post*, for instance, declared:

> *This is my home. I intend that it shall remain my home for the rest of my life. As long as I have any say in the matter, and I expect that I shall for a long, long time, the Washington Senators will stay here, too. Next year. The year after. Forever.*

Forever lapsed in 1961, with the shift of the franchise to Minneapolis. Even with the transfer, however, the owners were not ready to admit that a major U.S. city could not support big-league baseball, especially one with so many lawmakers and committee gavels. As part of the deal enabling Griffith to go to Minnesota, the AL expanded to ten teams, with a new (and seventh) franchise in the District of Columbia and local competition for the Dodgers in Los Angeles. The simultaneity of the transfer and the expansion not only whetted the appetites of other metropolitan centers for franchises, but also helped to create, in the financially wobbly cities of both leagues, an expectation they would be compensated somewhere along the line even if temporarily abandoned. Over the next decade, three cities—Kansas City, Milwaukee, and Seattle—would go to court or threaten to do so to have that expectation fulfilled, and all three would be rewarded sooner than later. For all the customary boardroom buccaneering that marked the sport's latest phase of development, in other words, the maneuvering took place within a new social climate that assumed that communities had a *right* to major-league baseball entertainment. While the legal basis for the sentiment was usually some stadium leasing arrangement that affected taxpayer money, that wasn't the only trigger. No less important was the embedment in the same social conciousnness of the generations-old claim that the sport represented the purest distillation of American values, leaving the insinuation that abandoned communities hadn't quite mastered the Pledge of Allegiance.

The New Breeds

E ight teams were added to the major leagues in the course of the sixties—Washington and Los Angeles (1961) in the AL, New York and Houston (1962) in the NL, Kansas City and Seattle in the AL (1969), and Montreal and San Diego in the NL (1969). With the exception of the Angels, they all distinguished themselves initially for how bad they were and for the relative degrees of patience their fans showed for their stumbling around. At the opposite extremes were the fans in New York, who turned their pain watching the Mets into an art, and those in San Diego, who didn't think their balmy climate should have been wasted on the Padres.

The Mets began as one of the worst teams in baseball history, with a record of 40–120 in their inaugural season. The New Breed (as they became known) that filed into the decrepit Polo Grounds to watch the club literally bannered its patience with ironic slogans scrawled across bed sheets and placards, turning the signs into as much of the entertainment as what was happening (or not happening) between the white lines. The television coverage given the sloganeering and artwork displays invited even more of them—a development that dour general manager George Weiss took long months to grasp was an essential part of the team's appeal; at one point, he even banned the bedsheets. The publicity given to the New Breed differed from the attention accorded previously to the Hilda Chesters and Mary

Otts in that its focus was the generic fan rather than some eccentric individual with claims to being colorful. It was an attention not easily surrendered, and in the years to come, grandstand crowds around the country would seek to entertain themselves with increasing regularity with beach balls, the Wave, and other distractions having nothing to do with hits, runs, or errors. More immediately, the New Breed filled the Polo Grounds in 1962 with numbers that easily eclipsed the last three years of the Giants in the park, went over a million in 1963, and, with the opening of Shea Stadium in 1964, made even the capacity crowds at Ebbets Field a diminished statistic.

For all the attention their fans earned them, the Mets were outdrawn by the Houston team in its first year. But the enthusiasm for big-league baseball in Texas didn't make fans the new franchise's number one priority. One symptomatic example was in the picking of a team nickname. For organization public relations chief George Kirksey, the ideal choice was Colt .45s since that would have sealed a pending advertising deal with the Colt Firearms Company. Kirksey was too far ahead of his time in the art of peddling naming rights, so that when even some of his bosses suggested that that might be seen as somewhat crass, he went through the motions of organizing a fan vote. After personally counting what he claimed were 10,000 ballots, he announced that, oddly enough, Colt .45s was the winner anyway. Ballpark amenities for fans were bait and itch. For three years, the club played in Colt Stadium, a temporary facility put under construction at the same time as the adjoining Astrodome; it was considered so temporary nobody bothered to mark the power alley measurements. But what it lacked in outfield wall numerals, Colt Stadium made up in giant mosquitos—so many of them that groundskeepers had to spray the park every half inning, lending a fine, acrid mist to summer evenings. Mosquito Heaven, as players called it, contributed as much as bad teams to declining attendances in 1963 and 1964 before the club—redubbed the Astros for the occasion—moved into the Astrodome.

While New York and Houston were defining the pejorative meaning of "expansion team" with their dim play, two other clubs with diametrically opposite records in baseball history were offering evidence that transferred franchises couldn't expect infinite rewards from a new location. The first was the Braves, the most successful city franchise of the twentieth century in that it never played below .500 in its thirteen years in Milwaukee. But as the club fell out of appointments with postseason play in the early sixties, the local press and fans found more and more reasons for going after owner Lou Perini, increasingly characterized as a carpetbagger as likely to leave Milwaukee for another city as he had left Boston for the Midwest. One of the biggest to-dos erupted over a policy forbidding fans to bring beer into County Stadium, forcing them to purchase it from ballpark concessionaires at inflated prices. The issue was aired to full censorious effect in the city that owed its fame to hops, so that Perini came off looking like not just another greedy baseball owner, but as an outsider who wanted to dictate to the region's chief industry. Attendance began to nosedive.

Worn down by all the criticism, Perini sold the club to a syndicate led by Illinois insurance broker William Bartholomay. Bartholomay took another couple of seasons of waning crowds, then announced in 1964 he was going to Atlanta. But the insurance man underestimated Milwaukee's public opinion. Prodded by a booster group that included future baseball commissioner Bud Selig, city agencies sued Bartholomay and the league for violating stadium lease contracts and for ignoring alternative local buyers for the team. The league prevailed in the suits, but only after the Braves had been forced to play a lame-duck 1965 season in Milwaukee. Against a backdrop of citywide resentment, many games drew fewer than a thousand people. Attendance for the final game—on September 22, 1965, against the Dodgers—was 12,577, about the same number that had welcomed the first Braves squad at the Milwaukee train station in 1953.

The converse of the Braves was the Athletics—the worst city

franchise of the century for the length of its survival (also thirteen years) and failure to reach .500. Over its first six seasons, Kansas City was openly regarded as a satellite for the Yankees, so much so that owner Arnold Johnson felt compelled to volunteer testimony before a congressional committee denying collusion between the franchises. The disgust of Kansas City fans at seeing such budding stars as Roger Maris shuffle off to Yankee Stadium in exchange for over-the-hill veterans and rookie busts showed in a dropoff of some 600,000 between the club's inaugural season in 1955 and 1960. And then Johnson died and things got worse.

The new owner, Indiana insurance executive Charlie Finley, was a blowhard, miser, and petty tyrant—with a Bill Veeck streak. His first public act on taking over the franchise was to stage the burning of an old bus—his grand way of saying that the era of the Yankee Shuttle was over. From that point on, Finley's dog-and-pony shows for fans overshadowed the relentlessly mediocre play of the team. He dressed up his squad in flamboyant kelly green and gold uniforms, intro-duced livestock in Municipal Stadium promotions aimed at farmers, had the players enter the ballpark on a mule train (and adopted one of the animals as a club mascot), set aside an area behind the outfield fences for grazing sheep, had a mechanical rabbit pop up behind home plate during games to resupply umpires with baseballs, and had players autograph game balls so that fans could catch what he described as "personalized" foul balls and home runs.

Even when they were on the road, Finley found ways to keep the Athletics the most talked-about topic in Kansas City. Responding to a dare, he hired Betty Caywood to do color on the club's broadcasts; the first woman to be part of a baseball radio team, Caywood con-centrated most of her remarks on events in the grandstands and in the dugouts—another way of keeping attention away from what was happening on the diamond. When the indignant owners of the White Sox refused to let him lead his mascot Charlie O around the field at Comiskey Park before a game, he rented a parking lot across the street and, with a ten-piece band and beautiful models to help draw a crowd, blasted the Chicago ownership for being "unfair to Charlie O the man, Charlie O the mule, baseball, and muledom."

But whereas such stunts from Veeck had usually increased attendance dramatically, Finley's ploys produced relatively few additional customers. One reason was a personality that reeked of business calculation, emitting none of Veeck's glee in his own gimmicks. Another difference was a parallel series of cost-cutting gestures—banning the telephone sale of tickets, eliminating a franchise practice of personally delivering season tickets to purchasers—that deterred fans from showing up at Municipal Stadium to be amused. More than anything, though, while the sport-shirted Veeck was a street-corner hustler who openly sought to profit from his Three-Card Monte salesmanship, the blue-suited Finley was too much the hypocrite to make such a commitment. After his public burning of the Yankee Shuttle, for instance, his first trade was to send Kansas City's best pitcher, Bud Daley, to New York in exchange for the kind of bodies Johnson would have accepted. Facing rising criticism for the sweetheart deal Johnson had worked out with the city for using Municipal Stadium, he staged another heavily publicized fire—this time of the ballpark lease, in the interests of demonstrating his community spirit. Only a couple of weeks later did he admit having torched a blank piece of paper and insist that the city was still obligated to the rental terms worked out with Johnson. While never without a word for the importance of keeping fans happy, it became increasingly difficult by the middle of the decade to pick up a local paper without reading a story about his intentions of moving the Athletics to any one of a dozen sites suggested by Rand-McNally.

When the AL finally authorized Finley to move to Oakland following the 1967 season, Kansas City mayor Ilus Davis moved to bring suit, and Missouri Senator Stuart Symington declared that he was ready to open another investigation of the antitrust exemption enjoyed by major league baseball. A panicked American League immediately promised a new expansion in 1969 that would include another franchise for Kansas City. Davis and Symington accepted the compromise, though the senator spent a few days describing Finley as "one of the most disreputable characters ever to enter the American sports scene" and comparing his impact on Kansas City to that of the atomic bomb on Nagasaki. What he was trying to say was that he thought the city had a right to a big league franchise.

Box Office Hits

Babe Ruth's power eruption in the twenties solidified the wisdom that hitting, especially home-run hitting, improved ticket sales. But just like the assertion that Jackie Robinson's arrival in Brooklyn dealt a mortal blow to baseball's color problems, this was, at best, a half-truth. If Ruth became the sport's greatest box-office attraction, it also had a little something to do with his extravagant personality and the fact that he played for a juggernaut of a club. Indeed, the only strong evidence for the siren powers of the long ball has been found in terrible teams where an individual slugger has represented the main reason for walking through a turnstile. In the wake of the Second World War, for example, many Pittsburgh fans descended on Forbes Field to see Ralph Kiner. The most jaded of them didn't hurry to be on hand for the home first inning, figuring cleanup hitter Kiner wouldn't get to the plate until the second inning; likewise, if he came to bat in the eighth inning, there was usually a rush to the exits after he had completed his turn at bat. In Washington in the mid-fifties, Calvin Griffith pulled in the Griffith Stadium fences in the hope that Roy Sievers and Jim Lemon, and later Harmon Killebrew, would sell more tickets with their slugging. The expansion Senators of the sixties also owed much of their income at D.C. (later Robert F. Kennedy) Stadium to the long balls of 6'7" Frank Howard. In such cases, it was very much in the interests of Organized Baseball as a whole, not just the specific franchises in question, to play up the seductive gate powers of the home run since noncompetitive teams like Kiner's Pirates and Howard's Senators had precious few other merits.

All of these questions came to the fore in the sixties, when a series of rulings first tried to tell fans what was important, then discouraged them from seeing what they were presumed to want, then reversed field to give them what they supposedly wanted anyway. The burlesque began when Ford Frick made sure not too much importance was attached to the most noteworthy home run of the decade. In 1961, as New York's Roger Maris, in tandem with teammate Mickey Mantle, began closing in on Ruth's single-season mark of 60 homers, the commissioner announced that the record would have to be surpassed within the 154 annual games of the Bambino's day to rate absolute mention in the record book; otherwise, the one-time Ruth ghost writer declared, the feat would be asterisked as a tainted product of the recently introduced, enlarged 162-game schedule. Frick's statistical scrupulosity, which he did not insist be applied to other record categories, kept average Yankee Stadium crowds to only 18,000 over the final days of the season when Maris first tied and then bested the Ruth standard; the 61st homer off Boston's Tracy Stallard came on October 1, the 162nd game, before a "crowd" of 23,154. The outfielder and 19-year-old fan Sal Durante supplied the grace for the occasion: Maris declining to accept the free gift of the ball caught by Durante and urging him to accept a restaurateur's offer of $5,000 for it. "The boy is planning to get married and he can use the money, but he still wanted to give the ball back to me for nothing," Maris told reporters. "It shows there's some good people left in the world, after all."

If Maris had harbored doubts on that score, it was hardly surprising. As he and Mantle had entered September in their joint pursuit of the record, it had become abundantly clear that Yankee fans both in the Bronx and around the league wanted their centerfielder, not the outsider obtained in one of the giveaway trades with Kansas City, to break the record. Between that obvious display of grandstand sentiment (sometimes spiked with objects thrown at him) and the pressures of having to answer the same questions day after day for a steadily growing press corps, the usually reserved Maris spent much of his final weeks snapping at fans and gazing at the clumps of hair falling into his hand whenever he touched his head. The leg infection suffered by Mantle in the closing hours of the season didn't polish Maris's achievement, either, simply creating a lot of what-ifs among Mantle fans.

But it was also those what-ifs—staples of the grandstand—that pointed up the tackiness of the Frick ruling. "What if Ruth had played the three games he had missed in 1927; would the record have been 63 instead of 60?" "What if Mantle hadn't batted behind Maris; would Maris have received at least one intentional walk during the season instead of having the opportunity to hit another ball into the stands?" "What if it hadn't been raining earlier in the season and Maris hadn't lost one homer to the failure to complete an official game?" Home runs, more than any other aspect of baseball, have engendered that kind of conjecture among fans. "How many home runs would Willie Mays have hit if he hadn't played most of his career in Candlestick Park?" "How many home runs would Ted Williams have hit if he hadn't lost so many years to military service in World War II and Korea?" Rather than elicit such fancifulness from his constituency, Frick and his diktat grounded it into an accountant's invoice numbers, while simultaneously rubber-stamping structural changes (expansion, divisional play) bound to require even more spreadsheets. In the last analysis, the widely heard charge that he was primarily interested in not having his personal hero's record eclipsed was the *least* insensitive explanation for Frick's asterisk.

But Frick didn't leave it at Maris. Although he didn't touch other achievements also affected to one degree or another by the enlarged schedule, he did conclude that hitting had become too easy, so he instructed umpires to widen the strike zone as of the 1963 season.

This brought about an immediate surge in strikeouts, a drastic cut in walks, and an even greater plunge in batting averages. In 1962, for example, the NL batted a combined .261 and the AL .255; a year later, the averages were .245 and .247, respectively. That trend continued through the sixties, with the AL dipping to .230 in 1968. In the latter year, the once-powerhouse Yankees batted .214 and still managed to finish four games above .500! Along with those numbers went descending attendance figures. The addition of four expansion teams, two of them in the super markets of New York City and Los Angeles, still left the combined totals of the leagues for most of the sixties a bare three million above pre-expansion levels. Between 1963 and 1965, the AL's ten clubs couldn't even reach 10 million.

The convergence of the diminished offense and decreased attendance suggested a straightforward cause-and-effect to the owners. In fact, there were plenty of both baseball and non-baseball reasons why running out to a ballpark had become less inviting in the sixties. Within the baseball world, there was the Yankee Effect. When the Twins won the pennant in 1965, they not only overthrew the New York dynasty, they undercut the AL's chief source of income for more than 40 years. Detroit and Cleveland fans simply didn't line up as avidly at their home parks for the Horace Clarke Yankees as they had for the Ruth Yankees, DiMaggio Yankees, and Mantle Yankees. Away from the diamond, professional football had taken its vows with network television, wasting little time in showing why the sport and the medium were a marriage made in Nielsen heaven. The enlarged 162-game schedule also coincided with longer basketball and hockey seasons, so that from mid-June to mid-July was about the only time baseball wasn't overlapping with another sport or, in the case of football, with well-publicized training camp events. The domestic turmoils occasioned by the civil-rights campaigns, the war in Vietnam, and, later, the assassinations of Martin Luther King and Robert Kennedy, were not just vaguely atmospheric conditioning factors, but, often, acutely polarizing agents; in other words, some people stayed away from stadiums as much from outright hostility as from indifference to Bob Gibson's shutouts. For many, the institution of major-league baseball—with its holier-than-thou pronouncements on the state of the nation, its record on minority players, and its dogged insistence on being identified with military virtues, most recently with the appointment of retired general William Eckert as Frick's successor—was not just irrelevant in the decade of Selma and Saigon, but very much part of the problem.

But more preoccupied by what they saw as the strict correlation between offense and attendance, the owners voted for a return to a narrow strike zone and the lowering of the pitching mound for the 1969 season. The hitters responded. In one year, the NL's average went from .243 to .250, while that of the AL soared a full 16 points to .246; far more stunning, the leagues combined for 1,064 more home runs from one year to the next. At the same time, in the NL only the Cardinals experienced a dropoff at the gate. But there the hard evidence of an offense-attendance correlation also ended.

The single biggest difference between 1968 and 1969 was not the additional 1,000 home runs, but a further expansion to include four more clubs that brought with it division play and a postseason playoff round prior to the World Series. The new teams not only swelled the overall attendance figures of both circuits, but also doubled the number of fans with real hopes of seeing their club reach the postseason. And yet, despite all the heavier offense and the better chance of playing in October, only the Orioles (the Eastern Division winner), Twins (Western Division winner), and 1961 expansion Senators (playing .500 for the only time in their 11-year D.C. existence) registered gate increases from 1968 in the AL. Conversely, the AL clubs with the most home runs for the year, the Red Sox and Tigers, lost customers. In the NL, if only St. Louis actually declined, merely three teams gained appreciably—the East-winning Mets, the West-winning Braves, and the Cubs, who blew the division flag to New York at the end of the season. Of these six teams—Baltimore,

Minnesota, Washington, New York, Atlanta, and Chicago—the only one to lead a league in any significant offensive category was the Twins, in batting average.

Whether achieved by hitting, pitching, fielding, running, or parading the best-dressed mascot, winning continued to offer the strongest correlation to a full grandstand. Once they stepped back from their own role to leave the stage to their improbable 1969 team, even Mets fans admitted losing wasn't everything.

Going to Market

Not counting Houston's temporary Colt Stadium and the expanded minor-league facilities of Minneapolis's Metropolitan Stadium and Seattle's Sick's Stadium, sixteen big-league ballparks opened between 1960 and 1973. While only the Astrodome (1965) was an indoor arena, just about all of them shared a greater sense of climatic control over the grandstand, in everything from actual temperature monitoring (in Houston) to stricter aisle policing. Cincinnati even contemplated bathing its new Riverfront Stadium in bakery smells for keeping patrons in a mellow frame of mind. Lacking the allure of crumb buns, Riverfront settled for being the epitome of the new installations that swapped the frequently obscured sightlines of such older fields as Fenway Park for completely unobscured views, but with a greater distance between the diamond and the seating. In the words of long-time Pittsburgh broadcaster Bob Prince, "When the Pirates left Forbes Field [for Three Rivers Stadium], they took the players away from the fans—you were near them, had the real smell of grass."

While generally true, some of the more cunning teams also exploited the contours of their new stadiums with the help of fans for use against visiting clubs. In effect, they sought to make fans not only the 26th player, but the 126th, 226th, and 326th. Commonly at the center of the ploys was the "batter's eye" seating section in center field—in most facilities closed off, except in cases of overflow crowds. In Dodger Stadium in the sixties, however, the management sold tickets to the right-centerfield slice of the batter's eye whenever left-hander Sandy Koufax was pitching against a righthander and to the left-center portion when righthander Don Drysdale was going up against a southpaw. In this way, opposing hitters were forced to pick up the ball out of the hands of the Los Angeles pitchers against an array of white shirts. (The gambit was not without precedent. In 1935, for instance, the Cubs encouraged fans to buy mirrors in honor of third baseman Stan Hack. The club feigned dismay when other teams protested that the "Smile with Stan" toys ended up reflecting the sun into the eyes of opposition hitters in the batter's box.)

The tradeoff of efficiency for remoteness in the new parks coincided with the sport's total commitment to a suburban fan base, either through the location of its stadiums in city zones with direct access to highways or by constructing the parks in the suburbs altogether. A brochure pitching the wonders of Kansas City's Royals Stadium (1973) boasted: "You get there by taking Interstate 70. You can see inside the stadium from your car."

Dodger Stadium (1962) was the lodestone of the riches Walter O'Malley scratched out of the California dirt. Emphasizing the family appeal of Dodger Blue entertainment and the ease with which motorists could get from parking lots to their seating tier, he transformed Chavez Ravine into the Taj O'Malley, drawing between 2.2 and 2.7 million over his first five years. The numbers were aided by another vindication of radio's impact on ticket sales and by a complete reversal of a policy in Brooklyn, permitting blanket television coverage (unless the opponent was the Giants, in the interests of re-stoking the East Coast rivalry between the teams). O'Malley entrusted the airing of games almost entirely to the radio play-by-play of Vin Scully, who made himself as critical to the Los Angeles version of the franchise as Red Barber had been to the Brooklyn edition. For all the very professional millions involved, however, Dodger Stadium fans projected a decidedly dilettante air to the rest of the country for their habit of arriving late for games and then, regardless of the score, leaving again in the seventh and eighth inning. When the image wasn't that of Hollywood hot shots just dropping in to "take a game," it was of O'Malley's two major selling points showing their other side: the families that had to get kids to bed early, or the thousands of drivers trying to beat one another to the expressway. One way or the other, Scully ended up doing a lot of play-by-play even for fans with tickets to the game.

The new ballparks were only the most visible sign that baseball was getting costly, and that William Cammeyer's strategy of waiting for people to come up and put a dime in his hand was no longer the silver path to profit. With the opening of the Astrodome came the first luxury boxes. The season-ticket holder moved rapidly from an ideal to a necessity of financial planning. As the sport's turnover soared into the hundreds of millions annually, fans became caught up in all kinds of marketing calculations. The new priority was to make customers—and whole communities—represent teams as much as the teams represented their locations. At the most rudimentary level, this meant giving away, especially to children, hats and other items bearing club logos. At another level, it meant public relations initiatives in which a club gained conspicuous circulation and gratitude for its emblem by sponsoring a junior league, contributing to a charity, or making its players available for visits to schools, hospitals, and other public venues. Politically, it meant more prominence for an owner or franchise official as the member of some civic board, showing that he was concerned about more than raising ticket prices. In the best of cases, it also meant exploiting a field success to the point that a team was sought out as a badge of identification by community leaders, such as John Lindsay's assiduous cultivation of the 1969 Miracle Mets when he ran as an independent candidate in New York's mayoralty elections ("If they can do it, I can do it"). Motorcades and ticker-tape parades were organized not only for World Series champions, but for teams arriving from spring training for the start of a season. From T-shirts to City Hall swearing-in ceremonies, the marketing objective was to have big-league baseball accepted in the community not just as a promising economic investment or cultural assumption, but as the flip side of a social right—as a social need.

Despite the constantly hovering controversy about taxpayers footing the bill for privately operated stadiums and growing economic pressures of various kinds, some franchises were slower than others about seeing the wisdom of more creative relations with the public. In its single year of wretched existence in 1969, the Seattle Pilots concluded that what it didn't have—a good team, television coverage, a viable ballpark—entitled it to charge the highest ticket prices in the AL. Another case study in counterproductivity was the Pirates of the early seventies. Between 1970 and 1975, Pittsburgh won five East Division titles and finished a slight 2 ½ games behind in the sixth season. But although second only to the Big Red Machine as the NL's best team of the period, it usually came nowhere near Cincinnati's attendance. In 1974, while drawing a million less than the Reds, the club could attract merely 22,725 to the last game of the regular season, when it had to defeat Chicago to nail down the division title. Most commentators were content to attribute the indifference to the simultaneous, long-awaited emergence of the Steelers as an NFL powerhouse and to characterizations of Pittsburgh as a football more than baseball town. For club historian Bob Smizik, however, the club itself was the chief culprit for the ticket-window apathy:

> *A lot of the blame for the poor attendance was placed on the people of Pittsburgh. It was a bad rap. Pittsburghers liked baseball . . . but it wasn't being presented to them properly. The Pirates didn't know a thing about marketing. The term was not used within the organization. When club officials first started to hear about other teams marketing their product, the Pirates thought they didn't need it. The Pirates' idea of marketing was to put a good team on the field.*

This was the same franchise that, only a couple of years later, would be setting the jock fashion pace with its turn-of-the-century black-and-gold caps and animating national business travel with a "city of champions" pitch for company conventions following another World Series victory over Baltimore.

FANS AND PHANATICS

Winning Ways

U nlike the football fan who can dream about it, even the most delirious baseball fan does not expect his team to win every game on its schedule. He is more than aware that, before every season, a club can be expected to win one third of its games, lose one third of them, and have its final standing determined by the remaining one third. But that numerically tested wisdom does not prevent him from approaching each individual game of the schedule in expectation of victory—or from resenting the practical impediments to his fantasy. On occasion, these obstacles have started with the owners, management, and players of his own team; other times, they have included the fan himself.

Connie Mack once argued that finishing second could profit a franchise more than winning a pennant because the players on a runner-up team, while performing well enough to draw big crowds, could not make the salary demands that those on a first-place club could. Mack made the point in an era when player contracts were negotiated from year to year under reserve-clause rules—a condition no longer prevailing in the current age of multi-year pacts. Also of account, today's greater economic reliance on season-ticket holders has provided more of a business incentive for winning everything, since a franchise will frequently draw more people the year *after* a successful flag drive; the Mets in 1969–70 (2.1–2.7 million) were just one of many exemplifying the social cachet in being identified with a championship club. But that said, Mack's observation remains pertinent for crystallizing the overriding objective of baseball ownership. As Leonard Koppett has put it:

> *Winning is not the goal of the* business. *It's a valuable means of attaining the goal of selling tickets—not only now but for future seasons. Winning is the goal of the individuals playing, and of that part of management responsible for choosing players. But the* club's *goal is to sell tickets. That's its reason for being.*

In the most outrageous circumstances, even *not* selling tickets can be an ownership objective. At one time or another, owners have deliberately depressed gates for such ulterior aims as transferring a franchise to another city, pressuring an organization sale, and facilitating the move of an owner himself to another market. Such episodes have served as reminders that not only has baseball always been a business; it has remained, in the face of all the institutional rhetoric and league superstructures implying otherwise, an *owner's* business.

General managers want to win for their employers and for their fans, but can possess a finer sense of reality than either. In the interests of holding on to their jobs, they sometimes resort to a lot of posturing for bridging the gap between the players on their roster and the pie in the sky. Most of those with reputations as great traders seemed to have trained for their expertise by rearranging the deck chairs on the *Titanic*. Seldom did a multi-player swap engineered by the likes of such mid-twentieth-century dealers as Paul Richards, Frank Lane, or Bing Devine amount to more than a distraction for restless fans, optimally turning fifth-place clubs into fourth-place clubs or .480 teams into .482 teams. In 1956, twenty years before free agency stirred complaints that players weren't loyal enough to the teams that had brought them to the major leagues, Richards, as Baltimore's general manager, had little problem with fan attachments in seriously proposing an entire 25-man roster trade with the equally shabby Athletics.

As head of baseball operations for the Indians in 1960, Lane swapped his manager Joe Gordon to the Tigers in exchange for Detroit dugout boss Jimmy Dykes, admitting the transaction was mainly for reviving fan interest in two also-ran teams. One reason fan interest needed reviving was that Lane had earlier sent Cleveland's most popular and productive player, Rocky Colavito, to Detroit because of fears the slugger would demand too much money after helping the team finish only five games out of first place in 1959. The most frantic of all the prestidigitators playing to the cheap seats was Devine of the Cardinals, who between 1969 and 1979 completed— or blueprinted for completion by others—193 deals involving more than 400 players (counting only transactions at the major-league level). None of the trades brought St. Louis a pennant in the period; what they did bring was an overall record of 887–888.

Throughout baseball history, players have sprinkled around evidence that a team victory was not always their most urgent priority. In the 1880s, pitchers like Tony Mullane thought it was more important to show up their black catcher Fleet Walker with hard deliveries in the dirt than to get batters out. In the World War I era, Hal Chase, Heinie Zimmerman, and Chicago's Black Sox were among the many throwing games for personal bets or as part of a fixing scheme. In 1927, Pittsburgh outfielder Kiki Cuyler mailed in his plate appearances to protest being switched from the third to the second spot in the Pirates lineup. Rogers Hornsby could never get a handle on why his Boston Braves teammates in 1928 paid so much attention to game situations and so little to giving him opportunities for driving in runs. In the seventies, Dick Allen talked his compliant manager Chuck Tanner into letting him leave games early even if the White Sox had the frailest of leads so he could avoid sportswriters. Across two generations, the Red Sox team had the reputation of being a squad of "25 players taking 25 cabs" after games for their self-absorption with personal statistics. In 1989, Kevin McReynolds and Darryl Strawberry abandoned the Mets dugout in Philadelphia while the game was still under way and headed back to New York because, as McReynolds's wife later explained, "they wanted to beat the traffic."

Notorious as some of these examples have been in themselves, they have also fed into a grandstand perception that failure in the field almost always owed as much to lack of effort as lack of ability; in other words, the player who strikes out in a clutch situation in the seventh inning simply "didn't want it enough." This view has permitted the fan to postpone thoughts that his team may not be quite as talented as his hopes—and franchise publicity—have been insisting. If he is not so far gone as to believe that wishing makes it so, he is usually rock-solid in the belief that it can never be so as long as everybody isn't putting his degree of energy into the wishing. Skill and luck, both completely beyond his control, are allowed to account only for the rest.

Some grandstands have voiced their exasperation with failure more pitilessly than others. Any straw poll would undoubtedly give the Golden Boo to Philadelphia fans, who have endured the most losses of any rooters in baseball history and who have been characterized for decades as being prone to hissing children, Santa Claus, and cancer patients. Their targets have almost always been the team's biggest sluggers—Del Ennis and Stan Lopata in the fifties, Dick Allen in the sixties, and Mike Schmidt in the seventies and eighties. As loud as the hostility has sometimes been, however, it has also contained a marked degree of haplessness—futility cheering on futility in the only way it knows how. There has been no better symbol of this relationship than Alice Roth, a fan who was struck by a Richie Ashburn foul ball at Shibe Park on August 17, 1957. As Roth was being carried out of the stands on a stretcher, the still-batting Ashburn lined another foul at her that toppled her off the stretcher to the ground. Such negative reinforcement has worked predictable wonders; or, as

Allen Barra has noted: "In their unshakeable pessimism, [Phillies fans] create a kind of Jungian collective paralysis that seems to infect their heroes at key moments. Like Bill Murray and Dan Aykroyd in the climactic scene of *Ghostbusters*, they bring to life the very image they fear the most."

While players have never relished the kind of booing the Phillies have had to get used to at Veterans Stadium, they have also indicated uneasiness with some of the alternatives. For all the comic relief Mets fans found in their Polo Grounds losers in 1962 and 1963, Gene Woodling and other veterans admitted hating the sardonic reactions their play triggered, saying it made them feel like less than major leaguers. Blue Jays players could have done without the polite applause Toronto fans conferred for years on just about anybody for anything at all (hits by opponents, outs by the home team) after the club joined the American League in another expansion, in 1977. During the 1998 duel between Mark McGwire and Sammy Sosa to break the Roger Maris home run record, players and managers around the National League moaned about their fans cheering on these two opposition sluggers even in the late innings of close games. Where was the priority of the fans for winning the game, they wanted to know.

Where it was was in that best of all entertainment worlds—being on hand to see some significant record broken in the top half of the inning, then watching the home team come back to win in the bottom half. Nobody said wish fulfillment had to follow a straight line.

On the Page

I f fans sometimes had to reach for explanations for player failures on the field, it wasn't just because of their own vapors. Since being old enough to read, most had been exposed to images of players in both newspapers and fiction where failure was either an aberration or the result of some wilful flaw. To judge by the writings, there weren't hundreds of players on major league rosters, but only about four. There was the stalwart family man who spent the season thinking about his wife and children back in Indiana or Missouri; the eager young bachelor who spent the season thinking about his fiancee back in Kentucky or Wisconsin; the big-city sharpie who brought his brazenness out on the field and won the respect of opposition players; and the "moody" guy who stayed away from his teammates and ended up being traded every couple of years. Beyond that, hitting and pitching statistics accounted for most of the biographical details served up by the press. In the definition of New York *Herald Tribune* sports editor Stan Woodward, beat writers were accustomed to "godding" players for readers.

The flimsy newspaper portrayals did little to contradict the idealistic or wholesomely antic portraits of players circulated by most fiction writers. A common motif of the earliest baseball fiction was a young hero in a prep school, college, or some other "respectable"

Eastern social setting that linked the sport to upper-middle-class Yankee values. Typical was Noah Brooks's *The Fairport Nine* (1880), which pitted the players from "better families" against a team of "ruffians" from working-class backgrounds. Far more popular were Gilbert William Patten's Frank Merriwell stories, originally aimed at boys but not without a substantial adult readership as well. Writing under the name of Burt L. Standish, Patten introduced Merriwell in *Tip Top Weekly* in 1896, presenting him as an Horatio Alger–type hero who, as an undergraduate at Yale, embodied as many superior skills on the field as his ambition, perseverance, and other estimable American virtues impressed off it. The Merriwell tales quickly became a franchise, with Patten turning out 20,000 words a week and *Tip Top Weekly* riding them to a weekly circulation of more than 200,000. Before the vein had been exhausted in the 1920s, there were more than 200 titles in print, with an astounding 125 million people estimated as having shared at least one Merriwell adventure.

Patten's influence on fan perceptions of baseball in the early part of the century was incalculable. He was Dr. Seuss, Dungeons and Dragons, and *Star Wars* rolled into one. He wasn't alone, either. The nickel-magazine and dime-novel markets were only too obvious for those looking to cash in: a popular subject, modest prices, simple writing, appealing equally to recent immigrants who wanted the rungs for their social climb clearly delineated and to the long-landed who appreciated being reminded why they were better than the immigrants. One who jumped aboard the gravy train was Giant pitcher Christy Mathewson who, with his ghostwriter John Wheeler, put his name to titles like *Won in the Ninth* and *First Base Faulkner*. Others prominent in the field were Ralph Henry Barbour (*For the Honor of the School, Wetherby's Inning*) and William Heyliger (*Bartley, Freshman Pitcher, The County Pennant*).

Edward Stratemeyer used dozens of pseudonyms while churning out (with the help of assistants) about 800 books, many of them series centered around Baseball Joe Matson. Later on, between the late forties and mid-sixties, Long Island University basketball coach Clair Bee found success with 23 books chronicling the walking Bible lessons of Chip Hilton on the hardwood, the diamond, and the football field. Whatever their literary merit, the Stratemeyer and Bee books needed only a couple of reviews praising them for their moral outlook to be guaranteed space on public library shelves long after commercial sales had come to an end.

The reply to "What did Virginia Woolf and H. L. Mencken ever agree about?" was that they both regarded Ring Lardner's *You Know Me Al* as a masterpiece. Created in 1914 as a series of short stories in *The Saturday Evening Post*, the Lardner tales took the form of correspondence between a minor leaguer and a friend (Al) back home. Their strength was a conversational vernacular that doggedly skirted parody and condescension in recounting the player's misadventures, misunderstandings, and missed chances, making him sound like a precocious codger on a porch rocker.

Uplift and reassurance continued to map the terrain of baseball literature between the two world wars, with sniping at the sport, even as passing dialogue in novels concerned with other matters, extremely rare. Although individual books won their adherents in the thirties and forties, character complexity in baseball figures largely had to await the work of Bernard Malamud (*The Natural*) and Mark Harris (*The Southpaw, Bang the Drum Slowly*) in the 1950s. Without completely neglecting the built-in dramatic arc leading up to the Big Game, Malamud and Harris also made it clear that their characters had more than one big game in them—personal contests that they lost as often as won.

It was in the same post–World War II period that Stan Woodward and other newspaper editors realized that they were in danger of becoming redundant by continuing to focus their baseball coverage on the play-by-play particulars already provided by radio (and later television). The result was more tales told out of school. By the 1960s, fans who read more than their horoscopes in the daily paper had a pretty good idea of whether that "moody" guy was a drunk, a misanthrope, or a Zen Buddhist. But there was also a limit to what reporters wanted shared with the public, and one of those limits was any unprocessed view directly from a player. When reliever Jim Brosnan published a best-selling diary about his 1959 season with the Cardinals and Reds under the title *The Long Season* (1960), he was welcomed by sportswriters about as effusively as radio broadcasters had been in the 1920s; even the rare positive review from the pressbox insinuated that Brosnan's ability to stitch together two consecutive coherent sentences without the mediation of a ghostwriter made him a footnote to the parting of the Red Sea. In 1970, Detroit catcher Bill Freehan published another diary, this one about the Tigers' 1969 season, and he too came in for a roasting from executives and the press.

But *The Long Season* and *Behind the Mask* turned out to be only a warmup for Jim Bouton's *Ball Four*. Also published in 1970, this memoir of the pitcher's 1969 season with the Seattle Pilots and Houston Astros, including extended reminiscences of his earlier days with the Yankees, caused a fit among the baseball establishment. While most of the uproar was because of the book's casual depiction of the sex-obsessed lives of major leaguers, it also unnerved front offices with its specific instances of settling rosters through racial quotas and of management hypocrisy in contract negotiations. When Commissioner Bowie Kuhn read some advance excerpts in *Look* magazine, he guaranteed the book's success by summoning Bouton to his office for another lecture on what was detrimental to baseball, and then, getting no satisfaction on that score, by angling for information on how he himself had been portrayed in the book. When Bouton revealed Kuhn's wheedling, *Ball Four* was on its way to four hardcover and four paperback editions and to global sales that eventually reached 3 million.

Reserve Causes

While the publishing world was attempting to cultivate the fan as reader with the Brosnan, Freehan, and Bouton books, Organized Baseball was trying to make him more of a customer. One step in that direction came in 1970, when the leagues turned All-Star Game voting back to the grandstand. The move followed several years when the exhibition had mirrored too well the sport's dominating pitching—not exactly an enticing development for a game at its most beguiling as a showcase for sluggers. If returning the vote to fans earned the sport public-relations points, they were needed. During the 1969–70 offseason, 14 of the existing 24 clubs announced the most significant price hikes ever recorded, many of them in coincidence with moves to stadiums that were already being underwritten by taxpayer money. Even more disaffecting were some of the consequences of the latest expansion in 1969, of the NL into Montreal and San Diego and of the AL into Kansas City and Seattle.

The only new franchise to appeal to fans immediately was the one that would later be labeled an albatross on big-league finances—Montreal. The first venture by Organized Baseball outside the United States produced six straight seasons of million-plus attendance for a team that didn't even reach .500 until its eleventh year. What the

Expos mainly offered over their first decade were players whose most conspicuous talent was in their names—Coco Laboy, Boots Day, and John Boc-ca-bel-la (as rendered with relish by the Parc Jarry field announcer)—and the exotic touch (for Americans, anyway) of having the game's most familiar terms translated into French. The Canadians also showed particular affection for outfielder Rusty Staub, one of the very small handful of players in the franchise's history who made an effort to learn French and who didn't treat Montreal as some kind of Houston North where they used Monopoly money and delayed the start of every game for a medley of North American anthems.

Seattle was an absolute disaster and entertained more with off-field lawsuits and as the raw material for Bouton's *Ball Four* than with on-field dramatics; it was transferred to Milwaukee after only a single season. San Diego boasted a grandstand apathy to match Seattle's one-year wonders. Over their first four seasons, the Padres averaged more than 100 losses while drawing little more than a half million fans. The chief talking point of the franchise, aside from its organizational disarray and lurid yellow and brown pajama-like uniforms, was Jim Eakle, a former Marine drill instructor who emerged as an unofficial team mascot by blowing out the great tunes of the day on his tuba while another San Diego reliever trotted in from the bullpen.

The reluctance of fans to watch the cellar-dwelling Padres bred some bizarre rationalizations. One favorite was that the weather was too ideal in San Diego for players to feel especially motivated on the field or for fans to want to watch them when there were so many zoos and battleships to visit. Finally, in January 1974, McDonald's hamburger king Ray Kroc stepped forward to buy the franchise, but not before the city had to advance it money to meet the payroll and a baseball card company issued a 1974 set with the *W* for Washington superimposed over the Padres pajamas on the assumption that the team was headed for the nation's capital.

The team that Kroc took over was as inept as the five that had preceded it—a fact noted by the owner on Opening Day when, in the midst of a pasting by the Astros, he grabbed the public address microphone to bewail "some of the most stupid ballplaying I've ever seen." Whims of the kind were embraced by the fans who, though exposed to another 102 losses, showed up more than a million strong, the first time the franchise had reached that mark.

But Kroc's popularity was hardly the norm for owners in the period. In 1969, Minnesota fans besieged Calvin Griffith with thousands of phone calls and letters for firing manager Billy Martin after he had led the Twins into the League Championship Series. Seattle was outraged by the clueless ownership that forced the Pilots to hurry off to Milwaukee on the eve of the 1970 season, Senators fans by the defection of still another Washington franchise, this time to Texas. Between 1970 and 1975, the White Sox, Indians, Giants, and even Yankees alienated their boosters with constant threats of moving elsewhere if they didn't get some stadium improvement or other community-financed concessions. Sensitivity wasn't too much in evidence, either, with some of the promotions organized for drawing bigger crowds. In 1973, the Brewers staged what they called a Chinese Aviator Look-Alike Contest, following a crack by Martin, moved on to manage Detroit, that "if the Brewers can win with what they've got, then I'm a Chinese pilot." When hundreds of fans showed up at County Stadium wearing outlandish makeup and outsized plastic teeth, the promotion drew protests from around the country for abetting stereotypes of the Chinese and other Asians. When Cleveland offered unlimited beers for a dime on June 4, 1974, 60,000 cups were sold, leading to a drunken riot, attacks on players and umpires, and a forfeit to visiting Texas. The Indian ownership was slammed all the way to Washington for the promotion.

Especially within a climate conditioned by so many franchise moves and threats of others, the owners won little public support for their ongoing battles with the players over repealing the reserve clause and granting greater player rights. Letters to the editor around the country ran markedly in favor of the Players Association. But that was also when the discussion was focused on the principle, rather than the practical ramifications, of free agency.

Battling the Blues

T he fan-umpire relationship has tantalized social critics since the first arbiter jerked his thumb in the air and the first spectator mistook it for another finger. What does the umpire's authority represent to the fan? Is he only a scapegoat for fan frustrations with a team, or is he a darker animal—the guard dog to all the order inherent in a game that the spectator would like to flout without really destroying? Or, vice versa, does the erratic performance of an umpire—at least in the eyes of the spectator—bring out the latter's insecurity that the game *isn't* as flawless as it should be? For sure, the umpire was intended from the very beginning of baseball not merely as an authority figure, but as an *absolute* authority figure. One of the very first rules adopted by the Knickerbockers for the New York Game on September 23, 1845, declared unequivocally: "All disputes and differences relative to the game [are] to be decided by the umpire, from which there is no appeal." There is even a touch of the romantically neat in the story about Alexander Cartwright having presided at the June 19, 1846, Hoboken game that has been widely accepted as the first true baseball contest; that detail subtly reinforces the seminal authoritativeness of the Hoboken exhibition and Cartwright's own role in the history of the sport. But it does so not only in the face of the earlier-mentioned particulars that he was not listed as an umpire and that New York Game rules had already been in use the previous October, but also in spite of the fact that William Wheaton, another Knickerbocker credited with a hand in formulating the new rules, was recorded as an umpire in a fall 1845 encounter between Brooklyn and New York squads.

Under the system then in force, Wheaton was actually one of three game arbiters—each team having its representative referee, with a neutral third voice for breaking deadlocks. This lasted until 1858, when the National Association of Base Ball Players, not up to spreading too many nickels around, stipulated the hiring of one umpire a game. For the next 25 years, the lone man on the field didn't hesitate to ask fans for their help on plays. As Connie Mack recalled the custom in his autobiography: "They would turn to the spectators when close plays were made and ask their opinion. The crowd was usually as divided in opinion as the United Nations, but they felt complimented by the umpire's consideration of them. The umpire would then make a decision. This was a practical method of stopping wars at their point of inception."

But the National League disagreed. In the name of avoiding unseemly disputes (but as much for asserting itself as a non-interactive entertainment), it banned the soliciting of fan views in 1882. At the same time, however, it offered no alternative help to the umpire who, long before he was mocked as a blind mouse, was assumed to have eyes in the back of his head. In 1890, the one-year Players League introduced the custom of two umpires, but, except for key games, that was not followed up as a requirement until 1911. Three became the stipulated minimum in 1933 and four in 1952.

At least for those sitting or standing closest to the field, fans were never more involved in the game than during the 25-year period when their advice was sought on calls. No coincidence, it was immediately after they were told to stick to their spectating that the most violent attacks on umpires assumed plague proportions in both the

National League and American Association. As David Voigt has chronicled:

> By the mid-1880s it became evident that the popular vilification [sic] of [umpires] was getting out of hand. . . . In 1884, Baltimore installed barbed wire to discourage mobbings by fans. That same year a mob assaulted league umpire [Tom] Gunning because he called a game a tie on account of darkness, and a Philadelphia mob turned on umpire Billy McLean. . . . McLean was goaded beyond endurance by taunts, and he threw a bat at a group of fans. Within minutes he was besieged, and it took a police escort to rescue him. The following day, the fiery Billy again needed a police escort to escape a mob.

Only too aware that protracted tantrums on the field stirred up home crowds, players and managers saw little reason to curb their baiting tactics. For Baltimore's Ned Hanlon, it was important to keep in mind that "players are not school children, nor are umpires school-masters. . . . Patrons like to see a little scrappiness in the game, and would be very dissatisfied to see the players slinking away like whipped schoolboys . . . afraid to turn their heads for fear of a heavy fine from some swelled umpire."

Occasionally, though, even officials and fans had enough. One of Ban Johnson's administrative premises for the American League was cracking down on players and managers who abused umpires, while simultaneously attracting better arbiters through higher salaries than those offered by the National League. In September 1906, Hilltop Park erupted against its shortstop Kid Elberfeld when his by-then-predictable antics with umpire Silk O'Loughlin forced a long delay in a tense game between the Highlanders and Athletics; Elberfeld had to be escorted off the field by police while his own fans pelted him with scorecards and other objects. The following September, at a game between the Browns and Tigers in St. Louis, Hugo Dusenberg, a clerk at the local German consulate, hurled a soda bottle that fractured the skull of umpire Billy Evans; before police could get to Dusenberg, fans sitting nearby had beaten him bloody.

Not that fans and umpires suddenly begam romancing each other. On Opening Day in 1907, Polo Grounds spectators pelted Bill Klem with snowballs so relentlessly that he declared a forfeit victory for the Phillies. On July 10, 1911, in Philadelphia, the same Klem figured in the first recorded instance of an umpire holding up a game until a fan was escorted from the premises; according to the arbiter, the unidentified culprit had been calling him a "fathead" past the point of tolerance. Fearing grandstand reactions much worse than simple name-calling, clubs routinely assigned bodyguards or had local policemen escort umpires away from parks after games.

The single biggest episode in baseball history affected by fan-umpire relations occurred on September 23, 1908, around the so-called Merkle Boner. With the Cubs and Giants deadlocked at 1–1 in the bottom of the ninth inning of a game crucial for the NL pennant, New York first baseman Fred Merkle failed to run the complete 90 feet from first base to second base after a single by Al Bridwell had apparently given the New Yorkers the win. When Chicago second baseman Johnny Evers saw Merkle veer off from the basepath to join his jubilant teammates, he yelled for center fielder Solly Hofman to throw him the ball so he could record a force-out that would have ended the inning without the run counting. Realizing what the Cubs were up to, Giant coach Joe McGinnity braved a cluster of celebrating fans on the field to retrieve the ball and fire it into the stands. A second ball from a never-disclosed source was thrown on the field, and Evers grabbed it and stepped on second to record the out. But when the infielder appealed to Bob Emslie for the call that would have sent the game into extra innings, the umpire claimed he hadn't been watching Merkle and passed the buck to colleague Hank O'Day. Even though he agreed with Evers, O'Day refused to say so because of the thousands of Giants fans around him, some of whom had also seen what Evers had done. As one New York newspaper described the Polo Grounds scene: "Everyone evidently recognized a good opportunity to get a shot at the umpire. Those within reach began pounding him on all available exposed parts not covered by the protector, while the unfortunate attackers on the outskirts began sending messages by way of cushions, newspapers, and other missiles."

Cowed by the mob, O'Day waited until he had been whisked away from the park by police to report his conclusion to NL president Harry Pulliam that the Giants run didn't count. Pulliam sat on his verdict for days before finally ruling that the game would have to be made up at the end of the season if the pennant was still in doubt. As it turned out, it was necessary, and Chicago ended up winning the game and the pennant. Giants manager John McGraw and the New York press were infuriated, not only because of the lost pennant but because of the claims by both O'Day and Pulliam that the temper of the Polo Grounds crowd had made an immediate decision and even a makeup game the very next day, on September 24, impracticable.

O'Day never again umpired in New York without threats of attack. Pulliam fared even worse. Already a somewhat melancholy personality, he broke under the constant savage attacks of McGraw and the New York dailies, requesting a leave of absence for a few months. It didn't help. Shortly after resuming his duties, on July 28, 1909, he blew his brains out at the New York Athletic Club at the age of 39. Asked for his reaction to the suicide, McGraw was said to have cracked: "I didn't think a bullet to the head could hurt him."

Episodes of fan-umpire violence grew more isolated as the twentieth century wore on. One important factor was the spate of new stadiums in the pre–World War I era that relieved overcrowding—always a fertile condition for impatience. Especially with the new dedication to administrative order they proclaimed with the appointment of Kenesaw Landis as commissioner, owners also had a harder time reconciling their pitch that baseball was the ideal family entertainment with the impression that they were egging on six-year-olds to throw rocks at Tom Connolly. No less important, the 50-year stability of the two leagues ultimately provided more exciting fan nemeses from the rivalries built up by such teams as the Dodgers and Giants, Yankees and Red Sox, Cubs and Cardinals. Given a choice of Bill Klem or Bill Terry, most Brooklyn fans would have run their first trolley over the latter.

Of course, there were always the McGraws, Ty Cobbs, and Leo Durochers around to play on home passions. Nor were any Gallup polls published indicating that teenagers wanted to become umpires instead of doctors or encyclopedia salesmen. If arbiters were defined as being at their best on the field when nobody noticed them, they were equally considered at their most ideal off it when they didn't exist, period. But then in 1963, Chicago attorney John Reynolds made it more difficult to ignore them when he announced the formation of the National League Umpires Association, a union vehicle that soon won members substantial contract benefits. A one-day strike by the association in 1970 startled fans more than the union agitation by players going on at the same time. For all his masks, chest protectors, and plated shoes, the umpire had basically been viewed as a "civilian." Fans might not be able to uncork a fastball at 95 miles an hour, blast a pitch into the upper tier of the right field stands, or steal second and third on successive deliveries to the plate, but they considered themselves capable of seeing the same slide as an umpire saw and judging whether it preceded or followed a second baseman's tag. Why should he have been praised—or paid more—for getting right something any normally sighted fan would have gotten right?

Free Agency

With the labor wars of the seventies, "I don't want to hear any more about that" became as much of a grandstand line as "Hey, beer, over here!" More often than not, the professed aversion to discussing the conflict between owners and players betrayed a fan insecurity as the bargaining issues grew in complexity and the sport's traditional contractual premises started peeling. If there was theoretical support for the right of players to get out from under the reserve-clause constraints that made them the property of a given team until the latter decided otherwise, there was an equal amount of sourness for the practical monetary consequences of having the players prevail; in other words, the player *cause* could be accommodated as part of baseball's fictional world, but the payment of very real and increasingly larger salaries could not. It was a contradiction that went right to the heart of the fan's relationship with the game.

A foretaste of the fan's "money" criticisms of free-agent signings was provided by the introduction of the amateur draft in 1965. With the previous season's reverse standings dictating the order of selection and with substantial cash in advance required for completing a signing, clubs had to put their intuitions in full public view. And what the public viewed were the vagaries of speculating about talent. While first-round picks in the initial years produced any number of solid major leaguers, including three future Hall of Famers (Reggie Jackson, Robin Yount, and Dave Winfield), they also yielded many times more young athletes who enjoyed their greatest days on a diamond before receiving their diplomas. The Mets would never be allowed to forget their enthusiasm for catcher Steve Chilcott (instead of Jackson), the White Sox for catcher Danny Goodwin (instead of George Brett), or the Padres for pitcher Jay Franklin (instead of Mike Schmidt). It was within this far-more-anxious public-relations climate that some clubs hustled ballyhooed signings to the big leagues to assure fans that they knew what they were doing; in more than one instance, they demonstrated precisely the opposite. The most notorious rush job occurred in Texas in 1973, when the Rangers put 18-year-old David Clyde on the mound over the warnings of manager Whitey Herzog. Clyde's 12 home starts during the season ended up accounting for almost one-third of the franchise's 686,000 attendance, but he won merely four games and was out of the league a few years later with a career record of 18–33.

By the time free agency arrived in the mid-seventies, the fan could thank the amateur draft for being practiced in knowing what his club should spend on Player A and what the ceiling should be on an offer to Player B. Whether or not he was bothered by the various local government subsidies extended to his team, in other words, he had little trouble thinking of himself as a shareholder as much as a booster. The pivotal event for the next phase of his commitment came on December 23, 1975, when a three-man arbitration panel ruled that pitchers Andy Messersmith and Dave McNally could not be tied to their teams by the customary automatic turnover of the reserve clause. The finding effectively authorized all players to become free agents a year after the expiration of the specific duration of their contracts. In the name of avoiding abrupt chaos, the players and owners agreed that only six-year big league veterans would be eligible to walk, but that didn't prevent a stampede to the door after the 1976 season. And the very first signings illustrated the extremes of free agency's potential impact. By giving Wayne Garland the first career-long contract ($2.3 million for 10 years) after merely one standout season for Baltimore, the Indians took out a mortgage on despair when the righthander first couldn't win and then suffered a rotator-cuff injury that cut short his playing days. By giving established slugger Reggie Jackson $2.93 million for five years, the Yankees helped assure themselves of another period of dominance on the field, in the headlines, and at ticket windows around the league.

But not even a free-agent's positive influence on a team exhausted the test papers he was expected to hand in to the average fan. His individual performance was scrutinized in an atmosphere of guilty until proven great, greater, greatest. Once the euphoria over a winning game or season had passed, the free agent was adjudged never worth the money he was getting. It was the nineteenth-century view of the first professional players emblazoned in neon. If there was any dulling of this prejudice with the passing of time, it was only because of the competing glares for the reckoned stupidity of the owners for shelling out so much and for their suspicious cries of poverty while adamantly refusing to open their ledgers for public examination.

The most common reason given by fans in the seventies and eighties for opposing the rocketing player salaries was that they were responsible for higher ticket prices. This surmise drew fire not only from Players Association director Marvin Miller, but from some owners as well. "If baseball had a payroll half as much as today's, or even a tenth as much, and if they found that at the present ticket-price level they were selling out their stadiums all the time," Miller noted, "they would raise ticket prices because that's what a good businessman does. People in sports who make the automatic assumption that you base ticket prices on player salaries just don't know what they're talking about." Milwaukee's Bud Selig agreed. "That the burden is passed along to the fans is a myth," the future commissioner averred. "If we passed along our increased cost of doing business because of the free-agent draft . . . we would have had to raise prices 10 times over what we have." Miller's rebuttal might have been comfortably syllogistic and Selig's altogether disingenuous, but both were buttressed by the fact that for every dollar doled out to a player, there were two more coming in, especially from broadcasting profits. As San Diego's Ray Kroc admitted more candidly: "Miller knows . . . that the latest figures show our attendance is up, our total revenue is up. . . . He also is armed with something even more important—He knows that there never has been a team in baseball that has gone bankrupt. And until some clubs go bankrupt, there is nothing to prove we can't stand the gaff." It was a diagnosis that eventually flowered into a tactic.

One of the immediate consequences of free agency was to resharpen focus on the Yankees, among both sympathetic and hostile fans. When George Steinbrenner, operator of the Cleveland-quartered American Ship Building Company, bought the franchise from CBS in January 1973, his first declaration to the press was: "We plan absentee ownership. I'll stick to building ships." The next three decades would be filled with similar truths and modesty, involving machinegun hirings and firings of managers and coaches, public lashings and instant demotions of rookies who made errors or yielded home runs in front of him, and rants against umpires and other owners who displeased him. Through it all, Steinbrenner affected a populist air about as convincingly as his declared role model, General George Patton. Whenever he talked about "the Yankee tradition," he sounded like he was referring to a special train to Maine; when he talked about "the average working guy," he sounded like he had once met one in a bar. But where he brought the Yankee tradition together with the average working guy was in his willingness to spend whatever it took to restore the franchise to its glory days. It was he more than any other individual who minted the popular impression that the free-agent era was about the team able to throw the biggest wad of cash on the table.

Not surprising, Yankee fans cultured the grandstand ambivalences of spending to win and winning the advantage to spend some more. There was what was described as Steinbrenner's "competitiveness"— not only in his dedicated pursuit of the biggest-name free agents on the market, but in his obsessiveness about not losing either exhibition games or the sports pages of the New York dailies to the Mets. "Nobody can say he doesn't want to win" was a common refrain; "At least he puts his money where his mouth is" was another. The equation of big spending for big winning was perceived as total. This meant that not even the owner himself got a pass for the legion of marginal pitchers who went straight from signing multimillion-dollar contracts to saying—and proving—how much they hated pitching in New York. The more blatant his free-agent strategy, the higher the expectations in the upper deck at Yankee Stadium. Steinbrenner could mock Dave Winfield as Mister May for slumping in the 1981 World Series, and nobody organized a protest march in the Bronx in defense of the out-fielder. He could apologize for the performance of the Yankees in losing that Series to the Dodgers, and without receiving an ava-lanche of letters saying "Oh, no, it's okay, George. Forget about it." Indeed, winning became the *minimum* for the Yankee fan's elevated expectations.

The extra—what distinguished the Bronx fan from his counter-parts around the country in the new free-agent era—came in the off-field entertainment provided by all the million-dollar egos. The Yankee players detested Jackson and Steinbrenner, and had the ghost writers to prove it with one Bronx Zoo book after another. Third baseman Graig Nettles rivaled Yogi Berra for quotability with such cracks as "When I was a kid, I wanted to play baseball and join the circus; with the Yankees, I've been able to do both" and "The more we lose, the more [Steinbrenner] will fly in from Florida, and the more he flies in, the better chance there'll be a plane crash." Steinbrenner never got tired of hiring, firing, and rehiring Billy Martin as his manager, making for the most thrilling clashes between a blustering egomaniac and a fractious manic-depressive to be seen outside a group therapy session. Thugs called Yankee Stadium security guards confiscated signs the owner didn't like, general managers and telephone operators were whimsically dispatched for being in the toilet at the wrong time, and a shakedown artist who lacked only a toothpick in his mouth was hired to get dirt on Winfield so the Yankees could get out of their contract with him. Between AL pennants in 1981 and 1996, Steinbrenner seemed to sense that the only way to stop the muttering about the big money was to turn New York into all-Yankees-all-the-time. And it seemed to work.

For many, it also offered further reason for despising Yankee fans —as identified with braying and smugness as Phillies fans were with booing and gloom. As Robert Lipsyte put it: "Yankee fans have long been the ugly Americans of sport. Like the old stereotype of Americans abroad, Yankee fans flaunt an assumption of wealth and dominance. In their case, it's from wearing pin-striped shirts bearing the numbers of the most storied players in baseball history. . . . Yankee fans never quite get this, wandering the baseball universe in their hero shirts, wondering 'Why do they hate us?'" Some players could have asked the same thing about fans in the seventies and early eighties.

Krank Cases:
The Late Century

FANS GO APE, TURNING SHEA INTO A JUNGLE! was a typical headline reporting the scenes unleashed by the Mets division-clinching victory over the Cardinals, pennant-clinching victory over the Braves, and World Series triumph over the Orioles in 1969. At least the Shea Stadium rampages, which thrice left the field more potholed than a Manhattan thoroughfare, had the veneer of celebrations. Other ballpark scenes over the next decade and more were as ugly in intent as in effect. More riots, demi-riots, and threats of violence were registered than at any time since the pre–World War I era. A common thread in many of the outbursts was the targeting of a high-priced free-agent acquisition. The crowd security problem was matched only by the rhinoceros-hided actions of some owners and executives who had missed all the Archie Bunker episodes about racism, sexism, and alcoholism. Native Americans stepped up efforts to get the Indians and Braves to change their logos, women's organizations protested the instructions of the Phillies management for female ushers to wear tight-fitting hot pants, and Ralph Nader backed a consumer group—FANS (Fight to Advance the Nation's Sports)—that sought to stem what it called "naked price gouging and runaway greed" on the part of the owners.

The first big ruckus of the period came in 1973–1974, around Hank Aaron's pursuit of Babe Ruth's career record of 714 home runs. Because of its holder, the mark had taken on the mystique of the game's most revered standard—something Aaron learned the hard way when he was assailed by hate mail and anonymous telephone calls from around the country for challenging the "white man's record." The Braves outfielder became all the more of a target when he ended the 1973 season with 713 home runs and had to go through the winter worrying about the seriousness of the threats. Taking no chances, the Braves asked the Atlanta Police Department to furnish a bodyguard and booked their star under the alias of Diefendorfer in a West Palm Beach hotel away from the rest of the team during spring training in 1974. Then matters became more complicated when Braves president William Bartholomay, disgruntled by his franchise's tepid attendance, announced that Aaron would sit out the season's opening series in Cincinnati so that home runs 714 and 715 could be hit before home crowds at Fulton County Stadium. Such an explicit acknowledgement of the record's box-office value was too much for traditionalists, who wanted to know what had happened to baseball as a team game more important than any single player's statistics. The *Sporting News,* for one, didn't understand the hostile reaction. "The Braves hardly could be faulted for wanting Aaron's historic achievement to occur in Atlanta," the weekly editorialized. "Estimates of the extra income it could generate range up to $1 million. If Henry got the job done in Cincinnati, the Braves would miss a chance for a big payoff. . . . The Braves have a right to play Aaron when and where they see fit."

The paper received a representative retort from its own Letters column, when University of Wisconsin Law Professor Donald W. Large observed that "if this implies that a team can play its star only when commercially feasible, why can't a player, on the same theory, play to win only when economically feasible? Perhaps the Chicago Black Sox were just misunderstood entrepreneurs." Commissioner

Bowie Kuhn agreed with the professor, ordering the Braves to have Aaron in the lineup Opening Day at Riverfront Stadium. Aaron responded by tying Ruth's mark with the first swing of his bat in the first inning in Cincinnati. But that was it. Bartholomay emerged with a compromise when 53,775 poured into Fulton County Stadium on the cold and miserable night of April 8, 1974, and saw the slugger tag Al Downing of the Dodgers for his 715th. The last scary moment came when a couple of fans jumped out onto the field as the slugger was rounding the bases and began pursuing him; they were proven to be publicity hogs rather than would-be attackers.

If the threats against Aaron were aimed at preventing him from accomplishing something, others reflected pathological responses to failure. In the spring of 1970, for example, an ex-convict in Chicago was arrested for threatening the life of Ernie Banks, apparently because the Cubs first baseman hadn't prevented the collapse of his team in the previous year's pennant duel with the Mets. In 1977, Angels designated hitter Don Baylor made the mistake of being the only one of several high-priced Angels free agents not to spend most of the season on the disabled list, so he had to ask for police protection for his family against threatening and abusive fans who jeered him through every strike of a second-half slump. But the single worst year for fan intemperance was 1981, especially in the weeks leading up to a June strike by players.

The biggest target, in more ways than one, was Pirates outfielder Dave Parker, who ended up on the receiving end of batteries, apple cores, and other objects both in Pittsburgh and on the road; in Philadelphia, police retrieved a .38-caliber bullet from the debris thrown at him. The singling-out of Parker stemmed from an expanding girth that he attributed to bad legs and that fans ascribed to a typical deterioration of fat-cat free agents; he was all the more visible because of Pittsburgh's bunny rabbit–yellow uniforms and his own on-field styling when he homered. Also in the course of the

1981 season, Baltimore pitcher Dennis Martinez required four stitches after being hit by a bottle thrown from the stands in Comiskey Park; Pete Rose had to be restrained by teammates from going after a heckler with a bat; and outfielders Cesar Cedeno and Reggie Smith broke through restraining arms to grab for fans who had tossed objects at them. Umpires also had their tense moments. In Atlanta, Jerry Crawford held up a game until a box-seat fan was ejected for spewing endless threats in his direction. In Chicago, Dale Ford warned the White Sox they would forfeit the second game of a doubleheader if they didn't stop broadcaster Jimmy Piersall from making allegedly obscene gestures in his direction and inciting fans to "riot."

For grandstand crassness, the hands-down winners were Fenway Park bleacherites. On May 4, 1982, Red Sox fans began taunting Twins outfielder Jim Eisenreich to "shake! shake! shake!" as the rookie fell prey to a breathing fit and accompanying tics. Eisenreich, who suffered from Tourette's syndrome, finally had to call time and quit the field—the start of an enforced retirement for a couple of years before he found the medication that enabled him to return as a pinch-hitter and platoon player. The fact that the Fenway Park episode occurred during a Game of the Week telecast prompted nationwide outcries against the Boston fans.

One of the angriest episodes extending beyond a ballpark occurred on June 15, 1977, when the Mets traded popular ace Tom Seaver to Cincinnati. The deal followed weeks of snide attacks on the pitcher by *Daily News* columnist Dick Young, widely thought to have been inspired by the team's front office. While Seaver broke down in tears on television, both fans and rival dailies laid equal blame on Young and Mets board chairman M. Donald Grant for forcing the hurler, a union activist and management critic, into a corner where he had to request the deal. In the words of a *New York Post* headline: YOUNG DROVE SEAVER OUT OF TOWN. Some fans picketed Shea Stadium, others cancelled season tickets, and cranks began bombarding Grant with phone and mail threats, so that he spent the rest of the season with a bodyguard at his side. The club's attendance didn't recover for years, after the team had been sold.

On other occasions, it was baseball executives writing primers on how not to attract fans. Speaking before the Waseca Lions Club immediately after the 1978 season, Twins owner Calvin Griffith dropped such pearls as the facts that he had welcomed the opportunity to move his club from Washington because of D.C.'s large black population, that blacks were more disposed to attending wrestling matches than baseball games, and that catcher Butch Wynegar had batted only .229 on the year because he had spent most of spring training chasing his new wife around their bedroom. According to Griffith, Wynegar would have been better off staying single and sticking to one-night stands since "love comes pretty cheap for ballplayers these days and they should take advantage of it."

Shortly afterward, Toronto general manager Peter Bavasi chilled his team's box office (not to mention the club itself) when, informed that an Exhibition Stadium ticket taker had been fired for being seen getting into the car of one of his players, cracked that "I certainly wouldn't want my daughter dating a Blue Jay."

Oakland fans didn't need any foot-in-the-mouth incentive for staying away. As part of a labyrinthian scheme to depreciate the Athletics franchise for sale or transfer purposes, owner Charlie Finley gave radio broadcasting rights for games to a weak-powered college radio station, stripped the Coliseum (redubbed the Mausoleum) of a working scoreboard and its rest rooms of plumbers, and made sure food-concession stands sold only what was gold and green. The result in 1977 was a dip below a half million in attendance.

The *Chicago Tribune* ownership that took over the Cubs in 1981 wasn't too friendly to fans, either—at least to some of them. Informed that some enterprising landlords were charging heavily for the rooftop seats across the street from Wrigley Field, the team mulled a plan for erecting a barrier along Sheffield Avenue that would screen out the familiar sign of EAMUS CATULI! (the Latin approximation for LET'S GO, CUBS!). The idea was scotched—at least temporarily—only when team announcers Harry Caray and Jack Brickhouse began screaming that it would ruin one of the most familiar features of Cubs baseball. Without interference from the team, the rooftop seats (advertised as "alternative skyboxes") became a source of quick cash for the landlords of thirteen neighborhood buildings; even the city got in on the poaching by selling "special club licenses." Inside Wrigley Field, meanwhile, the raucous Bleacher Bums added a wrinkle to their habit of dowsing enemy outfielders with beer—firing back onto the field any home-run ball hit by an opposition player. The practice was soon picked up in other parks, often to the discomfort of fans who wanted to hold on to the ball they had grabbed.

Even well-intended promotions frequently ended in misadventure in the period. On Opening Day in 1978, thousands of Yankee fans celebrated a first-inning home run by Reggie Jackson by raining down the Reggie Bars handed out at the gate. The earlier-mentioned Beer Night in Cleveland on June 4, 1974, was just one of several fiascos fueled by suds. At Dodger Stadium in 1977, the customary seventh-inning run out to parking lots was delayed while fans in the upper and lower decks exchanged volleys of beer, Dodger Dogs, and other Pentagon-priced foods. The worst scene of the period, however, had to do with music rather than beer.

In his latest boardroom appearance with the White Sox, Bill Veeck had been irritating other AL owners as regularly as he had been while running the Indians and Browns. Attempts to divert attention from his generally mediocre club had included sewing the names of players on the backs of their uniforms (initially opposed around the rest of the league as a blow to scorecard sales), attiring the team in short pants (ended after a year when the legs of the White Sox had begun looking like ads for a hospital emergency room), and encouraging his players to take curtain calls after home runs (enraging opposing teams). Along the way there had been such other promotions as Martian Night, in which Eddie Gaedel and other dwarves invaded Comiskey Park to zap fans with their X-ray guns, and Al Smith Night, when all fans named Smith were admitted free in order to give moral support to slumping and regularly booed outfielder Al Smith—only to see him drop a fly ball to cost Chicago the game against Boston.

But all of that was mere prelude to Disco Demolition Night on July 12, 1979, during Veeck's second stint as White Sox owner. The idea was supposed to have been a cross-promotion for getting Chicago fans to Comiskey Park and for reminding the city that the facility was being rented out regularly for rock concerts when the team wasn't in town. Instead, a local disc jockey's stunt of blowing up disco records produced a mob scene of thousands of fence-jumpers running wild on the field between games of a doubleheader, with policemen trying futilely to restore order and firemen trying to put out the blazes caused by the explosions. The chaos not only forced the forfeiture of the second game by the home team, but gave Veeck a big push out the door from his final ownership position.

The scenes of mass havoc didn't completely eclipse individual grandstand characters. But the most noted, like the Shea Stadium Sign Man who had a pre-scrawled observation for just about every diamond occasion, were benign in the extreme. Much of this reflected the influence of team-controlled TV cameras that had no interest in giving exposure to hecklers of the Kessler brothers stripe. As for the fans themselves, they were either camera-aware enough to know how to behave if they wanted attention, or indifferent to anything but the on-field objects of their taunts. Gone were the days of Pete Adelis, a Philadelphia heckler who was regarded as such an effective bane of visiting teams that the Phillies gave him a pass so he could indulge his specialty for every home game. In keeping with the new priorities, the most outlandish figure of the seventies was all show business—a Cincinnati stripper named Morganna Roberts.

The lavishly endowed (44–23–37) Kentucky native launched her baseball career at Riverfront Stadium in 1971, when a friend dared her to run across the diamond and kiss Pete Rose in the outfield. It turned out to be the first of some two dozen big-league kisses that she bestowed on players in the middle of games. Dubbed the Kissing Bandit by a Cincinnati sportswriter, Roberts went after the likes of Johnny Bench, Nolan Ryan, Cal Ripken, and Steve Garvey, but her favorite was George Brett, whom she managed to accost twice, the second time at the 1979 All-Star Game at Seattle's Kingdome. The relative ease with which she managed to get into ballparks and out onto fields, not to mention travel around the country, raised more than one suspicion that some clubs paid her to pep up the box office. Thanks to the publicity she gained from her jiggly sprints, Morganna ended up working as an exotic dancer in Las Vegas, Houston, Tacoma, and other cities.

If Morganna was show business, Novella O'Hara was closer to the cattle business. A fanatical Giants fan, she actually tried to buy pitcher John Pregenzer from the team in the sixties. When she learned his contract had been purchased from a low minor league for merely $100, she offered the Giants $110 for him. Rejected, O'Hara then organized a fan club for Pregenzer that swelled to a claimed 3,000 members, including good-sport Peace Corps director Sargent Shriver. When plans for a John Pregenzer Day at Candlestick Park were aborted by his demotion to the minors, she organized (to no greater success) a Bring Back John Pregenzer Day. A San Francisco restaurateur who had counted on a guest appearance from the pitcher posted a sign in his window reading: JOHN PREGENZER WAS GOING TO EAT HERE.

Aside from the influence of television, the decline in the notoriety of unofficial mascots owed to the decision by teams to create their own official ones. Some, such as announcer Harry Caray and owner Ted Turner, acquitted their tasks as sidelines to bigger interests. On Opening Day at Comiskey Park in 1976, Veeck noticed that Caray was singing

"Take Me Out to the Ball Game" along with fans at the seventh-inning stretch. Without telling the announcer, he stuck a microphone in the broadcasting booth, so that the following day Caray's rasping voice was heard throughout the park. When Caray protested, Veeck's answer was: "Anybody in the ballpark hearing you sing knows he can sing at least as well as you can, so they sing along." The announcer brought his routine over to Wrigley Field in 1982, where it became such an integral part of Cubs games that it was continued by guest celebrities even after Caray's death. By that time, the announcer himself had become enough of a Wrigley Field institution that his caricature rivaled the uniform bear as a franchise emblem.

Turner, meanwhile, had little hesitation about trying to play his own Atlanta club's most visible cheerleader. Bent on making the Braves "America's Team" through his cable TBS coverage, he played to the grandstand with such stunts as leaping out of his box seat onto the field to welcome hitters at home plate after a home run and joining the grounds crew in sweeping the infield in the fifth inning. The regular promotions included the very Veeck-like Wedlock and Headlock Night, during which 34 couples were married on the field before the game and wrestling matches held after it. In 1977, he decided the best way to have fans ignore their miserable club was to manage it himself. This lasted a single game (a 16th consecutive loss) before NL president Chub Feeney dug out an old regulation barring managers from owning stock in the club that employed them.

Big Victor was another controversial presence at Fulton County Stadium. A totem-sized figure that rolled its eyes whenever a Brave hit a home run, it was one of the first targets of Native American protests over the franchise's demeaning of Indian tradition. In 1967, the team warehoused Big Victor, but only to replace it with a teepee called Chief Noc-a-homa's Wigwam. The Wigwam stood on a platform behind the left field fence for four years, after which it began being shuffled back and forth from right field to left field for some years because of seating expansions. With the Braves favorites to reach the LCS in 1982, however, it was dismantled altogether for yet more seating, triggering two things: a losing streak that threatened to end in one of the worst swoons in baseball history, and fan protests that Chief Noc-a-homa was exacting revenge for having been left homeless. The wigwam was restored, and the Braves managed to slip into the playoffs. But in spite of that obvious lesson, the club once again shut down the teepee in 1983, provoking still another losing spin and another public outcry. This time, the teepee was restored for good, remaining in place until the Braves moved to Turner Field in the nineties. For Native Americans, it was just one more symbol of the franchise's racism.

The most famous animate team mascot was Ted Giannoulas, the San Diego Chicken, who went to work on Opening Day in 1974. For some years, the Chicken entertained Padres fans by cavorting atop dugouts and along outfield fences with an acrobatic dexterity the home team could have used. Giannoulas's tenure ended when he got into a squabble with the club over the patent rights on his costumed character and had to take it elsewhere in the majors and minors without any reference to San Diego. Over the next few years, some 24 teams adopted mascots—most of them animal creatures related to a club's nickname and almost all of them with routines seemingly born in the brains of the real birds and fish represented. The most accomplished by far was Dave Raymond's Phillie Phanatic, a flouncy, huge-bellied anteater that mocked visiting players and sped around on the Veterans Stadium turf on a scooter. Before being replaced by Tom Burgoyne in 1993, Raymond's stint (16 years) was the longest of any kind of Phillie in any kind of uniform except for Mike Schmidt.

The adoption of the Disneyland-like mascots was part of a strategy for building up baseball's profile as a family entertainment. It came amid rising criticism that by scheduling even World Series and All-Star games at night, the sport was becoming less accessible to children and jeopardizing its long-range fan base; or, as Leonard Koppett has succinctly stated it, "If you can't keep converting children into new fans, you can't stay in business." But the recourse to the toon creatures sent two other messages as well. The more obvious one was that the owners didn't consider the game on the field enough of an entertainment in itself; certainly, theaters and moviehouses weren't dressing up their ushers as kangaroos to go hopping among audiences in the middle of shows. The other was in the asexual fuzziness of the mascots: While football had its tassel-bra'ed, high-booted cheerleaders and other sports played up their "big bad boys," baseball marketing was pitched toward the harmless and the endearing. Logically enough, teams soon began using their oversized morphs the way local television stations used weathermen: as cheerful company representatives at civic functions.

THE NEW
COMPULSIVENESS

Getting Involved

T he players who have drawn fans to the ballpark haven't always been the ones who have most animated the grandstand. If sluggers and pitchers have dominated baseball history, it has been the speedsters who have more regularly involved fans as the 26th player. As far back as the nineteenth century, in the era of rabbits King Kelly and Billy Hamilton, a single or walk stirred spectators to shout mass encouragement for a steal of second, in the process unnerving the pitcher and agitating the infield defenders. The 1911 Giants established two records—for team steals in a season (347) and for grandstand volume. The last-place 1912 Yankees didn't have much else to shout about, but they woke up their fans whenever they advanced a runner as far as third base—in position to set the record for thefts of home (18). Jackie Robinson depended on the grandstand reaction for his intimidating tactics—not only at Ebbets Field, but through the apprehensive mutterings of fans in other NL parks as well. Like the 1911 Giants, the 1959 White Sox capitalized mightily on vocal fan involvement.

As owner Bill Veeck once said of his Go-Go Sox, "never did a team make less use of the lively ball." A classic Chicago rally consisted of leadoff man Luis Aparicio drawing a walk and then stealing second, number two batter Nellie Fox grounding out to advance Aparicio to third, and Jim Landis hitting a sacrifice fly for the one and only run the team's superior pitchers were expected to defend. Absurdity was reached with the punchless club on April 22, 1959, when it scored 11 runs in one inning against Kansas City on the strength of 10 walks, a hit batsman, three Athletics errors, and a lone single by outfielder Johnny Callison. As ludicrous as such an offense might have appeared on paper, however, the Go-Go Sox drew a franchise-high 1,423,144 fans who, when they weren't chorusing Aparicio on into another of his league-leading steals (56), were singing along with Captain Stubby and the Buccaneers to "Let's Go Go Go White Sox." Their payoff was a first-place finish, 5 games ahead of the Indians and 15 ahead of the powerhouse Yankees.

In the sixties and early seventies, while lack of offense was being blamed for diminished crowds around both leagues, two clubs not having gate problems were the Dodgers with Maury Wills and the Cardinals with Lou Brock. By that time, the running game had also become a focus of television coverage through the split screen, enabling the viewer to watch the prancings around first base and the swings at home plate at the same time. Television also had a lot to do with the hoopla around a handful of pitchers between the mid-seventies and mid-eighties. Ever-sharper closeups and mikings of glowering, sweating, grunting hurlers gave them a dramatic physical immediacy that the coiled but cool batter making four or five spot appearances didn't always project. Among those who galvanized attention in the period were Mark Fidrych, Fernando Valenzuela, Nolan Ryan, and Dwight Gooden. Although masterly from an athletic point of view, they also brought *shtick* to their game that gave them the sport's equivalent of the highest possible Q-rating.

Fidrych was as much a shooting star as baseball has ever seen. A nonroster player with the Tigers in 1976, he didn't start a game until five weeks into the season, but thereafter went on to mesmerize Detroit and the rest of the country with both his skills (19 wins and a 2.34 ERA earning him Rookie of the Year honors) and idiosyncrasies. The Bird (so-called for a caricatural resemblance to Big Bird of *Sesame Street*) talked to the ball, got down on his hands and knees to landscape the pitching mound, refused to use a ball that had been knocked for a base hit because it emitted "bad karma," and ran over to shake hands with infielders who had made difficult plays. Aside from attracting regular attention from the Game of the Week for his routines, Fidrych contributed critically to coffers around the AL: In his 29 starts at home and on the road, he drew more than 900,000 fans, with his 18 home appearances accounting for more than 40 percent of the Tiger Stadium gate. The Angels counted on him so much as an attraction that they organized an autograph day in Anaheim during a visit by the Tigers. But the phenomenon ended as quickly as it began when Fidrych tore up his right knee, then developed shoulder tendinitis the following year. He won only 10 more games before quitting in 1980.

Valenzuela's impact extended beyond national borders, to Mexico and other Latin American countries. Although there had been numerous Hispanic stars before him, the Dodger lefthander broke through marketing's glass ceiling over Latins with the "Fernandomania" that erupted on both sides of the U.S.-Mexican border with his every start. He also broke through a good 20 years of antagonism between the Los Angeles franchise and local Chicanos following the mass evictions at Chavez Ravine so the team could build the Taj O'Malley.

Valenzuela captured attention initially for a fireplug physique and an unorthodox delivery in which he glanced skyward while in his windup. On Opening Day in 1981, he was drafted as an emergency starter, going on to shut out the Astros. He then won seven more games in a row, four of them also blankings. His overall record of 13–7 with eight shutouts for the strike-shortened season gained him both Rookie of the Year and Cy Young honors. His starts caused millions of Mexican radio listeners and TV viewers to tune in to Los Angeles's Spanish-language networks and millions of Anglos across the U.S. to get into the habit of watching him on national television. In Mexico, his popularity even spawned a comic strip.

At an age that always remained hidden (official records made the highly dubious claim that he was born in 1960), the southpaw took the mound for 255 consecutive starts, not missing a turn until July 1988. There was little he didn't accomplish (20 wins, a no-hitter, a Silver Bat for best-hitting pitcher, a Gold Glove for best-fielding pitcher) before arm injuries began to wear him down. For some years, he drifted back and forth between the Mexican League and various big-league clubs. His last big moment in a major league uniform came on August 16, 1996, when the Padres tabbed him to start the first big-league game ever played in Mexico, at Monterrey, and he defeated the Mets.

The single biggest pitching lure toward the end of the century was the strikeout. On June 17, 1978, Yankee left-hander Ron Guidry sparked the habit of rhythmic grandstand applause at a two-strike count on his way to fanning 18 Angels. Thousands more fans showed up for Ryan's every start on the chance that he would add to what eventually became his career-best 5,714 strikeouts, not to mention the possibility that he would hurl another no-hitter (the last of a record seven being fashioned for Texas in 1991 at the ripe age of 44). Gooden's magnetism was concentrated in the mid-eighties for the Mets, when his power and tormenting curve gave him all the strike-out and many of the victory standards for a rookie and a teenager. In 1985 and 1986, he was so dominant that Las Vegas bookmakers would accept only game bets against him. Before gradually succumbing to drug and injury problems, the right-hander also inspired the "K Corner" at Shea Stadium—the start of the fan practice of posting cards numbering a pitcher's strikeouts during a game.

While not as influential at the ticket window, relief pitchers with set routines also increased the visibility of teams in the period. The Cardinals didn't win a division title in the early seventies, but they had the country's most familiar closer in Al Hrabosky. By his own admission, Hrabosky sought "standing boos" from opposition fans by standing at the back of the mound in apparent meditation for a few seconds, then pounding his glove, charging up to the slab, and firing fastballs. The Mad Hungarian, as he was marketed by the Cardinal press department, also shared with Goose Gossage and other contemporary relievers a Fu Manchu mustache aimed at giving him even more of a menacing look. (Conversely, it was the lack of such *shtick* that appeared to work against subsequent recognition for the most dominant closer of the period, Bruce Sutter.)

In helping to popularize the Fidryches and Hraboskys beyond their immediate markets, television made them the pitching equivalents of the Ralph Kiners and Frank Howards, but on a national level. There had been colorful pitchers for mediocre teams before; there had been TV-promoted aces on championship clubs before; but the national coverage given The Bird and his analogs encouraged even New York and Los Angeles fans to watch Detroit and Kansas City games without any particular interest in the clubs surrounding the pitchers. The assumption of all concerned was that the star was the story.

Seeing Rose

No player in recent decades has brought out the enormous gap between fan and official attitudes toward baseball more definitively than Pete Rose. The question of how a player's off-field activities should affect his diamond achievements has been merely one aspect of the question.

Rose had three major claims on national attention in the seventies and eighties—his 1978 pursuit of Joe DiMaggio's 56-game hitting streak, his 1985 chase after Ty Cobb's all-time hit record, and his 1989 lifetime suspension for gambling. He was Roger Maris, Hank Aaron, and Joe Jackson rolled into one, but with none of the stage anxieties of the first, the hovering threats over the head of the second, or the tentative public demeanor of the third. Even before taking on DiMaggio and Cobb, the versatile infielder-outfielder was a lightning rod for fan passions. The pageboy haircut framing a wrestler's mug, his trademark belly-flops into bases, and his incessant demonstrations of being Charlie Hustle made him the darling of his native Cincinnati and the bane of opposition grandstands during the Big Red Machine era.

The worst fallout from his rugged style among Rose haters occurred during the 1973 NLCS, when a hard slide into second base precipitated punches with Met shortstop Bud Harrelson and then mass disorder at Shea Stadium. Only when New York players begged fans to control themselves did Cincinnati lose a fleeting hope of winning a critical game by forfeit. On the other hand, Riverfront Stadium supported him even when he tore into teammates in the interests of getting a hefty pay increase out of the Reds. In 1977, he publicly scoffed at the idea that shortstop Dave Concepcion and outfielders George Foster and Ken Griffey should be worth the money he was getting from the club. What would have been taken as selfishness in other players erupted into a campaign of letters and phone calls demanding that the Reds give Rose a bigger contract before he walked off as a free agent.

The pact that was all but forced on the front office kept Rose in a Cincinnati uniform for his 1978 attempt at surpassing the DiMaggio record. After two weeks of building suspense and attendances around the league, he had to settle for tying Willie Keeler's NL mark of 44 games—and, again, not all that graciously, accusing Atlanta's pitchers of lacking the nerve to challenge him while keeping him hitless. The following year, the Reds made it clear that no amount of mail or telephone calls would help them find more money, so Rose walked off as a free agent to the Phillies. Philadelphia immediately joined Cincinnati in perceiving its new acquisition as "brash" rather than obnoxious. The first payoff came in 1980, when Rose proved to be the one of the sparkplugs for the only world championship ever won by the Phillies. All of baseball breathed a sigh of relief the following year on August 10, 1981, when 60,561 fans wedged their way into Veterans Stadium to see him pass Stan Musial for the most career hits by an NL player. The game was the first to be played after the 50-day players' strike that year and put to rest boardroom apprehensions that fans would carry through on threats to boycott ballparks because of the walkout.

It was back in Cincinnati as a playing manager in 1985 that Rose bore down on Cobb. And down to the finish line, he found himself facing the same question that had confronted Aaron eleven years earlier—

whether or not to save the record-breaker for a home crowd. But there were two differences from the home run quest: Rose himself made out the lineup cards, and he had as much of a reputation as a win-at-any-cost player as he did as a hit machine. With the Reds in Chicago on September 8 and Rose still two hits short of Cobb, the 44-year-old switch-hitting manager had the perfect out to remain on the bench and save his effort for a subsequent series against San Diego in Cincinnati: He had fallen off seriously enough as a right-handed batter to bench himself against southpaws, and lefty Steve Trout was scheduled to pitch for the Cubs. But at the last minute, Chicago substituted righthander Reggie Patterson for Trout, and Rose immediately inserted himself into the lineup. Before a capacity Wrigley Field crowd, he again emulated Aaron—getting two hits to tie the record, but saving for his home field the tie-breaker. Hit number 4,192 (of an eventual 4,256) came before a delirious crowd at Riverfront Stadium off Eric Show of the Padres on September 11.

Through all his field and self-promotion exploits, Rose had been held up as the model baseball player; among those contributing a shoulder to the lifting was A. Bartlett Giamatti, who had moved from the presidency of Yale to that of the National League before being sworn in as commissioner in April 1989. But hardly had Giamatti taken his place next to Kenesaw Landis, Ford Frick, and William Eckert than he disclosed that his office was looking into reports that Rose had been betting on baseball games and was in hock to gamblers for an estimated $500,000. What followed was a circus: months of accumulating evidence about Rose's addiction to betting on sports events, independent press investigations linking him to shadowy figures around the country, and his own repeated denials that he had ever wagered on baseball. Then, finally, with a suit challenging Giamatti's authority still bouncing around from courtroom to courtroom, Rose announced on August 24 that he had thought it over and would abide by the commissioner's decision to ban him permanently from baseball.

Although a behind-doors agreement between the sides made no explicit mention of Rose's alleged betting on baseball, Giamatti couldn't even get through his first subsequent press conference without charging that the manager had indeed been wagering on games, including some involving the Reds. For his part, Rose continued issuing denials, as well as spurning suggestions that his monumental losses to bookmakers (calculated in the millions) indicated an addiction. His public image didn't improve when, barely a week after the ban arrangement, Giamatti succumbed to a heart attack, prompting glib charges that the chain-smoking commissioner had been done in by his one-time hero—a diagnosis left to ripple in the breeze by Giamatti's successor and keeper of the flame, Fay Vincent. And even his keenest supporters in Cincinnati were taken aback when Rose, desperate for money, stepped up his appearances at card shows to sell his autograph at inflated prices and became a regular on home shopping networks to peddle the trophies and memorabilia he had accumulated over the years. Charlie Hustle suddenly looked too much like Charlie Hustler.

In 1990, a federal court found Rose guilty of tax evasion and sentenced him to several months' imprisonment. On top of that, the committee charged with overseeing Cooperstown election procedures ruled that his ban from the game also made him ineligible for consideration as a member of the Hall of Fame. The decision—based on stipulations about the moral character of candidates—made no mention of the fact that the museum was already honoring racists like Cap Anson and Ty Cobb, alcoholics like Grover Cleveland Alexander and Rabbit Maranville, and numerous others who would have come up as short of the nebulous standard as Rose did. Ironically, however, it was also Cooperstown's attempt at definitiveness that incited wide-ranging debate over the extent to which off-field activities should weigh on career accomplishments. Making allowances for the jiggery-pokery involved in phrasing public opinion poll questions, popular sentiment was very clear: In survey after survey, fans across the country declared by large margins that whatever Rose had done or not done off the field, it should not affect his right to Hall of Fame membership. The consensus was dramatized at the 2000 All-Star Game when, to the tremendous discomfort of Commissioner Bud Selig, Rose had to be honored along with other members of the so-called All-Century Team selected by fans from coast to coast; indeed, except for guest of honor Ted Williams, he received the loudest ovation from Fenway Park spectators. As one sportswriter would put it a couple of years later concerning the ongoing controversy: "Keep him out, and you're going against the will of the people, expressed repeatedly in opinion polls and, most persuasively, with their thunderous applause every time Rose is allowed to make a sanctioned public appearance."

As in the aftermath of the Black Sox revelations, fans simply refused to be as scandalized as baseball officials. And for the most part, their response wasn't based on any deep study of the Giamatti probe that Bill James and other commentators adjudged "grotesque." It didn't have to be. Instead, there was the fact that none of the charges collected by Giamatti investigator John Dowd pertained to Rose's playing days; what fans had paid to see during his years as a leadoff batter for Cincinnati, Philadelphia, and (briefly) Montreal had been delivered. Not even insinuations that he had also bet against the Reds while managing them—in themselves leaks of a highly suspicious kind—went so far as to accuse him of rigging games to protect his money. No less important, the charges against Rose weren't that he had participated in any illegal gambling, but that he had violated 60-year-old baseball strictures against gambling—an in-house statute that set up both the commissioner's office and the Hall of Fame as superior vigilantes of penal order and social custom. As a corporate norm within General Electric or Wendy's, this might have passed without much comment until the first lawsuit by an aggrieved employee, but major-league baseball was a public entertainment dependent on the witness and memory of its spectators. Institutional morality did not blithely trump statistical history, not with the former so relative (see Anson and Cobb) and the latter so firmly set down in black and white. As much as the game had always been a balancing act between the pragmatism of its administration and the fictionality of its diamond dramas, there was also the expectation that the sport's organizational structure would respect its diamond inventions and the inventions achieve some rational materiality through the conclusiveness of their numbers.

Through the first years of the new millennium, prior to Rose's admission in a book that he had bet on games, the hits King and Selig danced back and forth over reinstatement conditions the way the United States and North Vietnam had once argued over the shape of their tables at the 1972 Paris peace talks. "Character" discussions gradually took on an evangelical tone. If Giamatti and Vincent had addressed Rose within the atmosphere of a star chamber, Selig's administration seemed more intent on convening a nationally televised Gamblers Anonymous meeting at which Rose would tell everyone he was Pete and then admit his failings not only when it came to Arizona mule races and Malaysian soccer matches, but also to 1988 Pirate-Reds games. But not even this approach significantly altered public perceptions, nor for that matter did numerous television interviews with Rose in which he looked and acted like he had gone from a pageboy wrestler to a WWF flack. Even his belated admission of having bet on baseball came with a self-serving whine that maybe he would have benefited from a Gamblers Anonymous structure during his managing days. *What* character was the all?

Few fans in Cincinnati or anywhere else would have said "likeable" if asked to list Rose's most prominent virtues; what he had been perceived as more than anything else was a *winner*. The highest of all baseball reputations, the winner didn't have to be a batting champion or a 20-victory pitcher; sometimes he could be a utility player—the Jack Wardens or Joan Cusacks of the situation whose appearances stirred energies around them, driving toward more than individual accomplishment goals. The supreme winner, though, *was* a batting champion or dominant pitcher, employing his own specially honed skills as a catalyst for leading others into exploiting their own to the fullest. The winner never took time off on the field, never allowed teammates to coast. It was as this breed of player that Rose, for instance, hadn't hesitated to jeopardize the career of friend Ray Fosse by slamming brutally into the catcher to score an exhibition run in the 1970 All-Star Game. That he was (depending on one's ideology) an addict, chump, or moral blight off the field didn't change that appreciation from the grandstand.

Rose wasn't the only one accepted for having different zodiac signs on and off the diamond. In 1985, for example, immediately after testifying in court to drug use earlier in his career, Mets first baseman Keith Hernandez, then the motor in the team's revival, was given a standing ovation at Shea Stadium, enraging media moralists. In fact, a stronger argument could have been made for the influence of Hernandez's cocaine habit on his playing than for the effects of Rose's gambling. But no matter how much a loser Hernandez might have been thought of for having once done a lot of sniffing in his hotel room, he too had established his credentials as a winner on the field, and that was where the grandstand judgments were centered. Similarly, in 1987, Dwight Gooden received a warm welcome back to Shea Stadium after going through rehab for cocaine use. Conversely, fans in Pittsburgh and Kansas City hurled constant abuse at local team players caught up in other drug investigations of the time, forcing releases, trades, or other forms of departure. While some press organs found comfort in thinking of this reaction as an assertion of traditional moral rectitude, it also so happened that the players targeted didn't have the field leadership reputations as "winners" that Rose, Hernandez, and Gooden had.

It might have been true, as Giamatti had pontificated in August 1989, that "no individual is superior to the game," but it was equally true that no individual institutional regulation was superior to the general values and priorities promoted for generations by that same institution.

Hexes and Complexes

I n the summer of 1949, Charley Lupica decided that the Indians needed some help if they were to repeat as pennant winners. His contribution was to build a 60-foot-high flagpole platform above his delicatessen, where he perched for 117 days with the announced resolve of coming down only when Cleveland moved into first place or was mathematically eliminated from the AL race. In the end, he had to settle for the second option, but with the consolation that Bill Veeck, never one to ignore a promotional occasion, sent a truck out to the flagpole and packed it up to take it to Municipal Stadium. Only with 34,000 people on hand to watch the descent did Veeck allow Lupica, who had even missed the birth of a son during his vigil, to climb down into applause and prizes.

Losing has never come easy to the baseball fan. Identification with a team has led him to superstititions, rituals, even appeals to the arcane arts for invoking success or averting failure. "All baseball fans believe in miracles," as John Updike has said. "The question is, how many do you believe in?" The only answer, of course, is "as many as are needed." The physical, the mental, and the behavioral all become raw materials in the baseball fan's Cana. It can become essential to the fate of his club that he sit with his left leg crossed over the right one and not vice versa, that he tell himself his favorite player will strike out so he can in fact hit a home run, that he not take his second bite of a hot dog until the second pitch has been delivered. It can go without saying that his team's rally was thwarted because once again the loudmouth across the hall was yelling at his kids or an airliner flew over the city. What could be more obvious than that his team won because he gave a dollar to a panhandler or his subway seat to an old woman on the way to the ballpark? Winning is the reward for nimble thoughts, obedient behavior, and solid character.

But sometimes not even the strongest personal commitment helps, and explanations have to be found for losing. Fortunately for the desolated fan, the historical record has furnished some. It was on January 3, 1920, for instance, that Boston announced the sale of Babe Ruth to the Yankees, invoking that particular curse. And it was on October 6, 1945, at the fourth game of the Chicago-Detroit World Series, that Wrigley Field ushers refused admittance to tavern owner William Sianis's reeking goat Billy, bringing on the saloonkeeper's potent malediction that the Cubs never again take the field in late October. Following those two events, it was merely a question of choosing one's poison. Who were better off—Boston fans, because at least their team got into a few World Series that they proceeded to lose in excruciating ways; or Chicago fans, because they have never again had the opportunity to lose a World Series, excruciatingly or any other way?

It didn't really matter. The important thing, according to baseball's rich cultural tradition in losing, was that failure stem from the intercession of unnatural forces. While not as celebrated as their Red Sox and Cub counterparts, White Sox fans have been able to attribute their woes to the Cissell Curse—invoking a once-promising infielder of the late twenties who drank away his career and then spent years haunting Comiskey Park as an alcoholic laborer before dying of malnutrition at the age of 45. Before their 2002 championship, Angel fans had detected the supernatural in the decades of career-ending injuries and deaths that had ravaged the team; the more ardent in Houston still discern that kind of bloody hand in the sky when the Astros open the roof of Minute Maid Park.

Such curses are so self-evident that they have been visible to more than star-crossed fans. In 1900, for instance, it was that Presbyterian minister glimpsing Jesus Christ as the manager of the injury-plagued Pirates in retribution for playing on Sundays. Ninety years later, it was outfielder Brett Butler expressing relief to be leaving the Giants for the Dodgers because San Francisco would never win a championship as long as the city was so tolerant of homosexuality and other sins of the flesh. Of more recent vintage, and totally indiscriminate toward the fans it affects, has been the Money Curse.

Prior to the advent of free agency and the publication of money numbers as another measure of performance, it wasn't easy for fans to identify the opposite of a Pete Rose—the *losing* player. There might have been a lot of inadequate big leaguers who should have never been where they were, but that wasn't quite the same thing; the merely untalented wouldn't have been allowed to figure too often in the kind of clutch situations determining a true loser's soul. Part of what made losers harder to pinpoint were the normal percentages defining base-ball success (three hits in ten plate appearances, winning only half of 35 starts); such percentages made individual failure more likely than remarkable. Even that venerable threnody to diamond despair, Ernest Thayer's "Casey at the Bat," drew unashamed claims from marginal players that they were the inspiration for the poem; one of them, nineteenth-century Phillies pitcher Dan Casey, was still giving radio interviews on the eve of World War II trying to make a place for himself in the sport's grayest lore. When a player did not produce at a critical moment, such as Fred Merkle in detouring before touching second base in 1908 or Fred Snodgrass in dropping a fly ball in the 1912 World Series, he might have been guilty of a "boner" or a "$30,000 muff," but the plays were not sewn into his character the way that, say, Joe Morgan's twilight-year roamings around so-so teams that ended up in contention or in postseason play stamped him as an innate winner.

For most of baseball history, the primary grandstand perception of a losing player wasn't of one who didn't succeed, but rather of one who sought to dodge the challenge or was intimidated by it before even taking the field. New York baseball alone has provided numerous cases in point. Warren Spahn might have won more games than any other lefthander, but his aversion to pitching against the predominantly righthanded Boys of Summer Dodgers did not have anybody in Brooklyn rushing to submit his candidacy to Cooperstown. Conversely, Don Newcombe dominated the NL for the Dodgers in the fifties, but Brooklyn fans reached for the Suicide Hotline whenever he trudged out to face the Yankees in the World Series. More than one Met spoke of the "deer-in-the-headlights" look of Boston reliever Calvin Schiraldi, a former Met happy to have left New York, before he helped to blow the last two games of the 1986 World Series for the Red Sox. And in a classic instance of self-fulfilling prophecy, the local media have been so dedicated to sculpting the ideal "New York player" in recent decades that entire squads of impressionable all-stars have joined the Yankees and Mets, answered questions hourly about how cowed they were by playing in the city, suffered some kind of reversal on the diamond, then greased their slide by deciding yes, it absolutely was the fault of the Empire State Building.

With the instant evaluations encouraged by free agency, however, the grandstand definition of the losing player came much closer to equating a flawed nature with mere lack of field success. Only greed's slave would have struck out with the bases loaded or yielded that grandslam home run. Who else but that overpaid wretch would have stolen bases only for building up his personal statistics, hit home runs only in one-sided games, and thrown seven-hitters only against clubs playing below .500? The new loser isn't intimidated by anything (except the New York media); he just fails to deliver when it counts (often defined as being when he doesn't deliver). Admittedly, it sometimes isn't even his fault. It's the curse of the money, the money, and the money—what anybody in his place would grovel after. But how can a lot of losing millionaires *not* add up to a losing team?

There are, of course, several ways for a team to lose and continue to lose over an extended period of years. Hypothetically, a franchise like Boston could deal not only Babe Ruth, but other future Hall of Famers like Waite Hoyt and Red Ruffing, plus a slew of all-stars, to the Yankees; could ignore black players more adamantly than any other team in either league; could create a clubhouse atmosphere for the sovereign rule of superstars; could have a shortstop (Johnny Pesky) hesitate on a relay throw in the seventh game of a World Series, have a rookie with merely three big-league decisions (Jim Burton) the only bullpen help available in the ninth inning of another seventh game, and have a hobbled first baseman (Bill Buckner) on the field one out away from a championship in a sixth game; could drive away stars by forgetting to mail them their contracts (Carlton Fisk, Fred Lynn) or disparaging them in public (Roger Clemens, Mo Vaughn); and could become so mesmerized by the shape of its home field that it forgets to have a player who knows how to run or win on the road. For the purposes of conjecture, a franchise like the Cubs might overlook that the Wrigley Field winds blow in as much as out during an average season; might believe post-1945 players like the summer sun beating down on them so much that they don't even need the protection of the old-time late afternoon starting times for relentless day games; and might have no use for such players as Lou Brock, Bruce Sutter, Rafael Palmiero, and Greg Maddux. Also in the area of the purely speculative, the owners and general managers of every team in both leagues might be more obsessed about how much money they spend for free agents than about how, and for exactly whom, they spend it.

But none of these scenarios would leave much room for curses, jinxes, or complexes. They would propose incompetence and bad scouting instead of ineffability and bad karma. They would intimate that, given the right combination of cut-rate management and one-dimensional players, losing franchises don't have expiration dates on them any more than winning ones do (or, in the words of one of their managers, Jim Riggleman, "the Cubs have just had a bad century"). They would imply that, for all the novelists given to associating the Red Sox with *War and Peace* and for all the political commentators prone to viewing the Cubs as another bewildering national tax, the fans most realistic about losing have been those in Philadelphia, with their philosophy of booing everybody and everything because *somebody* is responsible. Lastly, such scenarios would compromise the mythology fans have developed about themselves—ardent and passionate in the face of preordained failure, exasperated little people hemmed in by the forces of Mo Vaughn's waistline, a public sometimes willing to be as satisfied by its expectations as by their fulfillment. Most of all, in defeat, fans have to be winners too.

Gambling Fantasies

However isolated and personal an addiction it was meant to appear, the Pete Rose controversy once again linked baseball to gambling. The fact was that, although there weren't all that many scandalous headlines in the second half of the twentieth century, the lifelong romance between the two activities had never flagged, had actually even blossomed, making the fan as prone to putting his money as a hot dog where his mouth was. Residents of Los Angeles and San Francisco weren't the only ones happy to welcome the Dodgers and Giants after the 1957 season; with the Pacific time zone suddenly in play, sports books in Las Vegas and elsewhere had reason for increasing their daily business hours. The huge media attention given to the record quests by Rose, Roger Maris, and Hank Aaron spawned all kinds of fan bets on exact dates, while the more inventive houses were open to unders-and-overs on game or season strikeouts by the Ryans and Goodens. Divisional play offered another betting category to go along with the astronomically rising millions wagered annually on pennant winners and World Series victors. In short, there was sideline action for the sport's every structural move or attempt to address its own history. And that was without counting baseball's own new goal (even as it was belaboring the Rose story) of getting fans more interested in blackjack and crap games.

By the new century, a dozen clubs had signed sponsorship or advertising agreements with casinos covering both broadcasting and ballpark billboards. Connecticut's Foxwoods and Mohegan Sun reservations were regular sponsors of the Mets, Yankees, and Red Sox. For the Dodgers, it was the Las Vegas Convention and Visitors Authority. The Padres plastered all their publications and advertising with promos for the Syucan tribal casino. No sooner had the Expos been taken over by the other 29 clubs than their English-language radio broadcasts were presented by the Golden Palace cyber-casino. Asked how his team could justify taking sponsorship money from Harrah's Cherokee Casino in light of the sport's long history of holier-than-thou pronouncements about gambling, Braves corporate sales director Jim Allen said simply: "Obviously, we're looking for revenues from wherever we can possibly get them."

Fans did not need to go on-line to the Golden Palace to find gambling action. Millions of them had already discovered another way of combining baseball with betting by joining rotisserie leagues. The idea originated with magazine writer-editor Daniel Okrent in November 1979, when he sketched out a parlor game during a flight to Austin. After unsuccessfully trying to interest Texas acquaintances in his fantasy concept, he brought it up again with fellow editors at a lunch in a Manhattan French restaurant. With the restaurant (La Rotisserie) providing the name for its undertaking, the group drafted competitive imaginary teams whose fortunes were determined by the combined real statistics of the players chosen. The money bid on individual players during the drafting phase went into a general pot that paid off winners in various categories at the end of the season. Within a few years, rotisserie baseball and its numerous variations had generated a multimillion-dollar business in fantasy guides, on-line statistic-gathering services, and contests. Weekly sports publications and daily newspapers began to feature columnists who wrote on the subject in the tone of half-sportswriter, half-lottery numbers analyst. Football, basketball, and hockey fans adapted the game to their own sports. Baseball team offices came under siege from rotisserie participants wanting to know the smallest details about some player's injury or status in the lineup to gauge the effects on their living-room rosters. Callers to radio talk shows spewed out hallucinatory trade proposals aimed more at improving their fantasy team than the one recognized by the National or American league. Club officials known to belong to their own after-hours rotisserie circles offered a big target for sportswriters who mocked their bad moves as being the result of too much fantasy and not enough reality.

Insofar as it allowed players to create their own fictional competition, rotisserie baseball was an extension of the board and dice games that have been around since the nineteenth century. But whereas in the earlier amusements players had doped out strategies just as field managers might have, the fantasy variations cast them in the role of owners and general managers—trading, acquiring, or dropping major leaguers from their rosters as they became available or expendable. As a pastime, it was also usually far more time-consuming than the old activities. Depending on the specific rules of the group, participants could trade with one another once a month, once a week, or incessantly, leading in the most manic cases to a substitute for life more than a hobby for leisure hours. Even those not given to daily negotiations with other league members pored over box scores and statistics with the assiduousness of Talmudic scholars.

One of the consequences of absorption in a rotisserie league was a grandstand rooting interest that went beyond, and sometimes clashed with, traditional team loyalties. The Red Sox fan normally eager for a Nomar Garciaparra home run found himself tempted to wish for the blast to be delayed until the following day if his fantasy club included the Toronto pitcher facing the Boston shortstop. If his league had special bonus payoffs for multiple home runs in a game, the Giants fan was not as exultant as his Pac Bell neighbors if Barry Bonds reached McCovey Cove (merely) once. Vice versa, he wasn't as crushed as his neighbors if the Rockies pulverized his Giants, in good part because of the three home runs hit by *his* player, Todd Helton. In fact, it became a common complaint of people dropping out of fantasy leagues that they had stopped "enjoying" games because of such ambivalent feelings.

Fantasy baseball's highlighting of individual player rather than major-league team achievements amounted to the fan's side of the coin in the free agency era. The same people who couldn't gripe enough about big leaguers not showing loyalty to a club were themselves parked in front of ESPN's *Baseball Tonight* as interested in the latest save by a Devil Rays reliever as in whether or not their Twins had won. It was a market that ESPN, Fox, and other cable networks exploited to the full with separate home-run lists for the day or other highlights that came close to reducing games to balls that went over the wall or to other details of importance to rotisserie participants. To say the least, none of this was bad for cable television's profitability or for its leverage with major-league baseball in working out new broadcasting contracts.

More generally, the instant gratifications promised by fantasy baseball heightened the fan's sense of involvement—if not empowerment—in the baseball medium. The financial investment in a rotisserie club brought him much closer to the racetrack bettor for whom emotional and imaginative participation in an outcome had never been sufficient. Commissioner Selig and baseball owners clearly agreed. The days when campaigns against gambling presences in the ballpark had supposedly been undertaken in the interests of rescuing the fan from his lowest instincts were long gone. With the endorsement of Selig's office and every club in both leagues, the embrace of a cyber-casino by the industry-owned Montreal Expos sent out a clear signal that compulsiveness was good—at least so long as it increased major-league revenues.

By the Numbers

Many rotisserie-league players had their mental convolutions abetted by a growing abstruseness in the statistical measurement of field performance. Because of some obscure numerical dynamic revealed by a rotisserie columnist, the fantasy player might be compelled at the last minute to choose Pitcher B instead of the more ostensibly logical Pitcher A within his betting pool. More often than not, the smoking statistic could be traced back to satellite fan organizations and individual researchers rather than to league offices (usually reluctant to review any findings that would contradict accepted wisdom). In the best cases, these researchers could illuminate, if not always redress, statistical injustices attached to baseball history (for example, the 1910 AL batting race between Ty Cobb and Nap Lajoie). In the worst cases, the massaging of numbers didn't stop at carrying on the scientification of the sport that had been under way since Henry Chadwick's day, but ran on to ludicrous pretensions to turning the study of Rickey Henderson's on-base percentage into a branch of higher mathematics. In all cases, deepening abstractions about the game's past and present made for callow solemnities even as the practicing analysts were insisting that they were interested only in the simple and the entertaining. The ethereality also favored a more widely accepted relativity about the statistics themselves, this in turn gnawing at one of the sport's traditional foundations.

Until the thirties, baseball's statistical research had largely consisted of compiling numbers on what players had or had not done. Then, deciding individual player production should have been as receptive to sophisticated projection as chewing gum marketing, Phil Wrigley set his company statisticans loose on the Cubs for determining the probabilities of success in given game situations (left-handed batters against southpaw pitchers, hitters at bat with the bases loaded, and the like). The Chicago club's findings ended up wadded in tinfoil, but the Wrigley initiative was not lost on Branch Rickey. In 1947, the same year in which he brought Jackie Robinson to the major leagues, Rickey also hired Allan Roth as the game's first full-time statistician. With the hiring of Roth, Red Barber and other Brooklyn announcers could routinely inform listeners in numerical detail about Duke Snider's feeble career against Bill Henry and Carl Furillo's penchant for slumping in June. While those paying close attention might not have needed the statistical verification, the numbers relieved the fan of doubts of some impressionistic bias, as well as strengthened his managerial convictions on the couch about when a pinch-hitter was needed.

In 1951, A. S. Barnes of New York issued *The Official Encyclopedia of Baseball*. Edited by Hy Turkin and S. C. Thompson, it was a major foray into both the statistics of the game and into the fan's perception of the sport as an historical institution heavily reliant on numbers (however inaccurate some of them might have been). The Turkin-Thompson collaboration wasn't a newspaper or a magazine or an annual guide. It wasn't even merely a book. It was an *encyclopedia*, with all the implicit authoritativeness of such a reference work. Over ten revised editions until 1979, by which time it had been superseded by Macmillan's *Baseball Encyclopedia,* it made the fan's possession of numbers in compact form a basic feature of the knowledgeable baseball experience. When Casey Stengel finished off one of his windy tales with the assurance to listeners that "you can look it up," they knew where to start.

Since 1971, the chief fan marketplace for all things statistical has been the Society for American Baseball Research (SABR). At an August meeting in Cooperstown that year, 16 researchers pledged themselves to "foster study of baseball as a significant social and athletic institution." By 2004, the organization had grown to 7,000 members in the United States and abroad; had standing committees on every conceivable aspect of the game (stadiums, nineteenth-century baseball, the minor leagues, and so on); was able to count on guest appearances from noted baseball figures (some of them members) for its various regional meetings and annual national convention; and published various periodicals and newsletters concerning its research findings and the doings of those who had done the finding.

Aside from having baseball at or near the center of their world, SABR members were not a particularly homogeneous bunch. Some simply liked the community of interests at its most general level, whether in the sheer identification of belonging to the organization, the opportunity to socialize with similars at periodic meetings, or the chance to read the group's publications. Some of the more active members had a vehicle for passions that sometimes seemed to speed right through trivia and drivia to obsession; for instance, a profile of a nineteenth-century pitcher who was the first to win a 1-0 game on his own home run or one on a third-string Washington catcher of the sixties who was "underrated" despite batting merely .196 over seven seasons. More common was SABR's predeliction, familiar to any expanding organization, for giving attention at its meetings and in its periodicals to people who had earned it not because they had been strikingly skilled at what they had done but simply because, by doing it at all, they had helped justify the group's orbit of interest; for example, the .235 Braves shortstop from the seventies as an article subject because he embodied .235 Braves shortstops from the seventies.

At least for outsiders, though, SABR was to become primarily identified with mathematical formulas (so-called *sabermetrics*) intended to convey fresh standards for measuring the efficiency of players and teams. The formulations gained added notoriety around the turn of the century when such decision-makers of the game as Oakland general manager Billy Beane and his Boston equivalent Theo Epstein were quoted as embracing them to one degree or another. One of Epstein's first moves after joining the Red Sox in 2002 was to hire sabermetrics pioneer Bill James as an assistant.

The fan confronting sabermetrics for the first time normally had an experience in two acts. The first act was the repeated disclaimers by practitioners that anything unusual was going on. If anything, compared to the statistics that fans were traditionally exposed to, in the words of SABR's Pete Palmer and John Thorn, "simplicity emerges from complexity." For James, sabermetrics was nothing more than "the search for objective knowledge about baseball." In the opinion of another researcher, James Fraser, "the principles behind sabermetrics are simple: find something about baseball that merits examination, collect as much information as possible, examine all the evidence as objectively as possible and then allow others to criticize it."

The second act was sampling some of the simplicity. "For evaluating runs contributed by any batter at any time," according to Palmer and Thorn, "there is no better method than Batting Runs," as expressed by the formula "Batting Run $(.47)1B+(.78)2B+(1.09)3B+(1.40)HR+(.33)BB+HB+(.30)SB-(.60)CS-(.25)(AB-H)-.50(OOB)$." In another article aimed at identifying the game's most effective pinch-hitters, Palmer concluded that the shortest path lay with the formula $\sigma = [(P \times Q)/N]^{.5}$. Why? Because "the binomial theorem tells us that, with a sufficiently large sample, about ⅔ of the values in the distribution will fall within one standard deviation. . . . of the mean, and that about 95 percent of the values will fall within two of the mean. . . ."

As impenetrable as this language might have been to non-adepts, it actually didn't define the sabermetrician perception of a fan's interests as much as the first-act disingenuousness about the "simplicity" to be encountered in such calculations. The mathematically inclined had their pursuits, moviegoers theirs. But just as endless TV cable documentaries on the step-by-step realization of the special effects and computerization tricks involved in the making of *The Matrix: Revolutions* presumed that the technical workings of the industry were as fascinating as the end product delivered to the screen, sabermetricians, for all their regular protestations of being concerned only with what went into scoring runs, presumed a fan given to equating technical interpretations of scoring probabilities with knowledge and enjoyment of the game itself. Tactfully left unsaid (usually) was the sorry alternative: defending the traditional here-take-it-and-shut-up attitude of Major League Baseball and its old numbers for preserving the game's mystique as sport and entertainment.

Whatever importance sabermetrics had as a reformist instrument for computing the achievements of individual players and teams, it was an integral part of a late-twentieth-century trend that threw into question the stability of statistics as a whole as a fan lure. There was in fact little about the game that didn't echo the theme of "you can make anything you want out of numbers." Whereas in years past, in such parks as the Baker Bowl and Ebbets Field, friendly outfield walls had been greeted as a charm of the game, the offensive numbers piled up by Rockie players in Colorado's thin air were simply greeted with suspicion. Winter arbitration meetings pitted player agents citing a client's 20 home runs as the third best for that position in the league and team representatives rebutting that those same 20 home runs were only the tenth best among players wearing his uniform number. The fan in front of the TV set was informed without hesitation that So-and-So had a 1.000 batting average against a given pitcher—based on one plate appearance. Little of this tightened the bonds between the grandstands and the field as intended by Chadwick, even as fans were aware that the scores compiled at Coors Field counted as much as those at Yankee Stadium and that the first baseman they were cheering on was there because he had lost his arbitration battle —or had succeeded the traded one who had won it.

At the same time, there were regular reminders that *not* going by the numbers could be costly in the new statistical climate. The managers who exasperated the bleachers by always playing by the book had never dogeared so many pages; they knew better than anyone that bleacher fans would have been the first to cite the more readily available percentages to them if some unorthodox move backfired. In the seventh game of the 2003 ALCS between the Red Sox and Yankees, Boston manager Grady Little earned himself infamy in New England by not lifting starter Pedro Martinez during an eighth-inning New York rally. When the Yankees went on to tie and later win the game for the pennant, Red Sox fans demanded his head. While the front office that included Theo Epstein and Bill James kept its own counsel for a couple of weeks, Little supplied his own axe for the beheading by defending his decision about Martinez as having been the result of "a hunch." Any fan could have told him that a hunch was not a statistical category.

Noise! Noise! Noise!

I n 1987, National League president A. Bartlett Giamatti warned owners they were driving away their own fans through maintenance and security negligence and with a new mania for filling every ballpark lull with screech-decibel music and spastic images on gigantic DiamondVision screens. Apparently unable, despite his title, to make this point persuasively enough at league meetings, Giamatti told readers of the *Boston Globe*:

> *If you cannot park and be sure you or your car will be safe; or if you are ignored by ushers or unable to find a decent or thug-free restroom; or if you cannot watch a contest free from the constant assault of obscene language or a mindlessly insistent scoreboard, seemingly run by people who dare not let the contest speak for itself; or if your child cannot watch without passively ingesting marijuana clouds; or if there are fights in the stands and on the field or arena of play that subtly and insidiously fuel and feed off each other—then you begin to wonder why you came. As time goes on, the stands increasingly become the private preserve of the roughneck who came in order to drink too much, and for whom the contest is simply an outlet for the aggressive, ultimately anti-social, impulses that physical sports are meant to re-direct into acceptable patterns.*

If that sounded a lot like William Hulbert at the foundation of the National League and Ban Johnson at the launching of the American League, Giamatti added the late-twentieth-century note that technology offered fans an alternative to the ballpark that had not existed before. Because of videos and satellite television, he declared, "the vast majority of the population in America that wants to consume leisure passively . . . will do so at home. . . . There will be very few incentives to go out to the ballpark or hockey rink or basketball arena or football stadium. . . ."

For the most part, Giamatti's warning was dismissed. Stadiums continued to incite fans with scoreboard urgings to make noise during a home-team rally and to saturate between-innings interludes with pointless snatches of pop music and shrill games inviting spectators to guess whether the red car, the blue car, or the yellow car would cross the finish line first. Even ignoring the fact that such scoreboard games encouraged the kind of betting baseball officials usually liked to ascribe to the Prince of Darkness, they introduced the tatty atmosphere of a Tenderloin arcade. The drinking criticism elicited a more textured hypocrisy. Budweiser, the most ubiquitous brewer in baseball circles, sensed enough trouble from sentiments such as Giamatti's to adopt a new public relations campaign around the theme of "responsible drinkers." It also made sure it wasn't caught putting up strong opposition to the introduction of non-alcoholic seating sections in parks or to a policy cutting off beer sales after the seventh inning. At the same time, however, the company leased ever-larger billboard space for reminding fans exactly what beer they should be responsible about drinking. For their part, concessionaires made up for the losses from the seventh inning by boosting prices significantly over the first six innings.

Fans weren't only on the receiving end of the new din. Individually, the loudest booster was Cleveland's John Adams, a telephone-company employee who in 1973 began urging the Indians on with the help of a bass drum. First at Municipal Stadium, then at Jacobs Field, Adams camped out in nosebleed outfield seats banging away relentlessly at the instrument, for which he had to buy a separate seat. The team's official position was that it had no objections to the booming as long as other fans didn't protest; when such protests did occasionally arise, however, the Indians decided Adams had become too much of a good publicity thing, so handled the complaints without demanding an end to the drumming.

Cavernous Olympic Stadium gave fans a way to use noise for making the best out of a bad situation. Even before Montreal's precipitous attendance decline in the late nineties, the more fervid Expos fans on hand for a game enlisted absentees for rally demonstrations by rattling the empty wooden seats around them up and down. For impact on diamond events, though, the echoes of Olympic Stadium were a silent movie compared to the Metrodome. In both the 1987 World Series against the Cardinals and the 1991 games against the Braves, the Twins were aided mightily to championships by shrieking capacity crowds that clamored and waved so-called Homer Hankies from the first to the last Minnesota batter. The club's perfect home record in both Series so angered one hearing expert (who also happened to be a St. Louis fan) that he produced research showing that the noise produced by the Twins fans could not have failed to affect those not accustomed to it (specifically, Cardinals players). According to Bill Clark, a scientist with the Central Institute for the Deaf and Washington University's Department of Otolaryngology, the decibel count at the Metrodome in 1987 rose to 92, while that at Busch Stadium had been 83. "Perceptually, 92 decibels is twice as loud as 83," Clark told a conference.

If there was any positive side to the heightened cacophony, it was that even the hectoring fans seemed satisfied with the vocal rather than the physical. By the same token, there was less reverence for the old taboo about not riling up opposition players. One noted example was Fenway Park's derisive "Dar-ryl! Dar-ryl! Dar-ryl!" chant to New York outfielder Darryl Strawberry in the 1986 World Series after he had managed only one single in his first ten at-bats and displayed some tentative fielding. This proved to be the mold for subsequent razzing around both leagues, including among Mets fans. Many years later, Shea Stadium would still be ringing with such sardonic chants as "Lar-ry! Lar-ry! Lar-ry!" (attempting to exorcise the nemesis of Atlanta's Chipper Jones by using the given name he was known to hate) and "MVP! MVP!" (aimed at Jeromy Burnitz, a highly priced outfielder going through a miserable season for New York).

Piling on players hardly went against the grain. By the end of the century, in fact, there was little about baseball that didn't emphasize the individual player over his team, including media rhapsodies about how the emphasized player was the ultimate team man. Even those not exposed to the finest-spun statistics compiled by the Elias Sports Bureau or the Society for American Baseball Research only had to glance at a scoreboard or a television screen to learn that the latest callup from Iowa had once hit three doubles in a game against Wichita. When batters walked toward the plate, they were accompanied by customized music themes. When fans entered the gate, they were given caps, photographs, collector cards, T-shirts, videos, or bobblehead dolls honoring franchise stars. Reggie Bars for Reggie Jackson in New York inspired similar promotions for Wade Boggs in Boston, Jose Canseco in Oakland, and Henry Rodriguez in Montreal. Weekly network games were soon being interrupted for relays from other contests because somebody was going after an annual record or a career mark, or was thought worthy of bulletin coverage simply because of who he was. It was the rare interview that wasn't pitched as "The Real (Ken Griffey, Jr., Mark McGwire, Randy Johnson, Barry Bonds)"—the assumptions being that the player in question had been coming across as too surly for his own good and that of the sport's publicity machine, that he had deep things to say about himself and the state of the game, and that fans were as breathless to hear them as they were about hearing Jennifer Lopez's marriage plans. In short, for all the movement of players and franchises, teams continued operating like the old movie studios, with publicists as vital as producers and directors for bringing stars before the public.

Not all the surliness emanated from the players. In August 1983, Cub manager Lee Elia exploded against fans who had jeered his club's play throughout an afternoon game, calling them "garbage" and getting off such gems as: "Eighty-five percent of people in this country work, the other fifteen percent come out to Wrigley to boo my players." Elia was fired a couple of days later. For their part, fans still didn't accept losing as part of the program. Following the 1986 World Series, Bill Buckner was plagued by so many poison-pen letters and unpleasant street confrontations because of his critical error in the sixth game that he had to move his family from Boston to Idaho. In the wake of yielding the home run to Joe Carter that gave Toronto its 1993 World Series victory, Phillie reliever Mitch Williams told reporters: "I'm not going to commit suicide." He then returned to his Philadelphia home to find that irate fans had broken all the windows in the house—the opening salvo in another harassment campaign that forced him to move out of the area.

Williams's crack about suicide struck some as a tasteless reference to another reliever's tragic end after giving up a critical home run. In 1986, Angel closer Donnie Moore yielded a ninth-inning blast to Boston's Dave Henderson when the Angels were only one out away from winning the American League Championship Series. Moore remained in the game in spite of a serious rib injury until the eleventh inning, when he gave up a winning sacrifice fly to the same Henderson. The following year, the right-hander's every appearance on the mound at home set off ugly shouting from Anaheim fans, and he was soon cut loose. After a hellish spell of drinking and scratching after dollars, Moore shot his estranged wife three times and then killed himself. His wife survived the shooting and laid much of the blame for the tragedy on the fans. "All those people that booed him, I wonder how they feel," Tonya Moore wondered. "Can they live with theirself, knowing each and every day that Donnie Moore might be dead because they didn't have enough courage to give him a hand?"

Whatever the responsibility of the Angels fans in Moore's demise, baseball continued a marketing strategy of rising or falling with its most prominent names, and never more so than in the mid-nineties. By then, it had taken enough new falls to be grateful for any strategy at all.

Weather or Not

I t became instant wisdom that the sport's greatest crisis in the nineties was the 1994 work stoppage that forced cancellation of postseason play for the first time since John McGraw had refused to let his Giants meet the Red Sox in the unplayed 1904 World Series. But in terms of long-range discomfiture to fans, the strike ranked merely third behind still further expansion and the scheduling required to accommodate the new teams, both during the regular season and in the postseason.

The NL's 1993 addition of the Colorado Rockies and Florida Marlins brought both gargantuan and minuscule numbers and debates about what they meant. From an attendance perspective, the Rockies started off as the single most successful franchise in baseball history, with both an Opening Day crowd of 80,227 and a season total of 4,483,350 demolishing all records. While that total wasn't reached again, the team continued to draw well over three million annually into the new millennium, vindicating decades-old attempts by Denver authorities to attract a major-league franchise. Nor, unlike most of the rest of baseball, did Colorado fans feel the need to apologize for the home team's bloated offensive numbers in the rarefied air of Mile High Stadium and, subsequently, Coors Field. On the contrary, they gorged themselves on a powerhouse (Andres Galarraga,

Larry Walker, Dante Bichette, Vinny Castilla) that was soon running up a string of years of leading the league (or coming close to it) in scoring, home runs, and batting average, while leaving Rockies pitchers to the same dire fate as those in opposition uniforms. It was the Offense-As-Box-Office philosophy magnified into the rueful lesson of having to be careful about what you wish for; but, Rockies fans and rotisserie league participants aside, the hitting numbers amassed by Colorado players were ridiculed as aberrations. For those not having a rooting or betting stake of some kind in the team, the endless home runs and games in double-figured runs represented the baseball fiction run amok, beyond comparison even with what had regularly taken place in such storied bandboxes as Philadelphia's Baker Bowl. For both hitting success and pitching failure, no team before had ever made statistics, the bedrock of baseball certitude, look so relative.

While the Rockies were attacking belief in the traditional virtues of statistics, the Marlins were having a go at the minimal standards fans might expect from owners. The Miami club was brought into the league with three strikes against it—a demographic fan base anathemic to the sport's soaring prices for its marked tilt toward recent Hispanic immigrants and retired Anglos; tropical rains that forced awkward late afternoon game starts and threatened constant evening interruptions; and furious Tampa–St. Petersburg interests that had been shut out after years of major-league teases that they would get Florida's first franchise. That all these obstacles were shunted aside owed largely to Wayne Huizenga, the 50-percent owner of Joe Robbie Stadium and 100-percent owner of Blockbuster Video, which handled all of baseball's video production, retailing, and rentals.

For a couple of years, neither Miami nor anyone else outside Tampa cared about Huizenga's Gordon Gecko-like approach toward ownership. In a poll of advertised experts on the "best and worst owners for the fans," *USA Today Baseball Weekly* even found him "determined to create a fan-friendly atmosphere," ranking him third behind only Toronto's Paul Beeston and Atlanta's Ted Turner for his concern for followers of the Marlins. Certainly, there seemed to be nothing but profit for everybody when he acquired enough high-salaried players through trade and free agency to propel Florida toward an improbable wild card postseason berth and even more improbable World Series championship in 1997.

But manager Jim Leyland had barely completed a tearful victory lap around Joe Robbie Stadium than Huizenga began dealing all his stars, with the contention that he was losing a fortune and needed to make the team's budget more attractive for prospective buyers. It was *Biscayne Boulevard* as a sequel to *Wall Street*.

Huizenga's laments of financial bleeding had become familiar by the nineties. When fans weren't responsible for torpedoing a franchise by not showing up in big-enough numbers, they were responsible for torpedoing a franchise by not pressuring a local government to build a new stadium for the club or by not being numerous enough to attract significant cable-TV advertising dollars. But few cases ranked with Huizenga's for *chutzpah*. As Andrew Zimbalist pointed out in analyzing the franchise's accounting manipulations, Huizenga's plaints were primarily based on some $38 million in revenues that had been shifted from the club's ledgers to those of the ballpark that he owned separately. In itself, there was no particular novelty in such a personal-profit-through-franchise-suicide tactic. Oakland's Charlie Finley had done it in the seventies, and even he had picked up a few pointers from some nineteenth-century Cleveland and Washington owners. As recently as 1993, San Diego had been so transparent about the ploy that season-ticket holders Paul and Nancy Marshall had filed an unprecedented class-action breach-of-contract suit against the team, basing it on a preseason solicitation form letter promising that the Padres would be a contender for years because of their young stars, even as the club was finalizing deals for getting rid of those players. (The Marshalls eventually settled their suit out of court, after which San Diego resumed its giveaway trades.)

What made the Florida grab-and-run more cynical to many was the 1997 championship—bald evidence that fans and owners had radically different ideas about what winning was all about.

The ramifications of expanding into Denver and Miami didn't end with debates over the worth of published numbers. The two new teams also prompted major changes in league schedules and division structures that, for most fans, added up to robbing Peter to pay Paul. As with the start of divisional play in 1969, the introduction of NL and AL Central divisions in 1994 permitted the sport to claim wider participation in the postseason; instead of only two pennant winners qualifying for the World Series or four teams earning eligibility for the LCS, the extra division winner and a wild card in each league made for excitement among the fans of eight cities. One tradeoff for the additional elimination round, however, was the increased vulnerability of a league's season-long best team to being knocked off well short of the World Series because of a single-series slump. Such a revaluation of chance at the expense of skill was reminiscent of the Rube Goldberg cavortings that had left the best clubs by the side of the road in the split season of 1981. In TV parlance, the system awarded priority to filling the time slot rather than to the quality of what was filling it.

The 1993 expansion also brought unprecedented stress to regular-season scheduling. Ever since the decision to go to divisional play in the sixties, basic geography had been paying the price for trying to make as many owners happy as possible. Much of the problem had originated in the demand for compensation by the Mets for the fact that the creation of a Western Division would mean fewer dates at Shea Stadium for the Dodgers and Giants and the fans they had left behind in going to California. Behind a threat of opposing the entire divisional play concept, New York insisted that St. Louis, then a league power, be included in the Eastern Division so that it would have to make three (rather than two) annual visits to Queens. The Cardinals agreed only on condition that the Cubs also be put into the East so as not to compromise the venerable St. Louis–Chicago rivalry. Once it agreed to the demands, the league office had little choice but to stick far more eastern Atlanta and Cincinnati in the West.

As it developed, the Mets could have saved themselves the trouble since St. Louis quickly turned mediocre and had no particular box-office cachet in the seventies. More generally, however, their ultimatum produced only the first of several tinkerings with schedules and geography that left fans increasingly at the mercy of the clock and the weather and of the stubbornness of owners about acknowledging the importance of either. To start off with, both leagues played a balanced schedule in which every team faced off in a proportionately equal number of games against those inside and outside its division. The main drawback to this format, stemming from the sheer number of teams involved, was that, instead of being able to see their Indians battling it out with the White Sox for first place in the AL Central in the closing weeks of September, Cleveland fans were likely to have to watch their club playing a cellar dweller from the Western Division while praying that the White Sox would be tripped up by a middle-of-the-pack team from the East. None of this made for suspense at the end of the baseball season.

Unwieldiness followed unwieldiness. 1997 brought the debut of interleague play—an idea that dated back to Cubs executive William Veeck, Sr., who had proposed it shortly before his death in 1933 as a tonic for sagging Depression gates. Imposed on the already-bulging leagues of the nineties, interleague play delivered a curiosity factor to the turnstiles in enabling NL fans to see AL stars and vice versa; in a few cases (Yankees–Mets, Cubs–White Sox, Dodgers–Angels), it stoked territorial rivalries to considerable commercial effect. But as soon as the novelty wore off, such faceoffs as Devil Rays–Pirates, Blue Jays–Marlins, and Reds-Royals had about as much midseason box-office allure as a late spring training game, and cries were soon going up for cutting back on the interleague contests in favor of more intradivision play. Instead, matters became even more complicated with yet another expansion in 1998—bringing in the long-coveted market of Arizona and the long-seething one of Tampa–St. Petersburg.

With all the additions and necessary accommodations for interleague play, teams entered the new century facing almost twenty different opponents a year—a throwback to the diffuse nineteenth-century schedules of the National Association of Base Ball Players. It was within this teeming context that the balanced schedule was jettisoned for an unbalanced one, providing for nineteen annual encounters among division rivals. Unfortunately for fans, this also meant only one home-and-away series against extradivision clubs, leaving next to no room for making-up rainouts or other kinds of postponements. As a consequence, rather than call off games in brutal weather, teams waited up to two and even three hours to avoid having to cancel the single visit by an extradivision team. Fans had little choice but to clean out concession stands during the long waits or forfeit their tickets. The same long delays in starting or resuming games made post-midnight finishes before seas of empty seats a common occurrence.

It was against this background of structural disarray and customer disservice that many found it more convenient to think of the 232-day strike between August 1994 and April 1995 as the sport's real traumatic event.

Krank Cases:
Today's Game

By the turn of the century, a lot of fans were walking into ballparks knowing they were prospective cast members for the show to follow. Going well beyond the banners toted by the early Mets fans, many brought along their own costumes and special props. In the late eighties, for example, younger Mets follow-ers with a particular attachment to pitcher David Cone and the "Saturday Night Live" TV show dressed themselves up as Coneheads in the expectation that their pointed latex skulls would be on cam-era several times during the game. Similar costuming grabs-for-attention played around both leagues through the nineties until, by the early 2000s, a Gary Sheffield who *didn't* have followers in Turner Field wearing chefs' hats (for Sheff's Chefs) would have caused more comment. In Philadelphia, the entire Phillies starting rotation had specially garbed followings (the Wolf Pack for Randy Wolf, the Padilla Flotilla for Vicente Padilla, etc.). Friends with more minimalist tastes were content to strip to the waist and stand shoulder-to-shoulder for the Magic Marker spelling-out of a team name across usually unaes-thetic torsos. For those more interested in having their ingenuity rather than their faces or ample guts on camera, there were increas-ingly elaborate variations on the K Corner cards for Dwight Gooden. A common motif of drawn and Xeroxed symbols was nicknames. At

Yankee Stadium, every Roger Clemens strikeout produced the hanging of a rocket over an upper-deck railing, every one by Mike Mussina of a moose.

Sometimes, awareness of cameras drew spectators with more on their minds than baseball. Born-again-Christian proselytizers regularly found box seats behind home plate so that every pitch of a game was delivered not only to a batter, but toward a homemade sign that contained a quotation from the Gospel of John warning of the perils of not seeking salvation. Dilemmas about what to show and not to show produced more than one red-faced moment for TV directors and for the fans they picked up. The years-long protests by Native Americans over Atlanta's logos reached a new level with the adoption of the Tomahawk Chop chant that accompanied every rally by the Braves. After not only Ted Turner, but his wife Jane Fonda and former president Jimmy Carter were seen joining in the gesture during postseason games in the nineties, the word was passed to cut down on the shots of the choppers. Network coverage of a game from Toronto included a lingering shot of a Skydome hotel window where a couple had clearly lost interest in whether the Blue Jays would pull one out.

The addition of giant TV screens in parks intensified the fan's love affair with the camera. Whether as closed-circuit shots between innings or as feeds from on-air telecasts, spectators got used to seeing themselves as the Fan of the Day or simply as the Hi-Mom Waver of the Moment. As though the grandstand needed any more encouragement, teams promoted such distractions as the Kiss-Cam, where couples caught within hearts on Jumboboards were encouraged by those around them to kiss. Whatever other challenges that might have posed for strangers sitting next to one another, it proved the undoing of David Horton at Cincinnati's Great American Ball Park in May 2003. A fugitive wanted on charges of cocaine trafficking, Horton was nudged into a kiss by the stadium screen before the watch of some 30,000 fans, who just happened to include his parole officer. He was arrested before he got out of the ballpark.

Horton was not the only fan whose name ended up on a police blotter, on a court docket, or simply in a newspaper as a victim of some ballpark misadventure. Intoxicated by beer or a need for attention, several spectators hurtled railings to go after players— and in every case, paid heavily for it. In 1995, bond trader John Murray was angry enough at Cubs pitcher Randy Myers for yielding a home run to Houston's James Mouton that he charged the closer on the mound at Wrigley Field; the martial arts practitioner Myers shortarmed him in the throat and had him on the ground by the time security men arrived. In 1999, one Berley Visgar got tired of watching the Brewers losing at County Stadium, so he assaulted Houston outfielder Bill Spiers; his punisher was Astros pitcher Mike Hampton, who ran all the way from the mound to return the attack and then some. In two separate episodes at U.S. Cellular Field, boozed spectators admitted frustration with TV's no-showing policy where outfield streakers were concerned, so they directed their assaults around first base. In the first attack, in September 2002, Kansas City coach Tom Gamboa was punched and kicked to the ground by William Ligue, Jr., and his son. The following April, also at Chicago's AL park, 24-year-old Eric Dybas sought to tackle umpire Laz Diaz. Both times, the assailants ended up the worse for wear under piles of umpires, players, and security guards. "I wanted to do something that would stick out a little more," Dybas said by way of explanation.

Some contentiousness involved fans not against players or umpires, but against baseball executives. In 1988, for example, Chub Feeney became so unpopular as president of the Padres that he couldn't walk into Jack Murphy Stadium without encountering SCRUB CHUB signs. Little more than hours after he was seen giving the finger to the bearers of one such placard, he was bounced from his post. Faring no better in the same ballpark was Dodgers general manager Kevin Malone on April 14, 2001. Irritated by San Diego fan Jim Esterbrooks's heckling of Los Angeles outfielder Gary Sheffield, Malone turned on the season-ticket holder, finally having to be led away; he too lost his job shortly afterward.

Malone was merely one of many public-relations problems that Los Angeles had around the turn of the millennium. In August 1995, Dodger fans, whipped on by endless arguments between umpires and manager Tom Lasorda, triggered the National League's first forfeit in 41 years by firing giveaway baseballs onto the field, one of which almost beaned St. Louis outfielder Brian Jordan. In May 2000, catcher Chad Kreuter and 15 other Dodger players invaded the stands of Wrigley Field after a fan had plucked the receiver's cap off his head. What ensued were three years of suits brought by Cubs fan Ronald Camacho, who charged that Kreuter and other Dodgers players had choked and pummeled him although he had had nothing to do with the grabbing of the hat. In the end, Camacho collected not only $300,000 from the Dodgers, but another $475,000 from the Cubs for their attempts to make him the scapegoat of the episode by cuffing him and charging him with disorderly conduct.

Only three months later, in August 2000, the Dodgers were back in the news when nine Dodger Stadium security guards converged on lesbians Meredith Knott and Danielle Goldey for kissing in the grandstand and ordered them never to return to the park. Fans sitting around the women made such a scene defending them that newsmen got wind of what was going on and reported Goldey's sorrow that she had been "bleeding Dodger blue all [her] life." The red-faced Dodgers not only counteracted the ban against Goldey and Knott (who worked as a porn star under the name of Nico Treasures), but announced a donation of 5,000 tickets to gay and lesbian organizations and special "sensitivity" training for Dodger Stadium's security personnel. According to club president Bob Graziano, the organization's response to the incident represented "the most important act" of his tenure. It wasn't long after the

Goldey-Knott brouhaha that the Dodgers, Giants, Braves, Cubs, and Twins all announced special promotions (Come Out to the Ballpark) aimed at local gay communities.

Even when the Dodgers weren't directly involved, they provided the setting for ugly incidents. On July 24, 1993, Mets outfielder Vince Coleman met with Los Angeles's Eric Davis in a Dodger Stadium parking lot on their way to dinner together. Coleman thought it would be funny to throw a firecracker into a group of departing Dodger fans, succeeding in injuring three people, two of them children. The Mets released him a few days later.

Ronald Camacho wasn't the only one who managed to collect from two teams for miseries suffered at a ballpark. In August 1993, Marlins fan Linda Postlethwaite was struck in the face by an errant warmup toss from Philadelphia's Mitch (Wild Thing) Williams. Postlethwaite was awarded $2.5 million when a Florida court found the Marlins negligent for having lowered a netting between the box seats and the visitors' bullpen. Home-team owner Wayne Huizenga and Joe Robbie Stadium were accounted the most to blame, with the Phillies also assessed a share of the damages payment. On April 7, 2000, the Marlins park was the site of more tragic mishap when Cardinals outfielder Ray Lankford hit a foul ball during batting practice into a group of youngsters known as Bullpen Buddies, inflicting permanent brain damage on Andrew Klein. The Klein family was eventually awarded $1.5 million.

Fan incidents in the postseason attracted even more attention because of the importance of the games. The single most notorious episode of the period occurred at Yankee Stadium on October 9, 1996, when 12-year-old Jeffrey Maier leaned over the right-field wall to snatch a fly ball when it was several feet above Baltimore's Tony Tarasco in the eighth inning of the opening game of the AL Championship Series; to the fury of the Orioles, umpire Rich Garcia ruled that the drive by Derek Jeter was a home run, enabling New York to tie the score. After the Yankees had won the game in extra innings, Garcia allowed as to how he had probably blown the call, but continued to insist that Tarasco wouldn't have caught the ball, that it would have probably fallen for a double if not grabbed by Maier. In the meantime, the boy became the media flavor of the week as a Yankees "hero."

With the innovation of arming fans with Thunderstix in 2002, teams all but explicitly invited spectators to cause interruptions. The most prominent follow-through came during the World Series, when an Angels fan leaned over a railing to whack Reggie Sanders with her Thunderstick as the Giants outfielder was bending down to retrieve an extra-base hit in the seventh game. "While officials scream zero tolerance and pay for extra security," Selena Roberts noted in the *New York Times,* "they also display decibel meters to egg on crowd noise, turn up the volume on baby sound effects when a player whines, juice up the thumping music during timeouts, and hand out Thunderstix before the game . . . while [the Angels fan] is a harebrained individual responsible for her own actions, her outrageous need to be part of the scene has a partner on the executive level these days."

In the sixth game of the 2003 NLCS, Cubs fans had little doubt that the "partner on the executive level" for another postseason Chicago debacle was the infamous Sianis goat. The hex was again the easiest explanation when, with the home team only five outs away from its first pennant in 58 years, Cubs fan Steve Bartman grabbed for a foul ball that appeared catchable for left fielder Moises Alou. Because the ball was ruled to be in the Wrigley Field stands, there was no interference call, despite ragings from Alou and Chicago manager Dusty Baker. Given another life, Florida second baseman Luis Castillo drew a walk, his teammates proceeded to rally for eight runs, and the Marlins advanced to a seventh game that they also won. Baker's questionable use of the bullpen and a key error by Chicago shortstop Alex Gonzalez notwithstanding, the twenty-six-year-old Bartman, a youth-league baseball coach, had to be escorted by security men out of an angry, disillusioned Wrigley following the Florida rally. When reporters tracked him down as a hot example of the Sianis Curse, he issued a statement declaring that he was "truly sorry from the bottom of this Cubs fan's broken heart."

The period heckler was Anthony Ercolano, a season-ticket holder at Safeco Field who filed suit against the Mariners for trying to get him to tone down his shouts from a fifth-row box seat behind home plate. Given the $32,000 he had invested in his tickets, Ercolano told reporters, he had hardly expected to be "belittled" by the team. According to the former Microsoft employee, he had never used foul language, never taunted an opposition player for a weak batting average, and never ridiculed a player's family. What he had done, the Mariners said, was annoy all those sitting around him in the costly Diamond Club section with a mind-sapping routine that seemed to have been borrowed from the book of Franklin Roosevelt's least favorite fan, Patsy O'Toole: loud shouts to short players that they should "stand up straight" and to young players about "their prom dates," as well as mock sobbing whenever a visiting player got into an argument with an umpire.

In Chicago, a lawsuit filed by Peter John Cavoto, Jr. accusing the Cubs of keeping tickets off the general market so they could be sold through a dummy subsidiary at astronomical prices prompted investigations inside and outside baseball. The *Chicago Tribune* owners of the Cubs defended the practice of funneling the tickets to Wrigley Field Premium Ticket Services by claiming that the brokerage house (owned by the newspaper chain) was only dealing VIP tickets that had been set aside under baseball rules. But the rival Chicago *Sun-Times* extracted a laconic statement from the commissioner's office that there was no such rule, going on to report that $45 tickets for an interleague series with the Yankees in June 2003 were being sold for as much as $1,500 by Premium Ticket Services.

A saga lending itself to a Solomonic denouement revolved around Giants fans Patrick Hayashi and Alex Popov. At PacBell Park on October 7, 2001, Barry Bonds's record-setting 73rd home run hit

Popov's glove in the outfield stands, but then fell out again when he was dropped to the ground by a crush of fans seeking the valuable piece of memorabilia. By the time the scuffling on the ground ended, Hayashi had the ball and a claim to being its owner. Judge Kevin McCarthy of the Superior Court agreed with him only halfway, ruling that the two men had equal rights to the ball. With their only option McCarthy's threat to slice the ball in two, Popov and Hayashi agreed to divide evenly the proceeds from its sale.

The opening of PacBell Park in 2000 brought added color to the practice of retrieving home run balls clouted out of stadiums. For decades, the point of reference for the pastime had been Cubs fans standing outside Wrigley Field. But San Francisco's new facility on the Bay spurred dozens of amateur sailors and divers to wait behind the right field wall in rowboats and other vessels hoping for the opportunity to jump in after a Bonds blast. (Bud Selig's Brewers, on the other hand, took all the chance out of shagging with the announcement that Miller Park was putting Guaranteed Foul Ball tickets on sale at $36, assuring fans they would be given a voucher to be redeemed for a game-used ball.)

As adventuresome as Giants fans were in diving into (the redubbed) McCovey Cove for home-run balls, theirs was not the most extravagant example of wanting to be part of the major-league experience at the turn of the century; that primacy went to fantasy camps. Started by former Cub catcher Randy Hundley in the early eighties, the camps charged between $3,000 and $4,000 for fans thirty and older to spend (usually) a week at spring-training sites in Florida and Arizona. In that time, customers wore team uniforms, were "coached" by former franchise stars in daily games, and got to linger into the evening over dinners and drinks, trading baseball stories. The quintessential fantasy camp experience was a reverse machismo—participants groaning about how much they hadn't been prepared for it physically. Reflecting on his week at the Cub facilities in Mesa, Arizona, for example, Larry Weitzman recalled:

By Tuesday evening, muscles were hurting that I didn't know existed. Walking became difficult and running was out of the question. On Friday I went down for a grounder which took a bad hop, bounced off my chest, and landed five feet in front of me. I yelled to my teammates, "I can't get up!" Eventually, after what felt like a month, I was able to retrieve the ball to prevent any base runner from advancing. When people asked how are my legs, I said, "What are those?"

It didn't take long for Hundley's idea to flower into a multi-million-dollar vacation business, with both big-league teams and private concerns offering variations on the idea, including campsites abroad. For most participants, it was the field of dreams brought achingly to life.

CONTRACTION
PAINS

Calling All Cals

T he biggest losers in the 1994 players' strike were Montreal fans. When the Players Association walked out on August 12 because of ownership attempts to impose a salary cap, their team had the best record in both leagues and appeared primed to end Atlanta's three-year reign over tbe NL East. As negotiations hiccoughed through the winter, Montreal's best players (Larry Walker, John Wetteland, Marquis Grissom) either went off as free agents or were dumped in fire sales behind laments that the Expos couldn't meet their pay demands within the labor climate. When fans showed lessened enthusiasm for watching the team's remains in 1995, they were told that Montreal residents were interested only in hockey, anyway. When the club continued to divest itself of such stars as Moises Alou and Pedro Martinez over the next few years, the fans were told that boycotting of Olympic Stadium reflected the increasing francophone hostility of Quebec province to Anglo-Saxon pastimes. Finally, after a franchise sale and more auctioning of key players, they were told their team was either going to be moved elsewhere or contracted out of existence altogether because they had refused to support it.

In many respects, the decline of the Expos franchise represented baseball's most successful disinformation campaign since Kenesaw Landis was denying that the sport was racially segregated, and for much the same reason: Fans, especially those outside Canada, were told what they wanted to hear. When Expos attendance began plummeting to all-time lows at the end of the nineties, it was the realization of a self-fulfilling prophecy that hadn't been all that mantic to begin with. For starters, the city that supposedly obsessed about hockey to the exclusion of all other professional sports (as Pittsburgh was once allegedly interested only in football) had been on target for sending two million fans to Olympic Stadium in 1994—a plateau that had already been reached four times. Even with the first gutting of the roster during the offseason, the club, despite finishing last, outdrew nine others in 1995, including the Mets and Giants. In 1996, with the team's resurgence to second place, attendance *rose* from the previous year, but without any learned analyses that still-trailing New York was interested only in marathon running or still-trailing San Francisco only in clam-eating contests.

The fact of the matter was, Montreal had simply outlived its *industry* usefulness by the mid-nineties. Its days as a decompression chamber for Jackie Robinson and as a vehicle for Walter O'Malley to profit from expansion through his International League Montreal Royals farm club were ancient history. Whatever fans cheered or groaned about on the field, in English or in French, the disparity between the American and Canadian dollar had created too many bookkeeping problems, only one of which was the resistance of free agent players to going north of the border for lessons in international currency. Whatever else the secessionist movement had demonstrated in Quebec by narrowly losing an October 1995 referendum, it clearly had a suspicious attitude toward directives from other North American places. For its ultimate industry goal of moving the franchise to a more controllable economic and political setting, it was much easier for Major League Baseball to denigrate Expos fans than to listen to complaints about the forced departure of the first true Canadian all-star playing in his home country (Larry Walker), about the need to watch games in the least accessible and least inviting stadium in the major leagues, or about persistent stories that Claude Brochu, the organization's first among equals, was collecting hefty bonuses for unloading players whose departures helped balance the club's books. And fortunately, the strike supplied the most evasive of all alibis for writing off the city; that is, that Montreal fans were "disgusted" by the 1994 labor strife.

Although management had to settle with the players without gaining its salary cap, it came away with the walkout itself as a consolation prize. The situation wasn't entirely dissimilar to the "moral renewal" drum-thumping that had obscured the pressing administrative reasons for bringing in Kenesaw Landis as commissioner. Rather than having attention focused on the organizational blunders that were threatening to make the game-going experience as enticing as an IMAX movie on a neighborhood multiplex screen, the plague-on-both-your-houses criticisms arising from the strike provided cover for the sport's two most important promotional campaigns in the decade—the consecutive game streak of Baltimore's Cal Ripken, Jr. (1995), and the home-run duel between Mark McGwire and Sammy Sosa for eclipsing Roger Maris's single-season home run record (1998). Both events were sold relentlessly as having rescued baseball from a nationwide hostility caused by the strike. ESPN said so, the daily sports pages said so, and Commissioner Bud Selig wanted lip readers to see that he was saying so.

The 1994 walkout found fans much more prepared than the 1981 job action, when there had still been widespread astonishment that the Players Association would truly go through with its announced intentions. The cancellation of the postseason also struck many as the collapse of some final frontier—a sign that the sport's principals held nothing sacred. At the same time, if the country could get through October cold-turkey, who really needed whom? Dave Anderson was one of thousands of sportswriters who took on the theme "Biggest Loss for Baseball: Do You Care?" Call-in shows, Letters columns, and Web sites became gathering places for the alienated, with professions of disillusionment vying with vows never to go to another major league game. In numbers, this translated as a 20 percent decline in the 1995 attendance as compared to the pre-strike season of 1993. At least some of that fall, however, was due to the fact that the conflict wasn't settled until the eve of the campaign, so season ticket-holders had kept their checkbooks in their pockets at the usual winter subscription renewal solicitations.

And that dropoff turned out to be the worst of it. In 1996, overall attendance climbed 10 million over the 1995 protest year; by 1998, it was back to pre-strike volume. Although the latter figure reflected the addition of Arizona and Tampa Bay, it equally included the start of Montreal's business suicide and contained no fewer than 11 teams showing sizeable increases from 1993 totals. Moreover, six of these clubs (Angels, Orioles, Indians, Yankees, Mariners, Rangers) were AL franchises with nothing to offer in, or gain from, the McGwire-Sosa duel. There was little reason for Furman Bisher to retract a prediction made during a brief walkout in the eighties: "Fans won't stop going to ballgames any more than tavern habitues will stop drinking beer because the brewers are on strike."

Not that resentment over the strike evaporated as soon as the players took the field again. Singled out for special acrimony were the team representatives for the Players Association, seen frequently on the evening news during the months of on-and-off negotiations. Conversely, minor leaguers who had been contracted as scab replacements in case an agreement had not been reached with the union were the recipients of "little guy" media profiles that made them as sympathetic to the grandstands as they were frozen out in clubhouses. For the most part, however, the 1995 season proceeded without much incident until the final countdown for Ripken's challenge to Lou Gehrig's record streak of 2,130 consecutive games. When the Orioles third baseman finally ran out to his position for the 2,131st time on September 6, it was within a Camden Yards production explicitly geared toward "redeeming" the sport in the eyes of its fans. As the centerpiece of the industrial purging, the graying, pleasant-looking Ripken couldn't help reminding half the media of Gehrig himself and the other half of Gehrig's film portrayer, Gary Cooper. His elaborate trot around Camden Yards in the middle of the game to shake as many hands as possible was turned into an orgy of self-congratulation—not for him so much as for baseball executives who wanted the world to know their product didn't have to be synonymous with the aloof and the greedy.

Even when sportswriters eventually snapped out of their trance, it was not to question the theme of Ripken the Redeemer, but to wonder about the intrinsic worth of the consecutive-game streak. A 1998 *Sports Illustrated* article, for example, described it as "The Most Meaningless Record in Baseball." Writers also found another secondary target when, seven years after the fact, fans exposed to the ESPN telecast of the Camden Yards spectacular voted the breaking of the streak as baseball's single most memorable moment. Conducted by Major League Baseball and a credit card company as a sidelight to the 2002 World Series, the Top Ten list was mocked in particular for having no room for Bobby Thomson's 1951 playoff home run or for anything accomplished by Babe Ruth. The same pundits who agreed that Ripken had saved the game chuckled plenty over how impressionable, short-sighted, or both, the voting fans were.

What all the propaganda agendas and media massaging ended up slighting was the genuine admiration a majority of fans *did* feel for Ripken and his accomplishment. Even those on the pro side of the debate that he might have benefited the Orioles more by having rested on occasion found in the infielder a paradigm of the American work ethic. As Steve Jacobson put it in *Newsday*: "Ripken glowed with the concept that a man goes to work on time and does his best every day whether he feels like going to work or not." Ripken was the diamond's blue-collar obligation to the grandstand's white-collar expectations at the same time that he represented white-collar achievement for blue-collar fantasy. If he was pocketing it as much as any other player and more than most, he still had the image of not being *about* money—and the statistic to prove the image was accurate. Where fans were concerned, Ripken represented a rare convergence of the seeing, the believing, and the wanting to believe.

The McGwire-Sosa run at the Maris record in 1998 provided an even bigger show than Ripken in that it extended over the entire second half of the season. As the Cardinals first baseman and Cubs right fielder jockeyed back and forth in the home-run column, they also marked off to dramatic effect their diametrically opposed personalities—the stoic white Californian with sensitivity issues and the exuberant black Dominican with dissimulation ones. More than one journalist would wonder about the racial component of their competition and how it affected one another's followings, but that angle was overwhelmed by the effusive gestures of friendship exchanged by the sluggers on the field and by baseball's adroitness in promoting such displays as some instinctive aspect of the national pastime. The feel-good race also had the Maris family on hand at Busch Stadium on September 8, when McGwire was the first to break the record; with melodramatic perfection, St. Louis's opponent was Chicago, so Sosa was present as well. The Cubs slugger continued on in pursuit of the all-time season mark, but finally fell four short of McGwire's 70. In a typical commentary on the race, Thomas Boswell told *Washington Post* readers:

> *The chase of '98, which consumed headlines for months, was more a summer-long cure for the chronically jaded soul of sport. It wasn't about greed, violence, drugs, or strikes. Instead, it celebrated the game's rich past while embracing friendship, sportsmanship and diversity in the present. Mac and Sammy were "I'm okay, you're okay" incarnate. America thought, "That's us at our best."*

The celebratory mood was barely grazed by disclosures that McGwire had been using a steroid banned by several other sports.

But his vow to cease taking androstenedione as soon as questions were raised about it shone light on another organizational problem having nothing to do with the priority of making sure people remembered the strike so they could be shown how to recover from it.

Neighborhood Plays

Sentimentalists weren't the only ones to object to the installation of lights at Wrigley Field in 1988. So did the CUBS—not the team, but the Citizens United for Baseball in the Sunshine. For that group in the Lakeview section of Chicago surrounding the ballpark, night games were a recipe for lower property values through increased crime, traffic congestion, street noise, and general rowdyism. Although CUBS lost an extended political and courtroom battle, it did so only after exacting a commitment from the club to schedule no more than 18 night games a year—and after the dispute had thrown the franchise into crisis with the owners of both leagues, the office of Commissioner Peter Ueberroth, and the television networks.

The Wrigley Field controversy was noteworthy for more than involving the last bastion of daytime-only baseball. It also foreshadowed the escalation of hostilities between citizen lobbies, on the one side, and local governments and Major League Baseball, on the other, over numerous ballpark-neighborhood issues in the nineties. Before the decade was out, such groups as Save Fenway Park (Boston), The Coalition Against Public Funding for Stadiums (St. Louis), Friends of Tiger Stadium (Detroit), Progressive Minnesota (St. Paul), Grassroots Against Government-Mandated Entertainment

(Minneapolis), The Oakland A's Fan Coalition (Oakland), and The Committee to Stop the Giveaway (San Francisco) would gain attention for their protests against city, county, or state intentions of opening the public till for financing stadium construction at the cost of tearing up or abandoning urban districts. And that was without counting New York, where George Steinbrenner's heavy-handed campaign to force a replacement for Yankee Stadium in midtown Manhattan won obeisant support from Mayor Rudolph Giuliani but so much laughter from the rest of the city that there was little need to organize much formal resistance. Although attempts were sometimes made to portray the protesters as radical environmentalists who had run out of bears and whales to save, the groups were in fact largely made up of fans who simply saw no reason why taxpayers should have to foot the bill for a private enterprise.

The most wizened argument for government-supported stadiums has been that they serve as a spur to economic development, specifically in the creation of more jobs. But the most generous estimate of numerous studies has been that pro sports in general generate no more than 0.5 percent of the jobs in a community, and that the overwhelming majority of these are in minimal-paying service sectors. In the words of one analyst: "Professional sports are not the swizzle stick that stirs any economy." The nearest thing to an exception has been found in special events, such as a tennis or golf tournament, a horse race, or even a baseball World Series that draws thousands of visitors to a location for a limited time period. In 1993, New York Mayor David Dinkins received blistering criticism as an elitist from his newly-elected successor Giuliani and the tabloid press for working out a deal with the U.S. Tennis Association for expanded facilities in Queens. What got lost in all the demagogic shrieking was that, aside from the fact that the tennis group was going to pay for the expansion itself, the U.S. Open brought more outside dollars to the city in two weeks through hotel, restaurant, and bar patronage than the Yankees and Mets did during their regular seasons.

But even the Dinkins-tennis investment spoke to a parasitic—economy sector with negligible impact on the creation of significant working positions. The second most heard argument for public financing of stadiums has concerned the intangibles mainly affecting that same sector—tourist and business interest being whetted by a community's reputation as the home of a club. Essential to this dynamic, however, has been a winning franchise (e.g., the "city of champions" pitch from World Series victors Pittsburgh, Philadelphia, and Baltimore around the turn of the eighties) or one with a winning tradition (e.g., Yankees); not too many vacationers in recent years have chosen Tampa over Rome because of the Devil Rays. The negative model for the importance of these intangibles was the decline of Brooklyn coincident with the departure of the Dodgers in 1957; the positive model by the nineties was Oriole Park at Camden Yards, credited with instigating a commercial and cultural renaissance in the city with its retro, idiosyncratic design and with inspiring fan-friendly architecture throughout baseball. But as soon became evident in cities like Pittsburgh and Milwaukee, other retro parks seeking to emulate the success of the Orioles could have used a few more wins on the field in addition to outfield nooks patterned after Ebbets Field. Happy-face propaganda to the contrary, most of them were also hard pressed to prove they had elevated the quality of their civic surroundings as much as their own organizational revenues. At best, the publicly funded stadiums meant grand entertainment complexes of the Lincoln Center or Kennedy Center kind—as much island as hub. While these have unquestionably added amusement industry jewels to municipal escutcheons, they have hardly deserved tribute for improving general civic well-being, as their construction has almost always been promoted as signifying.

Routinely mentioned in the same breath with Camden Yards, for example, was Cleveland's Jacobs Field, opened in 1994 as the centerpiece of a downtown reclamation project financed largely by taxes on cigarettes and alcohol. As Joanna Cagan and Neil deMause recorded in *Field of Schemes: How the Great Stadium Swindle Turns Public Money into Private Profit,* the campaign around a referendum for the Gateway Project included such promises as: "Gateway will create a development that will generate $33.7 million in public revenues every year and provide: 28,000 good-paying jobs for the jobless; neighborhood housing developments for the homeless; $15 million a year for schools for our children; revenues for City and County clinics and hospitals for the sick; energy assistance programs for the elderly." At the same time, project backers vowed "no property tax; no sales tax; no income tax" on Cleveland residents and "no tax abatement" for the Indians owners. It was around the same time that commissioner Fay Vincent visited the city to perfume the atmosphere with the warning that "should this facility not be available in Cleveland, should the vote be a negative one, it would be very bad for baseball, and I am opposed to Cleveland losing its team."

Whether because of Vincent's velvet subtlety or a mass desire to get away from the Municipal Stadium cavern dubbed the Mistake by the Lake, the referendum passed and Indians fans filled Jacobs Field so eagerly that it wasn't until 2002, when a previously contending club had been dismantled, that a game was played before less than a sellout crowd. If that amounted to enough riches for the team owners to sell the franchise for still more profit, it also left the city with continuing spirals upward in poverty and downward in education and health care. "While Cleveland has been lauded by the media as a classic comeback town," Cagan and deMause observed, "life is no better for the city's population, which continues to shrink. The huge projected tax revenues that were to go for hospitals, housing for the homeless, and help for the elderly never materialized."

Jacobs Field was merely a background character for *Field of Screams,* which primarily focused on similar fast shuffles around the 2000 move by the Tigers into Detroit's Comerica Park. Much the same story emerged from close looks by other journalists into the building of Miller Park in Milwaukee and Safeco Field in Seattle. One in-depth report on the Seattle facility concluded:

> *The scoreboard is a metaphor for the entire stadium project. A small portion benefits the public, while the greater part generates money for the Mariners. This project was always less about the aesthetics of playing on grass than about amassing the green stuff. It was less about ballpark intimacy than bottom-line vastness. It was also about the way sports teams can seduce a segment of the public and intimidate most of their elected representatives.*

The return by teams to downtown area facilities in the nineties did not mean a return to emphasizing an urban clientele. Infrastructure projects included elaborate access systems that made it possible for the suburban fan to drive past, over, or under weathered neighborhoods to his destination without real contact. The city encountered along such a route was not merely ignored, as had been the case in traveling to an extraurban stadium; more precisely, it was reduced to another remote presence, with the trip culminating in the artifice of the ballpark's nostalgic trappings. Far less of a virtual reality, on the other hand, was the cost of the outing and who was able to afford it. Referring to the practical changes wrought by Jacobs Field for the Cleveland fan, the AFL-CIO's John Ryan lamented: "The increase in prices and the decrease in low-priced tickets has made the crowd much more white. Incredibly much more white. And with the special parking and all that, the wealthier people don't mix with the working-class people for the most part." One local political commentator estimated that, rather than the 28,000 new jobs promised by referendum backers, the city had *lost* 26,000 during the construction of the park. An investigative series by *Newsday* into the impact of publicly funded parks on their cities came to the same conclusion about Jacobs Field. In the words of reporter John Riley:

*Cleveland remains, as it has long been, a racially divided, poor city—
divisions that are reflected in a new baseball stadium filled with whites
who can afford the luxury suites, premium seats, and higher ticket prices,
but relatively few blacks. In a city with 42 percent of its families under
the poverty line, a city that ranks 74th among the nation's 75 biggest
cities in per capita income, the tax-payers subsidize a baseball stadium
for a team that pays its players an average of $1.49 million a year.*

But what the stadiums might not have delivered for the community at large, they delivered to their own industry. Certainly, none
of the trends epitomized by the parks—more controlled environ-
ment, greater market visibility, steady variety in product setting—
discouraged television's commitment to the sport. Already in the
dispute over the lights at Wrigley Field, Ueberroth had made it clear
that the central issue wasn't Chicago's failure to get with the program after fifty years, but an agreement with the TV networks for
all weekday World Series games to be played at night. As the commissioner wrote to Cubs chairman Andrew McKenna on December
18, 1984: "I must warn you that in the absence of an appropriate solution being worked out by the Cubs, baseball will have no alternative
but to resolve the situation on its own. . . . This could include the
requirement that the Cubs' postseason games be played elsewhere but
Wrigley Field, perhaps not even in Chicago." Not even the flattering
assumption that the Cubs needed to concern themselves with postseason obligations brought any break in the stalemate between the
franchise and anti-lights forces for another four years. By that time,
the team's frazzled Chicago *Tribune* ownership was reduced to using
its editorial pages to denounce city council opponents of night
games as "boneheads" and "political bums." When Mayor Harold
Washington finally brokered a deal for the lights, Major League
Baseball and television immediately rewarded the Cubs by awarding
Wrigley Field the 1990 All-Star Game.

If the CUBS campaign was undertaken in the name of preserving

a neighborhood, Steinbrenner's maneuverings in New York sought
to pull the last props out from under a depressed district. Although
the issue caught fire only in the mid-nineties, it had in fact been sim-
mering since the 1977 World Series, when ABC cameras showed scattered blazes outside Yankee Stadium and Howard Cosell told
America: "Ladies and gentlemen, the Bronx is burning!" Two
decades later, with the compliant Giuliani in office, Steinbrenner
and his aides mused almost daily about relocating to the
Meadowlands, Yonkers, or some other venue outside New York City
control if the Yankees weren't allowed to leave the Bronx for a
brand-new stadium in Manhattan. The Yankees executives seldom
missed the opportunity to refer to the area around their park as
"crime-ridden," then tried to look gloomy as they reported that
declining attendance figures were evidence that fans didn't want to
visit the House That Ruth Should Have Left. All of it made for
month after month of speculation, by which time every resident of
the South Bronx had been interviewed for rendering such judgments as "It's Yankee Stadium that brings the neighborhood down.
Good riddance." As if the prospect of city voters endorsing a referendum calling for a $1 billion stadium bond issue for the multimillion-
aire Steinbrenner weren't unlikely enough, the Mets revealed that
they too expected backing for a new facility in Queens and, on the
basis of an agreement with City Hall, before the Yankees got theirs.

One of the lesser effects of the September 11, 2001 attack on the
World Trade Center was that both teams shut up about asking voters
for the better part of $2 billion.

The Cubs, on the other hand, had few qualms about using even
the 9/11 catastrophe for revisiting their decades-old complaints
about Waveland and Sheffield Avenue entrepreneurs selling rooftop
seats to watch games. In the spring of 2002, the team erected wind-
screens over the left-field chain-link fence to make it more difficult
for outsiders to peer in. According to an organization spokesman,
however, the move was not related to the "copyright infringment"

battles it had been waging with its neighbors across the street, but simply reflected "higher security concerns" following the attacks in New York and Washington.

Contractions

By the new century, even Major League Baseball was ready to concede that its latest expansions had mainly expanded the cracks in the sport's foundations. In particular, Tampa Bay proved to be an even tattier operation than the Marlins with its undercapitalization, constant boardroom brawls, gloomy indoor stadium, and lack of direction on the field, not to mention age-heavy demographics that had earned the market the sobriquet of "God's waiting room." But instead of acknowledging that Florida's two teams were a disaster or that such clubs as Milwaukee and Kansas City were less interested in fans than in the revenue-sharing compensation they could get for not drawing any, Commissioner Selig led the ownership chorus in other songs. One of the most popular was that the leagues had to contract and that the prime candidates were Montreal and Minnesota. If the Expos were an obvious target because of their location, the Twins (the first American League team to draw 3 million, in 1988) emerged as a candidate because they couldn't get the Minnesota legislature to spring for another taxpayer-supported stadium and because owner Carl Pohlad could pocket more money from dissolution than from trying to sell a franchise he had driven into the ground. Sportswriter Larry Stone was merely one of dozens who decided in the wake of the November

2001 contraction announcement that "there are other agendas at work here, one of which may be Selig's attempt to provide his long-time friend and ally (Pohlad) with a golden parachute out of a miserable situation in the Twin Cities."

Another favorite theme at the start of the millennium was what Selig termed a "crisis in competitive balance" between rich teams able to pay high free-agency or arbitration player salaries, and those unable to do so. What was striking about this "competitive balance" crisis was that it should appear when it did (2001): Over the previous decade, just six of the existing thirty clubs had *not* reached the postseason. These included the Expos, who had been on their way there before the 1994 strike; the Devil Rays, who came into existence only in 1998; and the Angels, who would become world champions the following year. The others were the Brewers (owned by Selig himself), Royals, and Tigers—none of which had a winning record between 1995 and 2002 and all of which were at the front of the line for the revenue-sharing handouts begun in the nineties.

If all this created puzzlement in other regions of North America, it made for pitched battle and then glee in Minnesota. First, various citizens' groups came together in courtrooms to block any contraction of the Twins. The key ruling came little more than a week after the explicit threat on the franchise, when Minnesota county district judge Henry Seymour Crump ruled out any abandonment of the team because "the welfare, recreation, prestige, prosperity, trade, and commerce of the people of the community are at stake." By the time higher courts in Minnesota had ratified Crump's verdict three months later, the Players Association had also filed a suit against any contraction move, sending Selig into retreat. Neither the Minnesota media nor fans were ready to let it go at that, however. For the vocal majority, the impasse over a new stadium for the club was a decoy issue—and not only for past favors Selig owed Pohlad for a personal loan, but also for the commissioner's ambition to have his own Brewers dominate the northern central television market.

"Let's hope Bud's family already hadn't budgeted in the extra TV and attendance revenue the Milwaukee Brewers were expected to rake in as a result of the elimination of the Twins," crowed *St. Paul Pioneer Press* columnist Tom Powers. "If so, they all have to do some major recalculating."

The response from the field and the grandstand was even louder. The Twins, dismissed as one of the clubs that couldn't compete, dominated the AL Central Division in 2002, then knocked off heavily favored Oakland in the Division Series before finally succumbing to Anaheim in the League Championship Series. Television cameras at the postseason games in the Metrodome were hard put to avoid fans holding up placards advocating CONTRACT BUD LITE. T-shirt and cap manufacturers couldn't sell wares around the contraction theme fast enough. Selig's response was to take out a full-page ad in both the *Minneapolis Star Tribune* and *St. Paul Pioneer Press* declaring: "Thank you, Minnesota, for your patience and enthusiasm . . . and congratulations, Twins, for a most memorable season. We look forward to building our future together." Lest anyone get the impression he was eating his words, however, he continued to talk throughout the winter about how Minnesota's field success in 2002 had been an "aberration" in the overall baseball picture. Nor did he back away from claims before the 2002 season that half the fans in the major leagues were wasting hopes if they went to their local parks expecting to see a team that would play in the postseason. This caused baseball business analyst Doug Pappas (among others) to wonder: "What other business would allow, let alone encourage, its chief executive and most visible spokesman to disparage its product with remarks like 'at the start of the spring training, there no longer exists hope and faith for the fans of more than half of our 30 clubs?' MLB has *more* competitive balance than any of the other major team sports . . . handicapping a season before spring training is a wildly uncertain venture. Selig's remarks can only reduce interest in baseball and depress attendance in the very markets he's trying to help."

For their part, Montreal fans had few illusions left about the "help" Selig and the other owners were trying to provide. But what not even the most jaded of Canadians had expected was that the twenty-first century would take off with a nostalgic replay of the most bare-faced nineteenth-century syndicate ownership schemes. As a first step in the process, Expos owner Jeffrey Loria sold the franchise to Major League Baseball in February 2002 for an estimated $120 million. This not only freed him up to buy the Marlins (with the help of a loan from Major League Baseball), but enabled Florida general partner John Henry to make a bid for the Red Sox. The final step came when Selig pressured Boston's sale to Henry's group even though others had submitted higher offers—a development described by Massachusetts Attorney General Thomas Reilly as "a bag job."

As in Minnesota, the payoff was lawsuits and fan eruptions. The most prominent legal action came from fourteen bought-out partners of the Expos who charged Loria, Selig, and Major League Baseball with fraud and racketeering for conspiring in the franchise switch. The fans had their loudest moment of rage on Opening Day at Olympic Stadium, when the presence of the Marlins as the opposition allowed a significant number of the 34,351 on hand to chorus "Loria sucks!" throughout the game. One fan carrying a sign with the lyric of the day managed to get atop the Florida dugout to lead a group sing before being apprehended. Others threw beer at Marlins outfielder Eric Owens, covered the field with O Henry bars passed out in honor of Montreal pinch-hitter Henry Rodriguez, and shook the foul pole so violently that manager Frank Robinson had to plead for calm. "That's not baseball," Loria was quoted from his Manhattan apartment where he had watched the game via a satellite dish, "that's hooliganism."

What it definitely was was useless, at least in terms of changing official minds about shuttering operations in Montreal. At first, the team's 2002 season didn't go as planned, with the Expos playing so credibly that the other owners had to hold their noses and approve requests to acquire marquee names Cliff Floyd and Bartolo Colon for a serious run at the NL East title. But as soon as that goal fell beyond reach, it was back to Program A, with Floyd dealt away again (to Henry's Red Sox), the open exploring of selling the franchise to interests in Washington, northern Virginia, or Portland, Oregon, and the announcement that the club would play 22 of its "home" games in 2003 in Puerto Rico. Even then, potential embarrassment remained in the air because the club's play had drawn enough customers to Olympic Stadium that the Marlins, rather than the Expos, appeared doomed to recording the league's lowest attendance. But then, by happy coincidence, an anonymous benefactor stepped forward to buy 18,000 tickets for Florida's last home game of the year. The final attendance count was Marlins 813,118, Expos 812,537.

Montreal's need to play 22 of its home games in San Juan in 2003 should have made its sporadic appearances at Olympic Stadium even more of a non-event. But although increasingly weary from all their traveling and hotel living, the players once again disappointed executive expectations by staying in contention for the NL wild card through late August. Having already been barred from making any more trades of the Floyd kind, the club was then told it couldn't even make the usual recalls from the minor leagues in September because of budgetary restraints. Whatever interest had been developing in Montreal for the team despite its irregular presence subsided in tandem with the club's record.

But Montreal wasn't the only team to exceed expectations in 2003. Throughout the campaign to eliminate the Expos, Selig and the other owners had little to say about the Marlins, as ripe a candidate for contraction as any that existed. What continued to be said in baseball corridors following the Montreal–Florida–Boston round-robin, on the other hand, was that Loria had agreed to go to Miami only with the understanding that, should the Marlins not show a profit for three years running, he would be able to cancel his loan from Major League Baseball and also have the freedom to move the club wherever he wanted. If there was any truth to the reports, the Florida owner had to be among the most disgruntled people in the country when his team defied all probabilities by winning the NL wild card and then charging through the postseason to a world championship. Along the way, Pro Player Stadium rocked with the kinds of crowds not seen since 1997. Throughout the team's surge, Loria assured Florida fans he would not do as Huizenga had done once the season was over.

The new readiness to transfer the Expos rather than eliminate them represented more than a belated awareness that anti-contraction lawsuits from various quarters might tie everybody up in courtrooms for years; it also signalled the end, for the immediate future anyway, of further expansion. Although there had been plenty of field and organizational motives for not adding clubs for some time, they had always taken second place to the eagerness of the owners to divvy up the buy-in fees paid by new teams. For this reason, clubs like the Athletics, Giants, and White Sox had been urged in the eighties and the early nineties to resolve their financial problems locally rather than resort to a transfer to a then-virgin market (Denver, Tampa, Phoenix) that would have squandered a buy-in-fee opportunity. If it had done nothing else, the fallout in Minnesota over the contraction attempt had made the owners cautious about daring to subtract teams with one hand and add them with the other. In this context, teasing talk about how regular-season games played by the Padres in Mexico and by the Expos in San Juan might mean expansion to Spanish-speaking lands in the near future, was just that—*hablar.*

Bonding Necessities

The anxieties raised by the 1994 strike brought on another wave of reaching out by teams toward fans, the media, and their surrounding community. The need was perceived as even greater following yet one more threatened walkout in the second half of the 2002 season. Camera days became almost obligatory. Players were warned about brushing off autograph seekers. Outfielders routinely ended innings by tossing third-out balls into the stands. Little League Days had the home team taking the field with each player flanked by a uniformed youngster. Deaf Days were held for the handicapped. Atlanta led the way in promoting designated drivers—serving free bottled water to the volunteers in return for donning bracelets that made them ineligible to buy beer during games. Public appearances at malls and hospitals were stepped up. Interviewing the manager became a standard weekly—when not daily—feature of local call-in sports shows.

Demographically, the fans being cultivated weren't quite who they had been a few years earlier. There were more of some and less of others. The steady addition of luxury boxes and field boxes (in some parks right up to the foul lines) translated to more corporate customers who regarded games as business entertainment expenses on clients. Women, who had been hovering around the 30-percent mark since the end of World War II, were estimated as accounting for as much as 35 or 36 percent of major league gates by the end of the nineties. In addition to the Little League Days, children were the object of the Baseball Is For Kids program for the underprivileged, as well as target customers for such private co-marketing deals as that between the Padres and Legoland California. Several parks also added playground slides and other game areas. Apart from immediate phil-anthropic or profit objectives, the campaigns aimed at the young reflected long-term concerns in that the average age of the baseball fan was calculated to be 45, as opposed to 44 in hockey, 41 in basket-ball, and 39 in football.

Age wasn't the only fan problem facing the sport in the new cen-tury. Entire social groups, most prominently African Americans, showed less interest every year. The decline began in the seventies, when the number of black *players* had also started becoming thinner on the ground. Study numbers included such findings as that only 10.6 percent of the African-American population was enthusiastic about baseball, only 9.5 percent of those who watched games on tel-evision were black, and that African Americans on big league rosters were dipping closer and closer to the 10-percent mark.

The factors behind the decline were hardly revelations. One was the soaring cost of attending games on inner-city family budgets. Well into the eighties, Major League Baseball was able to claim that going to a game cost only a fraction of most other mass-entertainment media. By the new century, however, with parking, concessions, and other extras added to ticket costs, that contention remained tenable com-pared to the extortive prices demanded by Broadway theaters and NBA arenas, but to little else. At the same time, there was the relent-less transfer of games from free television to cable; even basic cable service did not qualify as a priority spending item for economically stressed households.

Then there was baseball tradition. For all the symbolic significance of Jackie Robinson's breakthrough with the Dodgers in 1947 and the

Selig-led ceremonies at Shea Stadium to mark the 50th anniversary of that event, individual teams had never exactly put out a welcome mat for black customers. In talking once about Kansas City's acknowledged failure to draw black fans, Negro-league legend Buck O'Neil had only to change a few proper nouns for his remarks to apply to any number of franchises. According to O'Neil, the Royals merely carried on marketing plans begun by the Athletics when they had moved from Philadelphia to Kansas City in 1955. "The A's didn't sell baseball to the black fans," O'Neil observed. "They sold it to Johnson County. They sold it to the white fans. They had a built-in fan base with the Monarchs fans, but they didn't think they needed them." For every protestation by teams that they were doing everything possible to encourage greater attendance by black fans, there was some statistic or happening to suggest the opposite. The most notorious incident was the 1987 appearance by Los Angeles general manager Al Campanis on the ABC network show *Nightline* during which he asserted that African Americans did not have "the necessities" to become managers or general managers. Although the Dodgers fired Campanis for stirring up a storm of protests that embarrassed the franchise, the episode hardly reassured the black community about the sport's racial attitudes.

The opportunities (or lack of them) for fan identification also played a big role. With the help of Latins Roberto Clemente and Manny Sanguillen, the Pirates had been able to field the first all-black lineup in major-league history on September 1, 1971. But by the beginning of the 2003 season, only three of the 30 clubs—Colorado, Cleveland, and Tampa Bay—could manage even a theoretical majority of five African Americans among a starting nine, and that only by including disabled players. The most commonly heard explanation for this change was that black teenagers preferred basketball and football to baseball, that it was all the fault of NBA deals with Puma or NFL agreements with Gatorade. But, more pertinent, the initial sources of black talent for the major leagues, the Negro leagues, had always been an anomaly, a one-time pipeline; at most, their influence had stretched to a second generation of African Americans influenced by exposure to the Roy Campanellas and Hank Aarons. Otherwise, the main athletic structure for an inner city teenager had always been the schools where baseball (a summer recess sport) had never been valued as highly as basketball or football (whose seasons paralleled the academic year). Except for a few franchises, scouting players or proselytizing for the sport in black neighborhoods had *never* been a priority. It was only when the Negro-league pipeline began drying up, with most subsequent black players coming from schools with an exceptional athletic profile, that this oversight began to manifest itself. But whereas these schools (usually in the West and Southwest) went on supplying at least a modicum of black players, the continuously ignored black neighborhoods had still been left on their own to generate enthusiasm for the sport. By and large, the opportunity had been resisted.

The marketing of the few African-American stars around the turn of the century did little to bridge the gap. For a good part of the nineties, there was little argument that outfielder Ken Griffey, Jr., was the best all-around player in the game, and, despite playing for faroff Seattle, he had the commercial endorsements to reflect it. But then came the Ripken and McGwire-Sosa spectaculars, the failure of the Mariners to reach the World Series, and Griffey's decision to force a trade to his home-town of Cincinnati. Once a member of the Reds, one injury after another disabled him for extended parts of three seasons, crippling his box-office cachet as much as his diamond abilities.

Then there was Barry Bonds. Already a Griffey rival in debates about the best player of the nineties, the San Francisco outfielder went after bigger game at the start of the century, in 2001 compiling the single greatest offensive year by any player in baseball history. Among other things, his 73 home runs shattered the McGwire single-season record, his .863 slugging eclipsed Babe Ruth's 1920 record of

.847, his 177 walks broke another Ruth standard dating back to 1923, his 107 extra-base hits tied Chuck Klein's 1930 National League effort, and his .515 on-base percentage was the league's highest since John McGraw's .547 in 1899. The next year was more of the same. Although his home runs declined to 46, Bonds became the oldest (38) first-time batting champion by hitting .370, smashed the 61-year-old on-base mark held by Ted Williams by averaging .582, and drew an astonishing 198 walks. Moreover, he reached base 21 out of 30 times during the World Series against the Angels, including four home runs and seven intentional walks. Entering the 2004 season, he had collected an unprecedented six MVP trophies and was only two behind his godfather Willie Mays for third place among all-time home-run hitters.

But for all that, Bonds also remained the media's least favorite player. One Boston columnist, apparently soaking in some of the fumes from the Aaron-Ruth chase, allowed as to how the Giants outfielder shouldn't even be recognized for topping McGwire because he was "unlikeable." The more he achieved on the field, the more he bred articles with titles like "The Trouble with Barry Bonds" and "Why America Will Never Love Barry Bonds." The trouble, a majority agreed, was that he didn't like people much, starting with newspapermen and including numerous teammates. For David Halberstam, there was little mystery about why America would never love him:

> The stories [about Bonds] have always been quite shocking. They are not . . . about a distant, somewhat aloof, rather private young man who keeps himself apart from the amiable byplay that can make baseball a good deal of fun. Rather they are about unprovoked, deliberate, gratuitous acts of rudeness towards all kinds of people, other players, distinguished sportswriters. They are of a handsomely rewarded young man of surpassing talent, going out of his way to make the ambiance in which he operates as unpleasant as possible, and to diminish the dignity and pleasure

of other men . . . who also work for a living. This is about nothing less than the abuse of power-he has it by dint of his abilities, and he uses his power to make others' lives more difficult and less pleasant.

The depth of Bonds's truculence-interrupted-by-whimsy was seen by many more than Halberstam as going beyond the defensive mechanisms of a black star being asked the same questions a thousand times a day by white people holding microphones and notepads; he was his own crank, not ready to be anybody's role model. However misleading the image might have been, it not only didn't pull at the heartstrings of prospective black fans, it didn't draw too many quietly knowing, jaded assents of being "one of ours," either. Bonds wasn't much one of anybody's, black *or* white. This added up to an awkward market commodity. Or, as one sports-marketing consultant asked dubiously: "Where is the shelf space for Barry Bonds?"

Foreign Affairs

U nlike African Americans, Hispanic fans didn't have to fantasize to put together lineups with a majority of Latins; teams like the Rangers, Royals, Braves, Orioles, Expos, and Marlins did so regularly. In great measure because Latin American players could be signed cheaply, without the restrictions of the amateur draft, Hispanics had approached 30 percent of major league rosters by the early century—double what it had been a decade before. Included were the game's biggest stars—Dominicans Sammy Sosa, Pedro Martinez, Vladimir Guerrero, and Miguel Tejada; Puerto Ricans Juan Gonzalez, Carlos Delgado, Roberto Alomar, and Ivan Rodriguez; and the Cuban Rafael Palmiero. Then there were such U.S.-born franchise players as Alex Rodriguez, Edgar Martinez, and Nomar Garciaparra. At the same time, the Latin fan base was estimated as growing by 7.8 million between 1992 and 2002. It wasn't only concentrated in such customary Latino markets as New York, Miami, and Los Angeles, either; the Hispanic community in Kansas City, for example, increased at three times the national rate in the nineties. The trend propelled baseball into printing All-Star ballots in Spanish, providing greater Spanish-language radio and television coverage, organizing Hispanic Night and "Señoritas Days" promotions at ballparks, and even adding such items as Dominican flags at ballpark souvenir stands.

Dinosaurisms still hovered, however. In a controversy that threatened to become a Latino version of Al Campanis and the Necessities, Houston owner Drayton McLane was accused in June 1999 of smearing Hispanics as basically being too dim and too poor to merit the marketing priorities of the Astros. The charges stemmed from a conversation between McLane and two local KTMD-TV executives, general manager Marco Camacho and sales manager Rod Rodriguez. According to Camacho, "we asked him why he doesn't market toward Hispanics. He said it was hard to reach Hispanics because the game of baseball is strategy and skill and it's complicated and that's why more Hispanics don't go to Astros games. He said if you gave them a basketball and told them to put the ball through the hoop, they can do that."

Declaring himself "angry and outraged" by the allegations, McLane mounted a counter-campaign against Camacho and Rodriguez, going from a press conference to a telecast of an Astros-Twins game to make his case directly to fans. Commissioner Bud Selig was enlisted to characterize the owner as "honorable" and "sensitive" and to dismiss the claims by the two TV executives as "slander." A month later, KTMD's parent company, the Los Angeles–based Telemundo Group, apologized to McLane and praised him for "strongly supporting Hispanics."

The weathering of that storm still left some unconvinced, a few years later, of baseball's commitment to Hispanics. At the start of the 2003 season, for instance, *Houston Chronicle* sportswriter John P. Lopez warned against reading too much into San Diego's regular-season series in Mexico on a couple of occasions, or the decision to move a good slice of Montreal's home games to San Juan. "[Baseball] has sent teams to Puerto Rico and pandered to the culture," Lopez declared, "but it has failed to find ways to establish legitimate relationships with those who could pay the bills for years to come." *New York Times* columnist Harvey Araton also found the rescheduling of the Montreal games in Puerto Rico "a good idea, but lacking in good will." According to Araton, "the operation gave the appearance of drive-by baseball, at prices that can at best be described as highway robbery. The top ticket costs $85, more than the Mets charge in New York. The general admission price, $25, costs more than a box seat in Montreal. . . . In any language, it sounded like price gouging."

Suspicions about the game's attitudes toward Hispanics persisted despite the sale in early 2003 of the Angels to Arturo Moreno, a Phoenix-based Mexican-American who had made his money in the billboard industry. In paying the Walt Disney Company an estimated $180 million for the defending World Champions, Moreno became baseball's first principal owner from a minority group. One of his first crowd-pleasing moves in taking over the Anaheim franchise was to lower the price of beer at Edison Field.

In the meantime, extra thousands of fans continued to solidify their relationships with Hispanic stars. The attendance boosts were particularly noticeable in the case of Red Sox right-hander Pedro Martinez, with gates on the road fluctuating wildly between days when he pitched and those when he didn't. In Boston, his strikeouts became so much part of his charisma that Fenway Park took to booing him jocularly if he allowed a batter to pop up.

Even before becoming a familiar national television presence for his 1998 duel with Mark McGwire, Sammy Sosa had managed to rival Ernie Banks as Chicago's Mister Cub; his subsequent feats (including an unmatched three 60-plus home-run seasons) gave him pride of place in the den. In the most traditional of big-league parks, the outfielder added his own rituals of sprinting out to his position, sending the Bleacher Bums his tap-the-heart sign for peace and love, and topping off every home run by giving dugout TV cameras a kiss of his index and middle fingers (for his wife and mother). Nobody seemed more unaffected by the daily necessity of spewing out cliches about how personal performance was secondary to whether the team won or lost.

All the showmanship came in handy in June 2003, when Sosa was discovered using a corked bat in a game. Media commentators leaped all over him, accusing him not only of ruining his image, but of compromising the legitimacy of his power feats. "There can be no saving of Sammy Sosa from the stain he has now cast on the record books and his career," as Bill Madden of the *Daily News* put it. "He has told us it is so—he has been loading his bat and, as we scratch his name off our Hall of Fame futures list, we are left to only ask: Why?" Other columnists took to the familiar wheeze that he had let down not his race in this case, but his Dominican Republic homeland. Fans in Baltimore couldn't wait to pelt him with pieces of cork when he took the field at Camden Yards right after being caught. But Wrigley Field was another story, with his following accepting his excuse that he had picked up a corked batting practice bat "by mistake" and assurances that he had never used one in a game before. The standing ovation he received on his first plate appearance echoed the earlier reactions the Pete Roses and Keith Hernandezes had drawn after their problems had been aired. Even the *New York Times*, rarely given to front-page baseball stories, thought the Wrigley Field response deserved the Page One headline of AT CRIME SCENE, SOSA HEARS MOSTLY CHEERS.

Asian players brought not only fans, but their own press corps. The first to do so, in 1995, was Japanese pitcher Hideo Nomo, an all-star in his country who had much the same impact on Los Angeles that Fernando Valenzuela had had 14 years earlier. Like the Mexican southpaw, right-hander Nomo drew an ethnic group that had previously been cool to the local team, helped swell average attendances for his starts above 50,000 in a season filled with fan growling over a player strike, and took Rookie-of-the-Year honors. Like Valenzuela as well, he gained attention for an unusual delivery—a maddeningly slow windup and last-second Luis Tiant–like twist. Nomo's every move was dogged by dozens of Japanese reporters and photographers who relayed his smallest twitch back to Tokyo, where fans rose before dawn to watch Dodger telecasts. The phenomenon was repeated in Seattle in 2001, with the arrival of the first Japanese position player, outfielder Ichiro Suzuki. Ichiro, as he was called, not only was named Rookie of the Year, but was awarded MVP honors for becoming the first player since Jackie Robinson to lead a league simultaneously in batting and steals. As Nomo had done previously in Los Angeles, he also expanded home-park concession-stand fare with the introduction of sushi. Fears that the Japanese players might reawaken World War II animosities among older fans, especially around West Coast shipping ports, went largely unrealized. The ugliest incident of the kind took place in April 2001 when a group of Oakland fans fired ice-cubes and coins at Ichiro behind racial slurs before being escorted out of the Coliseum.

Much of Nomo's impact among the Japanese in Los Angeles had initially appeared reserved for Koreans responding to the arrival of countryman Chan Ho Park in the majors. But the right-hander Park failed in a 1994 trial and didn't stick with the Dodgers until two years later. By that time, he was also taking the mound with some serious complexes imported from Asian cultural and historical antagonisms. As he told one reporter: "Sometimes, when I see all the Japanese reporters [around Nomo], I feel bad. It reminds me of Japan being really powerful, big, and strong. It makes me sad. My country needs me." As it turned out, an injury to Nomo left Park the big man in the Dodger rotation in the late nineties and Korean fans far more numerous than the Japanese.

Korean lobbies were also among the most vocal in condemning racist remarks made by Braves closer John Rocker in the winter of 1999. In an interview with *Sports Illustrated,* Rocker described himself as "not a very big fan of foreigners," going on to lament that "you can walk an entire block in Times Square and not hear anybody speaking English. Asians and Koreans and Vietnamese and Indians and Russians and Spanish people and everything up there [in New York]. How the hell did they get in this country?" It was under pressure from such groups as the National Korean American Service & Education Consortium, the Korean Resource Center in Los Angeles, and the Korean American Community Center in Philadelphia that Selig suspended Rocker for spring training in 2000 and a handful of regular season games.

The influx of Asian players and the desire by teams to go after more of them spurred Major League Baseball to open the 2000 season in Tokyo with a two-game series between the Mets and Cubs. The games before packed houses came some eleven decades after Albert Spalding's Great World Tour, in a country he had bypassed.

Epilogue

I n the early days of television, NBC placed cameras and monitors in Rockefeller Center so passersby could glimpse themselves within the chassis of the new medium. Some people were amused by their image; others studied themselves and their background, pondering how the box differed from a mirror; and still others lingered to make faces or clown around with friends. What few recognized immediately was how indispensable they were to the novelty in the NBC window; how, once past grasping the rudiments of how the medium worked technically, they would be expected to keep returning to see smoother performers on the field of their watching, contemplating, and playing.

In the 1840s, the passersby were in Hoboken's Elysian Fields rather than in Manhattan's Rockefeller Center. Later, they congregated in Brooklyn, Washington, Chicago, Los Angeles, San Pedro de Macoris, and Tokyo. They increased in numbers from hundreds to thousands to millions to hundreds of millions. They went from small talk to the telegraph to daily newspapers to radio to television to the Web. They went from sitting on the grass to a hard bench to a slap-up seat to a lounger equipped with a computer. They used the sport's situations as simile, then as metaphor, then in unawareness that they were using metaphor. Upon such arcs, baseball has claimed

353

a relentlessly progressive growth, depth, and power in American culture. The game admits to no ties. Today beats yesterday because the numbers are bigger, the places more far-flung, the assumptions more instinctive.

But for the fan, this global ballpark has always had obstructed sight lines. He has known franchise gerrymandering and ownership carpetbagging since the smoke cleared from the Civil War. He has been told why he is minor and how much it will cost him to become major. He has been told to despair unless he votes for a publicly subsidized stadium, then told that the only place he can afford in it is somewhere in the upper right-field deck. He has been told to hope because of revenue sharing, then told the owners of capital-shy clubs weren't obligated to spend their supplementary income on improving their teams, could in fact pocket the money as a bonus for failure.

In some eyes, this has made for an ideal fan. As Yankees manager Joe Torre snapped when asked about a grandstand reaction to one of his moves, "it's not the crowd's job to understand. Their job is to cheer and boo." It has been in this spirit that the National League stopped umpires from asking for spectators' views on plays in the nineteenth century, that both leagues doubled up on All-Star games (and admissions) for a few years in the late fifties and early sixties while simultaneously taking the vote away from fans, and that tens of thousands sit in chilling rain for hours waiting for an interleague game to start because the visiting team won't be dropping by again and Fox has scheduling promises to keep.

The fan has been complicit in all this, presumably because he has found the exchange in entertainment worth it. Baseball has enraptured his imagination as vividly as a theatergoer's has been captivated by Shakespeare, a music lover's by Bach, and a TV viewer's by *The Top Ten Squad Car Crashes*. What has made this involvement more notable is that it has required no little projection for the fan to remain within the spell. If the game's appeal to him has been its seasonality, that has had to survive indoor Jiffy Bag stadiums, unchanging California weather patterns, and World Series played closer and closer to Thanksgiving. If the allure has been some of that legendary timelessness, that has had to survive three calls to the bullpen an inning, sitting in the mist within Pro Player Stadium's ban on umbrellas, and the tradition of naming parks not after the venerable Ebbetses, Comiskeys, and Griffiths, but after the latest cell phone companies setting off their wares all around him in the general admission section. If the sport's attraction has been its fine statistical accountings of struggle and imperfection, that has had to survive ever-finer mathematical conclusions that he has been paying too much attention to his passions and impressions, that his stars have actually computed as black holes, that, in sum, he has rarely understood what he has been watching.

Ultimately, what has made all these assaults less than fatal is that they have been crassnesses and manias imported from the real world; they have been as relevant to the central fiction as finding out that Morocco's Vichy policemen were as vicious as the Nazis, that they would have never licensed an American looking like Humphrey Bogart to open a nightclub, and that they would have never allowed a hunted European Resistance leader to run freely around Casablanca. What has made the time go by without the mass rejection that doomed cricket in the nineteenth century has been, to a significant degree, baseball's quality of fictional measurement—not merely of the ascents and descents in the career of a player or the fortunes of a club, but of the fan's own young, middle-aged, and elderly relationship to the game. The fan who has seen all three generations of Bells and Boones on the diamond isn't old, he is the witness to a saga unfolding outside himself that can suggest agelessness for all concerned, including for the institution hosting it. And more engrossing than in the case of the moviegoer who has watched era after era of Barrymores, Redgraves, and Fondas, his unfolding has been continuous—dependent not on one or two special events a year, but in game after game, box score after box score. In the last analysis, the seductiveness of baseball's rhythms is not in the fact that they are seasonal, but that they are *daily*—the quotidian filtered through the entertaining; not that they are timeless, but that they are *dated*—exactly when and where who did what, in front of whom.

The specific dramatic ingredients of the game—the constant evaluation of offensive and defensive alternatives, the short-term risks for long-term gains or vice versa, the sheerly athletic potential for making the most brilliant mental calculations moot, the climactic emergences or failures of individual players, the joys and horrors of outcomes—are not as incidental as aerial academic perspectives on sports-crowd dynamics have sometimes made them appear. No boxing fan has ever been told he is more of an American for watching a mouthpiece go flying across the ring; no racing fan has ever been scolded for approaching the $2 window, then been told by track officials where to place a $10 bet instead; no arena football fan has ever lamented that his sport wasn't introduced to Afghanistan in time to prevent the Taliban from gaining power. Baseball has always taken itself seriously, if not with absurd solemnity, and has exacted that attitude from its fans. Indeed, that has been its most durable legacy from the need to placate nineteenth-century Puritan scolds.

With increasing regularity, however, the fan's acceptance of the game's seriousness, his documented avidness for financing it, even his indispensability as an audience, have been denounced as insufficient. Over the last couple of decades in particular, Major League Baseball has shown more than the normal anxiety of the shopkeeper about whether the customer will return the following day, having all but announced that it *doesn't* trust him to come back. It has ignored the most obvious consistency in its ledgers since the start of the National League in 1876—that winning teams draw and losing ones don't—to wallow in declarations of crisis supposedly not of its own making. It's the players who are grasping, the cities that don't move their bulldozers fast enough, the fans who are angry, indifferent, or whimsical (i.e., unreliable). When Braves fans don't fill

Turner Field to capacity for the opening games of the Division Series, it's because they have grown blasé about a team that has won more consecutive division titles than any other club in the history of any professional sport, not because the Division Series itself might be a credibility-challenged gimmick for increasing TV revenues. When fewer and fewer people tune in to the All-Star game every year, it's not because interleague play and player mobility have coopted the novelty, but because the mob in the stands wants less baseball and more Norah Jones supplying the lyrics to a home-run–hitting contest. When modest-market teams like Minnesota and Oakland threaten to reach the World Series, baseball's Homeland Security chart zooms up to red-on-red. They are "aberrant" winners, in Selig's view, because they are the equivalent of the walkup fan—they haven't been provided for within what passes for Major League Baseball organization.

There have been numerous consequences to baseball's rising distrust of the fan, but none more conspicuous than the compulsiveness strategy. The shrill acoustic and visual atmosphere of the contemporary stadium has been of a piece with agitating yearnings to an ever-greater addictive degree. When Shea Stadium resorts to the evangelical lunacy of the Peter Finch character in *Network* as a DiamondVision signal for the grandstand to get behind a rally, it does so sardonically but without self-referential irony. Whether it's Major League Baseball Properties or some satellite industry, any junk item not previously claimed by the Franklin Mint is geared toward cashing in on collection cravings. Why be satisfied with a single Met cap when dozens and dozens of variations are for sale? Why hang just one Blue Jay jersey in the closet when there are copies of those worn for the road, for batting practice, and for when the opposing pitcher is from Aruba? Why be satisfied with the usual boring baseball cards when insert cards, redemption cards, and premium cards might one day produce another Honus Wagner facsimile worth millions? Why stop at going on the Internet to pick up the play-by-play of an

Expos-Brewers game when, with the right credit card, you can log on to a sponsoring cyber-casino and stay in front of your monitor until you've broken the bank?

There is nothing especially original about a mass medium exploiting addictiveness as insurance for profit-making. King Kong had his son, Frankenstein's monster his bride, Bing Crosby and Bob Hope a whole collection of road maps. The weekly TV sitcom formula proven so comfortable for tens of millions has developed on the big screen into the pre-insured familiarity of IV, X, and XV for boxers, whales, and serial killers in hockey masks. But in the specific case of baseball, where the caring is supposed to provide the entertainment, reliance on compulsiveness toys with the unique combination of partisan ardor and analytic detachment that has always characterized the grandstand spectator. It insists the fan choose less and demand more, turn into a true *fan-atic*—a formula over the long haul for abandoned loyalties and increased frustrations and angers. That Major League Baseball has not only embarked on this course, but relished it propagandistically, arguing it as a present reality rather than the menacing future it itself is laboring to bring forward, has been akin to putting Cassandra in charge of the gates to Troy.

The fan's last line of defense, of course, will always be the strength of the baseball fiction vis-à-vis the reality show under way at the latest press conference by a Bud Selig, a Players Association representative, or a City Hall aide. At the onset of the millennium, belief in it still excited more for being sustained than for wavering. The Rangers, Mets, and Rockies, most prominently, offered conclusive evidence that it wasn't how much you paid players, but what players you paid, that determined the quality of a club. The arrival of players not only from Latin America, Japan, and South Korea, but also from Taiwan and Australia, elevated the game's international luster at the same time that the creation of a successful Mets farm club in the Coney Island section of Brooklyn returned a light to baseball's origins. In 2001, Seattle shook off the successive losses of three of the game's greatest players (Ken Griffey, Jr., Randy Johnson, and Alex Rodriguez) to win an unlikely 116 games before record-breaking crowds. In 2002, Yankee fans by the thousands purchased satellite dishes when a greed duel between the team's YES network and its Cablevision provider blacked out games for the year over a wide swath of the Tristate area. In 2003, the Fox network's inspiration to telecast an inning of a May 17 Giants-Mets game over melodramatic movie music provoked enough of an outcry that the witlessness was curbed before it turned into a weekly "production value." In some quarters, the game was still the thing.

Since the first of these games in Hoboken more than 150 years ago, the fan has played many roles in the sport's history, social weight, financial manipulativeness, and hero worship, but not the part of an innocent. What has not been done in his name has been done in the name of his great-great-grandfather or great-great-grandson, and he has accepted it with his passion and his money. As much as the owners, players, and media, it has been his national pastime—not because Albert Spalding said so or because the latest *USA Today* poll reported a resurgence in its popularity over *Monday Night Football*, but because he has been integral to baseball's pioneering contribution to, and development of, the mass-entertainment media society the United States has given the world far more momentously than bats and balls. Unlike Abner Doubleday, the fan has had *everything* to do with baseball.

Endnotes

Introduction

xi. ". . . William Henry Nugent." *The Dickson Baseball Dictionary*, Paul Dickson, Facts On File, New York, 1989, p154. It should be noted that the most popular term for a fan for much of the 19th century was *krank* (sometimes rendered as *crank*). For the sake of simplicity, however, the present book will use the word *fan* throughout.

xii. "Quiet and respectable strangers." *Porter's Spirit of the Times 3*, December 12, 1857.

xii. "The caring is the entertainment." *Sports Illusion, Sports Reality*, Leonard Koppett, Houghton Mifflin Company, Boston, 1981, 15.

xii. ". . . the sum total of our historic life." britannica.com.

xiv. ". . . in one December edition." *Daily News*, December 19, 2002.

xvii. ". . . explanations of the difference." In his *Sports Fans: The Psychology and Social Impact of Spectators* (Routledge, New York, 2001), Daniel L. Wann makes a distinction between fan and spectator throughout.

Genesis Tales

3. ". . . dating to 1774." *The Baseball Reader*, edited by Charles Einstein, McGraw-Hill Book Company, New York, 1980, 18. "The ball once struck off/Away flies the boy/To the next destined post/And then home with joy."

3. ". . . Valley Forge in 1778." *Baseball: The Early Years*, Volume I, Harold Seymour, Oxford University Press, New York, 1960, 5.

3. ". . . a dollar a game." *Early Innings: A Documentary History of Baseball, 1825–1908*, compiled and edited by Dean A. Sullivan, University of Nebraska Press, Lincoln, 1995, 6.

3. ". . . reprinted that year in the United States." Seymour, *op.cit.*, 5.

3. ". . . in the mid-1830s." Seymour, *op.cit.*, 5.

8. ". . . moral or even physical health." *Sport and American Mentality 1880-1910*, Donald J. Mrozek, University of Tennessee Press, Knoxville, 1983, xiii.

8. ". . . pleasure to the spectators." Cited by (among others) Allen Guttmann in

From Ritual to Record—The Nature of Modern Sports, Columbia University Press, New York, 1978, 84.

10. "... activities that might have been pursued." Seymour, *op.cit.,* 76.

10. "... redemption of all mankind." *Sporting Life,* June 18, 1912.

11. "... there were thousands of people present." *Sporting News,* February 29, 1896.

11. "... their New York Game ..." The play of the Knickerbockers was referred to for many years as the New York Game to distinguish it from the Massachusetts Game, which was played widely in New England. The Massachusetts Game fielded teams of from 10 to 14 players on a 60-foot square with bases at the corners. There was no foul territory, runners could be retired by hitting ("soaking") them with the ball while between bases, one out was sufficient for ending an inning, and a specified number of runs had to be reached for declaring a winner. The Massachusetts Game barely survived into the 1860s.

11. "... City of Base Ball Clubs." *Porter's Spirit of the Times,* June 20, 1857.

12. "... cheek of the most fastidious." *Brooklyn Daily Eagle,* August 3, 1859.

12. "... a privilege, not a right." *Porter's Spirit of the Times,* December 12, 1857.

12. "... players by their presence." Seymour, *op.cit.,* 29.

13. "... in the late 1830s." A Boston cricket team was playing scheduled games as early as 1809.

13. "... their energy or their thought." *America's National Game,* Albert G. Spalding, American Sports Publishing Company, New York, 1911, 1–2.

14. "... took days to complete." *Touching Base,* Steven A. Riess, University of Illinois Press, Urbana and Chicago, 1999, 3.

14. "... cut into ribbons at cricket." *The Creation of American Team Sports—Baseball and Cricket, 1838-72,* George B. Kirsch, University of Illinois Press, Urbana and Chicago, 1989, 101.

17. "... openly in the grandstand." Seymour, *op.cit.,* 29.

18. "... fewer ladies were on hand." *Brooklyn Daily Eagle,* August 24, 1860.

19. "... blackguard manner they did." *Ibid.*

19. "... reference to Irish immigrants." *New York Clipper,* August 24, 1860.

19. "... further up the class ladder." *Playing for Keeps: A History of Early Baseball,* Warren Goldstein, Cornell University Press, Ithaca and London, 1989, 74.

22. "... cannot fail to elicit applause." *New Jersey Daily Advertiser,* May 14, 1860.

24. "... profoundly honorable pastime." On December 5, 1856, the *New York Mercury* made the first known printed reference to baseball as the "national pastime."

25. "... thrust and saber stroke." Spalding, *op.cit.,* 64.

25. "... the country was building." *A Great and Glorious Game: The Baseball Writings of A.*

Bartlett Giamatti, edited by Kenneth S. Robson, Algonquin Books of Chapel Hill, 1998, 83.

25. ". . . from New York to California." Primitive Baseball—The First Quarter-Century of the National Pastime, Harvey Frommer, Atheneum, New York, 1988, 5.

26. ". . . fine old live oaks." Seymour, *op.cit.,* 40.

26. ". . . like dysentery." *The Old Ballgame in Folklore and Fiction,* Tristram Potter Coffin, Herder and Herder, New York, 1971, 4.

26. ". . . summer of 1864." Seymour, *op.cit.,* 41.

26. ". . . skill as baseball players." "Sports, the Meter Stick of the Civil War Soldier," Lawrence Fielding, *Canadian Journal of History of Sport and Physical Education,* May 1978.

27. ". . . score of 41–15." *Diamonds in the Rough: The Untold History of Baseball,* Joel Zoss and John Bowman, Macmillan Publishing Company, New York, 1989, 83.

27. ". . . clean score and a home run." *Ibid.,* 234.

31. ". . . at baseball's expense." Carriages themselves would remain part of the sidelines scene into the next decade, but less and less prominently and certainly not to the detriment of the sightlines provided by the grandstands.

31. ". . . bootblacks, and so on. . . " *Wilkes' Spirit of the Times,* November 2, 1867.

32. ". . . group comprising everything." *Wilkes' Spirit of the Times,* June 6, 1868.

33. ". . . with the ball players." *New York Chronicle,* November 28, 1867.

33. ". . . the blackguards." *Ball Players Chronicle,* August 22, 1867.

36. ". . . betting of certain parties." *Baseball, from the Newspaper Accounts, 1845-1881,* Preston Orem, self-published, Altadena, California, 1961, 36.

36. ". . . $100,000 changed hands." *Newark Daily Advertiser,* August 23, 1867.

36. ". . . bet on the Haymakers." *Philadelphia Sunday Mercury,* August 16, 1868.

37. ". . . for the catch." Seymour, *op.cit.,* 53.

37. ". . . you yourselves should cheer" and ". . . opponent whenever possible" both cited by Allen Guttmann in *Sports Spectators,* Columbia University Press, 1986, 88.

38. ". . . suspected of baseness." *Harper's Weekly,* October 26, 1867.

The Professional Game

43. ". . . ever before held." *Brooklyn Daily Eagle,* June 25, 1866.

44. ". . . ball match yields." Chadwick Papers, Spalding Collection, New York Public Library.

44. ". . . biggest games every year." *New York Times,* April 10, 1869.

44. ". . . game's popular pull." *Wilkes' Spirit of the Times,* June 11, 1870.

44. "... bones and bruised flesh." *Brooklyn Daily Eagle*, February 5, 1861.

45. "... 30,000 fans." *Baseball and the American Dream*, Joseph Durso, The Sporting News, St. Louis, 1986, 50.

46. "... a proper restraint." *The Creation of American Team Sports—Baseball and Cricket, 1838–72*, George B. Kirsch, University of Illinois Press, Urbana and Chicago, 1989, 232.

46. "... drawing big crowds." *Brooklyn Daily Eagle*, July 27, 1868.

46. "... lose that title, either." *Rockford Register*, August 17, 1867.

47. "... hippodrome principle." *American Chronicle I*, February 20, 1868.

47. "... only 5,000 that year." *New York Clipper*, November 13, 1869.

47. "... hippodroming exhibition." *Wilkes' Spirit of the Times*, October 1, 1870.

50. "... helped out business, sir!" "Cash and Glory: The Commercialization of Major League Baseball as a Sports Spectacular, 1865–1892," David Quentin Voigt, Graduate School Dissertation, University of Syracuse, August 1962, 85.

50. "... the scheduled contest." *New York Clipper*, December 18, 1869.

51. "... the homers in baseball." *Primitive Baseball—The First Quarter-Century of the National Pastime*, Harvey Frommer, Atheneum, New York, 1988, 15.

52. "... possession of the sport everywhere." *America's National Game*, Albert G. Spalding, American Sports Publishing Company, New York, 1911, 125.

52. "... morality and respectability." *New York Times*, March 8, 1872.

52. "... seeing an honest game." *Blackguards and Red Stockings: A History of Baseball's National Association, 1871–1875*, William J. Ryczek, McFarland & Company, Jefferson, North Carolina, 1992, 214.

53. "... among the city's residents." *Baseball: A History of America's Game*, Benjamin G. Rader, University of Illinois Press, Urbana and Chicago, 1992, 33.

53. "... threatened its existence." *The National Game*, Alfred H. Spink, Southern Illinois University Press, Carbondale and Edwardsville, 2000.

55. "... *and What It Means*." *The Krank: His Language and What It Means*, Thomas W. Lawson, Rand Avery Company, Boston, 1888.

55. "... his loudmouth behavior." Much of the book offers flippant dictionary-like definitions of baseball terms popular in the nineteenth century; e.g., "circus catch (catching the ball between the upper and lower eyelid)" and "over the fence (this is what becomes of small boys who are caught in the act of crawling under it)."

58. "... church can approach it." *Baseball: The Early Years*, Volume I, Harold Seymour, Oxford University Press, New York, 1960, 83.

59. "... without such income." In his book *The Rise and Fall of American Sport: Mudville's Revenge* (University of Nebraska Press, Lincoln, 1981), Ted Vincent notes that the

usually pedantically scrupulous Henry Chadwick gave only approximate accountings of the exhibition games with non-league teams, implying that the so-called major leaguers had lost more than an anticipated share of them.

59. ". . . with much of a profit." Aside from exhibitions against independently organized clubs, the NLers took on artisan and trade squads if there was a promising gate.

60. "It did, and there wasn't." Following the 1876 season, a group of investors from thirteen big and small cities launched the so-called International Association of Professional Base Ball Players in competition with the NL. The initiative, which eventually included franchises in such major centers as Brooklyn and Washington and minor ones in Lowell and Holyoke, lasted only a few years before being outmaneuvered by the NL and has never been recognized as a true major league.

61. ". . . company in Rhode Island." When Wright retired after the season to concentrate exclusively on his new business, he became the only manager to win a pennant in his only season of managing.

63. ". . . singing society picnics." *Gotham: A History of New York City to 1898,* Edwin G. Burrows and Mike Wallace, Oxford University Press, New York, 1999, 975.

64. ". . . attacks on Irish immigrants." *Diamonds in the Rough: The Untold Story of Baseball,* Joel Zoss and John Bowman, Macmillan Publishing Company, New York, 1989, 120.

65. ". . . between NL and AA ballparks." *Touching Base,* Steven A. Riess, University of Illinois Press, Urbana and Chicago, 1999, p44.

69. ". . . The tricky and the bold." *Slide, Kelly, Slide,* Marty Appel, Scarecrow Press, Lanham, Maryland and London, 1996, 107.

70. ". . . outside after a game." *Ibid,* 114.

71. ". . . ascendancy in American society." The *Times* shift was signaled by a mean-spirited editorial on September 23, 1888 that took aim at New Yorkers who felt "local pride" over a successful pennant drive by the NL Giants. "A considerable number of intelligent and respectable citizens of New York are daily disgusted at the evidence of the interest taken by a still more considerable number of persons whom they assume to be less intelligent and respectable in the game of baseball," the paper declared. After deciding that the latter fools couldn't simply be dismissed and that any kind of local pride was noteworthy, the *Times* concluded: "If this sentiment were extended in more rational directions there might actually come an irresistable public demand that New York should become the best paved, cleaned, and policed city and the most attractive place of residence in the United States. Meanwhile, any stir of local

pride is to be welcomed that makes a beginning in the direction of that distant and utopian end."

Patronage and Patronization

75. ". . . Richmond, and St. Paul . . . " Counting ties, Altoona got through 25 games for the Union Association in 1884, Richmond 46 for the American Association in the same year, and St. Paul 9 for the Union Association.

76. ". . . Tiernan's club, as well." The 1890 Players League revolt gutted the NL Giants, with such stars as Buck Ewing setting up a rebel club of the same name and leaving only a shell of their former team.

78. ". . . was the theatrical press." *Playing for Keeps: A History of Early Baseball,* Warren Goldstein, Cornell University Press, Ithaca and London, 1989, 8.

78. ". . . aims and objects are." *Sporting News,* March 17, 1886.

79. ". . . for the coming season." *Baseball: The Early Years,* Volume I, Harold Seymour, Oxford University Press, New York, 1960, 185.

80. ". . . respose and soft indolence." "The Universal Athletic Sport of the World: Albert Spalding Takes Baseball on Tour," Lewis Carlson, *American History Illustrated,* Vol. XIX, No. 2, April 1984.

81. ". . . 'refined' and 'legitimate.'" *A Pictorial History of Vaudeville,* Bernard Sobel, The Citadel Press, New York, 1961, 27.

81. ". . . far from dead." *Gotham: A History of New York City to 1898,* Edwin G. Burrows and Mike Wallace, Oxford University Press, New York, 1999, 1162.

83. ". . . terrapin dinner." Washington Gazette, February 20, 1892.

86. ". . . bat-and-ball pendulum." *Big Leagues,* Stephen Fox, William Morrow and Company, New York, 1994, 62.

86. ". . . mad with joy." *Ibid,* 69.

87. ". . . on your nerves after a while." *The Glory of Their Times,* Lawrence S. Ritter, Vintage Books, New York, 1985, 27.

89. ". . . so frequently induces." Cited by Seymour, *op.cit.,* 328.

89. ". . . influence of the fair sex." *Diamonds in the Rough: The Untold Story of Baseball,* Joel Zoss and John Bowman, Macmillan Publishing Company, New York, 1989, 199.

90. ". . . serviceable future husband." *Porter's Spirit of the Times,* September 6, 1856.

91. ". . . waited for the next train." *Sporting Life,* December 24, 1884.

91. ". . . were without aprons." *New York Times,* August 19, 1883.

91. ". . . for their struggling intellects." *New York Times,* September 23, 1883.

92. ". . . they were watching." Fox, *op.cit.,* 75.

92. ". . . squeamish or even particular." *San Francisco Examiner,* August 5, 1888.

93. ". . . the rights of others." *Sporting Life,* May 5 and May 28, 1909.

94. ". . . decorous demonstrations." *America's National Game,* Albert G. Spalding, American Sports Publishing Company, New York, 1911, 3.

94. ". . . improvement in man breeding." *New York Times,* November 13, 1910.

96. ". . . amid the piling debris." *Philadelphia Inquirer,* August 10, 1903.

98. ". . . Polo Grounds practice." *New York Sun,* August 12, 1911.

99. ". . . Toledo, and Milwaukee." In Milwaukee, the scorecards were also printed in German.

100. ". . . Coney Island amusement park." *New York Sun,* August 12, 1906.

102. ". . . the results of games." *Sporting Life,* June 29, 1912.

103. ". . . keep it that way." Cited by *Sporting Life,* June 8, 1912.

104. ". . . supremacy on the ball field." *Lost Ballparks,* Lawrence S. Ritter, Viking Studio Books, New York, 1992, 103.

104. ". . . on the World Series." *Baseball: The Golden Age,* Volume II, Harold Seymour, Oxford University Press, New York, 280.

104. ". . . an end to an Evil." *Sporting Life,* December 2, 1911.

105. ". . . in that city alone." Seymour, *op.cit.,* Volume II, 280.

109. ". . . fundamental in religion and baseball." *Sporting Life,* May 28, 1910.

109. ". . . cleanest paper on earth." *Sporting Life,* March 14, 1908.

111. ". . . approved for most Pennsylvania communities." "The Fight for Sunday Baseball in Philadelphia," Robert D. Warrington, *Newsletter of the Philadelphia Athletics Historical Society,* July and August 1998.

112. ". . . great American game." *Chicago Tribune,* June 10, 1918.

113. ". . . by the present war." *Sporting Life,* July 14, 1918.

114. ". . . players for company teams." *Sporting News,* July 25, 1918.

Close Encounters

117. ". . . of our national life." *Harper's Weekly,* January 17, 1914.

118. ". . . individual parts, that counted." *City Games: The Evolution of American Urban Society and the Rise of Sports,* Steven A. Riess, University of Illinois Press, Urbana and Chicago, 1991, 66.

120. ". . . Mandarin rolled into one." "Baseball's Dictator," Frank Lane, *Baseball Magazine,* February 1921.

122. ". . . the heads of the kids." *New York Evening World,* September 30, 1920.

122. ". . . after hearing of the fix." "The Truth About Baseball," Walter Camp, *North American Review,* April 1921.

122. ". . . Comiskey and the Sox fans?" *Chicago Herald & Examiner,* September 30, 1920.

122. ". . . harsher steps by a 60–40 ration." *Chicago Tribune,* December 10, 1920.

123. ". . . annoying but not reprehensible." *Sporting News,* August 4, 1921.

124. ". . . business, and society generally." *Sporting News,* September 8, 1921.

124. ". . . good enough for America." "Kenesaw Mountain Landis," Frank Graham, *Baseball Magazine,* February 1945.

132. ". . . whenever he showed up." *Literary Digest,* November 29, 1929.

132. ". . . dropped by the end of May." *Sporting News,* June 2, 1932.

133. ". . . the dove as its national bird." *The Sporting News: First Hundred Years, 1886–1986,* Lowell Reidenbaugh, Sporting News Publishing Co., St. Louis, 1985, 106–107.

136. ". . . books recommended for children." "Adios to Ghosts," Christy Walsh, *Cleveland News,* September 21, 1937.

137. ". . . What's the matter with baseball?" Reindenbaugh, *op.cit.,* 127.

138. ". . . what they were seeing." *Baseball America,* Donald Honig, Macmillan Publishing Company, New York, 1985, 181.

139. ". . . That was the real world." *Ibid.,* 197.

139. ". . . crosswords, and other come-ons." Reidenbaugh, *op.cit.,* 152–153..

140. ". . . playing to such a small crowd." *Sporting News,* March 7, 1935.

142. ". . . Rickey's pioneering approach . . ." There had been previous attempts by major league clubs to set up a farm system, most notably by Cleveland's Ernest Barnard in 1910, but these had foundered on financial problems.

146. ". . . It was swell." *Cincinnati Post,* May 25, 1935.

148. ". . . year in that time." *Dallas Times Herald,* May 15, 1939.

148. ". . . but also the Phillies." "Baseball's Most Devoted Fan," Harry Robert, *Baseball Magazine,* December 1929.

148. ". . . road trips with them." Unsourced clipping from the Baseball Hall of Fame Library.

148. ". . . greatest Giants fan of all time." *New York World-Telegram,* August 29, 1935.

149. ". . . everybody can see them." *Sporting News,* October 3, 1935.

149. ". . . the night of May 9." *Sporting News,* May 16, 1940.

149. ". . . in the Brewer City." *Sporting News,* February 22, 1940.

149. ". . . he gave him $5." *Sporting News,* December 21, 1939.

149. ". . . one Hack Wilson Potts?" *Sporting News,* November 6, 1930.

149. ". . . in his miniature uniform." *Sporting News,* August 24, 1939.

150. ". . . to give them encouragement." *Sporting News,* May 23, 1940.

151. ". . . giving them a fare-thee-well." Unsourced clipping from the Baseball Hall of Fame Library.

154. ". . . seriously wounding another." *The Brooklyn Dodgers: An Informal History,* Frank Graham, Southern Illinois University Press, Carbondale and Edwardsville, 2002, 135.

155. ". . . Malamud novel *The Natural.*" "Fatal Attraction: The Woman Who Shot Eddie Waitkus," Ron Visco and Bruce Markusen, *Elysian Fields Quarterly,* Fall 1999.

155. ". . . as enjoyable pastime)." *Sports Fans: The Psychology and Social Impact of Spectators,* Daniel L. Wann et al., Routledge Press, New York, 2001, 31.

Minority Images

162. ". . . any of our . . . teams." *Diamonds in the Rough: The Untold History of Baseball,* Joel Zoss and John Bowman, Macmillan Publishing Company, New York, 1989, 212.

162. ". . . fingers in their mouth." *Baseball Digest,* October 1945.

164. ". . . his life in his hands." *Sporting Life,* April 11, 1891.

165. ". . . watching major league players already." negroleaguebaseball.com, September 30, 1999.

166. ". . . the woolly-haired race." *Sporting News,* December 6, 1923.

167. ". . . We just weren't recognized." *Invisible Men: Life in Baseball's Negro Leagues,* Donn Rogosin, Atheneum, New York, 7.

168. ". . . the world that Negro baseball made." *Ibid.,* 6.

168. ". . . they're going to rake leaves." Negro League Baseball Museum Collection.

168. ". . . next to the man in question." Cited by Rogosin, *op.cit.,* 89.

168. ". . . like it was the World Series." NLB Com *op.cit.*

169. ". . . something entirely different." NLB Com *op.cit.*

170. ". . . We played baseball." "Reading the Hops: Recollections of Lorenzo Piper Davis and the Negro Baseball League," Theodore Rosengarten, *Southern Exposure 5,* 1977.

171. ". . . whether he likes it or not." Cited by Rogosin, *op.cit.,* 149.

172. ". . . cracking the heads of niggers." *New York Times,* July 31, 1938. Because the remarks made to Elson were not taped, various versions of the exact quote have circulated. The *Times* version is the most widely quoted.

172. ". . . Adolf Hitler treats the Jews." "Before Rocker: The Jake Powell Incident," Chris Christensen, *Elysian Fields Quarterly,* Fall 2000.

172. ". . . businesses, and bars in Harlem." *Baseball: America's Diamond Mind, 1919–1941,* Richard C. Crepeau, University Presses of Florida, Orlando, 1980, 223.

173. ". . . hundreds of favors for them daily." Christensen, *op.cit.*

173. ". . . worse menace than anything Powell had said." *New York Times,* August 17, 1938.

175. ". . . a hundred different cars." *Voices of the Game,* Curt Smith, Diamond Communications, Inc., South Bend, 1987, 212.

176. ". . . with the then-first baseman . . . " Robinson was signed from the Kansas City Monarchs, where he had been playing shortstop. With Montreal and then Brooklyn, he was converted to first base. He had his greatest years for the Dodgers as a second baseman.

179. ". . . bat right up your ass." *Nice Guys Finish Last,* Leo Durocher with Ed Linn, Simon and Schuster, New York, 1975, 205.

180. "By his own accounting . . ." *Veeck As in Wreck: The Autobiography of Bill Veeck,* with Ed Linn, New American Library, New York, 1962, 173.

181. ". . . researchers pointed out in the late nineties . . ." "The Truth About Bill Veeck and the '43 Phillies," David Jordan, Larry Gerlach, and John Rossi, *National Pastime,* Volume 18, 1998.

184. ". . . after only one edition. . ." The newspaper called off the balloting, according to Veeck, because one of its editors thought it ridiculed the game.

188. ". . . the end of my world." "Memoir: The Boston Braves," Camille Minichino, *Elysian Fields Quarterly,* Opening Day Issue 1993.

192. ". . . Ebbets Field on August 26, 1939." Prior to the telecast, Barber also held the first televised interview with a player, with Reds pitcher Bucky Walters. In addition, he was the announcer for the first color cast of a game, on August 10, 1951.

193. "2,500 players under contract." "Our Game," John Thorn, *Total Baseball,* Total Sports Publishing, Kingston, 2001, 6.

193. ". . . out of minor league fans." *American Baseball: From the Commissioners to Continental Expansion,* Volume II, David Quentin Voigt, Pennsylvania State University Press, University Park, 1983, 297.

Market Lures

201. ". . . beefing, threatening, foxing, and conniving." *The Last Good Season: Brooklyn, the Dodgers, and Their Final Pennant Race Together,* Michael Shapiro, Doubleday, New York, 2003, 71.

201. ". . . something other than prejudice." *Ibid.,* 318.

202. ". . . game on Independence Day." *Daily News,* July 4, 2003.

206. ". . . just give the score." *Storied Stadiums: Baseball's History Through Its Ballparks,* Curt Smith, Carroll and Graf, New York, 2001, 204.

207. ". . . free box seat section for them." *Calvin: Baseball's Last Dinosaur,* Jon Kerr, Wm. C. Brown Publishers, 1990, 55.

207. "The year after. Forever." *Washington Post,* January 15, 1957.

211. ". . . at the Milwaukee train station in 1953." *Milwaukee Journal,* September 23, 1965.

212. ". . . collusion between the franchises." *Sporting News,* August 7, 1957.

214. ". . . right to a big league franchise." *New York Times,* April 12, 1968.

216. ". . . left in the world, after all." *Daily News,* October 2, 1961.

221. ". . . mellow frame of mind." "Gene Ruehlmann and Bob Howsam: Designing a Riverfront Winner," Robert Harris Walker, *Baseball in Cincinnati: From Wooden Fences to Astroturf,* Cincinnati Historical Society, Cincinnati, 1988, 48.

221. ". . . had the real smell of grass." Smith, *op.cit.,* 352.

222. ". . . inside the stadium from your car." Smith, *op.cit.,* 365.

224. ". . . put a good team on the field." *The Pittsburgh Pirates: An Illustrated History,* Bob Smizik, Walker and Company, New York, 1990, 2.

Fans and Phanatics

229. ". . . on a first-place club could." *My 66 Years in the Big Leagues,* Connie Mack, John C. Weston Company, Philadelphia, 1950, 131.

230. ". . . That's its reason for being." *Sports Illusion, Sports Reality,* Leonard Koppett, Houghton Mifflin Company, Boston, 1981, 38.

231. ". . . with the equally shabby Athletics." The deal was foiled only because Kansas City general manager Parke Carroll couldn't reach owner Arnold Johnson for formal approval before the June 15 trading deadline then in effect.

233. ". . . the very image they fear the most." *New York Times,* April 6, 2003.

234. ". . . 'godding' players for readers." *Sports Page,* Stan Woodward, Simon and Schuster, New York, 1949, 42.

237. ". . . portrayed in the book." *Ball Four Plus Ball Five,* Jim Bouton, Stein and Day, New York, 1981, 408.

238. ". . . already being underwritten by taxpayer money." *Sporting News,* April 11, 1970.

240. ". . . Twins into the League Championship Series." *Sporting News,* November 1, 1969.

242. ". . . from which there is no appeal." *Diamonds in the Rough: The Untold Story of Baseball,* Joel Zoss and John Bowman, Macmillan Publishing Company, New York, 1989, 292.

243. ". . . stopping wars at their point of inception." Mack, *op.cit.,* 145.

244. ". . . police escort to escape a mob." *American Baseball: From the Gentleman's Sport to the Commissioner System,* Volume I, David Quentin Voigt, The Pennsylvania State University Press, University Park, 1983, 185–186.

244. ". . . fine from some swelled umpire." *Sporting News,* April 10, 1897.

244. ". . . with scorecards and other objects." *New York Times,* September 4, 1906.

245. ". . . had beaten him bloody." *Sporting News,* September 19, 1907.

246. ". . . cushions, newspapers, and other missiles." *New York Herald,* September 24, 1908.

246. ". . . bullet to the head could hurt him." Zoss and Bowman, *op.cit.,* 345.

251. ". . . we would have had to raise prices 10 times over what we have." *Sporting News,* January 8, 1977.

251. ". . . we can't stand the gaff." *American Baseball: From Postwar Expansion to the Electronic Age,* Volume III, David Quentin Voigt, Pennsylvania State University Press, University Park, 1983, 216.

252. ". . . losing that Series to the Dodgers. . . " *New York Times,* October 29, 1981.

252. ". . . I've been able to do both." *Sports Quotes,* Bob Abel and Michael Valenti, Facts on File Publications, New York, 1983, 209.

252. ". . . there'll be a plane crash." *If You Don't Have Anything Nice to Say. . . Come Sit Next to Me.* Coral Amende, Macmillan Publishers, New York, 1994, 136.

253. ". . . Why do they hate us?" *New York Times,* November 4, 2001.

254. ". . . World Series triumph over the Orioles in 1969." *Sporting News,* October 11, 1969.

254. ". . . runaway greed on the part of the owners." *Sporting News,* June 3, 1978.

255. ". . . during spring training in 1974." *Sporting News,* March 16, 1974.

255. ". . . play Aaron when and where they see fit." *Sporting News,* March 9, 1974.

255. ". . . just misunderstood entrepreneurs." *Sporting News,* March 30, 1974.

256. ". . . pennant duel with the Mets." *Sporting News,* March 14, 1970.

257. ". . . inciting fans to riot." *Daily News,* June 1, 1981.

257. ". . . SEAVER OUT OF TOWN." *New York Post,* June 16, 1977.

258. ". . . they should take advantage of it." *Minneapolis Star & Tribune,* October 1, 1978.

261. ". . . Las Vegas, Houston, Tacoma, and other cities." *Seattle Post-Intelligencer,* July 6, 2001.

264. ". . . you can't stay in business." Koppett, *op.cit.,* 221.

The New Compulsiveness

271. ". . . use of the lively ball." *Veeck As in Wreck: The Autobiography of Bill Veeck,* with Ed Linn, New American Library, New York, 1962, 351.

277. ". . . money he was getting from the club." *Sporting News,* January 29, 1977.

277. ". . . most career hits by an NL player." *Philadelphia Inquirer,* August 11, 1981.

278. ". . . home field for the tie-breaker." *Chicago Tribune,* September 9, 1985.

278. ". . . Show of the Padres on September 11." *Cincinnati Enquirer,* September 12, 1985.

279. ". . . some involving the Reds." *New York Times,* August 25, 1989.

280. ". . . make a sanctioned public appearance." *Seattle Times,* March 9, 2003.

280. ". . . commentators adjudged 'grotesque.'" *Whatever Happened to the Hall of Fame?: Baseball, Cooperstown, and the Politics of Glory,* Bill James, Simon & Schuster, New York, 1995, 355.

282. ". . . no individual is superior to the game." *New York Times,* August 25, 1989.

283. ". . . climb down into applause and prizes." *Sporting News,* December 25, 2002.

283. ". . . how many do you believe in?" "Hub Fans Bid Kid Adieu," John Updike, *The New Yorker,* October 22, 1960.

290. ". . . wherever we can possibly get them." *Athens Banner-Herald,* April 8, 2003.

295. ". . . 1–0 on his own home run. . . " "The Short, Spectacular Career of Harry McCormick," W. Lloyd Johnson, *The Baseball Research Journal,* No. 16, 1987.

295. ". . . merely .196 over seven seasons." "Pardon My French," Merritt Clifton, *The National Pastime,* Winter 1987, Volume 6, No. 1.

296. ". . . simplicity emerges from complexity." "Sabermetrics," Pete Palmer and John Thorn, *Total Baseball,* Total Sports Publishing, Kingston, 2001, 532.

296. ". . . allow others to criticize it." "What is Sabermetrics?" James Fraser, *Baseball Primer,* www.baseballprimer.com, March 12, 2001.

296. ". . . -.50(OOB)." *Total Baseball, op.cit.,* 534.

296. ". . . fall within two of the mean." "Clutch Hitting One More Time," Pete Palmer, *The Best of "By The Numbers,"* Phil Birnbaum (ed.), Cleveland SABR, 2003, 43.

299. ". . . redirect into acceptable patterns." *Boston Globe,* July 20, 1987.

300. ". . . basketball arena or football stadium. . . " *Ibid.*

303. ". . . I'm not going to commit suicide." *Philadelphia Inquirer,* October 24, 1993.

304. ". . . courage to give him a hand." *One Pitch Away: The Players' Stories of the 1986 League Championships and the World Series,* Mike Sowell, Macmillan Publishing Company, New York, 1995, 322.

307. ". . . followers of the Marlins." *USA Today Baseball Weekly,* December 1–14, 1993.

307. ". . . ballpark that he owned separately." "A Miami Fish Story," Andrew Zimbalist, *New York Times Sunday Magazine,* October 18, 1998.

308. ". . . the split season of 1981." The essence of the 1981 split-season plan called for teams leading their divisions at the time of the June 12 strike to meet in an extra tier of playoffs with the clubs that led the way for the post-walkout August-September period. Such a formula made no allowance for clubs with the best season record overall, so that five teams (Cincinnati, St. Louis, Baltimore, Texas, and the Chicago White Sox) were denied access to postseason play in favor of those with inferior records.

313. ". . . he got out of the ballpark." Associated Press, May 30, 2003.

313. ". . . by the time security men arrived." *Chicago Tribune*, September 29, 1995.

313. ". . . return the attack and then some." *Milwaukee Journal*, September 25, 1999.

313. ". . . William Ligue, Jr. and his son." *Chicago Tribune*, September 20, 2002.

313. ". . . said by way of explanation." *New York Times*, April 21, 2003.

313. ". . . St. Louis outfielder Brian Jordan." *Los Angeles Times*, August 12, 1995.

314. ". . . charging him with disorderly conduct." *Chicago Tribune*, June 17, 2003.

314. ". . . bleeding Dodger blue all her life." *Los Angeles Times*, August 9, 2000.

315. ". . . eventually awarded $1.5 million." There have been numerous instances of fans being struck by balls over the years, some of them fatally. On September 30, 1943, for example, Clarence Stagemyer, a Civil Aeronautics Administration official, was killed while sitting in the first base boxes of Griffith Stadium, when Senators third baseman Sherry Robertson clipped him in the temple with a wild throw. On May 16, 1970, 14-year-old Alan Fish took a line drive in the head from Los Angeles's Manny Mota at Dodger Stadium; although he showed no signs of severe injury at first, Fish died a couple of days later. Numerous other fans have been killed falling out of upper decks or plunging from escalators while engaged in some stunt for friends. One of the more bizarre deaths recorded came at Candlestick Park on June 6, 1984, when infuriated Giants fan Anthony Perry ran down the steps of an upper tier shouting obscenities at the San Francisco players for losing their sixth game in a row, lost his balance at the railing, and toppled down into a concrete passageway.

316. ". . . the week as a Yankees hero." *Daily News*, October 10, 1996.

316. ". . . . . on the executive level these days." *New York Times*, November 17, 2002.

317. ". . . got into an argument with an umpire." *USA Today Sports Weekly*, September 4–10, 2002.

317. ". . . investigations inside and outside baseball." *Daily News*, October 11, 2002.

317. ". . . $1500 by Premium Ticket Services." *Chicago Sun-Times*, May 9, 2003.

318. ". . . the proceeds from its sale." *New York Times*, December 22, 2002.

318. ". . . redeemed for a game-used ball." *USA Today Sports Weekly*, June 4–10, 2003.

319. ". . . I said, 'What are those?'" "Playing the Game," Larry Weitzman, *The Mountain-Democrat*, February 2, 2000.

Contraction Pains

325. ". . . balance the club's books." *My Turn at Bat: The Sad Saga of the Montreal Expos*, Claude Brochu, Daniel Poulin, and Mario Bolduc, ECW Press, Toronto, 2002.

325. ". . . Do You Care?" *New York Times*, September 15, 1994.

326. ". . . because the brewers are on strike." *Atlanta Constitution,* July 25, 1985.

327. ". . . The Most Meaningless Record in Baseball." *Sports Illustrated,* September 3, 1998.

327. ". . . like going to work or not." *Newsday,* October 10, 2001.

328. ". . . affected one another's followings . . . " *New York Times,* September 20, 1998.

328. ". . . That's us at our best." *Washington Post,* December 25, 1999.

331. ". . . swizzle stick that stirs any economy." "Why Baseball Needs New York Just to Say No," Mark S. Rosentraub, *The Nation,* August 10–17, 1998.

333. ". . . Cleveland losing its team." *Field of Schemes: How the Great Stadium Swindle Turns Public Money Into Private Profit,* Joanna Cagan and Neil deMause, Common Courage Press, Monroe (Me.), 1998, 43.

333. ". . . the elderly never materialized." *Ibid.,* 46.

334. ". . . most of their elected representatives." "The Team That Mistook Its Stadium for a Hat," John Pastier, *Seattle Weekly,* July 15–21, 1999.

334. ". . . working-class people for the most part." Cagan and deMause, *op.cit.,* 49.

334. ". . . the construction of the park." *New York Times,* letter to the editor from Roldo Bartimole, September 9, 1994.

335. ". . . $1.49 million a year." *Newsday,* August 22, 1996.

335. ". . . not even in Chicago." *Newsday,* August 8, 1988.

336. ". . . Good riddance." *Newsday,* August 19, 1996.

339. ". . . miserable situation in the Twin Cities." *Seattle Times,* December 3, 2001.

339. ". . . owned by Selig himself." Selig's daughter, Wendy Selig-Prieb, took formal control of the Brewers with his move to the commissioner's office.

339. ". . . the community are at stake." Associated Press, November 16, 2001.

340. ". . . to do some major recalculating." *St. Paul Pioneer Press,* February 6, 2002.

340. ". . . building our future together." *Minneapolis Star Tribune* and *St. Paul Pioneer Press,* October 20, 2002.

340. ". . . the very markets he's trying to help." "Outside the Lines," *SABR Business of Baseball Committee Newsletter,* Fall 2001.

341. ". . . that's hooliganism." *Miami Herald,* April 7, 2002.

345. ". . . closer to the 10 percent mark." *Chicago Tribune,* June 15, 2003.

346. ". . . but they didn't think they needed them." "Royals Give Black Fans Little to Cheer," Greg Hall, The Pitch.com., June 21, 2001.

349. ". . . lives more difficult and less pleasant." "Page 2," David Halberstam, ESPN.com, July 2001.

349. ". . . shelf space for Barry Bonds?" "The Trouble with Barry Bonds," Mark Hyman, *Business Week,* October 15, 2001.

351. ". . . they can do that" and ". . . TV executives as slander." Associated Press, June 5, 1999.

351. ". . . strongly supporting Hispanics." Associated Press, July 13, 1999.

351. ". . . pay the bills for years to come." *Houston Chronicle,* April 15, 2003.

352. ". . . it sounded like price gouging." *New York Times,* April 12, 2003.

352. ". . . the price of beer at Edison Field." *New York Times,* April 17, 2003.

353. ". . . we are left to only ask: Why?" *Daily News,* June 5, 2003.

353. ". . . SOSA HEARS MOSTLY CHEERS." *New York Times,* June 5, 2003.

354. ". . . being escorted out of the Coliseum." *Asiaweek,* April 20, 2001.

354. ". . . My country needs me." *Asiaweek,* May 3, 1996.

354. ". . . How the hell did they get in this country?" *Sports Illustrated,* December 27, 1999.

Epilogue

358. ". . . Their job is to cheer and boo." *Daily News,* June 15, 2003.

361. ". . . Wagner facsimile worth millions?" A Wagner card issued by Piedmont cigarettes in 1910 was being sold and resold for around $1 million at the turn of the century. Its value as a rarity stemmed from the nonsmoking shortstop's objections to the card and Piedmont's decision to stop issuing it.

Acknowledgments

Numerous people were indispensable in helping the author cross all the t's, dot all the i's, and even in helping him find the letters in the first place. I would particularly like to thank David Quentin Voigt for sending me a copy of his 1962 dissertation "Cash and Glory: The Commercialization of Major League Baseball As a Sports Spectacular, 1865-1892." For one reason or another, I am also indebted to Evelyn Begley, Tim Chapin, George Kirsch, Dorothy Mills, John Thorn, and Robert Warrington. As always, Bill Francis and the staff of the Hall of Fame Museum and Library in Cooperstown supplied lights for many dark roads. Closer to home, I would like to thank my editor Philip Turner and his assistant Keith Wallman for their editorial suggestions and Nick Acocella and Sid Gribetz for surrendering their printers to my manuscript as it developed. It goes without saying they are fully to blame for any errors in the manuscript.

About the Author

DONALD DEWEY has published some seventeen books of fiction and nonfiction, including *The Biographical History of Baseball, The Ball Clubs, The All-Time All-Star Baseball Book, The Book of Baseball Lineups, The Greatest Team of All Time, Marcello Mastroianni,* and *James Stewart: A Biography.* He is a past winner of the Nelson Algren Prize and lives in New York City.

.

Index

(American Association), 62, 63–66, 76, 78, 79, 164, 244

Aaron, Hank, 255–56, 272, 273–74, 285, 343

Abbaticchio, Ed, 119

Adams, Daniel, 10–11

Adams, John, 296–97

Adelis, Pete, 260

African Americans and baseball, 166–67, 168, 172–73, 178, 342–45
  See also Negro leagues

AL (American League), 75, 77, 106, 109, 113, 123, 125, 129, 181, 184, 213–14, 244, 296

Alexander, Grover Cleveland, 275

Algren, Nelson, 121

All American Girls Professional Baseball League (AAGPBL), 162–63

All American Girls Softball League, 161–62

Allen, Dick, 231, 232

Allen, Jim, 286

Allen, Mel, 191

All-Star Games, 137, 261, 263, 276, 278, 331, 354

voting, 199, 238, 346

Alomar, Roberto, 346

Alou, Moises, 312, 319

Altrock, Nick, 131

American Association (AA), 62, 63–66, 76, 78, 79, 164, 244

American Association of Baseball Fan Clubs, 150

American League (AL), 75, 77, 106, 109, 113, 123, 125, 129, 181, 184, 213–14, 244, 296

America's National Game (Spalding), 48

Anaheim Angels, 256, 269, 280, 299, 305, 322, 335, 344, 348

Anderson, Dave, 321

Anson, Cap, 59, 67, 68, 71, 117, 275, 277

anti-trust provision in baseball, 59, 107, 213

Aparicio, Luis, 267

Araton, Harvey, 347–48

Arizona Diamondbacks, 306, 322

Arlin, Harold, 132

Ashburn, Richie, 232

Asians and baseball, 240, 349–50

Astrodome (Houston), 210, 221, 223

Atlanta Braves, 255–56, 262–63, 273, 286, 291, 297, 308, 319, 346
  See also Boston Braves; Milwaukee Braves

attendance
  celebrities, 83, 84–85
  decline in, 218–19, 258–59, 341
  during the Depression, 111, 132, 134, 138–40
  during expansion, 219–20
  gate receipts, 30, 33
  during McGwire/Sosa race, 321, 322
  Negro leagues, 169
  night games, 145–46, 147
  paid admission policies, 2–30, 31–33, 43–44
  and photography, 130–31
  and player compensation, 51–52, 139
  postseason incidents, 311–13
  and profits, 30, 105–6, 229–30
  and radio broadcasts, 132–35
  and rowdyisms, 154, 257–58
  season ticket holders, 51, 223

spring training sites, 314–15
and television broadcasts, 193–94
and umpires, 152–53
violence at games, 202–3, 232–33, 255–57
and women, 6, 89–90, 92–94, 98, 161, 162, 340–41
during World War I, 114
Averill, Earl, 140

Baker Bowl (Philadelphia), 96, 103–4, 293, 302
Baker, Dusty, 312
Baker, Newton, 113
Ball Four (Bouton), 237, 239
Ball, Phil, 120, 141, 145
Ball Players' Chronicle, 89
ballparks
batter's eye, 221–22
commercialization of, 97
concessions, 97, 98–100
facilities for women, 6, 98
government supported, 207, 327–33
grandstands, 97–98
leasing agreements, 206–8
marketability, 221–25
safety and security, 95–96, 100–101, 295
See also specific venues
Baltimore Orioles, 86, 219, 225, 250, 254, 311, 322, 323, 346
Baltimore Pastimes, 27
Bancroft, Dave, 162
Bang the Drum Slowly (Harris), 236
Bank One Ballpark (Phoenix), 97
Banks, Ernie, 256, 348
Barber, Red, 134, 135, 174, 191, 192, 222, 290
Barbour, Ralph Henry, 235
barnstorming, 20–21
Barra, Allen, 233
Barrow, Ed, 161, 172
Bartholomay, William, 211, 255
Bartley (Heylinger), 235

Bartman, Steve, 312
Baseball Andys, 150–53
See also kranks
Baseball Encyclopedia, 290
Baseball (publication), 148
Baseball Tonight, 288
Baseball Writers Association of America, 137
batting averages, 218, 219
Bavasi, Peter, 258
Baylor, Don, 256
Beadle's Dime Base Ball Player (Chadwick), 44–45, 164
Beane, Billy, 292
Bee, Clair, 236
Beech, George, 149
Beeston, Paul, 303
Bell, John, 27
Bench, Johnny, 261
Bendix, William, 200
Berle, Milton, 194
Berra, Yogi, 252
betting. *See* gambling/betting
Bichette, Dante, 302
Bilheimer, W. E., 141
Biot, Charlie, 168
Bisher, Furman, 322
Black Sox scandal, 105, 119–24, 121–24, 128, 231, 276
Blue collar workers and baseball, 14, 32–34, 62–66
Boccabella, John, 239
Boggs, Wade, 298
Bonds, Barry, 287, 298, 313, 314, 343–45
Bonura, Zeke, 175
books about baseball, 48, 55, 155, 235, 236, 237, 239, 290, 329
Boston Braves, 102, 105, 111, 134, 151, 177, 186–89, 231
See also Atlanta Braves; Milwaukee Braves
Boston Globe, 102–3, 295

Boston Red Sox, 125–26, 151, 186, 187, 193, 194, 195, 219, 231–32, 247, 280, 282, 283, 284, 286, 287, 292, 294, 299, 301, 337–38
Boston Red Stockings, 65, 70, 85, 87–88
Boswell, Thomas, 324
Bottomley, Jim, 135
Boudreau, Lou, 182–83, 185
Bouton, Jim, 237, 239
Bowman, John, 63–64
Braves Field (Boston), 186, 187, 188
Breadon, Sam, 140–41, 145
Breckinridge, John, 27
Brett, George, 249, 261
Brickhouse, Jack, 259
Bridwell, Al, 245
Brochu, Claude, 321
Brock, Lou, 268, 283
Brooklyn Atlantics, 11, 17–18, 20, 30, 36, 43, 46
Brooklyn Daily Eagle, 12, 18–19, 43, 44
Brooklyn Dodgers, 111, 147, 152, 153, 154, 160, 161, 175–76, 177, 179, 182, 188, 191, 192–93, 200–203, 247, 341 See also Los Angeles Dodgers
Brooklyn Eckfords, 11, 30
Brooklyn Excelsiors, 11, 12, 17–18, 20, 21, 22–23, 27, 36, 49
Brooklyn Resolutes, 19
Brooklyn Tip-Tops, 145
Brooks, Noah, 235
Brookside Park (Toledo, OH), 106
Brosnan, Jim, 237
Brown, Mordecai, 106
Browning, Pete, 67
Buckner, Bill, 283, 299
Burgoyne, Tom, 263
Burke, Kitty, 146–47, 148
Burnitz, Jeromy, 298
Burton, Jim, 283
Busch Stadium (St. Louis), 297, 324
business of baseball, 229–33, 281–86
Butler, Brett, 281

Cagan, Joanna, 329
Cahill, Daniel, 149
Cahill, George, 146
Cain, Bob, 184
Callison, Johnny, 268
Camacho, Marco, 347
Camacho, Ronald, 310, 311
Camden Yards (Baltimore), 322, 323, 328, 349
Cammeyer, William, 17, 29–30, 31, 43, 96, 223
Camp, Walter, 37, 122
Campanella, Roy, 178, 180–81, 343
Campanis, Al, 342, 347
Candlestick Park (San Francisco), 204, 261
Canseco, Jose, 298
Capitoline Grounds (Brooklyn), 12, 31, 32, 52
Caray, Harry, 259, 261–62
Carey, Max, 162
Carroll Park (Brooklyn), 12
Carter, Jimmy, 308
Carter, Joe, 299
Cartwright, Alexander, 4, 5, 25, 130, 242–43
Casey at the Bat (Thayer), 281
Casey, Dan, 281
Casey, Hugh, 153
Castilla, Vinny, 302
Castillo, Luis, 312
Cavoto, Peter John, Jr., 313
Caylor, O. P., 79
Caywood, Betty, 212
Cedeno, Cesar, 257
Cepeda, Orlando, 204
Chadwick, Henry, 30, 33, 37–38, 44, 46–47, 78–79, 289, 293
Chapman, Ben, 173, 177
Chase, Hal, 72, 93–94, 106, 117, 231
Chavez Ravine (Los Angeles), 202, 203, 222, 269
Chesbro, Jack, 87
Chester, Hilda, 153, 154, 175

Chicago American Giants, 168

Chicago Cubs, 87, 106, 107, 120, 131, 133–34, 135, 147, 148, 194, 202, 219, 222, 245–46, 247, 256, 258–59, 262, 274, 280, 283, 284, 290, 299, 305, 310, 312–13, 324, 332–33, 351

Chicago Daily News, 133, 257

Chicago Defender, 167, 168, 172

Chicago Excelsiors, 47

Chicago Herald & Examiner, 122

Chicago Sun-Times, 313

Chicago Tribune, 50–51, 105, 112, 122, 136, 137, 258, 313, 331

Chicago White Sox, 106, 123, 139, 147, 150, 212, 231, 240, 249, 257, 259–60, 267–68, 280, 305, 339

Chicago White Stockings, 47, 57–58, 67, 68, 70, 80, 94

Chilcott, Steve, 249

Christian, John, 154

Cincinnati Commercial-Gazette, 79

Cincinnati Reds, 98, 119, 146–47, 152, 177, 192, 199–200, 237, 255–56, 257, 272–73, 273–74, 275, 276, 305, 343

Cincinnati Red Stockings, 47, 49–50, 51–52, 55, 146, 199–200

citizen lobbies, 326–27, 331–32

Civil War and players, 23, 24–27, 37–38

Clark, Bill, 297

Clemens, Roger, 283, 308

Clemente, Roberto, 342

Cleveland Indians, 106, 140, 147, 154, 181–84, 185, 187, 231, 240, 250, 259, 279, 296–97, 305, 322

Cline, Maggie, 70, 84

Clyde, David, 249

Cobb, Ty, 71, 85, 117, 247, 272, 273–74, 275, 277, 289

Coffin, Tristram Potter, 26

Cohan, George M., 84, 148

Cohen, Andy, 160–61

Colavito, Rocky, 231

Coleman, Vince, 311

Colon, Bartolo, 337

Colorado Rockies, 287, 293, 301–2

Colt Stadium (Houston), 210, 221

Comerica Park (Detroit), 329

Comiskey, Charles, 112

Comiskey Park (Chicago), 121, 123, 139, 165, 167, 212, 257, 260, 261, 280

Commissioners of baseball. *See* individual names

Concepcion, Dave, 273

Cone, David, 307

Connolly, Tom, 247

contraction of baseball, 336–41

Cooperstown (New York), 1, 275, 282, 291

Coors Field (Denver), 294, 301

Cossell, Howard, 332

County Pennant, The (Heylinger), 235

County Stadium (Milwaukee), 187, 188, 211, 240

Cox, George, 82

Cox, William, 181

Crawford, Jerry, 257

Crawford, Sam, 85

Creamer, Robert, 175

Creighton, Jim, 21–23, 67

cricket, decline of, 13–15

criticisms of baseball, 12–13, 18–19, 62–63

Crosley Field (Cincinnati), 152

Crosley, Powel, 134, 199–200

Crump, Henry Seymour, 335

culturalization through media, 77–82

curses, 86–88, 280–81

Cusack, Joan, 277

Cuyler, Kiki, 231

Dahlgren, Babe, 150

Daley, Bud, 213

Darwin, Charles, 127

Dauvrey, Helen, 84

Davis, Eric, 311

Davis, Ilus, 213, 214

Davis, James Whyte, 5

Davis, Piper, 170

Day, Boots, 239
Day, Doris, 203
Day, John B., 75
D.C. Stadium, 215
Dean, Paul, 147
Decker, Reuben S., 31
Delgado, Carlos, 346
deMause, Neil, 329
Depression, impact of, 111, 132, 134, 138–40
Detroit Andys, 88, 150–53
    See also kranks
Detroit Tigers, 142, 160, 184, 219, 231, 237, 244, 268, 280, 329, 335
Detroit Wolverines, 65
Devine, Bing, 230, 231
Devyr, Tom, 35
Diaz, Laz, 309
DiMaggio, Joe, 272, 273
Dinkins, David, 327
Dixwell, Arthur, 84
Doby, Larry, 181
Dodger Stadium (Los Angeles), 222–23, 259, 311
Doubleday, Abner, 3, 21, 23, 27, 80, 111, 359
Douglas, Stephen A., 27
Dowd, John, 276, 277
Downing, Al, 256
Doyle, Barney, 202–3
Dreyfuss, Barney, 100, 104, 110
drinking, 64, 65–66, 99, 132, 296, 309
drug abuse, 278, 324–25
Drysdale, Don, 222
Duffy, Ed, 35
Duffy, Hugh, 119
Durante, Jimmy, 66
Durante, Sal, 216
Durocher, Leo, 140, 153, 154, 174, 175, 176, 179, 200, 247
Dusenberg, Hugo, 244–45
Dybas, Eric, 309
Dykes, Jimmy, 150, 231

Eakle, Jim, 239
Earley, Joe, 183
Ebbets, Charlie, 110
Ebbets Field (Brooklyn), 152, 153, 154, 174, 176, 177, 178, 179, 188, 192, 201, 202, 210, 267, 293, 328
Eckert, William, 219, 274
Eckford, Henry, 11
Edison Field (Anaheim), 348
Ehlers, Art, 184
Eisenhower, Dwight D., 205
Eisenreich, Jim, 257
Elberfeld, Kid, 244
Elia, Lee, 299
Elias Sports Bureau, 298
Elysian Fields (Hoboken NJ), 4, 5, 13, 26, 37, 130, 353
Emslie, Bob, 245
enclosure movement, 30–31
Englewood, 12
Ennis, Del, 232
Epstein, Theo, 292, 294
Ercolano, Anthony, 313
Esterbrook, Jim, 310
ethnicity, 160–61, 269, 341–51
Evans, Billy, 245
Evers, Johnny, 343–44
evolution and early organization of baseball, 3–7, 10–13
Exhibition Stadium (Toronto), 258
expansion of baseball, 43, 45, 209–14, 301–4
Exposition Park (Pittsburgh), 95

Fairport Nine, The (Brooks), 235
fan clubs, 85–88, 149–50, 261
    and kranks, 88, 150–53
fans
    African Americans, 166–67, 168, 178, 341, 342–45
    blue-collar workers, 14, 32–34, 62–66
    celebrities, 84–85, 203, 205

employment discrimination, 46
fantasy baseball, 285–88
and farm system, 143–44, 320
gambling/betting, 38–39, 102, 104–5
gay/lesbian, 310–11
Hispanic, 346–49
identification with players, 119
immigrant populations, 63–64, 112–14
kranks, 55–56, 84–88, 148–49,
  150–55, 254, 255–62, 307–15
and umpires, 242–47
See also fan clubs
FANS (Fight to Advance the Nation's
  Sports), 254
fantasy baseball, 285–88, 289
farm system, 143–44, 320
Farrell, James T., 121
Fashion Race Course (Corona NY), 16,
  17, 20, 29, 46
Federal League, 106–7, 145
Feeney, Chub, 262, 309
Feller, Bob, 165
Fenway Park (Boston), 87, 186, 187, 193,
  194, 221, 257, 276, 297, 348
Ferguson, Bob, 67
Fetchit, Stepin, 170
Fidrych, Mark, 268–70
Field of Schemes (Cagan & deMause), 329
Fight to Advance the Nation's Sports
  (FANS), 254
Finley, Charlie, 212–14, 258, 303
First Base Faulkner (Mathewson), 235
Fishel, Bob, 184
Fisk, Carlton, 283
Fitzgerald, John, 86
Fitzgerald, R. A., 14
Flanner, Joe, 79
Florida Marlins, 301, 302–3, 305, 311,
  312–13, 334, 337, 338, 338–39, 346
Floyd, Cliff, 337
Floyd, cliff, 338
Fonda, Jane, 308
For the Honor of the School (Barbour), 235

Forbes Field (Pittsburgh), 100, 101,
  132, 215
Ford, Dale, 257
Fosse, Ray, 278
Foster, George, 273
Foster, Rube, 164
Fox, Nellie, 267
Fox, Stephen, 85–86
Foxx, Jimmie, 162
franchise shifts, 186–89, 199–204, 207–8,
  238–41
Franklin Evening News, 109
Franklin, Lee, 165, 168, 169
Fraser, James, 292
Frazee, Harry, 126
free agency, 248–53, 282–83
Freehan, Bill, 237
Freeman, Harry H., 91
Freshman Pitcher (Heyliger), 235
Freud, Sigmund, 127
Frick, Ford, 136, 175, 177, 181, 216,
  217–18, 219, 274
Frisch, Frankie, 142, 147
Fullerton, Hugh, 121–22
Fulton County Stadium (Atlanta), 255,
  256, 262, 309
Furillo, Carl, 178, 290

Gaedel, Eddie, 184, 260
Galarraga, Andres, 301
gambling/betting, 17–19, 35–39, 276,
  277, 278–79
  banning of, 81
  and fans, 38–39, 102, 104–5
  fantasy baseball, 285–88
  hippodroming, 46–48
  media opinion of, 102–3
  and Pete Rose, 274, 275, 276–77
  and players, 22, 35–37, 38–39, 65,
    103–4
Gamboa, Tom, 309
game scheduling, 32–33, 44, 52, 145–47,
  188

and blue-collar workers, 14, 32–34, 62–66

Eastern/Western Divisions, 219–20, 304–5

expanded schedule, 216, 217

Garagiola, Joe, 195

Garcia, Rich, 311–12

Garciaparra, Nomar, 287, 346

Garland, Wayne, 250

Garvey, Steve, 261

Gas House Gang, 140–42, 176

Gehrig, Lou, 131, 132, 150, 161, 322, 323

Germano, Frank, 154

Giamatti, A. Bartlett, 25, 274–75, 278, 295–96

Giannoulas, Ted, 263

Gibson, Bob, 219

Gibsons, Josh, 165

Gilliam, A. M., 79

Giuliani, Rudolph, 327, 332

Goldberg, Rube, 304

Goldey, Danielle, 310, 311

Goldstein, Warren, 19, 78

Gonzalez, Alex, 312

Gonzalez, Juan, 346

Gooden, Dwight, 268, 270, 278, 307

Goodwin, Danny, 249

Gordon, Joe, 231

Gossage, Goose, 271

Grant, Cary, 203

Grant, M. Donald, 257–58

Grant, Ulysses, 49

Graziano, Bob, 310

Greenberg, Hank, 161

Grey, Zane, 84

Griffey, Ken, Jr., 273, 298, 343, 359

Griffith, Calvin, 206–7, 208, 215, 240, 258

Griffith, Clark, 159, 205–6

Griffith Stadium (Washington DC), 132, 151, 165, 172, 206, 207, 215

Grissom, Marquis, 319

Guerrero, Vladimir, 346

Guidry, Ron, 270

Guttman, Allen, 37

Hack, Stan, 222

Halberstam, David, 344–45

Hall of Fame, 1, 275–76, 282, 291

Hamilton, Billy, 267

Hamilton, Charles, 70

Hamilton Square (New York City), 12

Hampton, Mike, 309

Hanlon, Ned, 244

Harlem Globetrotters, 170

Harper's Weekly, 38

Harrelson, Bud, 272–73

Harridge, Will, 137, 184

Harris, Mark, 236

Harrison, Benjamin, 83

Hayashi, Patrick, 313–14

Haymakers, Troy, 36, 47

Heilmann, Harry, 136

Helton, Todd, 288

Henderson, Dave, 299

Henderson, Rickey, 289

Henry, Bill, 290

Henry, John, 337

Herman, Babe, 147

Hernandez, Keith, 278, 349

Herrmann, Garry, 82, 111, 113, 120

Herzog, Whitey, 249

Heydler, John, 109, 120

Heyliger, William, 235

Higham, Dick, 65

Hilltop Park (New York City), 94, 244

hippodroming, 46–48

Hispanics and baseball, 346–49

Hitler, Adolf, 127, 201

Hodges, Gil, 178, 200

Hodges, Russ, 191

Hoffman, Henry, 151, 152

Hofman, Solly, 245

Holder, John, 35

Hollis, Ira, 37

home run hitting, 215–17

Honig, Donald, 139
Hoover, Herbert, 132
Hopkins, Lolly, 150–51
Hopper, De Wolfe, 84
Hornsby, Rogers, 160–61, 231
Horton, David, 308–9
hot dogs, 99–100
Houston Astros, 209, 210, 237, 240, 281, 347
Howard, Frank, 215
Hoyt, Charles, 71
Hoyt, Waite, 283
Hrabosky, Al, 270–71
Huizenga, Wayne, 302–3, 311
Hulbert, William, 57–58, 59, 62, 296
Hundley, Randy, 314, 315
Hurley, Ed, 184

Ichiro, 350
immigrant fan base, 63–64, 112–14
Indianapolis Clowns, 169–71
industrialization of baseball, 53, 57, 58–59, 75–76, 77, 81–82
interleague play, 304–5, 305–6
International League Montreal Royals, 320
Irvin, Monte, 181

Jack Murphy Stadium (San Diego), 309
Jackson, Reggie, 249, 250, 252, 259, 298
Jackson, "Shoeless" Joe, 112, 120, 121–22, 272
Jacobs Field (Cleveland), 297, 328–31
Jacobson, Steve, 323
James, Bill, 276, 292, 294
Jennings, Hughie, 71, 85
Jersey City Mechanics, 19
Jeter, Derek, 311
Joe Robbie Stadium (Miami), 302, 303, 311
Johnson, Arnold, 189, 212, 213
Johnson, Ban, 77, 81–82, 88, 111, 113, 120, 121, 133, 244, 296
Johnson, Randy, 298, 359

Johnson, Walter, 105, 117, 140
Jones, Chipper, 298
Jordan, Brian, 310
Joyce, Robert, 154
Jurges, Billy, 154

Kansas City Athletics, 189, 209, 211–12, 216, 231, 238, 268
  See also Oakland Athletics; Philadelphia Athletics
Kansas City Call, 167
Kansas City Cowboys, 65
Kansas City Monarchs, 168, 171
Kansas City Royals, 278, 305, 334, 335, 346
Keeler, Willie, 273
Kelly, John, 70
Kelly, Michael "King", 66, 68–72, 118, 267
Kennedy, John F., 86
Kennedy, Robert F., 218
Killebrew, Harmon, 215
Kiner, Ralph, 215
King, Martin Luther, Jr., 218
Kingdome (Seattle), 261
Kirksey, George, 210
Klein, Andrew, 311
Klein, Chuck, 344
Klem, Bill, 245, 247
Kling, Johnny, 119
Knot House Gang, 141
Knott, Meredith, 310, 311
Koppett, Leonard, 230, 264
Koufax, Sandy, 161, 222
Krank: His Language and What It Means, The (Lawson), 55
kranks, 55–56, 84–88, 148–49, 150–55, 254, 255–62, 307–15
Kreuter, Chad, 310
Kroc, Ray, 239–40, 251
Kuhn, Bowie, 237, 256

Laboy, Coco, 239
Lajoie, Nap, 117, 289

Landis, Jim, 267
Landis, Kenesaw Mountain, 119–21, 122, 124, 137, 142, 159, 164, 169, 172, 181, 246, 274, 319, 321
Lane, Frank, 230, 231
Lankford, Ray, 311
Lardner, Ring, 236
Large, Donald W., 255–56
Larner, Winfield Scott, 28
Lasorda, Tom, 310
Lavagetto, Cookie, 152
Lawson, Thomas W., 54–56
Leach, Tommy, 87
League of Their Own, A (film), 162–63
League Park (Cleveland), 106, 140, 141
Lemon, Jim, 215
Leonards, Buck, 165, 167
Levy, David, 131
Levy, Ed, 161
Leyland, Jim, 303
Ligns, William, Jr., 309
Lincoln, Abraham, 24, 27–28, 80
Lindsay, John, 223–24
Lindstrom, Freddie, 138
Lipsyte, Robert, 253
Little, Grady, 294
Logan, John, 98
Lopata, Stan, 232
Lopez, John P., 347
Loria, Jeffrey, 337, 339
Los Angeles Dodgers, 200–203, 204, 208, 209, 211, 252, 256, 268, 281, 285, 304, 305, 310–11, 350
See also Brooklyn Dodgers
losing player, 281–84
Louisville Colonels, 177
Louisville Four scandal, 59, 119
Luecker, Claude, 85
Lupica, Charley, 279
Lynch, Thomas, 102, 103
Lynn, Fred, 283

Macaulay, Thomas, 8

Mack, Connie, 111, 137, 150, 184, 229, 243
MacPhail, Larry, 134, 145, 146, 147, 153, 174–76, 177–78, 188, 192
Madden, Bill, 349
Maddux, Greg, 283
Magee, Sherry, 117
Magerkurth, George, 154
Maier, Jeffrey, 311, 312
Malamud, Bernard, 155, 236
Malone, Kevin, 310
Managers. *See* individual names
Mantle, Mickey, 216–17
Maranville, Rabbit, 275
Maris, Roger, 136, 212, 216–17, 233, 272, 285, 321, 324
Marquard, Rube, 200
Marshall, Nancy, 303–4
Marshall, Paul, 303–4
Martin, Billy, 240, 252–53
Martin, Pepper, 142
Martinez, Dennis, 257
Martinez, Edgar, 346
Martinez, Pedro, 294, 319, 346, 348
mascots, 260–64
See also kranks
Massachusetts Historical Society, 25
Mathewson, Christy, 71, 93, 94, 110, 117, 235
Matrix: Revolutions (film), 293
Mays, Willie, 204, 344
McCarthy, Joe, 172, 173
McCarthy, Kevin, 314
McCormick, Robert, 137
McCovey, Willie, 204
McGinnity, Joe, 245
McGraw, John, 72, 103, 105, 110, 132, 137, 160, 179, 246, 247, 301, 344
McGreevy, Michael T., 85
McGwire, Mark, 233, 298, 321, 322, 324–25, 343–44, 348
McKenna, Andrew, 331
McLane, Drayton, 347

McLendon, Gordon, 190, 191

McNally, Dave, 249

McNamee, Graham, 132–33

McReynolds, Kevin, 232

McRoy, Rob, 87

Meany, Tom, 148

Medwick, Joe, 142, 150, 152

Memorial Coliseum (Los Angeles), 203, 204, 258, 350

Mercer, Win, 90

Merkle, Fred, 245, 281

Messersmith, Andy, 249

Metrodome (Minneapolis), 297, 336

Metropolitan Stadium (Minneapolis), 221

Mile High Stadium (Denver), 301

Miller, Marvin, 250

Miller Park (Milwaukee), 314, 330

Mills, Abraham, 26

Milton, W. H., 139–40

Milwaukee Braves, 187, 188, 194, 211, 219
    See also Atlanta Braves; Boston Braves

Milwaukee Brewers, 180, 240, 309, 314, 334, 335–36, 358

Minneapolis Star Tribune, 336

Minnesota Twins, 207–8, 218, 219–20, 240, 288, 297, 334–35, 357
    See also Washington Senators

minor leagues, 106, 110, 143–44, 145, 148–49, 193, 320

Minute Maid Park (Houston), 281

Montreal Expos, 209, 238–39, 276, 286, 288, 297, 319–21, 322, 334, 335, 337–38, 339, 346, 357–58

Montreal Royals, 177

Moore, Donnie, 299–300

Moore, Tonya, 299–300

Moreno, Arturo, 348

Morgan, Joe, 281

Morrissey, John, 47

Moses, Robert, 201–2

Mouton, James, 309

Mrozek, Donald, 8

Mullane, Tony, 67–68, 231

Mullin, George, 84

Mullin, Willard, 140, 179, 203

Municipal Stadium (Cleveland), 181, 183, 212, 213, 279, 296, 329

Murray, John, 309

Musial, Stan, 273

Mussina, Mike, 308

Myers, Randy, 309

NABBP (National Association of Base Ball Players), 18, 20, 43, 46, 49, 82, 243, 306

Nader, Ralph, 254

NAPBBP (National Association of Professional Base Ball Players), 51–53, 54, 55–56, 57, 60, 76–77, 81, 137

National Association of Base Ball Players (NABBP), 18, 20, 43, 46, 49, 82, 243, 306

National Association of Professional Baseball Players (NAPBBP), 51–53, 54, 55–56, 57, 60, 76–77, 81, 137

national game, 12–13

National League (NL), 35, 56, 59–60, 62–63, 75, 76, 77, 81, 82, 106, 109, 146, 243, 244, 296, 310, 354, 356

National League Umpires Association, 247

Natural, The (Malamud), 155, 236

Navin, Frank, 85

Negro American League, 166

Negro leagues, 164–73, 178, 180–81, 342–43

Negro National League, 166

Nettles, Graig, 252

Neun, Johnny, 177

New York Black Yankees, 168

New York Chronicle, 33

New York Clipper, 19, 47, 77, 78

New York Eagles, 11

New York Evening World, 121

New York Giants, 76, 87, 93, 103, 105, 110, 111, 120, 126, 147, 152, 154, 160,

161, 175, 179, 186, 189, 192, 194, 202–3, 245–46, 247, 267, 281
See also San Francisco Giants
New York Gothams, 11
New York Herald Tribune, 234
New York Highlanders, 82, 93, 244
New York Journal, 118
New York Knickerbockers, 4, 5, 10–11, 12, 26, 37, 38–39, 130, 242
New York Metropolitans, 11
New York Mets, 195, 209–10, 219, 223, 229–30, 232, 233, 249, 254, 256, 257, 269, 282, 286, 304, 305, 320, 327, 348, 351, 359
New York Mutuals, 11, 19, 35, 36, 43, 52, 58
New York Nine, 4, 5
New York Police Gazette, 78
New York Post, 257
New York Sporting Times and Theatrical News, 79
New York Sun, 98, 102, 103
New York Times, 44, 52, 64, 71, 91, 94, 173, 312, 349
New York Yankees, 110, 111, 125, 126–27, 131–32, 160, 161, 172–73, 175, 176, 185, 188, 189, 193, 194, 206, 212, 218, 240, 247, 250, 251–53, 267, 280, 283, 286, 294, 305, 311–12, 313, 322, 327, 332
Newark Daily Advertiser, 36
Newsday, 323
Nichols, Kid, 76
Nietzsche, Friedrich, 127
night games, 145–47
Nightline (television show), 342
NL (National League), 35, 56, 59–60, 62–63, 75, 76, 77, 81, 82, 106, 109, 146, 243, 244, 296, 310, 354, 356
noise, 295–300
Nolan, Lloyd, 200
Nomo, Hideo, 349–50
numbers on uniforms, 131–32

Oakland Athletics, 258, 292, 336, 339, 357
See also Kansas City Athletics; Philadelphia Athletics
O'Day, Hank, 245–46
Odd Fellows Hall, 6
Official Encyclopedia of Baseball, The (Turkin & Thompson), 290
O'Hara, Novella, 261
Okrent, Daniel, 286
Olmsted, Frederick Law, 63
O'Loughlin, Silk, 244
Olympic Stadium (Montreal), 297, 319, 320, 337, 338
Omaha Luxus, 106
O'Malley, Walter, 188–89, 201–2, 203, 222–23, 320
O'Neil, Buck, 171, 342
O'Toole, Patsy, 151, 313
Ott, Mary, 151–52
Ott, Mel, 160
Owen, Marv, 142
Owens, Eric, 337
owners, 29–30, 57–58, 251–53, 258–59, 302–4

PacBell Park (San Francisco), 313, 314
Padilla, Vincente, 307
Paige, Satchel, 180, 182, 183
Palmer, Pete, 292
Palmiero, Rafael, 283, 346
Pappas, Doug, 336
Park, Chan Ho, 350
Parker, Dave, 256
Paterson Olympics, 32
Patkin, Max, 181, 183
Patten, Gilbert William, 235
Patterson, Reggie, 274
Pearlstone, Hyman, 148
Pegler, Westbrook, 172
Penniman, James, 148
Perini, Lou, 187, 188–89, 211
Pesky, Johnny, 283
Philadelphia Afro-American, 172

Philadelphia Athletics, 58, 85, 100, 147, 148, 189, 244
  See also Kansas City Athletics; Oakland Athletics
Philadelphia Inquirer, 96
Philadelphia Phillies, 97, 117, 126, 132, 147, 148, 177, 180–81, 194, 233, 245, 253, 260, 273, 276, 281, 284, 299, 307, 311
Philadelphia Record, 79
Philadelphia Sunday Mercury, 36, 80
photography and fan familiarity, 130–31
Pierce, Jack, 152
Piersall, Jimmy, 257
Pittsburgh Courier, 167, 171
Pittsburgh Pirates, 86, 87, 100, 132, 133, 147, 193, 216, 224, 256, 277, 278, 281, 305, 342
Pittsburgh Steelers, 224
player compensation, 11, 48, 51, 139
players
  All-Star teams, 137
  Asian, 349–50
  attempts to personalize, 67–68, 72
  Civil War, 23, 24–27
  during the Depression, 138–40
  drinking, 69, 71
  drug abuse, 278, 324–25
  employment discrimination, 45–46
  and fan clubs, 149–50
  first organized teams, 4
  free agency, 248–50, 282–83
  and gambling/betting, 22, 35–37, 38–39, 65, 103–4, 274, 275, 276–77
  Hispanic, 346–49
  night games, 146–47
  popularity, 117–19, 267–71
  professionalism, 7, 49–53
  publicity, 71–72, 136–37, 234–37
  racism, 177, 350–51
  steroid use, 324–25
  touring, 20–21, 22
  and World War II, 159–61
  See also specific players
Players' Association, 241, 250, 319, 321, 322, 335
Players' League, 70–71, 76, 79, 243
players' strike, 319, 321–22, 340
Pohlad, Carl, 334, 335
Polo Grounds (New York City), 97, 98, 110, 126, 127, 132, 152, 160, 161, 179, 202, 209, 210, 233, 245, 246
Popov, Alex, 313–14
popularity of baseball, 13–15
Porter's Spirit of the Times, 12, 89–90
Postlethwaite, Linda, 311
Potts, Hack Wilson, 149
Potts, Harry, 149
Potts, Rogers Hornsby, 149
Powell, Jake, 172–73
Powers, Tom, 336
Pregenzer, John, 261
Presidents of the U.S.. *See* individual names
Price, Jackie, 181, 183
Prince, Bob, 221
Pro Player Stadium (Miami), 339, 355
professionalism, 7, 49–53, 57
profits, 105–6, 229–33
Prohibition, 108, 132
Protestant influences on baseball, 7, 8–11, 81, 108–9
Providence Grays, 119
publicity, 140–42, 279, 298–99

Quinn, Bob, 192

racism and players, 177, 350–51
Rader, Benjamin, 53
radio broadcasts, 132–35, 190–92, 212
Raymond, Bugs, 108
Raymond, Dave, 263
Raymond, Herbert, 200
Red House, 12

Redheaded Outfield and Other Baseball Stories, The (Grey), 84
Reese, Peewee, 179
Reilly, Thomas, 337
Reiser, Pete, 153
Reynolds, John, 247
Rice, Grantland, 132
Rice, Tom, 123
Richards, Paul, 230–31
Richter, Francis, 78, 79, 91, 109
Rickey, Branch, 141–43, 174, 176, 177, 179, 180, 181, 193, 201, 290
Riess, Steven A., 14, 118
Riggleman, Jim, 284
Riley, John, 330
Ripken, Cal, Jr., 261, 321, 322–24, 343
rituals and superstitions, 86–88, 279–84
Riverfront Stadium (Cincinnati), 221, 261, 273, 274
Roberts, Morganna, 260–61
Roberts, Selena, 312
Robinson, Frank, 337
Robinson, Jackie, 174, 176–78, 181, 192, 215, 267, 290, 320, 341, 350
Robinson, Wilbert, 87, 200
Rocker, John, 350
Rockford Forest Citys, 46, 47
Rodriguez, Alex, 346, 359
Rodriguez, Henry, 298, 337
Rodriguez, Ivan, 346
Rodriguez, Rod, 347
Rogosin, Donn, 167–68
Roosevelt, Franklin D., 146, 151, 159, 313
Roosevelt Stadium, 202
Rose, Pete, 257, 261, 272–78, 281, 285, 349
Roth, Alice, 232
Roth, Allan, 290
rotisserie leagues, 285–88, 289
rowdyisms, 18–19, 33–34, 36, 45–47, 52, 63–64, 95–96, 140, 154, 257–58, 259, 337
See also violence at games

Rowe, Schoolboy, 142
Royal Rooters, 85–88
Royals Stadium (Kansas City), 177, 222
Rubenstein, Helena, 162
Rudolph, Andrew, 84
Ruffing, Red, 283
Runaway Colt, A (Hoyt), 71
Runyon, Damon, 165
Ruppert, Jacob, 172
Rusie, Amos, 76
Ruth, Babe, 125–29, 132, 136, 137, 165, 178, 216, 255, 280, 283, 323, 344
Ryan, John, 330
Ryan, Nolan, 261, 268, 270
Ryczek, William J., 52

sabermetrics, 292–94
See also statistics
SABR (Society for American Baseball Research), 291–92, 298
Safeco Field (Seattle), 313, 330
Saint. *See* St.
San Diego Padres, 209, 238, 239–40, 249, 263, 270, 274, 286, 303–4, 309, 339
San Francisco Examiner, 92
San Francisco Giants, 203–4, 210, 240, 281, 285, 287, 301, 304, 320, 339, 359
See also New York Giants
Sanders, Reggie, 312
Sanguillen, Manny, 342
Saturday Evening Post, 236
Saucier, Frank, 184
Schacht, Al, 131
scheduling. *See* game scheduling
Schiraldi, Calvin, 282
Schmidt, Allie May, 141
Schmidt, Mike, 232, 249
Schoonmaker, Edward Davies, 117
scorecards, 45, 98–99, 131
Scully, Vin, 195, 222, 223
Seals Stadium (San Francisco), 203
Seattle Mariners, 322, 343, 358–59
Seattle Pilots, 209, 224, 237, 238, 239

Seaver, Tom, 257

segregation policies and Negro leagues, 164–66

Selig, Bud, 211, 250–51, 276, 277, 288, 314, 321, 334, 335, 336, 337, 338, 351, 357, 358

Sells, Ken, 162

Seymour, Harold, 9–10, 12, 26, 37, 104

Shea Stadium (New York City), 210, 254, 257, 270, 272–73, 278, 298, 304, 357

Sheffield, Gary, 307, 310

Sherman, William, 26

Shibe Park (Philadelphia), 100, 101, 150, 232

Show, Eric, 274

Shriver, Sargent, 261

Sick's Stadium (Seattle), 221

Sievers, Roy, 215

Simmons, E. H., 92–93

Sinatra, Frank, 203

Sisler, Dick, 178

Slaughter, Enos, 177

Smith, Reggie, 257

Smith, Wendell, 171

Smizik, Bob, 224–25

Snider, Duke, 178, 204, 290

Snodgrass, Fred, 281

Society for American Baseball Research, 291–92

Society for American Baseball Research (SABR), 298

Sockalexis, Lou, 119

Somers, Charles, 106

Sosa, Sammy, 233, 321, 322, 324, 343, 346, 348–49

Southpaw, The (Harris), 236

Spahn, Warren, 282

Spalding, Albert, 3, 13, 14, 15, 21, 25, 27, 28, 46, 48, 52, 58, 59, 61, 62, 68, 69, 79, 80–81, 94, 124, 148, 155, 359

Sparrow, Bill, 149

Spiers, Bill, 309

Spink, Alfred, 53, 78, 79

Sporting Life, 77, 78, 79, 91, 92, 104, 109, 113, 164

Sporting News, 11, 77, 78, 79, 113, 114, 123–24, 133, 137, 139, 148–49, 150, 165–66, 255

Sports Illustrated, 323, 350

Sportsman's Park (St. Louis), 79, 97, 141, 143, 145, 152, 183, 185

sportswriters, 38, 45, 128, 136–37, 141–42, 215–17, 237

weeklies, 47, 78–82, 118–19, 286–87

and women, 90–92, 92–94

spring training sites, 314–15

St. Louis Browns, 120, 133, 141, 147, 160, 182, 183–85, 189, 205, 206, 244, 259

St. Louis Cardinals, 102, 133, 140–42, 145, 146–47, 152, 175–76, 177, 191, 205, 219, 237, 247, 268, 270–71, 277, 297, 304–5

St. Louis Globe-Democrat, 184

St. Paul Pioneer Press, 336

stadiums. See ballparks or specific venues

Stalin, Joseph, 201

Stallard, Tracy, 216

Standish, Burt L., 235

Star Spangled Banner (Key), 30

statistics, 79, 218, 219–20, 289–94

Staub, Rusty, 239

Steinbrenner, George, 251–53, 327, 332

Steinhagen, Ruth Ann, 154–55

Stengel, Casey, 182, 290–91

Stephens, Vern, 182

Stern, Bill, 27

steroid use, 324–25

Stevens, Harry M., 98

Stevens, John Cox, 4

Stone, Larry, 334–35

Stoneham, Horace, 202, 203

Stratemeyer, Edward, 235–36

Strawberry, Darryl, 232, 297–98

strike, players', 319, 321–22, 340

strike zone, 217–18, 219

Sullivan, John L., 67
Sunday games, 64, 109–11
superstitions and rituals, 86–88, 279–84
Sutter, Bruce, 271, 283
Suzuki, Ichiro, 350
Swift, Lucy, 151
Sylvester, Johnny, 128
Symington, Stuart, 213, 214

Taft, William Howard, 205
Taj O'Malley (Los Angeles), 222, 269
Take Me Out to the Ball Game (Norworth), 90, 262
Tampa Bay Devil Rays, 288, 305, 306, 322, 328, 334, 335
Tanner, Chuck, 231
Tarasco, Tony, 311–12
Taylor, Zach, 184, 185
Tejada, Miguel, 346
telegraph and game reporting, 21, 58, 59
television broadcasts, 192–95, 268, 298, 308, 331
Tener, John, 58
territorial exclusivity, 57–61
Terry, Bill, 200, 247
Terrys, Bill, 136
Tessie Curse, 86–88
Texas Rangers, 249, 270, 322, 346
Thayer, Ernest, 281
The Long Season (Brosnan), 237
Thobe, Harry, 152
Thompson, S. C., 290
Thomson, Bobby, 178–79, 192, 323
Thorn, John, 292
Three Rivers Stadium (Pittsburgh), 221
Tiant, Luis, 171
Tiernan, Mike, 75–76
Tinker, Joe, 106
Tip Top Weekly, 235
Toledo Blue Stockings, 164
Toledo White Autos, 106
Toronto Blue Jays, 287, 299, 305
Torre, Joe, 354

Totten, Hal, 133
Tucker, William, 5
Tuckness, Kenneth, 149
Turkin, Hy, 290
Turner Field (Atlanta), 307, 357
Turner, Ted, 261, 262, 303, 308
Twain, Mark, 80
Tweed, Boss, 36, 47

Ueberroth, Peter, 326, 331
umpires, 52, 65, 152–53, 242–47, 257, 310
uniform numbers, 131–32
Union Grounds (Brooklyn), 29–31, 32, 43, 59
Union Park (Baltimore), 64–65
Unions of Morrisania, 32
Updike, John, 279
U.S. Cellular Field (Chicago), 309
USA Today Baseball Weekly, 302–3

Valenzuela, Fernando, 268, 349
Valli, Violet, 154
Vander Meer, Johnny, 150, 174
Vaughn, Mo, 283, 284
Veeck, Bill, 180–81, 182, 183–85, 189, 212, 213, 259–60, 261–62, 267, 279, 305
Veterans Stadium (Philadelphia), 233, 273
Vincent, Fay, 275, 329
violence at games, 202–3, 232–33, 255–57, 324
  See also rowdyisms
Visgar, Berley, 309
Vitt, Ossie, 154
Voigt, David, 244
Von der Ahe, Chris, 63, 65–66, 79

Waddell, Rube, 108
Wagner, Honus, 86–87, 117, 119
Waitkus, Eddie, 154–55
Walker, Dixie, 176
Walker, Fleet, 164, 231

Walker, James, 111
Walker, Larry, 302, 319, 320
Walsh, Christy, 136
Waner, Lloyd, 139
Wansley, William, 35
War and Peace (Tolstoy), 284
Ward, Arch, 136–37
Ward, John Montgomery, 84
Ward, Robert, 145
Warden, Jack, 277
Washington Evening Star, 28
Washington Gazette, 83
Washington, Harold, 331
Washington Nationals, 43, 46, 47, 49
Washington Park (Brooklyn), 145
Washington Post, 207, 324
Washington Senators, 90, 131, 133, 151, 160, 172–73, 205–7, 216, 219, 240, 291. *See* attendance
Weed, Hamilton, 31
Weeghman, Charles, 107
Weeghman Field (Chicago), 107, 114
weeklies, 47, 78–82, 118–19, 286–87
Weiss, George, 209
Weitzman, Larry, 314–15
West Side Park (Chicago), 107
West Texas-New Mexico League, 149
Wetherby's Inning (Barbour), 235
Wetteland, John, 319
Whales of Chicago, 106
Wheat Hill (Brooklyn), 12
Wheaton, William, 5, 243
Wheeler, John, 235
White, Jack, 152
Whitner, Clarence, 161
Wilkes' Spirit of the Times, 32, 44, 47
Williams, Elisa Green, 94
Williams, Lucas R., 148
Williams, Mitch, 299, 311
Williams, Ted, 276, 344
Wills, Maury, 268
Winfield, Dave, 249, 252, 253
Winman, Erastus, 63
Wolf, Randy, 307

Woman's Christian Temperance Union, 108
women
  and amenities at ballparks, 6, 98
  and gambling/betting, 39
  as players, 161–63
  as spectators, 89–90, 92–94, 161, 340–41
  and sportswriters, 90–92, 92–94
Won in the Ninth (Mathewson), 235
Wood, Frank H., 84
Woodward, Stan, 234, 236
World Series, 86, 97, 103, 119, 124, 127, 132, 133, 142, 151, 192, 193, 195, 202, 234, 254, 263, 281, 282, 297, 299, 303, 304, 312, 323
  See also Black Sox scandal; individual player names
World War I and baseball, 111–14
World War II and baseball, 159–63, 278–79
Wright, Al, 79, 80
Wright, George, 59, 60–61, 62, 146
Wright, Harry, 49, 50, 51, 57, 59, 60–61, 62, 97, 117
Wrigley Field (Chicago), 107, 134, 180, 202, 203, 258–59, 262, 274, 280, 283, 309, 310, 313, 314, 326, 331, 349
Wrigley, Phil, 161–62, 290
Wrigley, William, 133
Wyatt, Whitlow, 153
Wynegar, Butch, 258

Yankee Stadium (New York City), 127, 131, 162, 167, 178, 185, 212, 216, 252, 294, 308, 311, 327, 332
You Know Me Al (Lardner), 236
Young, Cy, 117
Young, Dick, 257
Yount, Robin, 249

Zimbalist, Andrew, 303
Zimmerman, Heinie, 231
Zoss, Joel, 63–64
Zulu Cannibal Giants, 169, 171